COMPETENCE, CONDEMNATION, AND COMMITMENT

The LAW AND PUBLIC POLICY: PSYCHOLOGY AND THE SOCIAL SCIENCES series includes books in three domains:

Legal Studies—writings by legal scholars about issues of relevance to psychology and the other social sciences, or that employ social science information to advance the legal analysis;

Social Science Studies—writings by scientists from psychology and the other social sciences about issues of relevance to law and public policy; and

Forensic Studies—writings by psychologists and other mental health scientists and professionals about issues relevant to forensic mental health science and practice.

The series is guided by its editor, Bruce D. Sales, PhD, JD, ScD, University of Arizona; and coeditors, Bruce J. Winick, JD, University of Miami; Norman J. Finkel, PhD, Georgetown University; and Stephen J. Ceci, PhD, Cornell University.

***

COMPETENCE, CONDEMNATION, AND COMMITMENT

AN INTEGRATED THEORY OF MENTAL HEALTH LAW

ROBERT F. SCHOPP

American Psychological Association
Washington, DC

Published by
American Psychological Association
750 First Street, NE
Washington, DC 20002

Copies may be ordered from
APA Order Department
P.O. Box 92984
Washington, DC 20090-2984

In the U.K., Europe, Africa, and the Middle East, copies may be
ordered from
American Psychological Association
3 Henrietta Street
Covent Garden, London
WC2E 8LU England

Typeset in Times Roman by EPS Group Inc., Easton, MD

Printer: Sheridan Books, Ann Arbor, MI
Cover Designer: Nini Sarmiento, NIDESIGN, Baltimore, MD
Technical/Production Editor: Catherine Hudson

The opinions and statements published are the responsibility of the
authors, and such opinions and statements do not necessarily represent
the policies of the APA.

Library of Congress Cataloging-in-Publication Data
Schopp, Robert F.
    Competence, condemnation, and commitment : an integrated theory of mental health
law / Robert F. Schopp.—1st ed.
        p. cm.—(The law and public policy)
    Includes bibliographical references.
    ISBN 1-55798-745-9
        1. Mental health laws—United States.   2. Insanity—Jurisprudence—United States.
3. Insane—Commitment and detention—United States.   4. Mentally ill offenders—
United States.   I. Title.   II. Series.

    KF3828 .S36 2001
    344.73′044—dc21

                                                                            00-050273

British Library Cataloguing-in-Publication Data
A CIP record is available from the British Library.

Printed in the United States of America
First Edition

*For those who participate so deeply
in our lives as to become part of us.*

CONTENTS

ACKNOWLEDGMENTS

Many colleagues and friends have contributed in various ways to this project. I can mention only a few of those who have had the most direct influence. Marc Pearce, Mike Quattrocchi, Mario Scalora, and Barb Sturgis served as coauthors on previous articles in which we developed the initial formulations of various arguments upon which I have built in this book. Mike and Barb have also participated in many conversations and commented on several other articles relevant to the analysis in this book. Marc served as a research assistant and reviewer of several chapters. Several of my colleagues in the College of Law and the Department of Psychology at the University of Nebraska have participated in various conversations and colloquia in which I have gradually developed some of the positions presented here. I am grateful to these individuals and others who have influenced my thinking regarding these matters.

I am also grateful to some teachers and colleagues who have influenced my more general preparation and background in mental health law. These include David Wexler, who influenced my understanding of mental health law as an interdisciplinary undertaking, as well as Bruce Sales and Bruce Winick, who have influenced my general thought in the area of mental health law and who have provided an outlet for this type of work in this book series. More generally, my former colleagues and patients at the Milwaukee County Mental Health Complex provided much of the early experience that stimulated my thought in this area. It is customary at this point to absolve these individuals of any responsibility for any errors in this work. In light of the pervasive influence of Mike and Barb, however, it only seems reasonable that they should also share in the risk, so I shall refrain from absolution.

Several of the ideas and arguments in this book were initially formulated in previous papers. I am grateful to the copyright holders for permission to make use of these ideas and arguments in developing the analysis presented here. John Wiley & Sons holds the copyright and grants permission regarding the following works: *Sexual Predators and Legal Mental Illness for Civil Commitment*, 13 BEHAV. SCI. & L 437 (1995) (with Barbara Sturgis); *Predicting the Present: Expert Testimony and Civil Commitment*, 13 BEHAV. SCI. & L. 159 (1995) (with Michael Quattrocchi); *Therapeutic Jurisprudence and Conflicts Among Values in Mental Health Law*, 11 BEHAV. SCI. & L. 31 (1993). The American Psychological Association holds the copyright and grants permission regarding the following works: *Expert Testimony and Professional Judgment: Psychological Expertise and Commitment as a Sexual Predator After Hendricks*, 5 PSYCHOL., PUB. POL'Y & L. 120 (1999) (with Mario Scalora & Marc Pearce); *Civil Commitment and Sexual Predators: Competence and Condemnation*, 4 PSYCHOL., PUB. POL'Y & L. 323 (1998); *Sexual Predators and the Structure of the Mental Health System: Expanding the Normative Focus of Therapeutic Jurisprudence*, 1 PSYCHOL., PUB. POL'Y & L. 161 (1995).

COMPETENCE, CONDEMNATION, AND COMMITMENT

INTRODUCTION:
Seeking Coherence and Justification in Mental Health Law

I. Formulating the Problem

Central provisions of mental health law authorize legal institutions to treat persons who are mentally ill in a manner that departs significantly from the way they treat persons who are not mentally ill. Ordinarily, these provisions of mental health law indicate either explicitly or implicitly that mental illness justifies differential treatment, but they rarely provide any clear conception of mental illness for the specific legal purpose, nor do they clearly and explicitly explain why such impairment justifies differential treatment. Although legal development and scholarly inquiry tend to address each of the institutions governed by these provisions in relative isolation from the others, they interact significantly in three ways. On a practical level, changes in one institution can affect the interpretation and application of others. Restrictions in use of the insanity defense, for example, can result in broader interpretation and application of civil commitment and of incompetence to stand trial. On a conceptual level, several institutions share common notions such as mental illness or dangerousness. Vague or inconsistent interpretations of these notions can generate circumstances in which various institutions of mental health law address individuals inconsistently or inappropriately. On a normative level, these conceptual inadequacies can generate practices that fail to comport with the underlying principles that justify specific applications of these institutions, the institutions themselves, or the broader legal system in which they are embedded.

Consider, for example, legal institutions that address sexually violent offenders. Sexually violent acts are crimes subject to criminal penalties, including quite severe penalties for the more serious offenses.[1] Legal systems also provide a variety of commitment and involuntary treatment interventions for those who commit sexual offenses, however, which suggests that these crimes are thought to be related in some important manner to psychological impairment.[2] Insofar as the mental health system addresses those who engage in violent conduct related in some important manner to psychological impairment, and the criminal justice system addresses those who engage in violence that does not bear this relationship to impairment, civil commitment and criminal incarceration appear to function as complementary institutions through which the state exercises police power. Sexual predator statutes raise serious questions regarding the coherence of these institutions, however, because these statutes provide for civil commitment, ostensibly for long-term care and treatment, of sexual offenders who have been convicted of their crimes and served their criminal sen-

---

[1] AMERICAN LAW INSTITUTE, MODEL PENAL CODE AND COMMENTARIES, art. 213 (Official Draft and Revised Comments, 1985).

[2] SAMUEL JAN BRAKEL, JOHN PARRY, & BARBARA A. WEINER, THE MENTALLY DISABLED AND THE LAW 739–43 (3rd ed. 1985).

tences.[3] Thus, if one accepted the complementary interpretation of civil commitment
and criminal incarceration, one would be driven to the contradictory conclusions that
the offenses committed by these individuals both were related and were not related
to impairment in the specified manner.

By raising important questions about the relationship between civil commitment
and criminal incarceration, sexual predator provisions elicit careful examination at
two levels of analysis. At the specific level, review of the statutes and the related
court cases raises serious questions regarding the coherence of and justification for
these statutes. Although these questions are important, the sexual offenders addressed
by these statutes constitute a relatively small and nonrepresentative subset of violent
criminals. Thus, the questions of broader significance arise at the level of the institutional structure within which these statutes are imbedded. These questions address
the proper role of the mental health and criminal justice systems as legal institutions
through which the state exercises police power regarding those who engage in violent
behavior, including sexual violence. For the purpose of this book, the sexual predator
statutes serve primarily to illustrate these questions of more general significance.

Mental health law includes several central components designed to address those
who demonstrate psychological impairment while engaging in conduct that harms or
endangers others or themselves. These include some provisions explicitly related to
the criminal justice system, such as the law of criminal responsibility, criminal competence, and postinsanity acquittal commitment.[4] Other provisions, such as civil commitment, lack the explicit association with the criminal justice system, but they are
related to that system insofar as they provide alternative institutions of coercive social
control for some of those who engage in violent or otherwise harmful conduct.

The sexual predator statutes are controversial partially because they blur the
boundary between the mental health and criminal justice systems. These statutes
provide no clear conception of the required mental abnormality or personality disorder that would explain and justify the commitment of offenders who have been
criminally convicted and who do not manifest severe impairment of the type ordinarily associated with civil commitment. This defect in the sexual predator statutes
pervades civil commitment more generally in that commitment provisions often fail
to provide any clear account of the mental illness requirement that would reliably
identify those appropriate to social control through commitment. Thus, these statutes
draw our attention to the need to examine the requirements of a "mental abnormality" in the sexual predator statutes and of "mental illness" in general civil commitment statutes in order to understand the meaning of these terms and their significance in justifying confinement through the mental health system rather than through
the criminal justice system.

Although the sexual predator statutes draw attention to this lack of clarity and
integration regarding police power interventions specifically, similar defects permeate
legal institutions of *parens patriae* intervention. Civil commitment statutes allow
police power and *parens patriae* commitment, but they provide neither an account
of the conception of mental illness required for each nor a justification for each type
of intervention. Most statutes accommodate both underlying powers simply by in-

---

[3] *See* chapter 2 for discussion of these provisions.

[4] MICHAEL L. PERLIN, MENTAL DISABILITY LAW, chap. 15 (criminal responsibility), chap. 14 (criminal competence), §15.20 (postacquittal commitment) (1989).

cluding a phrase that allows commitment on the basis of dangerousness to self or others.[5] Ordinarily, nothing turns on which power forms the basis for a particular commitment, and the court order might not explicitly identify the power under which the individual is committed.[6] Thus, common civil commitment statutes often address *parens patriae* and police power commitments as minor variations within the same commitment process. Neither the statutes nor the courts explain why the same parameters of commitment and conceptions of legal mental illness should apply to both types of commitment.

Parens patriae civil commitment appears to be closely related in principle to provisions authorizing findings of incompetence for person and appointment of a guardian. These provisions fail to adequately specify the nature of the impairment that suffices to render one subject to intervention under each statute, however, producing theoretical concern regarding the parameters of and justification for intervention under each. Furthermore, this lack of clarity generates troubling practical situations in which individuals are treated as subject to *parens patriae* commitment but not to *parens patriae* treatment. Similarly, police power civil commitment of those who harm or endanger others appears to be closely related in principle to the requirements of criminal responsibility, yet the relationship between the two is rarely addressed.

The sexual predator statutes provide no clear conception of the required mental abnormality that makes one likely to commit acts of sexual violence, and the civil commitment statutes provide no clear conception of the mental illness and dangerousness criteria. Similarly, the sexual predator statutes fail to articulate a clear relationship between commitment and criminal incarceration, and the civil commitment provisions fail to articulate clear parameters that differentiate *parens patriae* and police power commitment and explain the relationships between each of these and closely related legal institutions for involuntary intervention. Thus, the pattern of vague criteria and boundaries illustrated by the sexual predator statutes pervades civil commitment and mental health law generally.

In summary, the sexual predator statutes starkly illustrate the lack of clarity and integration that pervade many aspects of mental health law. This book adopts the methodological premise that some central issues in mental health law have proven intractable partially because legislatures, courts, and scholars have tended to address them as relatively self-contained questions.[7] A satisfactory approach to these issues must address them as central components in an integrated body of mental health law reflecting a coherent normative structure. Such an approach must provide a coherent conception of mental illness that has psychological content and is amenable to specification for particular purposes. This approach must explain the manner in which the principles underlying the relevant legal institutions justify differential treatment for a particular legal purpose of those who manifest such mental illness. It must integrate these specific conceptions of mental illness and the corresponding legal institutions in a manner that renders them coherent and justified by appeal to the

---

[5] Some include variations on danger to self such as grave disability or inability to meet one's basic needs. John Parry, *Involuntary Civil Commitment in the 90s: A Constitutional Perspective*, 18 MENTAL & PHYSICAL DISABILITY L. REP. 320, 323 (1994).

[6] Rogers v. Okin, 634 F.2d 650, 658 (1st Cir. 1980).

[7] For examples of scholarship that integrates some aspects of mental health law, *see* PAUL APPLEBAUM, ALMOST A REVOLUTION (1994); DAVID B. WEXLER, MENTAL HEALTH LAW (1981).

principles of political morality that support the larger legal system. It should clarify the empirical and normative components of the central notions, and by doing so, it should delineate the proper roles and responsibilities of clinical and legal actors. This book begins to develop such an integrated approach in which the distinction between police power and *parens patriae* interventions provides a central organizing principle.

II.   Synopsis of the Project

This book clarifies the distinction between *parens patriae* and police power commitment and the relationships between each and the related notions of civil competence and criminal responsibility. This clarification is central to understanding the function and justification of civil commitment specifically and of coercive state intervention through the mental health and criminal justice systems more generally. The book advances a revised system of coercive intervention that allocates *parens patriae* and police power interventions to separate legal institutions that reflect distinct underlying justifications. The familiar notion of civil competence for person provides the organizing principle that generates a revised structure for *parens patriae* institutions. This revised structure eliminates *parens patriae* civil commitment as an independent institution. It addresses involuntary inpatient admission and involuntary administration of various treatment modalities as dispositional questions that arise only after a judicial determination of incompetence. Thus, it consistently maintains the conceptual and justificatory relationship between incompetence and *parens patriae* intervention, and it precludes the practical difficulties that arise when an individual is subject to involuntary commitment but is considered competent to refuse treatment.

The book then develops a parallel notion of retributive competence that provides the organizing principle for the police power institutions. This notion of retributive competence explains and justifies the exercise of police power through the criminal justice system for those who possess such competence and through the mental health system for those who lack such competence. This restructured set of police power institutions provides for the social control of those who engage in violent or dangerous conduct, including but not limited to the sexual offenses addressed by sexual predator statutes, in a manner that conforms to the principles of political morality underlying liberal societies.

The relevant conceptions of mental illness for the police power and *parens patriae* interventions have clinical and normative components. The clinical aspects include the functional impairment of psychological processes, and describing and explaining this functional impairment falls within the expertise of clinicians. The normative components reflect the underlying principles of political morality that provide the common normative framework for the *parens patriae* and police power institutions. These principles support the judgments that certain types of functional impairment are sufficient to justify treating persons as incompetent to qualify as subjects of the criminal justice system that orders the public domain or as incompetent to direct their lives in the nonpublic domain. These judgments provide the basis for addressing these persons as subject to social control through the mental health system rather than through the criminal justice system or as subject to *parens patriae* intervention.[8] These normative components necessarily fall beyond the scope of clinical expertise because they involve legal or moral judgments. Thus, legislatures and courts must recognize and discharge their responsibilities to address these normative components in order to determine whether each individual is mentally ill for the legal purpose at issue.

This integration of the mental health and criminal justice institutions can provide a coherent legal approach to those who engage in violent or otherwise harmful conduct, as well as to those who suffer impairment that renders them subject to *parens patriae* intervention. By clarifying the criteria that render an individual appropriately subject to involuntary intervention by either the mental health or criminal justice systems, this integration should improve the ability of each institution to successfully discharge its practical tasks such as punishment, deterrence, containment, or involuntary care and treatment. By accurately and clearly representing widely accepted principles of political morality, this approach might reinforce and shape widely accepted principles of public morality in such a manner as to encourage voluntary compliance with these legal institutions.

Finally, by clarifying the clinical and normative components of various central determinations and criteria, this structure might promote the likelihood that legal actors and clinicians are able to identify and pursue their respective responsibilities. This clarification of the underlying principles and of the appropriate distribution of responsibilities should reduce the tendency to misuse these institutions in an oppressive manner, at least insofar as that misuse results from unintentional misinterpretation and misapplication. In summary, this book provides an abstract conceptual and normative framework for an integrated body of mental health law. This abstract framework does not purport to replace doctrinal, empirical, or policy analysis relevant to specific issues within mental health law. Rather, it provides an abstract context for more specific inquiries of these types, and it facilitates the design, interpretation, and application of legal institutions in a manner that implements and reinforces widely endorsed principles of public morality while protecting the nonpublic domain from intrusion. Furthermore, this framework clarifies the defensible parameters of involuntary clinical intervention, and it provides guidance regarding the appropriate distribution of responsibility for these interventions to clinicians, social scientists, and legal officials.

Part I presents and clarifies central legal and conceptual concerns. Chapter 1 presents some of the central concerns raised by sexual predator statutes and explores the manner in which these concerns permeate mental health law generally. Chapter 2 examines the brief passages in *Kansas v. Hendricks* in which the Supreme Court discusses and rejects the petitioners' claim that the sexual predator statute at issue in that case violates the criteria of validity imposed on civil commitment statutes by the Due Process Clause of the Constitution.[9] The chapter then examines a series of earlier Supreme Court cases addressing civil commitment and argues that these cases neither establish the criteria of commitment that they are often cited as establishing nor provide any meaningful guidance regarding the appropriate interpretation of commitment criteria framed in terms of mental illness or related phrases. Chapter 3 develops a formal conception of legal mental illness for general application to legal

---

[8] *See* chapter 3, section III.
[9] Kansas v. Hendricks, 117 S.Ct. 2072, 2079–81 (1997).

provisions that authorize differential legal treatment of those who are mentally ill. It then applies that formal conception to sexual predator and general civil commitment statutes in order to derive appropriate substantive interpretations of mental illness or mental abnormality requirements in those statutes.

Part II presents an integrated approach to the central institutions of *parens patriae* intervention. Chapters 4 and 5 provide a normative structure for the analysis of *parens patriae* interventions in a liberal society, with specific attention to statutes addressing *parens patriae* civil commitment and civil incompetence for person generally or health care specifically. These chapters propose a revised approach to these matters that abolishes *parens patriae* civil commitment as an independent institution and addresses involuntary hospitalization and treatment as dispositional decisions following a judicial determination of incompetence. Chapter 6 examines the current debate regarding the right to refuse treatment and the professional judgment standard (PJS) as applied to this issue. It proposes a revised interpretation of the PJS and integrates this standard with the central role of competence in *parens patriae* interventions in order to develop a coherent and defensible distribution of responsibilities among patients, clinicians, and courts for the purpose of delineating the scope of involuntary treatment.

Part III develops an approach to police power intervention. Chapters 7 and 8 develop a conception of retributive competence and a normative structure for the analysis of police power interventions, including sexual predator commitments. This structure provides a coherent and defensible foundation for the criminal justice system as the primary legal institution for police power interventions and for police power civil commitment as a complementary institution for the social control of those who fail to qualify as responsible subjects of the criminal justice system. This normative structure also coheres with the corresponding structure advanced in chapter 4 for *parens patriae* interventions. Thus, chapters 4 and 7 provide a consistent normative structure for the integrated *parens patriae* and police power institutions. Chapter 9 applies the normative structure developed in chapters 4, 6, and 7 in order to delineate the limits of the right to refuse treatment in the context of a police power intervention.

Part IV explores the significance of the interaction between this normative framework and the PJS for the professional responsibilities of clinicians, social scientists, and legal actors. Chapters 10 and 11 address the clinician's roles as information provider, including the role of expert witness. Chapter 12 addresses alternative responsibilities of clinicians. Chapter 13 returns to the Supreme Court cases reviewed in Chapter 2 and contends that the normative framework and revised institutional structure proposed in this book are consistent with principles implicit in these cases.

I do not contend that this framework provides an exhaustive theory of mental health law or that it represents the only interpretation of mental health law consistent with the principles underlying a liberal society. I contend only that the normative framework presented in this book provides a defensible example of the types of foundation needed to develop an integrated theory of mental health law that coheres internally and with related legal institutions such as the criminal law. Thus, the analysis advanced in the following chapters is intended to serve both as model for the development of an integrated theory of mental health law and as a substantive application of that model.

Part I

Mental Illness and Legal Intervention

Chapter 1
SEXUAL PREDATOR STATUTES AND THE FRAGMENTED STRUCTURE OF MENTAL HEALTH LAW

This chapter examines some of the central concerns raised by sexual predator statutes. These statutes reveal two levels of important conceptual and normative questions. At the specific level, the statutes raise important concerns about the appropriate interpretation of certain terms and provisions they include and about the justification for commitment authorized by them. At a more general level, they raise troubling questions regarding the coherence of and justification for the more comprehensive set of legal institutions that represent and apply mental health law. The questions raised at this more general level also implicate the appropriate relationships among the institutions of mental health law and related components of the legal system.

I.   Sexual Predators

Consider four hypothetical sex offenders. All four would meet the diagnostic criteria for pedophilia according to the diagnostic nomenclature most commonly referred to in the United States (DSM–IV).[1] All four would qualify for coercive legal intervention under various components of the criminal justice or mental health systems.

> *Anderson* suffers no impairment of orientation, consciousness, perception, comprehension, reasoning, or reality testing, but he is a socially anxious and inadequate individual who finds adult relationships uncomfortable because he lacks social skills and fears rejection and criticism. Anderson seeks small children in parks or on the street, befriends them, and lures them into isolated situations in order to engage in sexual activity. He carefully avoids causing physical injury to the children and rewards them with candy. When apprehended, he claims that he was merely providing the children with sex education and that some of the children approached him with questions about sexuality and requests for candy. It seems plausible that Anderson may use this rationalization to avoid the discomfort of guilt. He qualifies for the diagnoses of pedophilia and avoidant personality disorder under the DSM–IV.[2] Upon conviction for several counts of sexual assault on children, he is sentenced to a term of years in the state prison.[3]
>
> *Baker* suffers no impairment of orientation, consciousness, perception, comprehension, reasoning, or reality testing, but since adolescence, he has engaged in a broad pattern of criminal activity including a variety of crimes against persons. He has been arrested several times, and on a few occasions he has been convicted of various crimes. He has served a few relatively brief criminal sentences in the county jail and

---

[1] AMERICAN PSYCHIATRIC ASSOCIATION, DIAGNOSTIC AND STATISTICAL MANUAL OF MENTAL DISORDERS 527–28 (4th ed. 1994) [hereinafter DSM–IV].

[2] *Id.* at 527–28 (pedophilia), 662–65 (avoidant personality).

[3] NEV. REV. STAT. §28-320.01 (1995).

one longer sentence in the state prison. He regularly engages in sexual activity with adults, adolescents, and children, largely on the basis of convenience and often involving the abuse of his partner. Baker sometimes injures or threatens his victims in order to force them to submit, and he sometimes threatens to kill them if they tell anyone of his conduct. He qualifies for the diagnoses of pedophilia, sexual sadism, and antisocial personality disorder (APD) under the DSM–IV.[4] Upon conviction for several counts of sexual assault on children, he is sentenced to a term of years in the state prison.[5]

Cook is a moderately retarded adult who lives in a group home, works at a sheltered workshop, and engages in sexual activity with children and young adolescents in the neighborhoods around both the home and the workshop. He engaged in similar activity in previous neighborhoods. Sometimes he responds to advances by the adolescents, but on other occasions he approaches younger children in playgrounds and parks in order to solicit sexual activity. Cook neither physically injures nor threatens those with whom he engages in sexual activity. When a child rejects his advances, he looks for a more willing partner. He qualifies for the diagnoses of pedophilia and moderate mental retardation under the DSM–IV.[6] Upon arrest for engaging in sexual activity with children, he is charged with criminal offenses, but he is found incompetent to stand trial and committed to a secure mental health facility.[7] He appears to be honestly distraught and perplexed when the judge does not allow him to return home after he says "I'm sorry."

Davis suffers chronic paranoid schizophrenia. He frequently experiences sexual fantasies and urges regarding young children. During periods of relative remission of his schizophrenia, he experiences guilt and distress regarding these urges, and he intensifies his religious activities in order to distract himself from them. During his periods of psychosis, however, he sexually molests young children in response to auditory hallucinations and an ongoing delusional system in which he fuses his sexual fantasies about children with delusional thought about a special mission from god to establish a "sacred family of chosen acolytes." He qualifies for the diagnoses of pedophilia and paranoid schizophrenia under the DSM–IV.[8] Following trial for sexually assaulting children, he is found not guilty by reason of insanity (NGRI) and committed to a secure mental health facility.

These candidates all fulfill the diagnostic criteria for pedophilia, and each also qualifies for at least one other diagnosis under the DSM–IV. Many readers will find that the impairment supporting these diagnoses intuitively suggests differences in appropriate clinical treatment and legal disposition. Baker is a criminal who engages in a broad range of conduct ordinarily understood as falling within the jurisdiction of the criminal justice system. There is no obvious reason why the state should address his conduct constituting sexual offenses in a fundamentally different manner than it addresses his other criminal conduct, including nonsexual assaults. Cook and Davis suffer serious impairment that renders them appropriate subjects for treatment, training, and supervision through the mental health system. Davis was acquitted

---

[4] DSM–IV, *supra* note 1, at 527–28 (pedophilia), 530 (sexual sadism), 645–50 (APD).

[5] NEV. REV. STAT. §28-320.01 (1995).

[6] DSM–IV, *supra* note 1, at 39–46 (mental retardation), 527–28 (pedophilia).

[7] MICHAEL L. PERLIN, MENTAL DISABILITY LAW §§14.14–14.16 (1989).

[8] DSM–IV, *supra* note 1, at 273–87 (schizophrenia), 527–28 (pedophilia). Although he has experienced these urges and fantasies since adolescence, Davis usually acts on them only during periods of psychosis. When he is not psychotic, he either obsesses about the sinful nature of these urges and fantasies or attempts to avoid them by engaging in a series of compulsive rituals.

through the insanity defense, and Cook might have been a plausible candidate for the same defense, had he been competent to stand trial. Both are committed to secure mental health facilities that are intended to provide behavior control as well as care and treatment.

Anderson, in contrast, might elicit ambivalence among some readers regarding his most appropriate disposition. Although he would qualify for conviction and imprisonment, some might consider him an appropriate candidate for commitment to the mental health system. One can argue that among the four hypothetical offenders, only Anderson should be considered a "primary" pedophile for the purpose of social control through state intervention. That is, the conduct that qualifies Baker for the diagnosis of pedophilia is secondary in the sense that it is one part of a broad pattern of aggressive criminal conduct that requires social control. The pedophilic behavior of Cook and Davis is secondary in the sense that it reflects a pervasive pattern of impairment, rendering appropriate special institutions designed for persons with such impairment who require social control. Only Anderson limits his antisocial conduct to pedophilic behavior and lacks a broader pattern of severe impairment. Thus, Anderson is the only one of the four whose pedophilic conduct is primary in the sense that this conduct constitutes the primary reason for state intervention and the primary determinant of the appropriate form for that intervention. Should the state control Anderson and similar offenders through social institutions that address these offenders as psychopathological, criminal, both, or as falling into some unique category?

Two observations regarding these four offenders are particularly relevant to the purpose of this book. First, ordinary legal institutions provide some form of coercive behavior control for all four offenders. The criminal justice system currently provides the primary legal institution of coercive control for Anderson and Baker through criminal conviction and incarceration. Although Anderson may elicit some ambivalence regarding his most appropriate disposition, he is clearly competent to stand trial, and he fulfills the culpability requirements for conviction and punishment in the criminal justice system. Some might consider him an appropriate subject of mental health treatment before he engages in criminal conduct, during his prison sentence, or after he completes that sentence, but many individuals who are criminally responsible and subject to conviction and punishment might benefit from some form of mental health care. The criminal justice system provides the primary legal institution of coercive social control for these two offenders because that system provides society's primary legal institution for the coercive social control of those who culpably engage in criminal conduct. Alternative institutions apply to certain classes of offenders who are excluded from the criminal justice system by some special condition such as age or incapacity or by some special status such as diplomatic immunity.

Special commitment procedures confine Cook and Davis in secure mental health facilities. The precise relationships between the criminal justice and mental health systems vary across jurisdictions, but neither Cook nor Davis is convicted of a crime or sentenced to criminal punishment. Although the criminal courts might maintain jurisdiction over their commitments in some jurisdictions, they are committed to mental health facilities for custody and treatment. In some jurisdictions, Davis's postacquittal commitment could last only as long as the length of the maximum sentence he could have received if he had been convicted. At that time, the state could either release him or initiate commitment under the general civil commitment statute.[9] Cook's commitment following the finding that he is incompetent to stand trial must terminate if it becomes clear that he is not likely to become competent to stand trial, and at that time, the state could initiate civil commitment proceedings regarding him.[10] Thus, the state exercises coercive social control over Cook and Davis through some variation of the process of civil commitment, although criminal courts may retain jurisdiction over these commitments in some circumstances. In summary, it seems relatively clear that the criminal justice system provides the primary institution of coercive social control for Anderson and Baker and that the mental health system provides the primary institution of coercive social control for Cook and Davis.

The second observation that can be made about these four offenders is that although they differ significantly in the nature of their pathology and the legal dispositions that many readers might find intuitively appropriate, all four fall within the scope of the recently passed sexual predator commitment statutes.[11] Thus, their standing under these statutes apparently bears no direct relationship to the type of psychopathology they manifest or to the dispositions that are otherwise available and that seem intuitively appropriate. These two observations raise questions at two levels of analysis. At the specific level, do the sexual predator statutes represent a coherent and justifiable approach to coercive behavior control? At the more general level, does this inquiry regarding the sexual predator statutes inform our understanding regarding the coherence of, and the justification for, the more comprehensive structure of mental health law and its relationship to the criminal justice system?

II. Sexual Predator Statutes

The Washington Sexually Violent Predator statute provides the prototype for several recently enacted sex offender commitment statutes, including the Kansas statute at issue in *Kansas v. Hendricks*.[12] Although the Kansas and Washington statutes differ in some respects, they share several key provisions. Both statutes provide for indefinite civil commitment of sexually violent predators.[13] Both statutes define "sexually violent predator" as "any person who has been convicted of or charged with a crime of sexual violence and who suffers from a mental abnormality or personality disorder which makes the person likely to engage in the predatory acts of sexual violence if not confined in a secure facility."[14] Both statutes define a "mental abnormality" as "a congenital or acquired condition affecting the emotional or volitional capacity which predisposes the person to the commission of criminal sexual acts in a degree constituting such person a menace to the health and safety of others."[15] Although neither statute provides a definition of "personality disorder," the Washington Su-

---

[9] Perlin, *supra* note 7, §15.20.

[10] *Id.* at §§14.14-14.16.

[11] *See* section II.

[12] 117 S.Ct. 2072 (1997); Kan. Stat. Ann. §59-29 (Supp. 1997); Wash. Rev. Code Ann. §71.09 (Supp. 1998).

[13] Kan. Stat. Ann. §59-29a07 (Supp. 1997); Wash. Rev. Code Ann. §71.09.060 (Supp. 1998).

[14] Kan. Stat. Ann. §59-29a02a (Supp. 1997); Wash. Rev. Code Ann. §71.09.020(1) (Supp. 1998).

[15] Kan. Stat. Ann. §59-29a02(b) (Supp. 1997); Wash. Rev. Code Ann. §71.09.020(2) (Supp. 1998).

preme Court interpreted this statutory term with reference to the category of personality disorders as defined in the third revised edition of the DSM.[16]

These statutes resemble more general civil commitment statutes insofar as the requirements of a mental abnormality or personality disorder that makes the individual likely to engage in sexual violence are analogous to the more general civil commitment criteria of mental illness and dangerousness.[17] Indeed, either the general civil commitment statutes or the sexual predator statutes could provide for the commitment of individuals who commit relevant offenses while suffering severe impairment that supports the findings that they are incompetent to stand trial for those offenses, or that they are not guilty for those offenses by reason of insanity. Cook and Davis, for example, were committed to secure mental health facilities through the criminal justice system after respective findings of incompetence to stand trial and of NGRI. Either the sexual predator statutes or ordinary civil commitment provisions could accommodate Cook and Davis, however, because their serious impairment and the behavior constituting their criminal offenses would provide the basis for establishing the mental illness and dangerousness required under general civil commitment provisions or the mental abnormality and likelihood of engaging in acts of sexual violence required for commitment under the sexual predator statutes.

The variety of commitment provisions can generate some ambiguity regarding terminology. Most courts and commentators refer to commitment under the general civil commitment statutes as "civil commitment." Courts and commentators may refer to commitment following a finding of incompetence to stand trial or NGRI as "criminal commitment" because the criminal court retains jurisdiction, but they may refer to these commitments as "civil commitment" because such confinement does not require criminal conviction. Strictly speaking, however, these commitments and commitment under the sexual predator statutes remain civil in the sense that they do not require conviction and they at least purport to provide control, care, and treatment, rather than punishment.[18] For the sake of clarity, this book adopts the following conventions. "Commitment" and "civil commitment" refer broadly to confinement authorized by provisions addressing general civil commitment, sexual predator commitment, or commitment following findings of incompetence to stand trial or NGRI. Such commitments do not require criminal conviction and at least purport to provide control, care, and treatment, rather than punishment. "Sexual predator commitment," "post-NGRI commitment," and "postincompetence commitment" refer to commitment under provisions that address each of these conditions specifically. "General civil commitment" and "general commitment" refer to commitment under a state's general civil commitment statute.[19]

---

[16] In Re Young, 857 P2. 989, 1002–03 (1993); AMERICAN PSYCHIATRIC ASSOCIATION, DIAGNOSTIC AND STATISTICAL MANUAL OF MENTAL DISORDERS 629–34 (3d ed., rev.) [hereinafter DSM–III–R]. This was the current edition of the DSM at the time.

[17] John Parry, Involuntary Civil Commitment in the 90s: A Constitutional Perspective, 18, MENTAL & PHYSICAL DISABILITY L. REP. 320 (1994).

[18] Hendricks, 117 S.Ct. at 2072.

[19] Thus, suppose that X and Y are two criminal defendants who are found incompetent to stand trial; X is committed to a mental health facility under a provision that specifically provides for the commitment of those found incompetent to stand trial in order to provide for treatment intended to render them competent for that purpose. In contrast, the prosecutor drops criminal charges against Y and successfully seeks civil commitment of Y under the general civil commitment statute. According to the

Anderson, Baker, and other offenders who lack severe impairment raise the most pressing questions regarding the sexual predator statutes. Commitments of convicted sex offenders, such as Anderson and Baker, at the end of their prison terms provide the most common and most controversial applications of the sexual predator statutes, and these commitments most clearly differentiate these provisions from general civil commitment statutes.[20] The legislative findings indicate that the purpose and justification of the distinct sexual predator commitment provisions rest on the premise that the general commitment statutes do not apply to individuals who do not manifest the severe impairment usually associated with general civil commitment but whose proclivity to commit sexual offenses has not diminished following the completion of their criminal sentences.[21] The sexual predator statutes allow commitment partially on the basis of prior criminal acts, requiring no more recent overt act indicating dangerousness for those who have been confined during the period since those criminal offenses.[22] This failure to require more recent indicia of risk reflects the tacit assumption that the characteristics of these offenders that led to the perpetration of the sex offenses that resulted in their initial criminal convictions endure through the time of their mandatory release dates.

Sexual predator statutes such as those in Washington and Kansas invite controversy partially because they authorize commitment of individuals who manifest no serious impairment of a type that would ordinarily support civil commitment and who demonstrate no evidence of deterioration in their psychological capacities since they were convicted of their sexually violent offenses. Cases brought under these statutes frequently demonstrate this pattern. The subjects of the petitions for commitment had recently completed, or were approaching completion of, sentences for multiple violent sexual offenses. None of these offenders carried diagnoses that indicated serious impairment of orientation, consciousness, perception, comprehension, reasoning, or reality testing. They carried diagnoses (e.g., APD, the paraphilias) that can be based heavily upon the demonstrated propensity to commit such offenses. Although the appellate opinions provide only partial reference to the expert testimony supporting the diagnoses and commitments, these references indicate that the diagnoses and the findings of mental abnormality or personality disorder under the statutes emphasized the pattern of criminal conduct that generated the conviction and sentences.[23] These statutes and cases raise important questions regarding the nature of and justification for commitment under these statutes and regarding the relationships among sexual predator commitment, criminal conviction, and commitment under the more general civil commitment statutes.

---

terminology adopted here, X is subject to postincompetence commitment, but Y is subject to general civil commitment. If X is later released from his postincompetence commitment and committed under the general civil commitment statute because it becomes clear that he remains severely impaired and is not making progress toward regaining competence to stand trial, he moves from the status of postincompetence commitment to the status of general commitment. That is, this terminology reflects the type of provision under which the individual is committed.

[20] KAN. STAT. ANN. §59-29a03-07 (Supp. 1997); WASH. REV. CODE ANN. §71.09.030 (Supp. 1998).

[21] KAN. STAT. ANN. §59-29a01 (Supp. 1997); WASH. REV. CODE ANN. §71.09.010 (Supp. 1998).

[22] WASH. REV. CODE ANN. §71.09.060 (Supp. 1998).

[23] In Re Hendricks, 912 P.2d 129, 131, 137–38 (Kan. 1996); State v. Carpenter, 541 N.W.2d 105, 108–09 (Wis. 1995); In Re Linehan, 557 N.W.2d 171, 175–79 (Min. 1996); State v. Post, 541 N.W.2d 115, 119 (Wis. 1995); In Re Young, 857 P.2d 989, 994–96 (Wash. 1993).

III.   Police Power Civil Commitment

The traditional police power supports the state's authority to wield coercive force in order to protect the community from harm. It has relatively noncontroversial application in the administration of the criminal justice system as the primary legal institution of coercive social control over adult citizens who engage in culpable conduct that harms the legitimate interests of others.[24] Conviction and incarceration through the criminal justice system and some cases of civil commitment, including commitment under the sexual predator statutes, constitute applications of the traditional police power for the purpose of protecting the public from harm. Insofar as commitment applies to individuals like Cook and Davis, who suffer impairment that renders them inappropriate for conviction and punishment in the criminal justice system, commitment functions as an alternative institution of social control. The courts commit impaired individuals like Cook and Davis to secure mental health facilities partially because their impairment renders them either unable to participate in the adjudicative process of the criminal justice system (Cook) or unable to meet the culpability requirements for criminal punishment (Davis).

Although Cook and Davis are committed through proceedings associated with the criminal justice system, general civil commitment statutes authorize commitment on the basis of mental illness and dangerousness through an entirely civil proceeding intended to protect the community from harm. If one interprets the mental illness criterion as addressing impairment that renders the individual unable to function as a fully responsible subject of the criminal justice system, then general civil commitment statutes provide an alternative institution of coercive social control for those who are not eligible for social control through the criminal justice system. According to this interpretation, impairment would qualify as mental illness or mental abnormality for the purpose of commitment precisely because it renders the individual unable to function as a responsible subject of the criminal justice system. Using the sexual predator statutes to commit individuals, like Anderson and Baker, who remain fully culpable under the criminal law seems to preclude this interpretation, however, and reveals the need for an explicit conception of mental illness (or mental abnormality) for the purpose of civil commitment. These cases also demonstrate the need for a clear explanation of the relationship between the criminal justice and mental health institutions of social control under the police power.

In summary, commitment under the sexual predator statutes of individuals such as Anderson and Baker, who have completed criminal sentences for the conduct that precipitates their commitment, raises at least three important questions regarding sexual predator commitment specifically and police power commitment more generally. First, what type of psychological impairment constitutes a mental abnormality for sexual predator commitment specifically or a mental illness for police power commitment more generally? Second, in what manner does such a mental abnormality or mental illness justify the state in exercising the police power through institutions distinct from the criminal justice process? Third, in what manner can impairment justify purportedly civil commitment under the sexual predator provi-

---

[24] BLACKS LAW DICTIONARY 1156 (6th ed. 1990); SAMUEL JAN BRAKEL, JOHN PARRY, & BARBARA A. WEINER, THE MENTALLY DISABLED AND THE LAW 23–25 (3rd ed. 1985).

sions but neither justify commitment under general civil commitment statutes nor reduce culpability for criminal conduct?

IV. *Parens Patriae* Civil Commitment

Some passages in the sexual predator statutes and in the Supreme Court's ruling in *Kansas v. Hendricks* suggest that these statutes are intended to provide care and treatment for the offender as well as to protect the public.[25] The statutory language presents a rather puzzling picture regarding the role of treatment in sexual predator commitment. The legislative findings suggest that the individuals targeted by these statutes are not appropriately committed for treatment in that they do not manifest a disorder that ordinarily supports civil commitment and they are not amenable to ordinary treatment modalities. Yet, the statutes authorize commitment for long-term care and treatment and specify that this care and treatment must conform to constitutional standards.[26] Interpreted collectively, the legislative findings apparently claim that these offenders should be subject to a mental health commitment for long-term care and treatment because they have no serious mental health impairment of the type ordinarily appropriate to commitment, and they are not amenable to mental health treatment. A reasonable reading of these provisions suggests that they are intended primarily as a means of confining the individual in order to protect the public and secondarily as a means of providing such treatment as might be expected to improve the individual's condition in a manner that promotes the public safety.[27]

Although the sexual predator statutes apparently contemplate treatment as instrumental to the central goal of protecting the public, general civil commitment statutes explicitly include promoting the interests of the committed individual among the primary purposes of commitment. General civil commitment statutes ordinarily apply the traditional *parens patriae* power of the state as well as the police power. The *parens patriae* power classically supports the state's authority to intervene in the lives of citizens who lack the capacity to care for their own basic needs. It authorizes state officials to provide care for these citizens and to manage their property. It has relatively noncontroversial applications in the processes of guardianship and conservatorship for those who are unable to competently manage their own affairs or to care for themselves as a result of conditions such as severe retardation or senescent decline.[28]

General civil commitment statutes ordinarily require mental illness and dangerousness to self or others as criteria of commitment.[29] The distinction between *parens patriae* and police power is sometimes discussed as analogous to the distinction between dangerous to self and dangerous to others, although some writers interpret commitment to prevent persons from harming themselves as falling under either the

---

[25] *Hendricks*, 117 S.Ct. at 2072, 2084–85.
[26] KAN. STAT. ANN. §§59-29a07, 09 (1994 and Supp. 1997); WASH. REV. CODE ANN. §§71.09.060(1), 080(2) (Supp. 1998).
[27] *Hendricks*, 117 S.Ct. at 2083–85.
[28] BLACKS LAW DICTIONARY, *supra* note 24, at 114; BRAKEL ET AL., *supra* note 24, at 23–25.
[29] MICHAEL L. PERLIN, MENTAL DISABILITY LAW §2A-1 (2d ed. 1998).

parens patriae or the police power category.[30] The normative framework advanced in this book indicates that the conditions required to justify state intervention in order to protect the individual's interests differ from those required to justify state intervention in order to prevent injury to others. Thus, clearly distinguishing the *parens patriae* and police powers as protecting (respectively) the individual who is the subject of the intervention or others facilitates the development of legal doctrine that consistently reflects the underlying justification. For this reason, this book addresses commitment under the danger to self condition or its variants as falling within the scope of the *parens patriae* function of the state.

Although courts often refer to the criteria of commitment simply as mental illness and dangerousness, statutes and proposals sometimes supplement the subcategory of dangerousness to self with some additional conditions such as grave disability or the need for treatment to avoid harm, distress, or deterioration.[31] One might interpret these additional conditions as components in an extended conception of danger to self or as an alternative to the danger to self criterion. These additional conditions clearly fall within the scope of the *parens patriae* power in that they address those whose impairments render them unable to make reasoned decisions needed to protect themselves from harm or deterioration. If one interprets the mental illness criterion as requiring psychological impairment that prevents individuals from making similarly reasoned decisions about the dangers to which they expose themselves, the danger to self condition also represents an exercise of the state's *parens patriae* function because it addresses those who lack the capacity to protect themselves from harm.

Under ordinary conditions, competent adults have a right to refuse health care, including life-sustaining care.[32] Furthermore, many contemporary civil commitment statutes explicitly deny that commitment entails incompetence.[33] Thus, commitment under these statutes does not establish incompetence to accept or reject routine treatment, absent an emergency or a court determination of incompetence. These circumstances generate an apparent paradox regarding those who are committed under the *parens patriae* provisions of the civil commitment statutes. That is, they are involuntarily committed to a mental health facility for their own welfare because they suffer psychological impairment that renders them unable to protect their interests by making reasoned decisions regarding the risk of harm or deterioration to which they expose themselves, but they retain the authority to accept or reject health care for the purpose of protecting and promoting their interests.

Some cases address claims of a right to treatment or of a right to refuse treatment by applying the PJS according to which courts review professional decisions regarding treatment only to the extent that the courts affirm that the professionals exercised professional judgment in their treatment decisions.[34] Commentators criticize the ap-

---

[30] *See, e.g.,* Donald H. J. Hermann, *Barriers to Providing Effective Treatment: A Critique of Revisions in Procedural, Substantive, and Dispositional Criteria in Involuntary Civil Commitment,* 39 VAND. L. REV. 83, 95–96 (1986).

[31] Parry, *supra* note 17, at 322–23, 330–36.

[32] BRUCE J. WINICK, THE RIGHT TO REFUSE MENTAL HEALTH TREATMENT 1 (1997).

[33] BARBARA A. WEINER & ROBERT M. WETTSTEIN, LEGAL ISSUES IN MENTAL HEALTH CARE 86–87 (1993). WINICK, *supra* note 32, at 289–91.

[34] Youngberg v. Romeo, 457 U.S. 307 (1982); U.S. v. Charters, 863 F.2d 302 (4th Cir. 1988); Rennie

plication of the PJS to the right to refuse treatment, contending that the PJS reduces this right to a right to a second opinion and that by applying the PJS in this manner, courts forfeit judicial responsibility to clinical professionals who confront a variety of institutional pressures other than the patients' rights or interests.[35]

This intersection of the rights to treatment or to refuse treatment with *parens patriae* civil commitment raises a series of important questions regarding the *parens patriae* function of the mental health system. It explicitly raises questions about the appropriate roles of legal and clinical actors in decisions regarding treatment and treatment refusal. To what extent should courts directly address questions of involuntary treatment for committed patients, and to what extent and in what manner should clinicians address these decisions? This question generates additional questions regarding the nature of the mental illness required for *parens patriae* interventions. What type of impairment justifies *parens patriae* civil commitment, and in what manner, if at all, does that impairment differ from that required to justify a determination of incompetence for person generally or for health care decisions specifically? If impairment sufficient for *parens patriae* civil commitment does not entail incompetence for person generally or for health care decisions specifically, how can it justify involuntary confinement to a mental health facility for the purpose of protecting that person's interests? Finally, in what manner do clinical and normative factors interact in defining the meaning of "mental illness" for these purposes, and how does this interaction inform the appropriate parameters of legal and clinical responsibilities? These questions reveal the need to clarify the conceptual and normative relationships among provisions providing for *parens patriae* civil commitment, determinations of incompetence for person generally or health care specifically, guardianship for person, and protective placement.

V. Civil Incompetence and Guardianship

All states have established authority and procedures for adjudicating civil competence and for appointing guardians for those declared civilly incompetent by the court. The specific provisions currently in place vary significantly from state to state. This section introduces the broad general structure and purpose of this category of statutes, recognizing that specific provisions may depart from this general description in a variety of ways. Competence is the threshold issue in that the court does not address the appointment of a guardian, the authority and duties of the guardian, or substantive decisions such as placement or specific health care procedures unless it has already determined that the individual lacks competence.[36] These statutes ordinarily address competence for person and for property. Competence for person addresses the individual's ability to make reasoned decisions regarding his own personal well-being, and it includes but is not limited to competence regarding health

---

v. Klein, 720 F.2d 266 (3rd Cir. 1983); Susan Stefan, *Leaving Civil Rights to the "Experts": From Deference to Abdication Under the Professional Judgment Standard*, 102 YALE L. J. 639, 670–72 (1992).

[35] Alexander D. Brooks, *The Right to Refuse Antipsychotic Medications: Law and Policy*, 39 RUT-GERS L. REV. 339, 354–61 (1987); Stefan, *supra* note 34, at 646–85.

[36] UNIFORM PROBATE CODE §§5-101-04, 5-301-12 (Official Text with Comments, 10th ed., 1991); BRAKEL ET AL., *supra* note 24, at 370; WEINER & WETTSTEIN, *supra* note 33, at 287–92.

care. Competence for property addresses the individual's ability to manage any property or income that he or she maintains. Courts can declare individuals competent or incompetent for either or both domains of decision making.[37] The court exercises no further authority over the individual if it finds that person competent. If the court declares the individual incompetent for either or both domains, it appoints a guardian for that sphere of decision making.[38]

The court appoints a guardian for the appropriate domain in a court order that specifies the scope and limits of the guardian's authority. That authority can range from plenary authority to make decisions regarding person and property in the ward's stead to narrowly limited authority to address a specific decision or issue that extends beyond the individual's competence. Some statutes specifically define certain health care decisions, such as those authorizing psychosurgery, electroconvulsive therapy, or inpatient commitment, as beyond the authority of the guardian. Under these statutes, the court must make these decisions directly. Regardless of these specific statutory exclusions, the court can limit the scope of the guardian's authority by excluding certain matters in the court order or by defining the scope of guardianship narrowly.[39] The court delegates the decision-making authority to the guardian and retains jurisdiction over the case. Thus, the court can modify its own order; make certain decisions directly; and supervise, discipline, or remove the guardian.[40]

In summary, these statutes governing incompetence and guardianship can provide for inpatient care in a mental health facility either by direct court order or by decision of the guardian pursuant to a court order that provides the guardian with this authority. In either case, the court order requires a prior finding of incompetence for person generally, for health care decisions generally, or for this decision specifically. That finding of incompetence requires that the individual suffer some impairment that renders him or her unable to make and communicate reasoned decisions regarding these matters. The relationship between admission to a mental health facility under these statutes and *parens patriae* civil commitment under general civil commitment statutes raises puzzling yet familiar questions regarding the nature of the impairment that satisfies each type of provision and the justification for *parens patriae* intervention under each type of statute.

Admission directly authorized by court order under the authority of a statute addressing incompetence, guardianship, or protective placement, or by a guardian within the scope of that guardian's authority under such a statute, constitutes a *parens patriae* intervention requiring a prior finding of incompetence based on impairment that prevents the person from making reasoned decisions regarding these matters. Prior to the most recent generation of civil commitment statutes, civil commitment

---

[37] UNIFORM PROBATE CODE, *supra* note 36, at §§5-306, 5-401; BRAKEL ET AL., *supra* note 24, at 370; WEINER & WETTSTEIN, *supra* note 33, at 284–86.

[38] UNIFORM PROBATE CODE, *supra* note 36, at §§5-306, 5-401; BRAKEL ET AL., *supra* note 24, at 384–88; WEINER & WETTSTEIN, *supra* note 33, at 287–90.

[39] The recent trend in the statutes is toward narrower guardianship, allowing the ward to retain as much discretion as possible, but practical limitations may lead courts to rely more heavily on general guardianship orders. UNIFORM PROBATE CODE, *supra* note 36, at §§5-306(a), (c), 5-407(a) and comments at 368–69; BRAKEL ET AL., *supra* note 24, at 284–88; WEINER & WETTSTEIN, *supra* note 33, at 287–90.

[40] UNIFORM PROBATE CODE, *supra* note 36, at §§5-306(c), 5-311(a); BRAKEL ET AL., *supra* note 24, at 386–88; WEINER & WETTSTEIN, *supra* note 33, at 287.

represented a *de jure* or a *de facto* determination of incompetence in that committed individuals were presumed incompetent and treated as if they were incompetent. The more recent commitment statutes reject this approach, however, often explicitly rejecting any presumption of incompetence based merely on commitment, absent a judicial finding of incompetence.[41]

If the impairment that fulfills the mental illness requirement for civil commitment does not render the individual incompetent for self-regarding decisions, how can it justify a *parens patriae* intervention in the form of civil commitment? Given the foundation of the *parens patriae* rationale in the individual's inability to care for himself or herself, how can impairment satisfy the requirements of *parens patriae* civil commitment if it does not render the individual unable to make reasoned decisions regarding admission and health care? Furthermore, why would the conduct that satisfies the dangerousness to self or likelihood of deterioration requirement in the commitment statute justify *parens patriae* commitment unless it is the product of impaired decision making that renders the individual unable to decide competently whether to engage in that conduct and accept that risk or harm? In summary, by severing the prior relationship between civil commitment and incompetence, the more recent commitment statutes and cases raise serious questions regarding the putative justification for *parens patriae* commitment.

VI. Conclusion

Sexual predator statutes raise important questions regarding the coherence of and the justification for those provisions. Perhaps more significantly, however, they draw attention to a series of conceptual and normative concerns that permeate the central institutions of mental health law. Furthermore, these statutes draw attention to the relationships among these institutions and related areas of law such as the criminal justice system. These questions have important ramifications for any attempt to develop a coherent and defensible set of legal institutions. They also carry significance for the appropriate delineation of responsibility among legal and clinical actors in the operation of those institutions. Chapter 2 begins to clarify the legal foundations of mental health law by examining Supreme Court decisions that address civil commitment, including commitment under the sexual predator statutes.

---

[41] WEINER & WETTSTEIN, *supra* note 33, at 86–87; WINICK, *supra* note 32, at 289–91.

Chapter 2
THE SUPREME COURT ON
CIVIL COMMITMENT

The Supreme Court has addressed civil commitment in a series of cases that can be usefully understood as representing two distinct phases. The more recent cases address special circumstances of commitment such as commitment under sexual predator provisions or following NGRI acquittal. These cases rely on but do not carefully examine earlier cases that address civil commitment more generally. This chapter reviews the reasoning in the more recent cases in order to clarify the manner in which that reasoning relies on the earlier cases. It then examines those earlier cases in order to determine whether they provide the foundation the Court relies on for the latter cases. Finally, this chapter identifies the critical concerns left unaddressed by the entire series of Supreme Court cases.

I.   Recent Cases: *Foucha* to *Hendricks*

Although the Supreme Court's decision in *Hendricks*[1] directly addresses commitment under the sexual predator statute at issue in that case, it also represents the most recent Supreme Court opinion addressing the broader topic of civil commitment. Prior to the *Hendricks* decision, the sexual predator statutes divided the appellate courts. Some appellate courts upheld sexual predator statutes as consistent with the constitutional criteria of civil commitment established in a series of Supreme Court cases culminating in *Foucha v. Louisiana*.[2] Other appellate courts overturned sexual predator statutes as failing to satisfy the requirements of this series of cases.

Foucha involved the extension of a post-NGRI commitment on the basis of continued dangerousness under a statute that authorized indefinite commitment of NGRI acquittees until they carry the burden to prove that they are no longer dangerous.[3] Although the plurality and concurring opinions overturned Foucha's indefinite commitment to a mental health facility that was based only on his failure to prove that he was no longer dangerous, these opinions provided neither an explicit statement of constitutionally required commitment criteria nor a clear rationale for constitutionally valid civil commitment. After the Supreme Court handed down its decision in *Foucha*, some courts overturned sexual predator statutes because they interpreted *Foucha* and a prior series of Supreme Court cases as requiring mental illness and dangerousness for indefinite civil commitment.[4] Although these courts recognized that *Foucha* allowed brief confinement under narrowly circumscribed

---

[1] Kansas v. Hendricks, 117 S.Ct. 2072, 2078–81 (1997).

[2] 504 U.S. 71 (1992).

[3] *Id.* at 74–75.

[4] Young v. Weston, 898 F.Supp. 744, 749 (W.D.Wash. 1995); In Re Hendricks, 912 P.2d 129, 133–38 (Kan. 1996); State v. Post, 541 N.W.2d 115, 141–42 (Wis. 1995) (Abrahamson, J., dissenting).

conditions without mental illness, they understood the Supreme Court's ruling in *Foucha* as overturning the Louisiana statute at issue because it allowed indefinite commitment to a mental hospital absent mental illness.[5] *Foucha* addressed a postinsanity defense commitment statute, rather than a sexual predator provision, but these courts interpreted the sexual predator statutes before them as analogous to the provision at issue in *Foucha* insofar as they allowed indefinite civil commitment to a mental hospital without requiring mental illness.[6]

Other courts upheld sexual predator statutes as consistent with *Foucha*. These courts did not disagree with the overturning courts regarding the interpretation of the series of Supreme Court cases culminating in *Foucha* as requiring mental illness and dangerousness for indefinite civil commitment. Rather, these courts distinguished the sexual predator statutes before them from the Louisiana provision at issue in *Foucha*, interpreting these sexual predator statutes as requiring mental illness for commitment.[7] They also distinguished these statutes as applied in the cases before them from the specific application of the Louisiana statute in *Foucha* in that Louisiana had not contended that Foucha was mentally ill, but the states and experts in the cases before these courts argued that the petitioners were mentally ill.[8]

Thus, *Foucha*, the courts that overturned sexual predator statutes, and the courts that upheld sexual predator statutes all accepted consistent interpretations of prior Supreme Court doctrine as developed in the series of cases prior to *Foucha*; they understood these cases as requiring mental illness and dangerousness for indefinite civil commitment to a mental hospital. The upholding and overturning courts differed, however, in their assessments of requirements phrased as "personality disorder," "mental abnormality," or "mental disorder" as adequate to meet the mental illness requirement.

The courts that upheld sexual predator statutes advanced negative and positive arguments in supporting their interpretation of these provisions as consistent with the requirement of mental illness for indefinite civil commitment. They denied that there is a single canonical meaning for "mental illness," that the magic words "mental illness" were necessary, and that the clinical meaning would necessarily control interpretation of the statutes in light of *Foucha*.[9] They noted the courts' responsibility to respect legislative prerogative and to implement legislative intent, and they reasoned that experts had testified that these petitioners manifested disorders that qualified under the statutes and that these disorders either appeared in the current diagnostic manual or were consistent with diagnoses included in that manual.[10] However,

---

[5] *Young*, 898 F.Supp. at 744, 749–51; In Re Hendricks, 912 P.2d at 133–34; *Post*, 541 N.W.2d at 115, 141–45.

[6] *Young*, 898 F.Supp. at 744, 794–51; In Re Hendricks, 912 P.2d at 136–38; *Post*, 541 N.W.2d at 115, 142–45.

[7] Parrish v. Colorado, 78 F.3d 1473, 1477–78 (10th Cir. 1996); Matter of Linehan, 557 N.W.2d 171, 183–85 (Minn. 1996); In Re Blodgett, 510 N.W.2d 910, 914–16 (Minn. 1994); In Re Young, 857 P.2d 989, 1001–05 (Wash. 1993); *Post*, 541 N.W.2d at 115, 122–25.

[8] Hubbart v. Superior Court, 58 Cal.Rptr.2d 268, 289–90 (Cal. App. 6 Dist. 1996); *Parrish*, 78 F.3d at 1473, 1478; Matter of Linehan, 557 N.W.2d at 182–85; In Re Young, 857 P.2d 989, 1007 (Wash. 1993); *Post*, 541 N.W.2d at 115, 119, 122–24, 127.

[9] *Hubbart*, 58 Cal.Rptr.2d at 289–90; *Parrish*, 78 F.3d at 1473, 1477; In Re Blodgett, 510 N.W.2d at 910, 914–15; In Re Young, 857 P.2d at 989, 1001–03; *Post*, 541 N.W.2d at 115, 122–24.

[10] *Parish*, 78 F.3d at 1473, 1478; Matter of Linehan, 557 N.W.2d at 184; In Re Young, 857 P.2d at 989, 1001–03; *Post*, 541 N.W.2d at 115, 119, 123–24.

these courts did not articulate any legal criteria or test for mental illness or any of the alternate terms used in the various statutes. They provided no analysis that would guide lower courts or officials in applying the statutes. Although the courts denied that the clinical meaning of "mental illness" controls for statutory purposes, they relied heavily upon expert testimony by clinicians and upon the current diagnostic manual. A reasonable reading of these cases would support the interpretation that an individual fulfills mental illness, mental abnormality, personality disorder, or analogous statutory requirements in any case in which clinical expert witnesses testify that he or she does.

The courts that overturned sexual predator statutes as failing to meet the requirement of mental illness interpreted the statutory phrases such as "mental abnormality" or "personality disorder" as circular in that they merely restated the pattern of criminal conduct that generated the charges or convictions that preceded and supported the commitment petitions.[11] These courts relied partially on the common characterization of Foucha and of the petitioners in their cases as manifesting antisocial personalities, concluding that the Supreme Court apparently did not find an antisocial personality sufficient to constitute a mental illness for the purpose of indefinite confinement in a mental hospital.[12] Thus, the overturning courts, like the upholding courts, provided no analysis or criteria of mental illness for this purpose.

Although the overturning courts relied partially on the Supreme Court's characterization of Foucha as someone with an antisocial personality but not mental illness, the Foucha opinion does not explicitly rule that an APD cannot satisfy a requirement of mental illness for civil commitment. Rather, because the plurality and concurring opinions refer to and rely upon the characterization of Foucha, by the state and by the experts, as an individual who had an antisocial personality but who was not mentally ill, the Court's decision does not directly address the more general question regarding the adequacy of APD as a form of impairment sufficient to constitute mental illness for the purpose of commitment.[13] Similarly, the Court cited prior cases in order to support the contention that civil commitment requires mental illness and dangerousness, providing no rationale or justification for these two criteria as necessary conditions of legitimate civil commitment.[14]

The plurality opinion in *Foucha* cites *Addington v. Texas*[15] as establishing that in order to commit an individual to a mental institution the state must prove by clear and convincing evidence that the individual meets the statutory commitment criteria (i.e., that the individual is mentally ill and that hospitalization is required to protect his or her own welfare or the welfare of others).[16] The plurality's discussion of this

---

[11] *Young*, 898 F.Supp. at 744, 749–50; *Post*, 541 N.W.2d at 115, 143–44.

[12] *Young*, 898 F.Supp. at 744, 750; In Re Hendricks, 912 P.2d at 129, 137–38; *Post*, 541 N.W.2d at 115, 142.

[13] *Foucha*, 504 U.S. at 71, 74–75, 78–80, 86. *But see* Bruce J. Winick, *Ambiguities in the Legal Meaning and Significance of Mental Illness*, 1 PSYCHOL. PUB. POL'Y & L. 534 (1995). Winick argues that the case can be interpreted as ruling that antisocial personality does not qualify as legal mental illness and provides an interesting analysis of the ramifications of this interpretation. This question remains unaddressed after *Hendricks* because the *Hendricks* Court did not clarify the *Foucha* decision, and the opinion discussed Hendricks's diagnosis as pedophilia rather than as APD. *Hendricks*, 117 S.Ct. at 2072, 2078–81.

[14] *Foucha*, 504 U.S. at 75–78.

[15] 441 U.S. 418 (1979).

[16] *Foucha*, 504 U.S. at 75.

case is somewhat ambiguous; it is not clear whether the plurality reads *Addington* as requiring only that the state prove any required statutory commitment criteria by clear and convincing evidence or as requiring also that these criteria include mental illness and the need for hospitalization in order to protect welfare. The plurality's discussion of *Jones v. United States*[17] suggests the later interpretation; it discusses *Jones* as allowing commitment of post-NGRI acquittees without meeting the clear and convincing burden because the insanity acquittal establishes mental illness as the reason that the individual committed a crime. The plurality describes this acquittal as supporting the inference that the individual remains mentally ill and dangerous and thus subject to commitment.[18]

The plurality also cites *Jones* for the proposition that the state must release the committed individual who is no longer mentally ill or no longer dangerous.[19] The plurality finds support for this requirement in language from *O'Connor v. Donaldson*[20] in which the Court precluded the state from continuing to confine an individual when the conditions that legitimated the initial commitment no longer obtained; and thus from continued commitment of a nondangerous mentally ill person.[21] The *Foucha* plurality opinion relies upon *Jones* and upon *Jackson v. Indiana*[22] as establishing the principle that the nature of a commitment must bear some reasonable relationship to the state's purpose for that commitment, and it reasons that because Foucha is not mentally ill, this reasonable relationship principle precludes the state from holding him as a mentally ill person. Justice O'Connor's concurrence appeals to similar reasoning; she concluded that acquittees may not be confined as mental patients absent a medical justification because such confinement would not provide the necessary connection between the purpose and nature of confinement.[23]

In summary, the plurality and concurring opinions in *Foucha* rely upon the reasonable relationship principle from *Jackson* and upon precedent that they read as requiring current mental illness and dangerousness for civil commitment to a mental hospital. These opinions provide no analysis that would support a contention that only mental illness and dangerousness can satisfy the reasonable relationship principle, however, nor do they provide any other rationale for these criteria.[24] Finally, these opinions provide no analysis indicating what type of impairment should satisfy a mental illness criterion. Thus, the *Foucha* opinions provided state and federal courts that encountered sexual predator statutes with neither a Supreme Court standard of mental illness for the purpose of civil commitment nor a Supreme Court justification for the mental illness requirement that the lower courts could use for guidance in developing appropriate conceptions of mental illness for this purpose.

Two additional recent Supreme Court cases contain language suggesting that civil commitment requires mental illness and dangerousness, but these opinions provide neither reasoning to support these criteria nor explication of their meaning. *Zinermon v. Burch* cites *O'Connor v. Donaldson* for the proposition that the state

---

[17] Jones v. United States, 463 U.S. 354 (1983).

[18] *Foucha*, 504 U.S. at 76.

[19] *Id.* at 77–78.

[20] O'Connor v. Donaldson, 442 U.S. 563, 576 (1975).

[21] *Foucha*, 504 U.S. at 77.

[22] 406 U.S. 715, 717–19 (1972).

[23] *Foucha*, 504 U.S. at 88 (O'Connor, J. concurring).

[24] *Id.* at 79, 88 (O'Connor, J. concurring).

may not constitutionally confine a harmless mentally ill person who can live safely outside the hospital.[25] This proposition indicates that mental illness is not sufficient for involuntary civil commitment, but it neither establishes that mental illness is necessary nor provides any clear conception of mental illness for this purpose. *Riggins v. Nevada* cites *Addington* for the proposition that due process allows civil commitment upon a showing by clear and convincing evidence that the individual is mentally ill and dangerous.[26] The claim that the Constitution allows commitment on this basis does not establish that the Constitution requires these findings, however, and the opinion provides no reasoning requiring these criteria or clarifying what types of impairment would suffice as mental illness for this purpose. In summary, *Foucha, Zinermon,* and *Riggins* cite to earlier cases in asserting or suggesting that the Constitution requires mental illness and dangerousness for involuntary civil commitment, but these cases provide little or no reasoning that supports these criteria or provides guidance regarding the proper interpretation of the mental illness requirement for this purpose. Thus, the Court addressed *Hendricks* in the absence of a clearly articulated and well-reasoned body of law regarding civil commitment generally.

The majority opinion in *Hendricks* upheld the Kansas sexual predator statute against claims that it violated the due process, double jeopardy, and ex post facto requirements of the Constitution. The central concern for the purpose of this chapter involves Hendricks's claim that the statute violated the Due Process Clause because it authorized indefinite civil commitment absent mental illness. The Court's opinion in *Hendricks* rejects this claim, accepting the statutory requirement of a "mental abnormality" and Hendricks's diagnosis of pedophilia as sufficient to fulfill that requirement.[27] The opinion recognizes a protected liberty interest in freedom from physical restraint, but it also recognizes exceptions for those who are confined according to appropriate procedures and standards because their inability to control their behavior endangers the public health and safety. The opinion cites to *Foucha* and *Addington* as support for such exceptions,[28] and it reasons that the Kansas sexual predator statute clearly requires dangerousness in that it applies to those who have been convicted or charged with sexual offenses and who manifest mental abnormalities that make them likely to engage in future acts of sexual violence.[29]

The majority opinion also recognizes that dangerousness is not sufficient for commitment. Previously approved commitment statutes also include an impairment criterion, phrased in terms such as "mental illness," "mental abnormality," or "psychopathic personality." The Court rejected any suggestion that the statutory terms or their definitions must converge with their clinical counterparts or that the statutes must include the magic words "mental illness."[30] Although the opinion provides no clear explication of this mental illness criterion, several passages characterize the appropriate impairments as volitional disorders that render the individual unable to control dangerous behavior.[31] The Court provides no account of the types of im-

---

[25] Zinermon v. Burch, 494 U.S. 113 (1990).
[26] Riggins v. Nevada, 504 U.S. 127 (1992).
[27] *Hendricks*, 117 S.Ct. at 2072, 2079–81.
[28] *Id.* at 2079–80.
[29] *Id.* at 2080.
[30] *Id.* at 2080–81.
[31] *Id.* at 2079–80.

pairment that constitute volitional disorders, but it accepted Hendricks's diagnosis of pedophilia and his claim that when "stressed out" he could not control the urge to molest children as sufficient to establish such a disorder and to distinguish him from those "who are perhaps more properly dealt with exclusively through criminal proceedings."[32]

In summary, the *Hendricks* majority opinion appears to recognize mental illness and dangerousness as constitutional criteria for civil commitment, and it characterizes the impairment appropriate to fulfill the mental illness criterion as volitional impairment that renders the individual unable to control dangerous conduct. It does not make clear whether these criteria are necessary as well as sufficient for commitment. It does not explain why these criteria are necessary or sufficient, why only impairment that renders the individual unable to control conduct would suffice, or what type of impairment would render the individual unable to control his conduct for this legal purpose. Although the opinion indicates that Hendricks's disorder suffices for commitment because it renders him incapable of controlling his conduct, it provides no description or explanation of the impairment asserted and no reason to believe Hendricks's unsupported assertion that he was unable to control his planned, organized, and goal-directed conduct.[33] Thus, the Court recognized that the mental illness criterion does not require the magic words "mental illness," but it provided very little substantive analysis of the required impairment.

The Court's opinion in *Hendricks* resembles the opinions in *Foucha* and at least two other recent cases insofar as it accepts mental illness and dangerousness as sufficient conditions for involuntary civil commitment, but it provides no substantive analysis to clarify and justify these criteria. Rather, these opinions cite to earlier Supreme Court cases as support for these requirements.[34] Similarly, although the lower courts that have encountered sexual predator statutes have differed in their evaluations of those statutes, they have accepted the mental illness and dangerousness criteria, citing to *Foucha* and an overlapping series of prior Supreme Court cases.[35]

II.   Early Cases: *Jackson* to *Jones*

Four cases comprise the set of earlier Supreme Court cases recently cited by the Supreme Court and by other courts in support of the proposition that civil commitment requires mental illness and dangerousness. *Jackson v. Indiana* involved the indefinite confinement of an individual pursuant to a finding that he was incompetent to stand trial. Jackson's impairment and the conditions of confinement were such that no one contended that Jackson was progressing toward competence or that he was expected to do so. Consequently, the indefinite commitment pursuant to the finding of incompetence to proceed effectively constituted confinement of unlimited

---

[32] *Id.* at 2081.

[33] *Id.* at 2080–81; Stephen J. Morse, *Culpability and Control*, 142 U. PA. L. R. 1587 (1994); ROBERT F. SCHOPP, AUTOMATISM, INSANITY, AND THE PSYCHOLOGY OF CRIMINAL RESPONSIBILITY §6.3 (1991). Both sources argue that psychological impairment rarely supports the claim that the individual is unable to control his or her behavior.

[34] *Foucha,* 504 U.S. at 75–78 and at 92 (Kennedy, J., dissenting); *Riggins*, 504 U.S. at 127, 135; *Zinermon,* 494 U.S. at 113, 133–34.

[35] *See supra* notes 16–23 and accompanying text.

duration on the basis of an unadjudicated criminal charge without the benefit of either a criminal trial or a civil commitment proceeding. The experts who evaluated Jackson's competence to proceed with the criminal trial testified that he was unable to understand the trial process or communicate with his attorney and that the prognosis for his developing the necessary abilities was poor. Furthermore, Indiana lacked the facilities that might assist him in developing his extremely limited capacities in order to achieve any potential he might have.[36]

The Supreme Court recognized that the states have broad powers to commit mentally ill persons and that the states may establish a variety of statutory structures appropriate to the purposes for which they exercise these powers.[37] At that time, Indiana had separate statutes for the commitment of individuals as mentally ill or as feebleminded. Each provision established commitment and release criteria, and the Court concluded that the record before it did not establish that the state could confine Jackson under the criteria of either statute.[38] Thus, the Court reasoned that the case did not require it to consider constitutional limits on legitimate state purposes for commitment generally or for these statutes specifically because the proceedings under which Jackson had been committed did not purport to address any of the bases for indefinite civil commitment contained in either of Indiana's statutes. The Court articulated the reasonable relationship principle, according to which "due process requires that the nature and duration of commitment bear some reasonable relation to the purpose for which the person is committed."[39] The Court then applied this principle to commitment pursuant to a finding of incompetence to stand trial.

O'Connor v. Donaldson held ambiguously that "a state cannot constitutionally confine without more a nondangerous individual who is capable of surviving safely in freedom."[40] This passage seems amenable to at least two readings. "More" might refer to additional criteria of commitment, supporting the interpretation that commitment requires dangerousness in addition to mental illness. Alternately, "more" might refer to conditions of confinement, indicating that the state must provide more than mere confinement and thus, that the state must provide treatment to those whom it confines under civil commitment provisions. The facts of the case seem consistent with either reading in that it involved the extended commitment of an individual who had demonstrated no evidence of dangerousness and who had been subject to simple custodial confinement with no treatment despite repeated requests for treatment and for release.[41] The cases reviewed previously demonstrate that this holding has been interpreted in the former manner as establishing mental illness and dangerousness as required criteria of commitment.[42]

An integrated reading of the entire opinion cannot sustain that interpretation, however, because the Court's reasoning explicitly rejects it. The Court characterized the jury findings as establishing that Donaldson was not dangerous and that if he

---

[36] *Jackson*, 406 U.S. at 715, 717–19.

[37] *Id.* at 736–37.

[38] *Id.* at 727–29.

[39] *Id.* at 738.

[40] *O'Connor*, 422 U.S. at 563, 576. For a different analysis leading to a similar conclusion, *see* Stephen H. Behnke, *O'Connor v. Donaldson: Retelling a Classic and Finding Some Revisionist History*, 27 J. AMER. ACAD. PSYCHIATRY & L. 115 (1999).

[41] *O'Connor*, 422 U.S. at 568–69.

[42] *See supra*, Recent Cases: *Foucha* to *Hendricks*.

was mentally ill, he was not receiving treatment. On the basis of these jury findings, the Court explicitly set aside as unnecessary to decide for this case questions regarding the constitutional status of the criteria and conditions under which states ordinarily justify commitment or whether the state can confine a nondangerous mentally ill person for treatment.[43] Thus, the case merely rules out the practice of committing nondangerous mentally ill persons for treatment but keeps those individuals in simple custodial confinement without the treatment that represents the ostensible purpose and justification of their commitments. That is, this case only precludes as contrary to the Constitution commitment that involves neither dangerousness that would invoke the police power nor the provision of treatment under the *parens patriae* rationale.

Cases and commentators sometimes support the interpretation of this case as requiring dangerousness by quoting the following passage: "there is still no constitutional basis for confining such persons involuntarily if they are dangerous to no one and can live safely in freedom."[44] Although this passage might appear to support this interpretation when read in isolation, it occurs as part of a paragraph addressing simple custodial confinement. That is, it rejects as contrary to the Constitution the practice of holding indefinitely in simple custodial confinement persons who are not dangerous and who are capable of living safely outside the hospital. Thus, it reflects the interpretation of the case advanced here according to which the Court's reasoning precludes commitment that serves neither the police power nor the *parens patriae* rationales.

The Court's opinion explicitly applies the reasonable relationship principle from *Jackson* to support the proposition that constitutionally permissible initial commitment is insufficient to justify continued confinement if the basis that rendered the initial commitment constitutional no longer applies.[45] The interpretation advanced here of the ambiguous holding comports with that principle in that simple custodial commitment of a nondangerous person who can live safely outside the hospital bears no reasonable relationship to either the police power or *parens patriae* purposes. The lack of dangerousness precludes a police power rationale, and the lack of treatment or the need for custodial care precludes a *parens patriae* rationale. Thus, *O'Connor* represents a narrow application of the reasonable relationship principle in that it prohibits simple custodial confinement without treatment when such confinement bears no reasonable relationship to either of the state interests that justify commitment. This reasoning requires neither dangerousness as a criterion for all commitments nor treatment of all committed persons.

Although some cases discussed previously cited *Addington v. Texas* as a case that requires mental illness and dangerousness as criteria of civil commitment, *Addington* addresses the burden of proof the state bears in meeting the statutory criteria for commitment rather than the substantive criteria.[46] The appellant in this case was committed under a statute that required a finding of mental illness and the need for hospitalization for welfare and protection. He had been arrested on a misdemeanor assault charge, and the evidence at the hearing established that he was delusional

---

[43] *O'Connor*, 422 U.S. at 573–75.

[44] *Id.* at 575.

[45] *Id.* at 574–75.

[46] *Addington*, 441 U.S. at 418.

and had been threatening and assaultive. The judge instructed the jury that in order to commit they must find both mental illness and the need for hospitalization for welfare and protection. The appellant objected to the instructions because they required only clear and convincing evidence, rather than proof beyond reasonable doubt, but he did not object to the substantive criteria of commitment.[47]

The Supreme Court's analysis explicitly referred to the criteria of mental illness and dangerousness as established by the Texas statute. It did not endorse those criteria as constitutionally required, but it reasoned that the state had no interest in committing an individual unless its own statutory criteria were met.[48] The Court's opinion addressed only the procedural question regarding the proper standard of proof. It adopted the clear and convincing standard, rejecting both the preponderance and beyond reasonable doubt standards. The Court's reasoning emphasized the importance of the individual and state interests and the appropriate risk of error that each should bear in light of the severity of the potential injury that would occur to each as a result of erroneous conclusions under conditions of uncertainty regarding diagnosis and predictions of harm.[49]

Jones v. United States, the final case in the series, addressed several aspects of commitment under a postinsanity acquittal commitment statute.[50] The petitioner challenged the burden of proof, the extension of his commitment beyond the maximum duration of the criminal sentence he could have received for the crime of which he was acquitted, and the sufficiency of an insanity acquittal to establish the statutory commitment criteria of mental illness and dangerousness. He did not, however, challenge those criteria. Thus, the Court never addressed the necessity or sufficiency of those criteria.

The appellant directed his arguments primarily toward criteria for release, rather than criteria of initial commitment. The applicable federal statute provided for release from commitment when the acquittee was no longer mentally ill or no longer dangerous.[51] Similarly, the Court's language indicates that the acquittee is entitled to release when he has "regained his sanity or is no longer a danger to himself or society."[52] In isolation, this language appears amenable to interpretation as requiring mental illness and dangerousness as criteria of commitment. The entire opinion, however, fails to support this interpretation. The appellant did not challenge the statutory substantive criteria of commitment, and the Court's analysis provides no reasoning that directly addresses the issue of constitutionally adequate criteria of commitment.[53] The passages that appear susceptible to interpretation as requiring these criteria occur in the context of the Court's discussion of the duration of post-NGRI commitment as opposed to criminal sentence, and the Court upheld the indefinite nature of such commitment as consistent with the congressional purpose in

---

[47] *Id.* at 420–22.

[48] *Id.* at 426.

[49] *Id.* at 425–33.

[50] *Jones*, 463 U.S. at 354.

[51] *Id.* at 356–66.

[52] *Id.* at 370; *compare* similar language at 368.

[53] The Court cites only for this the legislative record and O'Connor v. Donaldson to support this interpretation. *Id.* at 368. As previously discussed, *O'Connor* does not establish dangerousness as a criterion of commitment.

writing the statute.[54] The Court accepted the congressional determination that the primary purposes of this type of commitment are treatment of the acquittee's mental illness and protection of the acquittee and of society from the danger produced by this mental illness. Thus, these passages are most consistently interpreted as another application of the reasonable relationship principle from *Jackson* in that the Court upheld the statutory criteria of release that were consistent with the articulated statutory purpose for the postacquittal commitment. These statutory criteria authorized release from commitment when the circumstances changed such that the mental illness and the resultant dangerousness that supported the congressional purposes of treatment and protection no longer applied.

In summary, these cases have been cited as establishing mental illness and dangerousness as required criteria of commitment, but they neither require these criteria nor do they provide any analysis from which one can directly infer such substantive requirements. Because these cases lack any analysis providing a justificatory foundation for civil commitment, they provide no guidance for lower courts called upon to interpret constitutional parameters for the meaning of statutory criteria articulated as "mental illness," "mental abnormality," "personality disorder," or related terms. Had the Supreme Court provided some account of the conditions that render commitment constitutionally acceptable, lower courts could apply ordinary principles of statutory construction by interpreting these terms in a manner that would render constitutional the commitment statutes that contained them.[55]

III.   Conclusion

One can interpret the reasonable relationship principle as mandating only minimal instrumental rationality in the sense that the state intrusion must provide some likelihood of advancing some state interest.[56] As such, it would carry no justificatory significance. Eliminating defense counsel and the rights to cross examine and to testify on one's own behalf might promote the state's interest in reducing the cost of criminal trials, for example, but this instrumentally reasonable relationship would not suffice to justify these limitations of individual rights. When combined with the requirement that the state interest take the form of a legitimate state interest of sufficient importance to justify the intrusion in question, however, the reasonable relationship principle becomes a formal principle of justice in constitutional adjudication. That is, it requires a certain relationship between the intrusion and substantive principles of political morality that are consistent with the Constitution and that justify the intrusion. It provides only a formal principle of justice, however, in that it provides no guidance regarding the substantive interests or principles that a court should accept as sufficient to justify state intrusions. Thus, a complete analysis requires both formal and substantive principles.

---

[54] *Addington*, 441 U.S. at 368–70.

[55] *See, e.g.*, Lessard v. Schmidt, 349 F.Supp. 1078, 1093–94 (E.D.Wis. 1972) (interpreting the Wisconsin commitment statute in order to render the substantive criteria consistent with constitutional principles).

[56] Stephen J. Schulhofer, *Two Systems of Social Protection: Comments on the Civil–Criminal Distinction, with Particular Reference to Sexually Violent Predator Laws*, 7 J. CONTEMP LEG. ISSUES 69, 83–84 (1996).

Cases and commentators tend to appeal to the traditional *parens patriae* and police powers of the state in order to provide the substantive justification of commitment, but these powers and the parameters of the justification they can provide rarely receive careful analysis.[57] A satisfactory justification for commitment under the *parens patriae* or police powers would articulate precise conceptions of the applicable notions of mental illness, dangerousness, or grave disability. This justification would explain why the presence of these or other specified conditions justify state intrusion into ordinarily protected liberty according to the principles of political morality underlying the *parens patriae* and police powers in the context of the more comprehensive set of legal institutions. This explanation would clarify the relationships among various forms of intervention through the mental health system and related legal institutions. Furthermore, it would articulate the particular conception of mental illness relevant to these forms of intervention.

To understand the meaning and justificatory significance of mental illness, dangerousness, and related notions in the context of specific legal institutions, one needs clear conceptions of these notions in the abstract and an account of the manner in which the underlying principles of political morality support the specific legal institutions at issue. To understand why mental illness justifies *parens patriae* interventions by the state and what "mental illness" means for this purpose, for example, one needs an abstract conception of mental illness applicable to legal contexts and an account of the principles of political morality represented by the legal institutions at issue. Chapter 3 provides an analysis of a formal conception of mental illness for legal purposes and identifies the central defect that renders it difficult to develop a satisfactory substantive conception of mental illness for the purposes of civil commitment generally and of sexual predator commitment specifically.

---

[57] *See, e.g., Addington*, 441 U.S. at 418, 426; Donald H. J. Hermann, *Barriers to Providing Effective Treatment: A Critique of Revisions in Procedural, Substantive, and Dispositional Criteria in Involuntary Civil Commitment*, 39 VAND. L. REV. 83 (1986) (providing a more detailed discussion than most commentary of the *parens patriae* and police power bases for commitment); Clifford D. Stromberg & Alan A. Stone, *A Model State Law on Civil Commitment of the Mentally Ill*, 20 HARV. J. LEGIS. 275, 280–81 (1983).

Chapter 3
LEGALLY SIGNIFICANT MENTAL ILLNESS

A formal conception of mental illness for legal purposes provides a conceptual framework for the analysis of the relationships among various types of psychological impairment and various legal functions. Application of this conceptual framework to a particular legal purpose allows one to identify the types of psychological impairment that qualify as legally significant mental illness for that purpose. This chapter examines the central defects in the statutory formulations of mental abnormalities or personality disorder in sexual predator statutes. It also demonstrates that these defects permeate civil commitment provisions generally. The chapter then develops a conceptual framework that enables one to clearly articulate the nature of these defects and to specify the requirements of a satisfactory formulation. Consistent application of this framework enables one to specify a conception of legally significant mental illness for each legal purpose, and it promotes the development of an integrated body of mental health law.

I.   Sexual Predator Statutes: Mental Abnormality or Personality Disorder

The sexual predator statutes authorize indefinite civil commitment of sexually violent predators who suffer a mental abnormality or personality disorder, but these provisions provide no clear conceptions of these disorders. Neither do they explain why the presence of such disorders justify intervention through the mental health system.[1]

Anderson, Baker, Cook, and Davis all qualify for clinical diagnoses under the most common nomenclature and for commitment as sexual predators under the statutory categories of mental abnormality, personality disorder, or both.[2] They vary significantly, however, regarding their standing under a variety of other legal provisions that authorize differential legal treatment of those who are mentally ill and those who are not. Neither Anderson nor Baker manifests the type of severe functional impairment ordinarily associated with civil commitment, although both qualify for commitment under the sexual predator statutes. Both Cook and Davis suffer severe impairment of a type often associated with general civil commitment, rendering the sexual predator statutes redundant for them. Cook, who is moderately retarded, is incompetent to stand trial, although the other three offenders are competent to proceed with criminal trials despite their clinical diagnoses. Davis suffers a psychotic disorder that renders him NGRI, and Cook's moderate retardation might well exculpate him under the same provision, if he were competent to proceed with the trial. Anderson and Baker, in contrast, were convicted despite their clinical diagnoses including pedophilia and personality disorders.

---

[1] *See* chapter 1, section II for a more complete discussion.
[2] *See* chapter 1, section I.

These cases suggest that no single clinical category or set of clinical categories will identify all and only those individuals who qualify for differential legal treatment under provisions including criteria phrased in terms of "mental illness," "mental disease," "mental abnormality," or similar terms. Provisions including these criteria clearly cannot apply to everyone manifesting any diagnosable disorder because all four offenders manifest diagnosable disorders, yet some fail to qualify under some of the legal provisions. Severely impaired individuals, such as Cook and Davis, fall within the scope of many statutes, suggesting that these criteria might refer to all clinical disorders that meet some threshold of severity. This strategy cannot provide a satisfactory approach, however, because some individuals manifest severe impairment yet fail to qualify for differential treatment under certain provisions. Davis, for example, remains competent to stand trial. Although it seems reasonable to classify Cook and Davis as seriously impaired for most purposes, it seems misleading to compare disorders on a general scale of severity. Moderate mental retardation and severe anxiety, for example, seem to differ qualitatively in a manner that would render each more or less disabling for different purposes.

Individuals committed under the sexual predator statutes frequently resemble Anderson and Baker more closely than they resemble the severely impaired Cook and Davis. These statutes invite controversy partially because they authorize commitment of individuals, like Anderson and Baker, who manifest no serious impairment of a type that would ordinarily support civil commitment under a general commitment provision and who demonstrate no evidence of deterioration in their psychological capacities since their convictions for their sexually violent offenses. The individuals committed in several recent cases under these statutes had recently completed, or were approaching completion of, sentences for repetitive violent sexual offenses. These offenders carried no diagnoses that indicated serious impairment of orientation, consciousness, perception, comprehension, reasoning, or reality testing. Rather, they resembled Anderson and Baker in that they carried diagnoses, including APD and the paraphilias, that can be based heavily upon the demonstrated propensity to commit the offenses for which they had been convicted. The appellate courts' discussion of the expert testimony in these cases indicate that the reasoning supporting the diagnoses and the findings of mental abnormality or personality disorder under the statutes emphasized the pattern of criminal conduct that generated the conviction and sentences.[3] These cases suggest that the propensity to commit criminal offenses carries substantial weight in establishing mental abnormalities under these statutes.

Insofar as they carry clinical diagnoses of paraphilia or personality disorder, and insofar as these diagnoses are predicated largely on their patterns of criminal activity, the offenders committed under the sexual predator statutes resemble the general population of sex offenders. Consider, for example, sex offenders who qualify for paraphilic diagnoses. The general diagnostic category of paraphilia includes a series of specific diagnoses applicable to those who experience significant distress or impairment of functioning associated with recurrent intense sexual urges, fantasies, or behavior of specified types. These urges ordinarily involve nonhuman objects, children, or suffering. Individuals with pedophilias, for example, experience distress or

---

[3] In Re Hendricks, 912 P.2d 129, 131, 137–38 (Kan. 1996); State v. Carpenter, 541 N.W.2d 105, 108–09 (Wis. 1995); In Re Linehan, 557 N.W.2d 171, 175–79 (Min. 1996); State v. Post, 541 N.W.2d 115, 119 (Wis. 1995); In Re Young, 857 P.2d 989, 994–96 (Wash. 1993).

impairment of functioning associated with their urges, fantasies, or behavior involving sexual activity with prepubescent children.[4]

When these individuals act upon their urges to engage in sexual activity with children, the behavior that constitutes the criminal conduct for which they are convicted also partially fulfills the criteria for the clinical diagnosis. To the extent that the pedophilic urges and fantasies are inferred from the criminal pedophilic behavior, that criminal behavior may provide the entire basis for the diagnosis. Thus, for a particular offender, it is possible that criminal sexual behavior with children can provide the basis for criminal conviction, the pedophilic diagnosis, and the determinations for the purpose of the sexual predator statutes that he suffers a mental abnormality and that he is likely to engage in predatory acts of sexual violence.

Commentators have developed a variety of systems for classifying people who act on their sexual urges in a manner that violates the law. The most common distinction, based on the age of the victim, is between those who assault adults (rapists) and those who assault children (child molesters).[5] Further distinctions are made within each of those categories according to how much aggression is involved and whether that aggression has been sexualized (sadism).[6] Within the child molester category, the primary differentiation addresses the degree of fixation on children, that is, the strength of the offender's sexual interest in children.[7] Systems also examine the level of social competence of these offenders,[8] and all recognize a category of offenders (that would include people like Baker) for whom the sexual offenses are secondary to a larger pattern of antisocial behavior.[9]

Attempts to identify psychological impairment generally characteristic of sex offenders have consistently failed. Psychological assessment of these offenders reveals marked heterogeneity.[10] Some sex offenders resemble Anderson insofar as they

---

[4] AMERICAN PSYCHIATRIC ASSOCIATION, DIAGNOSTIC AND STATISTICAL MANUAL OF MENTAL DISORDERS 522–28 (4th ed. 1994) [hereinafter DSM–IV].

[5] Leonard A. Bard et al., *A Descriptive Study of Rapists and Child Molesters: Developmental, Clinical, and Criminal Characteristics*, 5 BEHAV. SCI. & L. 203, 205 (1987); Gordon C. Nagayama Hall et al., *Three Methods of Developing MMPI Taxonomies of Sexual Offenders*, 56 J. PERSON. ASSESS. 2 (1991); Raymond A. Knight & Robert A. Prentky, *Classifying Sexual Offenders: The development and Corroboration of Taxonomic Models* in THE HANDBOOK OF SEXUAL ASSAULT: ISSUES, THEORIES & TREATMENT 23 (W.L. Marshall et al. eds., 1990); Raymond A. Knight et al., *Classification of Sexual Offenders: Perspectives, Methods, and Validation*, in RAPE AND SEXUAL ASSAULT 222 (Ann Wolbert Burgess ed., 1985).

[6] KENNETH V. LANNING, CHILD MOLESTERS: A BEHAVIORAL ANALYSIS (1992); Raymond A. Knight et al., *A System for the Classification of Child Molesters*, 4 J. INTERPERSONAL VIOLENCE 3 (1989); A. Nicholas Groth, An unpublished handout copyrighted (1981) by Forensic Mental Health Associates, 7513 Pointview Circle, Orlando, FL 32819 (adapted from A. NICHOLAS GROTH ET AL., SEXUAL ASSAULT OF CHILDREN AND ADOLESCENTS (1978) and A. NICHOLAS GROTH with H. JEAN BIRNBAUM, MEN WHO RAPE: THE PSYCHOLOGY OF THE OFFENDER (1979)).

[7] Groth, *supra* note 6; Knight et al., *supra* note 5; Knight & Prentky, *supra* note 5; LANNING, *supra* note 6.

[8] Gene G. Abel et al., *Sexual Offenders: Results of Assessment and Recommendations for Treatment* in CLINICAL CRIMINOLOGY: THE ASSESSMENT AND TREATMENT OF CRIMINAL BEHAVIOR 191 (M. H. Ben-Aron et al., eds., 1985); Groth, *supra* note 6; Knight et al., *supra* note 6; Knight et al., *supra* note 5; Knight & Prentky, *supra* note 5; LANNING, *supra* note 6.

[9] Groth, *supra* note 6; Knight & Prentky, *supra* note 5; LANNING, *supra* note 6.

[10] Bard et al., *supra* note 5, at 204; Hall et al., *supra* note 5, at 2; Gordon C. Nagayama Hall et al., *The Utility of the MMPI With Men Who Have Sexually Assaulted Children*, 54 J. CONSULTING & CLIN.

are socially anxious and inadequate in ordinary adult interaction, engaging in avoidant social behavior to a clinical or subclinical degree.[11] The distribution of diagnostic categories resembles that found in the general prison population.[12] The most common diagnostic category is that of APD, which requires a long-term pattern of maladaptive behavior but does not require impairment of psychological capacities.[13] Some studies of sex offenders document a pattern of comorbidity similar to that found in the sexual predator cases in that sex offenders meet the diagnostic criteria for paraphilia as well as for other diagnostic categories, particularly personality disorder and substance abuse. Although a few individuals may demonstrate psychotic process, the studies consistently find little evidence of psychosis or major psychiatric disorder in the large majority of sex offenders.[14] The only diagnostic features that consistently characterize most sex offenders involve the illegal conduct that provides the basis for the criminal convictions and the pattern of illegal conduct and arousal that fulfills the criteria for the diagnoses of paraphilia or personality disorder.[15]

The majority opinion in *Hendricks* suggests that some sex offenders qualify for social control through civil commitment, rather than solely through the criminal justice system, because they manifest mental abnormalities involving volitional impairment that renders them unable to control their sexual conduct. The court provided no basis for this interpretation, however, with the exception of Hendricks's claim that he is unable to control his sexual conduct under stress. The opinion provides neither an explication of this putative inability nor any reason to believe this unsubstantiated assertion regarding a pattern of planned and organized conduct.[16]

In summary, neither the sexual predator statutes, the *Hendricks* opinion, nor the studies of the general population of sex offenders provide any account of the required mental abnormalities or volitional impairments that differentiate the perpetrators subject to commitment as sexual predators from sex offenders generally or from those suffering "robberitis." Consider, for example, a defendant charged with armed robbery who claims that he suffers the mental abnormality of robberitis, which consists of a condition affecting his emotional capacity (greed) that predisposes him to the commission of criminal acts (armed robbery). The sexual predator statutes and cases provide no explanation why the mental abnormalities manifested by those committed

---

PSYCHOL. 493, 495 (1986); Knight et al., *supra* note 5, at 223; Jim Mann et al., *The Utility of the MMPI–2 with Pedophiles*, 18 J. OFFENDER REHABILITATION 59, 68 (1992).

[11] Abel et al., *supra* note 8, at 197; Bruce Duthie & Daniel L. McIvor, *A New System for Cluster-Coding Child Molester MMPI Profiles*, 17 CRIM. JUST. & BEHAV. 199 (1990).

[12] William D. Erickson et al., *Frequency of MMPI Two-Point Codes Types Among Sex Offenders*, 55 J. CONSULTING & CLIN. PSYCHOL. 566, 569 (1987); Knight et al., *supra* note 5, at 239.

[13] Erickson et al., *supra* note 12; Hall et al., *supra* note 5; Hall et al., *supra* note 10.

[14] Abel et al., *supra* note 8, at 196; Knight et al., *supra* note 5, at 234; FAY HONEY KNOPP, RETRAINING ADULT SEX OFFENDERS: METHODS & MODELS 7 (1984); Vladmir Konecni, Erin Mulcahy, & Ebbe Ebbeson, *Prison or Mental Hospitals: Factors Affecting the Processing of Persons Suspected of Being "Mentally Disordered Sex Offenders"* in NEW DIRECTIONS IN PSYCHOLEGAL RESEARCH 87, 112–15 (Paul Lipsitt & Bruce Sales, eds., 1980); Richard M. Yarvis, *Diagnosing Patterns Among Three Violent Offender Types*, 23 BULL. AM. ACAD. PSYCHIATRY & L. 411, 412 (1995).

[15] Christopher M. Earls & Vernon L. Quinsey, *What Is to be Done? Future Research on the Assessment and Behavioral Treatment of Sex Offenders*, 3 BEHAV. SCI. & L. 377, 380 (1985). For further discussion of diagnosis of sex offenders, *see* chapter 11, section II.A.

[16] *See* chapter 2, section I.

under these statutes would establish a better justification for treating these individuals differently from the general population of sex offenders than this robber's claim would provide for treating him differently from the general population of robbers. Although the sexual predator statutes starkly illustrate the lack of any clear conception of legally significant mental illness, this problem pervades general civil commitment.

II. Ellen and Francine

Consider Ellen and Francine, single women in their thirties with histories of involvement with the mental health system. Each began to manifest symptoms of psychological impairment during adolescence. Each has been hospitalized in mental health facilities several times during her twenties and thirties. On some occasions they have been persuaded to enter the inpatient wards voluntarily, but on other occasions they have been involuntarily committed following risky conduct or threats associated with their psychopathology. When discharged from the inpatient wards, each has participated in outpatient care intermittently. They manifest similar patterns of participation in that their attendance at scheduled aftercare appointments becomes irregular when they begin to deteriorate psychologically, and both cease attendance when they become overtly psychotic.

Both carry diagnoses of paranoid schizophrenia, and during periods of active psychosis, both evince delusional thought with persecutory and grandiose content.[17] Ellen's delusional process leads her to believe that she has a special gift from God that enables her to cure all illness by touching the sick person. She also believes that physicians want to kill her in order to prevent her from demonstrating their inadequacy and putting an end to their profitable control of health care. Francine's delusional process leads her to believe that she has a special mission from God to establish world peace by spreading God's word through her books. She is convinced that her books are repetitively rejected by every publisher to whom she submits them only because she is the target of a conspiracy among the "military–industrial complex" to protect their wealth and power by preventing her from bringing world peace by spreading God's word.

Both commit simple assaults related to their pathology, but neither causes significant injury. When a public health nurse visits Ellen to ask why she has not returned to the clinic, Ellen concludes that the nurse is part of the conspiracy and has come to kill her. Ellen attacks the nurse with her umbrella in delusional "self-defense." When Francine refuses to leave the offices of the latest publisher to reject her manuscript, a uniformed security guard attempts to escort her out of the building, and Francine attacks the guard with her umbrella, convinced that the guard has been sent by the military–industrial complex to kill her.

Both are arrested and charged with simple assault. Ellen confers with a public defender and understands the nature of the proceedings to a degree that allows her to participate adequately in the trial. The court finds Ellen competent to stand trial and NGRI. The court then commits Ellen to the state hospital for a period of observation and treatment pursuant to a post-NGRI acquittal provision. Francine refuses to talk to any lawyer because she believes they are all involved in the conspiracy to

---

[17] DSM–IV, *supra* note 4, at 274–87 (paranoid schizophrenia).

kill her. From her delusional perspective, the public defender, the prosecutor, and the judge are all interchangeable participants in the conspiracy by the military–industrial complex. She refuses to participate in any manner in the trial, and she constantly disrupts the proceedings by praying loudly and preaching to the participants and spectators in an attempt to spread God's word. The judge finds Francine incompetent to stand trial. Although she would be eligible for commitment pursuant to the finding of incompetence to stand trial, the court, the county attorney, and the clinical experts agree that the minor nature of the offense and the chronic course of her pathology support the decision to divert her from the criminal justice system to the civil commitment system. The county attorney files a petition for civil commitment, and after a civil commitment hearing under the state's general civil commitment statute, the court commits Francine to the same state hospital to which Ellen was committed after her acquittal.

During their commitments, physicians diagnose both Ellen and Francine as suffering from diabetes, which requires careful control through diet and may require ongoing insulin treatment. Ellen rejects the diagnosis and the proffered treatment because she interprets the physicians' diagnosis and advice as attempts to kill her under the guise of treatment. She concludes that she will protect herself from the ongoing threat to her life by forgoing all worldly nourishment, relying upon God to supply manna when it is necessary and upon her ability to heal any physical problem she experiences through the use of her divine gift. Francine accepts the diagnosis of diabetes and attends carefully to her physician's advice. She conscientiously follows the dietary plan in the hospital and develops an aftercare plan for continued treatment and monitoring of her diabetes with a public health nurse after she is discharged.

At approximately the same time, Ellen and Francine receive routinely scheduled 90-day reviews of their commitments. Both remain delusional but neither is grossly disorganized, assaultive, or threatening. Ellen's commitment is extended because her refusal of all food and medical treatment has seriously complicated her diabetic condition, and she requires artificial nutrition and careful monitoring in the hospital. Francine is discharged from the hospital with the aftercare plan she has developed and agreed to pursue.

In summary, Ellen and Francine demonstrate that general civil commitment and related areas of mental health law manifest conceptual and justificatory difficulties similar to those revealed by the sexual predator statutes. We lack a clear conception of mental illness that justifies differential treatment in various components of mental health law and allows a coherent integration of these components. Ellen and Francine demonstrate the same type of functional impairment of psychological process in that both demonstrate delusional thought processes with persecutory and grandiose content, and both qualify for the same clinical diagnostic category of paranoid schizophrenia. Ellen is competent to stand trial, she is found NGRI, and she is subject to postacquittal commitment as well as to continued commitment at the 90-day review. Francine is incompetent to stand trial, she is subjected to civil commitment under the general civil commitment statute, and she is discharged to outpatient care at the 90-day review.

How do we explain these variations in legal standing despite the common patterns of functional impairment and common clinical diagnoses? One can easily respond that there are different legal standards for different legal purposes, but this response generates two additional questions. First, what is the meaning of the mental illness requirement in these various legal provisions such that all require mental illness (or some alternative term referring to psychological impairment) as a criterion for differential legal treatment in some circumstances, but people with the same types of functional impairment and the same clinical diagnoses do not consistently qualify for similar treatment under these statutes? Second, can the principles of political morality underlying these legal institutions justify these results in a manner that renders these institutions coherent with one another and with the broader legal system in which they are embedded?

III. A Formal Conception of Legal Mental Illness

A. Impairment, Diagnostic Categories, and Legal Mental Illness

Legal criteria of commitment phrased in terms such as "mental illness," "mental disease or defect," "mental abnormality," or "mental disorder" can raise problems of interpretation partially because the legal rule may not clarify the intended relationship between the legal criteria and related terms of health care or ordinary language. According to one view, the basic distinction in health care is that between health and pathology. The notion of pathology refers primarily to parts or processes rather than to persons. Parts or processes are healthy when their ability to perform species-typical functions falls within some central range of statistical distribution for members of the species. They are pathological when they fall below that range.[18]

A person is sick or ill when pathological process impairs his or her functioning as a system.[19] Thus, the notion of functional impairment is central to both pathology and illness. A person is ill when his or her ability to function as a system is impaired by some pathological process of a biological or psychological subsystem. A person is mentally or psychologically ill when some pathology of psychological process impairs his or her ability to function at some previously defined level of psychological health in some intrapersonal or interpersonal aspect of ordinary life.[20] Psychological processes such as perception, memory, comprehension, mood, or reasoning are pathological if they fall significantly below the range of ordinary functioning.

Diagnostic nomenclatures ordinarily define diagnostic categories as identifiable patterns of impaired psychological processes that are thought significant for the normal functioning of the person as an intrapersonal and interpersonal system, and thus, for the clinical purposes of diagnosis and treatment.[21] Schizophrenia, for example, is currently defined as an extended pattern of pathological process involving psychotic

---

[18] Christopher Boorse, *Concepts of Health*, in HEALTH CARE ETHICS 364–71 (Donald VanDeVeer & Tom Regan eds. 1987). Strictly speaking, a part or process might fall beyond the central range without falling below it. When parts or processes fall beyond the central range by functioning well above that range, however, we do not ordinarily consider such functioning pathological. Visual acuity or reasoning that exceeds the ordinary range, for example, would not ordinarily be considered pathological.

[19] *Id.* at 364; MICHAEL S. MOORE, LAW AND PSYCHIATRY 189–95 (1984).

[20] Boorse, *supra* note 18, at 375–79.

[21] DSM–IV, *supra* note 4, at xxi (disorders are syndromes); *see* Seymour L. Halleck et al., *The Use of Psychiatric Diagnosis in the Legal Process: Task Force Report of the American Psychiatric Association*, 20 BULL. AM. ACAD. PSYCHIATRY & L. 481, 482–84 (1992) (recognizing most clinical diagnoses as syndromes that are useful for clinical or research purposes).

disturbance of perception and thought that impairs the individual's ability to function interpersonally or occupationally.[22]

In ordinary usage, therefore, "mental illness" can refer either to impairment of psychological process that undermines the person's ability to function effectively in ordinary life or to clinically significant patterns of impairment that diagnostic nomenclatures recognize as diagnostic categories. For the sake of clarity, this book uses "psychological impairment" or "psychological dysfunction" to refer to impairment of psychological processes including, for example, distorted thought process such as delusional thought, perceptual distortions such as hallucinations, or disturbed affect such as depressed mood. This book refers to clinically significant patterns of impairment recognized by clinical nomenclatures as "diagnostic categories." Notice that according to this terminology, a diagnostic category requires a pattern of impaired psychological process. Thus, the mere fact of inclusion in a diagnostic nomenclature is not sufficient. A diagnosis made purely on the basis of a pattern of socially maladaptive behavior, for example, would not constitute a diagnostic category in this sense because it would not involve impairment of psychological processes.[23] Similarly, "legal mental illness" refers to psychological impairment that renders a person incapable of meeting some legally relevant standard of adequate functioning.

Legal mental illness is specific to a particular legal purpose in that it involves psychological impairment that renders one ineligible for a specified legal status and thus, for rights or liabilities associated with that status. Legal standards for some purposes define criteria of eligibility positively as the capacities required to qualify for a particular status, whereas other legal standards define the criteria of eligibility negatively as the type of impairment that prevents one from qualifying for that status. Competence to stand trial, for example, defines eligibility positively as the capacities to understand the proceedings and consult with one's attorney. In contrast, standards for the insanity defense define eligibility for the status of criminally responsible negatively by identifying the types of impairment that constitute excusing conditions, undermining one's status as criminally responsible for one's conduct. Common legal standards identify the lack of ability to know that one's conduct is wrongful, for example, as a type of impairment that renders one NGRI, and therefore, that undermines eligibility for the status of criminally responsible regarding that conduct.[24]

For the sake of clarity, this book uses "eligible" positively to refer to those who possess the capacities necessary to qualify for the status and the associated rights or liabilities. Persons are ineligible when they suffer impairment that prevents them from qualifying for that status according to the applicable legal criteria. Such impairment constitutes legal mental illness for that purpose because it renders them inappropriate subjects of those rights or liabilities. Those who are civilly competent, competent to stand trial, or responsible for their criminal conduct, for example, are

---

[22] DSM–IV, *supra* note 4, at 285 (diagnostic criteria A, B, C). In ordinary language, we often classify permanent disabilities as distinct from illness. Mental retardation, for example, might be considered a mental defect or deficiency rather than an illness. It is included in the most common diagnostic nomenclature of psychological disorders, however, and it would fit the conception of illness articulated here. *See* DSM–IV, *supra* note 4, at 39–46; MOORE, *supra* note 19, at 194.

[23] *See, e.g.*, DSM–IV, *supra* note 4 at 645–50 (discussing APD).

[24] MICHAEL L. PERLIN, MENTAL DISABILITY LAW §§14.03 (competence to stand trial), 15.03–.09 (insanity tests) (1989).

eligible by the respective standards. In contrast, those who are civilly incompetent, incompetent to stand trial, or NGRI are ineligible for the applicable legal status by the relevant legal standards.

The presence of psychological impairment entails neither that the individual qualifies for a diagnostic category nor that the person suffers legal mental illness. Similarly, neither qualification for a diagnostic category nor a legal mental illness entails the other. Just as individuals qualify for diagnostic categories if and only if they manifest psychological impairment recognized by the applicable nomenclature as the criteria for those categories, they suffer legal mental illness for a particular legal purpose if and only if they manifest psychological impairment that renders them ineligible for the legal status at issue. Qualification for either a clinical diagnostic category or a determination of legal mental illness entails psychological impairment, however, because each of these categories represents a pattern or type of impairment recognized for a particular clinical or legal purpose. Those who manifest patterns of psychological impairment that are not recognized by the applicable diagnostic nomenclatures suffer psychological impairment but do not qualify under any diagnostic category. Such impairment may or may not constitute legal mental illness for a specific legal purpose. It does so if and only if it precludes eligibility for that legal purpose according to the applicable legal criteria.

Expert testimony regarding clinical diagnosis can have two types of relevance for the court's determination that an individual is (or is not) legally mentally ill. As ordinarily understood, testimony is relevant if it makes a fact at issue more or less probable than it would be without the testimony.[25] Testimony is directly relevant if the substantive content of that testimony bears a logical relationship to the fact at issue such that it renders that fact more or less probable, and it is indirectly relevant if it does not bear this logical relationship to the fact at issue but informs the credibility or weight of directly relevant testimony. Testimony that an individual qualifies for a particular diagnostic category is not directly relevant to the court's determination because it addresses the relationship between the person's impairment and the criteria for clinical diagnostic categories, whereas the court's determination of legal mental illness requires evidence addressing the relationship between the person's psychological dysfunction and the legal criteria of eligibility. Testimony that an individual qualifies for a recognized diagnostic category can have indirect relevance, however, in that the court might interpret such testimony as supporting the credibility of the expert and as decreasing the probability of malingering by the subject of the hearing. In contrast, expert testimony contending that an individual manifests a pattern of impairment that is not recognized by any accepted nomenclature might lead the court to doubt the expertise of the witness or to suspect malingering by the subject of the hearing.

Second, expert testimony regarding descriptive diagnosis is directly relevant to a court's determination that an individual is (or is not) legally mentally ill. "Diagnosis" refers either to a term identifying a specific disease or syndrome or to the process of establishing the nature and cause of a person's impairment.[26] Expert testimony that an individual qualifies for a diagnostic category constitutes diagnosis in the former sense, but expert testimony providing descriptive diagnosis involves di-

---

[25] FED. R. EVID. §401.
[26] TABER'S CYCLOPEDIC MEDICAL DICTIONARY 535 (ed., Clayton L. Thomas 1993).

agnosis in the latter sense. This descriptive type of diagnostic testimony carries direct relevance to the court's determination of legal mental illness because it provides description and explanation regarding the nature of the individual's impaired capacities and the effect of this impairment on the individual's capacity to perform the psychological operations relevant to a particular legal status. Thus, descriptive diagnosis but not diagnostic category is directly relevant to civil commitment and other legal determinations.

Most individuals who manifest a pattern of impairment that qualifies as legal mental illness also meet the criteria for some diagnostic category because the current diagnostic nomenclatures are highly inclusive.[27] The substantive legal significance of any psychological impairment rests upon its meeting the criteria of legal mental illness for a specific legal purpose, however, and not upon its qualifying for a clinical diagnostic category. Thus, most people who are legally mentally ill are also clinically diagnosable, but they are legally mentally ill because their impairment meets the legal standard and not because it qualifies for a recognized clinical diagnosis.

According to this view, a determination of legal mental illness requires an integrated legal and clinical analysis. First, lawmakers must specify criteria of eligibility in the form of a legal standard of adequate functioning for the relevant legal purpose. Second, this standard of adequate functioning generates a description of the types of functional impairment that render an individual legally mentally ill for this purpose in that any psychological impairment that prevents the individual from fulfilling the legal criteria of eligibility constitutes legal mental illness for this purpose. Third, to the extent that available evidence allows, clinicians must describe an individual's psychological impairment and explain the manner in which it might affect psychological functioning in various circumstances. Most often, this description will also generate a clinical diagnosis, but this fact carries no substantive legal significance or direct evidentiary relevance. Fourth, the fact finder must integrate the description of the individual's impairment with the criteria of legal mental illness in order to determine whether this individual's impairment renders him or her legally mentally ill for this purpose.[28]

B. Legal Standards, Eligibility, and Legal Mental Illness

Courts admit expert testimony regarding psychological impairment that is relevant to the legal issue. In order to evaluate the relevance of proffered testimony regarding

---

[27] See, e.g., DSM–IV, supra note 4, at 375 (Mood Disorder NOS), 444 (Anxiety Disorder NOS), 673 (Personality Disorder NOS).

[28] Two clarifications are in order. First, by articulating four distinct steps, I do not suggest that they must occur in this temporal order. In practice, for example, the lawmaker might complete the first and second in a single process, or a clinician might complete Step 3 before the lawmaker addresses Steps 1 and 2. The four steps are conceptually distinct but not necessarily completed sequentially.

Second, if the lawmakers articulate criteria of legal mental illness in terms that are compatible with clinical expertise, clinicians might be able to state a professional opinion regarding the significance of the psychological disorder for the criteria of legal mental illness. That is, the critical parameters of expert testimony require that it fall within the scope of the expert's expertise and that it has relevance to the legal issue. Such testimony may or may not address the ultimate legal issue. As law is currently formulated, expert testimony usually should not address the ultimate issue, but this reflects the manner in which current law is formulated rather than any principled lack of compatibility between expert testimony and ultimate issues.

psychological impairment, the court must apply a legal standard that provides criteria of legal eligibility for some purpose, and it must evaluate the significance of the purported impairment for the criteria of eligibility. In this manner, the court determines whether the impairment undermines eligibility, thus qualifying as legal mental illness for this purpose. Legal standards for competence to stand trial, and civil competence, for example, provide positive criteria indicating some legal theory of eligibility. Insanity standards fulfill a similar function in a somewhat different manner by articulating negative criteria of ineligibility. Either type of standard enables the court to identify certain types of functional impairment that undermine eligibility, constituting legal mental illness for these purposes.

Courts can apply the most common NGRI standards by admitting testimony regarding functional impairment of defendants' capacities to perceive, comprehend, recognize reality, reason, or engage in other psychological processes relevant to understanding the nature or wrongfulness of their conduct. Some insanity standards also include volitional clauses, but courts, commentators, and experts find it difficult to interpret and apply these standards as criteria of eligibility because they are unable to develop any clear conception of the putative volitional impairment, and therefore, they are unable to determine whether any recognized form of functional impairment of psychological process corresponds to these volitional criteria. Thus, courts are unable to articulate any clear conception of legal mental illness for the volitional clause, and they are unable to identify or interpret the significance of relevant testimony.[29] Contemporary standards addressing the ability to know or appreciate may not represent the most defensible account of insanity, but they provide the courts with some recognizable criteria of eligibility and, therefore, with some intelligible conception of legal mental illness for this purpose.[30]

The Supreme Court frames the standard for competence to stand trial in terms of the defendant's ability to understand and consult.[31] Sufficient disruption of comprehension or communication caused by mental retardation, cognitive disorganization, distorted reality testing, or other forms of psychological dysfunction constitutes legal mental illness for this purpose. Courts can admit expert testimony describing such impairment and explaining the manner in which the impairment affects the defendant's comprehension of the proceedings and ability to consult with counsel. In order to evaluate the significance of this testimony, the court must establish some minimal criteria of understanding and communication for this purpose, and it must interpret the expert testimony according to those criteria.

Similarly, statutes and case law define civil competence as the ability to understand the nature and significance of decisions regarding health care, contracts, property, or other legally relevant transactions. Impairment of psychological capacities that renders the individual unable to understand the likely results or significance of certain decisions or the alternatives undermines that person's competence for those

---

[29] Stephen J. Morse, *Culpability and Control*, 142 U. PA. L. REV. 1587 (1994); ROBERT F. SCHOPP, AUTOMATISM, INSANITY, AND THE PSYCHOLOGY OF CRIMINAL RESPONSIBILITY §6.3 (1991); Halleck et al., *supra* note 21, at 492–94, discuss the difficulty encountered with volitional impairment, but they seem to address it as a problem with current accuracy of measurement rather than the lack of any clear understanding of its meaning.

[30] SCHOPP, *supra* note 29, at §§2, 6.

[31] Drope v. Missouri, 420 U.S. 162, 171–72 (1975); PERLIN, *supra* note 24, at §14.03.

decisions and constitutes legal mental illness for those purposes.[32] Again, experts can describe the individual's level of comprehension and reasoning as well as any impairment of those capacities, and they can explain the manner in which that impairment influences decisions of the type at issue. Courts must then interpret that description and explanation in light of legal standards regarding the level of understanding that is sufficient to establish competence for this purpose.

One might criticize any of these standards as representing inadequate or misguided criteria for these legal purposes. The important point for this book, however, is that these standards all provide some criteria of eligibility in terms of the capacities that must be present (or impaired) in order to qualify the individual as eligible (or ineligible) for the legal status at issue. Terms such as "mental illness," "mental disease or defect," or "disease of the mind" indicate that ineligibility requires impaired capacity. That is, these terms preclude a finding of ineligibility because of factors such as disinterest, lack of due care, or personal preference rather than impaired capacity. Thus, one could rephrase these provisions in the following standard form.

Persons are not eligible for legal status S if and only if:

1. They suffer impairment of psychological capacities
2. rendering them unable to competently perform
3. psychological operations O.

In this formulation, S specifies a legal status in positive terms such as "criminally responsible for one's conduct" or "competent to stand trial." Clause 1 states the requirement of impaired capacity more clearly than do the usual terms such as "mental illness," "mental abnormality," or "disease of mind." Clause 3 specifies a set of psychological operations O, the ability to perform which constitutes the criteria of eligibility for S. For criminal responsibility or competence to stand trial under the most common current standards, for example, O specifies respectively knowing or appreciating wrongfulness or understanding the trial process and consulting with one's attorney. By specifying criteria of eligibility in terms of the capacity to perform certain psychological operations, these legal rules define legal mental illness for each legal purpose as any type of psychological impairment that renders one incapable of performing those operations. Clause 2 explicates the relationship between the psychological impairment and the operations O in that the impairment must prevent the individual from performing operations O to some threshold of competence established by lawmakers and evaluated by legal decision makers.

Clinicians can describe and explain the individual's impairment and the manner in which it affects the ability to perform operations O. The court must determine whether that impairment constitutes a legal mental illness rendering the person ineligible for the status at issue. That is, the court must determine whether the impairment constitutes legal mental illness by deciding whether it undermines the capacity to perform operations O as required by Clause 2. As most legal standards are currently formulated, clinicians cannot speak directly to the criteria of eligibility for two reasons. First, these are often stated in terms with no clear meaning or with a

---

[32] SAMUEL J. BRAKEL, JOHN PARRY, & BARBARA A. WEINER, THE MENTALLY DISABLED AND THE LAW 383–85 (1985) (civil competence for person and property).

meaning that does not translate directly into descriptive clinical language. It remains unclear, for example, what it means to appreciate wrongfulness or to be unable to conform to the requirements of law.[33] Second, criteria of eligibility ordinarily require a judgment of sufficiency that involves normative components that necessarily fall beyond the expertise of clinicians. Competence to stand trial, make health care decisions, or face execution, for example, requires the capacity to comprehend, but the level of comprehension that suffices to render one competent for each purpose varies with the complexity of the decisions faced and a variety of normative considerations involving error preference and the justification of various state actions.[34]

In current practice experts sometimes offer opinions that the defendants are (or are not) legally mentally ill for the purpose at issue, and courts sometimes allow or require such opinions. The point here is a prescriptive one regarding the appropriate roles of the expert and of the court, rather than a descriptive one regarding current practice. Consider, for example, the determinations of competence to stand trial and criminal responsibility regarding Cook and Davis. As initially described, Cook was found incompetent to proceed, but Davis was competent for this purpose.[35] Clinical testimony might describe the generally reduced level of comprehension and reasoning associated with Cook's mental retardation. Clinical testimony might also explain the manner in which those cognitive deficits affect Cook's understanding and ability to communicate in these circumstances. The clinician might ascertain, for example, that Cook understands that his defense attorney is "my friend" and that the prosecutor is a "bad guy." Cook might find it completely baffling, however, that the judge is neither his friend nor a bad guy because Cook might lack additional categories by which he understands the roles of other people.

Similarly, Cook may be able to provide simple factual answers to very specific questions from his attorney, but he may be unable to answer questions that are at all abstract or complex. He may also fail to form simple associations and to draw simple inferences, and thus, he may fail to inform his attorney about matters that any person of ordinary intelligence would recognize as obviously relevant and important to the case. Experts can describe and explain these impaired capacities and the manner in which they influence Cook's comprehension and communication regarding the trial. Experts cannot legitimately offer an opinion that such impairment renders (or fails to render) Cook incompetent to proceed, however, because this determination requires the application of normative considerations that fall beyond the range of clinical expertise. The court must make a normative judgment regarding the nature and degree of impairment of Cook's capacities to comprehend and to communicate that is required to justify denial of competence and suspension of the socially critical process of adjudicating responsibility for this criminal activity.

The legislature could define statutory criteria of competence to proceed that would render appropriate expert opinions by clinicians that specific defendants were (or were not) competent to proceed. The legislature could do so by making the relevant normative judgments in the legislative process by establishing statutory criteria of competence in purely psychological terms. The legislature might pass a statute defining a person as competent to proceed with trial, for example, if and only

---

[33] SCHOPP, *supra* note 29, at §§2.1.1, 6.3.

[34] *See* chapter 11, section V.

[35] *See* chapter 1, section I.

if that person achieves a full-scale intelligence score of at least 60 on an individually administered intelligence test. By defining the criteria of competence in terms that fall within the scope of clinical expertise, the legislature would enable clinicians to offer opinions that specific defendants are (or are not) competent to proceed. Unfortunately, criteria of competence defined in such a manner are highly likely to generate unjust outcomes because they fail to accommodate the wide variety of clinical and normative factors that are relevant to the justification for the competence requirement.

The criteria of exculpation represented by common insanity standards preclude expert testimony in the form of opinions that individuals meet (or fail to meet) these criteria for similar reasons. Recall that Davis was found NGRI and that Cook might well have qualified for exculpation had he been competent to proceed. Clinical experts might elicit strong evidence to believe that during his psychotic phases, Davis knew that the law prohibited sexual activity with children. He might also have understood that most people would consider such activity morally wrongful. He might also have believed, however, that his conduct was morally required because he was following a divine directive and that most people would agree that his conduct was morally required if they realized that he was following God's orders.

Similarly, clinical experts might ascertain that Cook knew that his conduct was wrongful. The experts might establish that Cook only approached potential sexual partners when no adults were present and that Cook always asked the children with whom he engaged in sexual activity if they would promise "not to tell." When exploring Cook's understanding of what it means to say that behavior is wrong, however, the experts learn that Cook's ability to explain why his conduct was wrong is limited to his statement that "mama will yell."

The determination that Cook's awareness that "mama will yell" constitutes (or fails to constitute) sufficient understanding to satisfy the requirement that he knows or appreciates the wrongfulness of his conduct necessarily falls beyond the scope of clinical expertise. This determination requires an evaluation of the principles and factors that justify the state in holding some persons criminally liable and in excusing others. The expert can describe and explain Cook's impairment and the resulting level of understanding of wrongfulness, but clinical expertise does not include the normative determination that such understanding justifies criminal punishment or exculpation from such punishment. This normative determination requires legal and moral evaluation of the information provided by the clinical experts in the context of additional evidence. Similarly, the clinical experts might be able to describe and explain the various senses in which Davis knew or did not know that his conduct was wrongful, but an evaluation of the exculpatory significance of the various senses of knowing requires the evaluation of legal and moral principles that fall beyond the scope of clinical expertise.

Although the limits of expert testimony are often discussed in terms of the legitimacy of expert testimony regarding the ultimate issue, the critical concerns are expertise and relevance, rather than whether the testimony goes to the ultimate issue.[36] Clinical experts cannot legitimately offer testimony regarding most ultimate issues because most plausible legal criteria of competence or culpability include legal and normative factors that fall beyond clinical expertise. Thus, clinicians ordinarily

---

[36] FED. R. EVID. §704.

cannot legitimately offer testimony regarding ultimate issues because such testimony exceeds the scope of expertise, rather than because it addresses an ultimate issue. Clinicians cannot legitimately offer expert opinions regarding other matters that do not qualify as ultimate issues for precisely the same reasons.

The legal criteria of eligibility serve two critical functions. They serve a discriminative function by providing courts with a description of the characteristics they should recognize as identifying those who are (or are not) eligible for the legal status at issue. That is, the criteria guide the fact finder in identifying the psychological impairment that distinguishes the eligible from the ineligible. They also serve a justificatory function by providing, at least implicitly, a justification for treating some citizens differently than others. Common criteria of eligibility for the insanity defense, for example, implicitly appeal to the principle that the justification of punishment requires that we limit punishment to those who violate the criminal law while knowing what they are doing and that their conduct is wrongful. The criteria for competence to stand trial appeal to the principle of fairness that requires that we try only those who have the capacities needed to defend themselves during the process of adjudication.[37]

IV. Legal Mental Illness: Ellen and Francine

This formal conception of legal mental illness provides the conceptual structure needed to clarify the initially perplexing series of legal judgments regarding differential treatment of Ellen and Francine. Despite common patterns of impairment and common diagnoses, Ellen is competent to stand trial but Francine is not. The justification for the requirement of competence to stand trial requires that defendants have at least a minimally adequate opportunity to participate in the process in order to defend themselves. Ellen and Francine differ regarding their eligibility for the legal status of competent to stand trial despite sharing common types of functional impairment and diagnostic categories; Francine's pathology renders her unable to perform the psychological operations required by the justification for the competence requirement, but Ellen's pathology does not prevent her from performing those operations. In summary, Ellen and Francine differ in their eligibility for this legal status because of the differential manner in which their functional impairments interact with the legal criteria of eligibility; thus, Francine is legally mentally ill for this particular purpose but Ellen is not.

A similar analysis explains why Ellen and Francine would realize similar outcomes under the insanity defense despite differential standing regarding competence. As initially described, Ellen is found NGRI, and Francine apparently would qualify for exculpation under the same standard, although her diversion to the civil commitment system precludes trial on the question. Thus, both qualify as legally mentally ill for this purpose. The critical requirement of the insanity defense for both defendants addresses knowledge of wrongfulness. Most insanity standards require the ability to know or appreciate the wrongfulness of one's conduct because the justification for criminal punishment is ordinarily understood to require that the defendant is

---

[37] SCHOPP, *supra* note 29, at §6.3 (discussing the corresponding functions as the epistemic and justificatory functions of insanity provisions).

culpable for the criminal conduct, and the ability to recognize that one's conduct is wrong is ordinarily considered a requirement of culpability. Thus, the criteria of eligibility for the status of criminally responsible include the ability to perform the psychological operations required to accurately identify conduct as wrongful.

Ellen and Francine engaged in delusional thought that led them to believe that their assaultive conduct was necessary in order to protect themselves from imminent unlawful assault. Had those beliefs been accurate, their conduct would have constituted justified self-defense, and justified conduct is not wrongful. Thus, their pathology generated inaccurate beliefs regarding justification, which prevented them from realizing that their conduct was wrongful. In summary, their impairment constituted legal mental illness for this purpose because it prevented them from performing the psychological operations required as criteria of eligibility for the legal status of criminally responsible.

The formal conception of legal mental illness developed in this chapter provides the conceptual structure that explains why common patterns of impairment generate similar results regarding legal mental illness for the purpose of the insanity defense but divergent results for the purpose of competence to proceed with trial. Furthermore, the structure of the analysis demonstrates the manner in which the functional impairment interacts with the legal criteria of eligibility in order to identify those who are appropriately subject to differential treatment consistent with the underlying justification for the applicable legal rules. In contrast, application of the same framework to the civil commitment standards under which Ellen and Francine are committed raises some questions about the legal criteria of eligibility and the applicable conceptions of legal mental illness for this purpose.

Ellen was initially committed under a post-NGRI acquittal provision, and Francine was initially committed under a general civil commitment statute. Both commitments were made under the state's traditional police power in that the commitment criteria required a showing of mental illness and dangerousness to others, although Ellen's NGRI acquittal established these criteria without a separate showing for the commitment.[38] In both cases, the delusional assaults provided evidence of dangerousness and of a delusional disorder. At review, both remained delusional, but neither was grossly disorganized, assaultive, or threatening. That is, the type of psychological impairment and the applicable diagnostic category remained constant for both across time, but the impairment became less severe. Francine was discharged because she no longer demonstrated evidence of dangerousness, but Ellen's commitment was extended because she continued to demonstrate evidence of dangerousness, although she endangered herself rather than others.

At first glance, this sequence of events appears to conform to the formal conceptual structure for legal mental illness. One might argue that Ellen's impairment constitutes legal mental illness for this purpose but that Francine's does not because the principles that justify civil commitment require legal mental illness in the form of impairment that endangers oneself or others. Two concerns raise questions regarding the adequacy of this initial analysis, however, and these concerns also expose deficiencies in the criteria of eligibility represented by common civil commitment statutes. First, some commitment statutes require mental illness and dangerousness rather than dangerousness by virtue of mental illness. Insofar as these statutes are

---

[38] Jones v. United States, 463 U.S. 354, 363–66 (1983).

interpreted and applied as written, they address mental illness and dangerousness as independent criteria, providing no indication of the psychological operations O that psychological impairment must undermine in order to qualify as legal mental illness. To the extent that statutes require dangerousness by virtue of mental illness, the required causal relationship between the two criteria appears to provide some guidance in that it indicates that the impairment must be of a type that renders the individual dangerous.

The causal relationship represented by statutes framed in this manner does little to illuminate the mental illness requirement, however, because it fails to identify legal criteria of eligibility in terms of the capacity to engage in psychological operations. Consider, in contrast, the requirements that the individual lack the capacity to know the wrongfulness of the conduct in the NGRI provisions or that the individual have the capacity to understand the proceeding and communicate with the defense attorney in the competence to proceed provisions. Each standard articulates criteria of eligibility for a particular legal purpose in the form of the capacity to engage in identifiable psychological operations, generating an applicable conception of legal mental illness as impairment that prevents the individual from engaging in those operations. The dangerousness requirement identifies no psychological operations, however, and therefore it generates no applicable conception of legal mental illness as impairment of the capacity to perform those operations. One might interpret these provisions as establishing that any impairment that plays a causal role in harmful conduct constitutes legal mental illness for the purpose of civil commitment, but review of actual and potential cases suggests that this interpretation cannot establish a satisfactory conception of legal mental illness for this purpose.

V.   Civil Commitment and Eligibility

A.   *Commitment as a Sexual Predator and Legal Mental Illness*

The sexual predator statutes are fundamentally defective precisely because they provide no account of the operations one must be able to perform in order to qualify for the status at issue and thus, no criteria of legal mental illness for this purpose. Although these statutes refer to "mental abnormalities affecting emotional or volitional capacities," they provide no account of the capacities one needs to qualify as eligible for the status of liberty from preventive commitment under these provisions or of the functional impairment of psychological processes that constitutes legal mental illness that renders one ineligible because of emotional or volitional disorder.[39]

The Supreme Court apparently adopts a conception of legal mental illness as volitional impairment, identifying Hendricks's putative inability to control his sexual conduct as a mental abnormality that differentiates him from those whose behavior is most appropriately addressed exclusively through the criminal process. The Court's opinion provides no account of the volitional capacities required for eligibility, however, nor does it explain what kind of impairment would constitute volitional impairment or what would count as evidence of such dysfunction. Furthermore, the

---

[39] KAN. STAT. ANN. §59–29a02(b) (Supp. 1997); WASH. REV. CODE ANN. 71.09.020(2) (1992).

Court does not explain what type of impairment would render an individual unable to control his conduct for the purpose of a postsentence commitment without undermining his culpability for the prior conviction.[40] Thus, the Court provides no guidance for the lower courts in interpreting and applying their decision and no explanation that would justify committing Hendricks or others under the statute. The appropriate conception of legal mental illness for the statute remains mysterious.

Prior appellate opinions addressing commitments under sexual predator statutes fail to articulate any intelligible criteria of eligibility or conception of legal mental illness. The conduct of the petitioners in *In Re Young*, like that of Hendricks and sex offenders generally, was organized, directed, and planned.[41] The "mental abnormalities" and "personality disorders" discussed in *Young* were identified primarily by the patterns of proscribed conduct and by the aberrant emotions and desires that motivated that conduct.[42] Emotional states include hate, greed, anger, or desire to engage in certain activity. Motivating emotions are involved in virtually any action. Thus, their mere presence provides no plausible justification for differentiating among actors and no discriminative criteria for selecting certain offenders for commitment under the statute. The mere fact that some individuals act upon aberrant desires or other emotional states provides no evidence of impairment of the capacities that most people use in constraining their conduct in order to avoid violating social rules and suffering the consequences of such violations. Thus, the conduct provides no evidence of legal mental illness as impairment that would differentiate these individuals from criminals generally and render them ineligible for the status at issue.

Both petitioners in *Young* had been convicted of multiple violent sexual offenses, and both were diagnosed by expert witnesses as qualifying for diagnoses of paraphilia.[43] Neither sexual assault nor the paraphilias entail impaired psychological processes apart from the specified sexual fantasies, urges, or behavior and the associated distress or impaired functioning.[44] These desires may be socially deviant in that they are directed toward socially aberrant content, but they provide no evidence of impaired capacities. That is, the mere fact that some individuals experience and act upon such desires does not support the contention that these individuals suffer impairment of the capacities ordinarily available to most people for use in understanding the relevant social constraints and directing their conduct in light of these constraints.[45] Insofar as "mental illness" or "mental abnormality" means a pattern of impaired psychological capacities, the court opinions in the sexual predator cases provide no bases for concluding that these offenders manifested such illness or abnormality.

Certain defendants charged with sexual offenses may suffer psychological impairment associated with their conduct. The impairment manifested by some of these individuals might justify government intervention through civil commitment or com-

---

[40] Kansas v. Hendricks, 117 S.Ct. 2072, 2080–81, 2088–89 (1997).

[41] In Re Young, 857 P.2d 989, 994–95 (Wash. 1993); KENNETH V. LANNING, CHILD MOLESTERS: A BEHAVIORAL ANALYSIS 19–20 (1992); W. L. Marshall & H. E. Barbaree, *An Integrated Theory of the Etiology of Sexual Offending*, in HANDBOOK OF SEXUAL ASSAULT: ISSUES, THEORIES, & TREATMENT 257, 268 (W. L. Marshall et al. eds., 1990).

[42] In Re Young, 857 P.2d at 989, 1001–03.

[43] *Id.*

[44] DSM–IV, *supra* note 4, at 522–32.

[45] SCHOPP, *supra* note 29, at §6.5.

mitment following a finding of insanity or incompetence to stand trial. Cook and Davis, for example, arguably fall within this category.[46] The impairment that justifies such intervention, however, is not constitutive of pedophilia, paraphilia, or any other diagnostic category common to offenders who would be subject to the predator statute. Rather, it represents impaired psychological process that could have similar significance if Cook or Davis were charged with nonsexual assault, robbery, or theft, and it differentiates them from Baker and from the petitioners in *Young*.

The supreme courts of Washington and Minnesota recognized that the statutory terms articulating the mental illness requirement as "mental abnormality," "personality disorder," and "psychopathic personality" represented legislative categories rather than clinical diagnostic categories. Neither court accepted clinical expertise or diagnostic categories as authoritative regarding these categories, and the Washington court explicitly rejected the current diagnostic manual as dispositive.[47] Yet, neither court provided any interpretation of legal mental illness for this statutory purpose, and neither identified the psychological operations one must be able to perform in order to remain eligible for independence from such commitment or the types of impairment that would qualify as a legal mental illness for this purpose. The *Young* court provided no basis for differentiating the petitioners from those who claim to suffer robberitis produced by the emotional disorder of greed. Similarly, neither the Minnesota statute nor the Minnesota supreme court opinion in *Blodgett* provide any account of the disorders discussed in that case to suggest that these "disorders" consist of anything other than desire to engage in criminal conduct and willingness to act on that desire.

The directly relevant question is whether the person manifests a pattern of psychological impairment that constitutes a legal mental illness, that is, one that renders that person unable to perform the operations that specify the criteria of eligibility for the legal status at issue. Sexual predator statutes provide neither criteria of eligibility nor any basis from which to infer such criteria. For this reason, they fail to fulfill the discriminative function in that they provide no guidance to decision makers in identifying those who are legally mentally ill in this sense, and they fail to address the justificatory function in that they provide no explicit or implicit justification for subjecting certain individuals to both commitment and criminal prosecution.

B. General Civil Commitment and Legal Mental Illness

General civil commitment statutes manifest the same defect as that contained in the sexual predator statutes. Civil commitment statutes either fail to define mental illness for this purpose or define it so vaguely as to provide little or no indication of the capacities that render one eligible for the status of liberty from involuntary civil commitment. Thus, these provisions provide no grounds from which courts can infer an appropriate conception of legal mental illness. The Wisconsin civil commitment statute, for example, defines mental illness as "a substantial disorder of thought, mood, perception, orientation, or memory which grossly impairs judgment, behavior,

---

[46] *See* chapter 1, section I.
[47] In Re Blodgett, 510 N.W.2d 910, 911–16 (Minn. 1994); In Re Young, 857 P.2d at 989, 1001–03.

capacity to recognize reality, or ability to meet the demands of ordinary life."[48] It is difficult to explain what impaired behavior means in this context.

One might construe this statutory definition broadly by interpreting the notion of a disorder of mood that impairs behavior to include any emotional state that generates aberrant behavior. According to this interpretation, any emotional state that motivated deviant conduct, including desires to engage in such behavior, would qualify as an emotional disorder. Such an interpretation might include offenders such as those convicted under the sexual predator statutes, but it would also include virtually anyone who engages in serious antisocial conduct. Thus it would distort the meaning of "illness" by including within it those who suffered no impairment of any capacities. According to this interpretation, for example, the previously discussed robberitis apparently qualifies as a legal mental illness; greedy bank robbers who steal because of a desire for money would seem to demonstrate an emotional disorder and resulting impairment of behavior. Such an interpretation is implausible on its face, distorts the meaning of "illness," and fails to fulfill either the discriminative or justificatory functions. It provides no account of the characteristics the fact finder should accept as differentiating "impaired" behavior from ordinary conduct in service of desire, and it provides no account that justifies treating these individuals differently than ordinary criminals.

Alternately, one could construe the Wisconsin statute narrowly by interpreting the category of disorders that "impair behavior" as limited to those that produce aberrations in behavior that result from substantial impairment of the listed processes of thought, mood, perception, orientation, or memory through which individuals ordinarily direct their behavior as minimally competent practical reasoners. Such an interpretation of legal mental illness for this purpose might reflect defensible criteria of eligibility in that those who suffer legal mental illness in this sense would demonstrate dysfunction similar to that which undermines civil competence or criminal responsibility under common standards for civil competence and guardianship or criminal responsibility.

This interpretation would establish minimal competence in practical reasoning regarding the conduct or decision at issue as the eligibility criterion for the status of independence from involuntary commitment as well as for civil competence and criminal responsibility. Impairment undermining the capacity to direct one's behavior through a minimally competent process of practical reasoning regarding the conduct or decision at issue would constitute legal mental illness for each of these purposes. This interpretation appears to hold some promise, but it also calls into question the purpose and justification for civil commitment as an institution distinct from civil competence and criminal responsibility. Later chapters pursue these matters in more detail.

Dangerousness as an additional criterion of commitment provides no indication of any legal theory of eligibility generating a conception of legal mental illness appropriate to mental health commitment. A judicial determination that a person is dangerous attributes a separate socially relevant property to that person in the circumstances. In finding that a person is dangerous, a court makes the judgment that this person presents a risk of harm sufficient to justify state intervention through the

---

[48] WIS. STAT. ANN. §§51.01(13)(b) (West 1997).

commitment process.[49] The determination of dangerousness is distinct from the finding of "mental illness" in that it generates no description of the types of impairment the court should accept as legal mental illness for commitment. That is, the statutory requirement of "mental illness" signals the requirement of psychological impairment, but dangerousness provides no account of the capacities to perform operations O that would establish the criteria of eligibility and that the impairment must undermine in order to qualify for legal mental illness, rendering the person ineligible.

Persons with various types of psychological impairment, including psychosis, retardation, mild depression, mild anxiety, or learning disabilities, might also be dangerous. The criteria of "mentally ill and dangerous" provide no principled basis for discriminating between the person who is an arguably appropriate candidate for civil commitment because he is psychotic and dangerous from the person who suffers mild depression or a learning disability and who engages in a pattern of criminal conduct for profit. These criteria could serve the discriminative function for commitment if one wanted to select all people who provide evidence of dangerous conduct and psychological impairment of any kind, but such criteria would defeat the justificatory function. No plausible principles would justify treating all those selected alike and as appropriate for commitment.

Statutes defining the criteria of commitment as "mentally ill and dangerous by virtue of the mental illness" do not solve the problem because they provide no indication either of the type of impaired process that qualifies as mental illness or of the relationship needed between the functional impairment and the dangerousness. Consider, for example, the criminal who suffers mild depression, rendering it somewhat more difficult for him to get up in the morning, so he steals rather than works because theft does not require him to rise at a regular time.[50] Alternately, consider the criminal who is mean and stutters. He assaults those who seem to be laughing at his stuttering, or he commits armed robbery rather than deal with the frustration of interacting with people on a job.[51] Another habitual criminal never learned to read because he suffers a learning disorder.[52] He walks into a bus station and asks a driver which bus goes to Chicago. When the driver replies "check the signs on the buses," the angry criminal assaults the driver.

In each of these cases, the defendant's psychological impairment plays a causal role in producing the dangerous conduct, but few readers would argue that these types of impairment should exculpate the actors for criminal conduct or justify mental health commitment. The mere fact that psychological impairment contributes in some manner to dangerous conduct provides no reason to treat these people differently than ordinary criminals. Only criteria of eligibility appealing to some underlying principles justifying mental health commitment for those whose impairment prevents them from satisfying those criteria serve both the discriminative and justificatory functions. General civil commitment statutes provide no basis from which to infer plausible criteria of eligibility and an appropriate conception of legal mental illness.

These statutes, like the sexual predator provisions, fulfill neither of the two

---

[49] See chapter 10, section V.
[50] DSM–IV, supra note 4, at 345–49.
[51] Id. at 63–65.
[52] Id. at 48–50.

central functions identified previously. They fail to advance the discriminative function because they provide the fact finder with no guidance regarding the type of impairment the court should recognize as legal mental illness that differentiates eligible from ineligible persons. They also fail to advance the justificatory function because they identify no principles that justify subjecting some persons who endanger themselves or others to civil commitment while addressing others through the procedures for establishing incompetence and guardianship or through the criminal justice system. Later chapters in this book examine the defects of general civil commitment provisions and advance an alternative formulation of civil commitment that addresses the defects that the sexual predator statutes bring into stark focus.

VI.   Conclusion

Many legal provisions addressing concerns that are traditionally understood as central to mental health law authorize differential treatment of some people for certain purposes by virtue of their mental illness. As used in these legal provisions, "mental illness," "mental disease," "mental abnormality," and related terms do not refer to psychological impairment generally or to clinical diagnostic categories. Rather, these terms refer to those types of psychological impairment that render individuals unable to competently perform the psychological operations that constitute the criteria of eligibility for a particular legal status. Those who manifest impairment that prevents them from competently performing those operations qualify as legally mentally ill for the particular purpose at issue.

The sexual predator statutes are fundamentally defective in this regard because they provide no account of the capacities that constitute the applicable criteria of eligibility, and thus, they generate no intelligible conception of legal mental illness. Although the sexual predator statutes demonstrate this defect in a stark form, the same problem pervades general civil commitment. This lack of any clear criteria of eligibility or corresponding conception of legal mental illness renders these provisions vulnerable to deliberate abuse, and perhaps more important, it renders them vulnerable to unintended misuse by those who must interpret and apply them in the absence of any meaningful guidance. To remedy these central defects, satisfactory civil commitment statutes must provide explicit criteria of eligibility in terms of the capacities to engage in the appropriate psychological operations. Such criteria of eligibility generate the appropriate conception of legal mental illness, fulfilling both the discriminative and justificatory functions of the statutes.

Identifying the criteria that fulfill these functions requires clarification of the underlying normative structure that justifies these particular legal institutions as components in a larger legal system. Part II develops a framework for an integrated system of *parens patriae* intervention through the mental health system of a liberal society. Chapter 4 presents a normative structure for *parens patriae* intervention. Chapters 5 and 6 integrate central functions of mental health law within that normative structure.

Part II

Parens Patriae Intervention

Chapter 4
NORMATIVE STRUCTURE I

This chapter applies the formal conception of legal mental illness to *parens patriae* interventions through the mental health system. It advances an interpretation of legal mental illness for this purpose as incompetence for person, and it integrates this conception of legal mental illness with the well-established right to refuse treatment and with the broader set of legal institutions within which this right is embedded. First it interprets this conception of legal mental illness as consistent with the widely accepted values of autonomy and well-being underlying the right to refuse treatment specifically and health care more generally. Then, it integrates this conception of legal mental illness and this analysis of the basis for the right to refuse treatment into the broader principles of political morality underlying the legal institutions of a liberal society. This chapter does not attempt to provide an exhaustive analysis of the principles underlying health care delivery specifically or of liberal political morality generally. Rather, it provides only the limited sketch of these projects needed to advance a plausible normative structure for *parens patriae* interventions through mental health law.

I. Ellen Revisited

Ellen's initial commitment rested on grounds that differed fundamentally from those that supported her extended commitment at the 90-day review. Her initial commitment rested on the police power and on her assault against the visiting nurse as conduct that demonstrated that she endangered others. Her psychopathology qualified as legal mental illness for the purposes of precluding criminal responsibility and of civil commitment following an NGRI acquittal. In contrast, the *parens patriae* rationale supported the extension of her commitment at the 90-day review because she was unable to recognize the danger to her health represented by diabetes. Ellen's case resembles that of the petitioner in *Jones v. United States*[1] insofar as the statute at issue in *Jones* addressed postinsanity acquittal commitment, but the criteria of continued commitment included mental illness and dangerousness to others or to oneself.

Although the *Jones* Court concluded that an insanity acquittal sufficed to establish mental illness and dangerousness for the purpose of commitment following the insanity acquittal, it provided no analysis to explain what kind of impairment would satisfy the mental illness requirement for commitment or why impairment sufficient to qualify as legal mental illness for an insanity defense necessarily sufficed for commitment.[2] Initial commitments under postinsanity acquittal provisions ordinarily

---

[1] Jones v. United States, 463 U.S. 354 (1983).
[2] *Id.* at 366.

involve harm or risk to the interests of others. Yet, the statute and the Court discuss protection of the acquittee and of society from the risk caused by the acquittee's disorder.[3] The Court's opinion does not explain why commitment predicated upon conduct demonstrating risk to others should continue until the acquittees are no longer dangerous to others or to themselves.

Ordinary civil commitment statutes reveal a similar pattern in that they allow police power and *parens patriae* commitment, but they neither provide an account of the type of impairment needed to establish mental illness for each nor explain why certain types of impairment justify state intervention under each power. Most statutes accommodate both underlying powers simply by including a phrase that allows commitment on the basis of dangerousness to self or others.[4] Ordinarily, nothing turns on which power forms the basis for a particular commitment, and the court order might not explicitly identify the power under which the individual is committed.[5] Thus, common civil commitment statutes, as well as postacquittal commitment statutes like that at issue in *Jones*, often address *parens patriae* and police power commitments as minor variations within the same commitment process. Neither the statutes nor the courts explain why the same parameters of commitment and conceptions of legal mental illness should apply to both types of commitment. In summary, the statutes and courts provide no conception of legal mental illness that addresses the discriminative and justificatory functions discussed in chapter 3.

A jurisdiction that lacked a civil commitment statute or had one that authorized only police power commitments could exercise *parens patriae* control over Ellen at the 90-day review under the authority of an appropriately drafted statute providing for a finding of incompetence for person regarding health care decisions. A finding of incompetence for person under an appropriately drafted statute would result in an appointment of a guardian and a protective placement intended to prevent Ellen from suffering harm resulting from her failure to maintain necessary nourishment and treatment for the diabetes. The court would address the determination of competence as the threshold question; it would address the appointment of a guardian, the authority and duties of the guardian, or substantive decisions regarding the necessity of protective placement or specific health care procedures only after it had already determined that Ellen lacked competence.[6] Although these statutes ordinarily address competence for person and for property, Ellen's circumstances raise concern specifically regarding competence for person. In determining whether Ellen was competent for person, the court would address Ellen's ability to make reasoned decisions regarding her personal well-being. These decisions include but are not limited to her competence regarding health care for her diabetic condition. The court could declare Ellen incompetent for person only, or if the conditions warranted, it could declare her incompetent for both person and property.[7]

---

[3]*Id.* at 354, 357–59, 363–70.

[4]Some include variations on danger to self such as grave disability or inability to meet one's basic needs. John Parry, *Involuntary Civil Commitment in the 90s: A Constitutional Perspective*, 18 MENTAL & PHYSICAL DISABILITY L. REP. 320, 323 (1994).

[5]Rogers v. Okin, 634 F.2d 650, 658 (1st Cir. 1980).

[6]UNIFORM PROBATE CODE §§5-101-04, 5-301-12, 8 U.L.A. 325–31, 354–77 (1998). BARBARA A. WEINER & ROBERT M. WETTSTEIN, LEGAL ISSUES IN MENTAL HEALTH CARE 287–92 (1993).

[7]UNIFORM PROBATE CODE, §§5-306, 5-401, 8 U.L.A. 365, 378 (1998); WEINER & WETTSTEIN, *supra* note 6, at 284–86.

Ellen's delusional disorder that generates her beliefs regarding her divine ability to heal and the conspiracy among health care providers to kill her would constitute legal mental illness for this purpose because it interferes with her ability to accurately comprehend the potential risks and benefits of prescribed treatment and to make reasoned decisions regarding that treatment. Civil competence statutes generate relatively clear conceptions of legal mental illness because they describe criteria of eligibility in functional terms. Individuals are competent for a particular domain if they have the capacities needed to understand the relevant concerns and to make and communicate reasoned decisions regarding those concerns. Impairment that distorts such understanding or impairs a person's ability to make and communicate such decisions constitutes legal mental illness for this purpose. This conception of legal mental illness reflects the formal conception of legal mental illness presented in chapter 3, and it fulfills the discriminative and justificatory functions because it reflects the principles of political morality embodied in these legal institutions of competence and guardianship. The following sections of this chapter extend this conception of legal mental illness to *parens patriae* interventions generally.

II.   Conflicts Among Values in Mental Health Law

Many ordinary citizens might find it intuitively obvious that health care providers should intervene in Ellen's decision to refuse treatment designed to control the harmful effects of her diabetes. Some of these citizens might think that health care providers should always have the authority to deliver the treatment expected to protect the patient's well-being. Others might agree that adults should ordinarily have a right to decide regarding their own treatment but conclude that providers should treat Ellen without her consent because she is "mentally ill." Those who hold this view may understand "mental illness" as a relatively broad phrase of ordinary language rather than as a technical phrase corresponding to the notion of legal mental illness. Some substantial percentage of citizens might well endorse the position that health care providers should treat anyone who is mentally ill in a manner designed to promote that person's well-being, regardless of whether or not the mentally ill person agrees. It might seem obvious to those who held this view that mental illness renders concerns for individual liberty inapplicable. They might say of Ellen or other mentally ill people that these individuals "don't really understand what they are doing."

Contemporary mental health law strives to protect individual liberty as well as to promote well-being through effective treatment, however, rejecting the premise that psychological impairment of any type overrides the individual's right to accept or reject proffered treatment. Many of the important developments in legal doctrine and scholarship in mental health law during the past quarter century have been directed toward establishing a body of legal rules and procedures designed to protect the individual liberty of those who interact with the mental health system. Legal doctrine established from this perspective sometimes constrains the manner in which mental health care providers pursue their therapeutic mission, but in other circumstances legal protection of liberty and the therapeutic mission of the mental health system converge.[8] When

---

[8] The research program known as therapeutic jurisprudence seeks this convergence, exploring potential developments in mental health law intended to promote both liberty and therapeutic effectiveness. DAVID B. WEXLER & BRUCE WINICK, LAW IN A THERAPEUTIC KEY (1996).

liberty interests and therapeutic effectiveness conflict, however, legal doctrine designed to maximize therapeutic effectiveness infringes upon individual liberty, and uncompromising protection of liberty impedes effective treatment.

When therapeutic interests conflict with individual liberty, one can advocate either of two plausible relationships between the competing values. First, one can grant a priority to one value over the other such that the first serves as a constraint on the second. According to this approach, for example, liberty might constrain therapeutic efforts such that any therapeutic program must give way when it conflicts with protected liberty, regardless of the magnitude of the potential gains or losses to each value. Alternately, one can balance the two competing values, selecting a rule or deciding a case by weighing the relative gains and losses to each value in the circumstances. Empirical data can inform the decision to endorse one of these approaches by providing a reasonable estimate of the likely results of each, but empirical premises alone cannot determine the correct choice. The justification for endorsing a particular relationship between these two values must take the form of normative argument, appealing to broader moral principles underlying the legal and ethical systems in which mental health law and treatment are embedded.

Some controversial developments in contemporary case law, statutory law, and the associated commentary involve apparent conflicts between therapeutic goals and the need to protect liberty. Although the participants in these debates sometimes differ regarding the therapeutic efficacy of specific forms of treatment or of involuntarily administered treatment generally, they also dispute the relative importance of effective treatment as compared to the right to decide for oneself whether to accept or reject such care. Recent disputes regarding the appropriate statutory criteria for involuntary civil commitment involve both levels of dispute.[9] Empirical evidence of the therapeutic effectiveness of involuntary treatment would supply a premise that is relevant to but not sufficient for the justification of involuntary commitment solely for the purpose of providing treatment. A complete justification of involuntary commitment for this purpose must also provide normative argument justifying *parens patriae* intervention into individual liberty for the purpose of promoting that individual's well-being through effective treatment. A normative argument of this type might reflect a categorical priority for well-being over liberty, or it might take the form of a balancing approach that grants priority to relatively strong interests in well-being over relatively mild intrusions into liberty.

In contrast, one could advance a normative analysis reflecting a categorical priority for protecting individual liberty over promoting well-being. Mental health law based on this normative foundation would preclude involuntary *parens patriae* commitment regardless of the cost to the individual's well-being. Alternately, a legal system reflecting a strong but not categorical priority for liberty might recognize a general right to refuse *parens patriae* commitment with limited exceptions for ex-

---

[9] *See generally*, Mary Durham & John Q. LaFond, *A Search for the Missing Premise of Involuntary Therapeutic Commitment: Effective Treatment of the Mentally Ill*, 40 RUTGERS L. REV. 303 (1988); Mary Durham & John Q. LaFond, *The Empirical Consequences and Policy Implications of Broadening the Statutory Criteria for Civil Commitment*, 3 YALE L. & POL'Y REV. 395 (1985); Stephen J. Morse, *A Preference for Liberty: The Case Against Involuntary Commitment of the Mentally Disordered*, 70 CALIF. L. REV. 54 (1982); Alan Stone, *Broadening the Statutory Criteria for Civil Commitment: A Reply to Durham and LaFond*, 5 YALE L. & POL'Y REV. 412 (1987) (rejecting the arguments of Durham and LaFond, 1985).

treme circumstances. In summary, specific provisions of mental health law involving such matters as involuntary civil commitment and the right to refuse treatment reflect underlying principles of political morality. An ideal system of mental health law would reveal a consistent underlying normative structure. Although an actual system will probably fall substantially short of complete coherence, analysis of the provisions in a particular system should provide some evidence of a relatively clear and consistent set of principles. That analysis can then generate proposals for revisions in the current system intended to render it more consistent with the underlying normative structure.

As manifested in statutes and judicial opinions, contemporary American mental health law reflects a normative structure that vests value in protecting individual liberty and in promoting well-being by providing for the care and treatment of those in need.[10] A series of cases addressing the right of involuntarily confined patients to refuse psychotropic medication directly raises the conflict between the therapeutic mission of the mental health system and the individual's right to accept or reject potentially beneficial treatment. In *Washington v. Harper*, for example, a prisoner asserted a right to refuse antipsychotic medication, absent a judicial determination of incompetence.[11] This prisoner did not contest the state's claims that he had been psychotic and assaultive and that the medication had previously improved his condition. Rather, he claimed the liberty to refuse admittedly beneficial treatment absent a judicial determination of incompetence.

Although *Harper* specifically addressed involuntary treatment in the prison setting, the petitioner framed the case as one involving a judicial determination of incompetence for person, and the Court addressed the case in terms that involved dangerousness to self or others and treatment in the individual's interests.[12] Other cases address the right of civilly committed patients to refuse treatment, and they discuss this issue in terms of dangerousness to self or others and judicial determinations of incompetence or alternative statutory procedures.[13] This series of cases reveals a complex pattern of concerns that calls upon both the police power and the *parens patriae* authority. This chapter pursues the *parens patriae* branch of the analysis by examining the framework underlying mental health law as a legal institution governing the delivery of health care to those who manifest psychological impairment.

III. Patient-Centered Health Care and the Right to Informed Consent

A. *Informed Consent, Autonomy, and Well-Being*

The widely endorsed patient-centered approach to health care contemplates a process of shared decision making in which competent patients retain final authority over

---

[10] David B. Wexler & Robert F. Schopp, *Therapeutic Jurisprudence: A New Approach to Mental Health Law* in HANDBOOK OF PSYCHOLOGY AND LAW 361–62 (Dorothy K. Kagehiro & William S. Laufer eds. 1992).

[11] Washington v. Harper, 110 S.Ct. 1028, 1032–35 (1990); Alexander D. Brooks, *Law and Antipsychotic Medication*, 4 BEHAV. SCI. & L. 247, 253–54 (1986).

[12] *Harper*, 110 S.Ct. at 1037–40.

[13] Rennie v. Klein, 653 F.2d 836 (3rd Cir. 1981), *vacated and remanded*, 102 S.Ct. 3506 (1982); Rogers v. Okin, 643 F.2d 650 (1st Cir. 1980), *vacated and remanded sub nom.* Mills v. Rogers, 102 S.Ct. 2442 (1982).

their own treatment. Providers diagnose their patients and recommend treatment, explaining the advantages and disadvantages of the available alternatives. Patients exercise the right to informed consent and the concomitant right to refuse treatment by selecting from among the options.[14]

In ordinary circumstances, the underlying values of autonomy and beneficence converge through the competent adult's exercise of the right to informed consent. The moral principle of autonomy includes a right to self-determination within a sphere of personal sovereignty.[15] Health care delivery traditionally emphasizes the principle of beneficence, requiring that the provider actively promote the well-being of the patient.[16] The doctrine of informed consent reflects respect for autonomy: Under the appropriate conditions, either informed consent or treatment refusal constitutes an exercise of self-determination regarding a matter that falls within the domain of personal sovereignty, because it is primarily and directly self-regarding. It promotes well-being according to the widely endorsed conceptions of well-being because in ordinary circumstances, fully informed and competent patients are in the best position to make treatment decisions likely to promote their interests.[17]

When patients who are competent refuse treatment that reasonably can be expected to produce a clear balance of benefits over costs, however, institutional decision makers confront a direct conflict between autonomy and individual well-being; they must either respect the patient's choice at the expense of well-being or override that choice in order to promote the patient's well-being. Some perennial debates in mental health reveal this tension between the more abstract values underlying the law and ethics of health care. Those debates involve such issues as the appropriate standard for *parens patriae* civil commitment and the committed individual's right to refuse treatment intended to promote his or her well-being.

B. Autonomy

Although autonomy is widely accepted as a core value in contemporary health care ethics, the precise conception of autonomy at issue often remains vague. When used to identify a right, "autonomy" refers to a right to self-determination within a sphere of personal sovereignty. The individual who holds this right enjoys discretionary authority within this sphere in that his or her competent, voluntary decision is necessary and sufficient to settle matters falling within the scope of the right. Theorists differ as to the proper boundaries of this sphere, but it generally encompasses central self-regarding life decisions regarding one's body, work, family, privacy, and prop-

---

[14] Cruzan v. Director, Missouri Dept. of Health, 110 S.Ct. 2841, 2846–52 (1990); TOM L. BEAUCHAMP & JAMES F. CHILDRESS, PRINCIPLES OF BIOMEDICAL ETHICS 74–79 (3d ed. 1989); ALLEN BUCHANAN & DAN BROCK, DECIDING FOR OTHERS 26–29, 90–93 (1989); RUTH R. FADEN & TOM L. BEAUCHAMP, A HISTORY AND THEORY OF INFORMED CONSENT 274–97 (1986); W. PAGE KEETON ET AL., PROSSER AND KEETON ON THE LAW OF TORTS 189–93 (5th ed. 1984). Although the patient-centered model is well established in law and commentary, some writers contend that the traditional paternalistic approach still dominates in clinical practice. FADEN & BEAUCHAMP, *id.* at 53–101.

[15] BEAUCHAMP & CHILDRESS, *supra* note 14, at 67–74; BUCHANAN & BROCK, *supra* note 14, at 36–40; JOEL FEINBERG, HARM TO SELF 27–97 (1986).

[16] BEAUCHAMP & CHILDRESS, *supra* note 14, at 194–97.

[17] BUCHANAN & BROCK, *supra* note 14, at 29–30, 36–40.

erty.[18] The right to informed consent and the concomitant right to refuse treatment fall squarely within this domain for competent adults, unless they suffer some condition, such as a contagious disease, that endangers others.

Autonomy-as-a-condition is a set of virtues derived from the conception of a person as a self-governing being. These include self-reflection, direction, reliance, and control; moral authenticity and independence; and responsibility for self.[19] Those who have attained a relatively advanced development of these virtues critically reflect upon and endorse or alter their own motives and values. Autonomous persons develop integrated lives by reviewing and shaping their projects, motives, and conduct according to their higher order values. They are self-governing in that they define their lives and the principles they live by through this process of self-evaluation and development. By doing so, they reaffirm their lives as their own.[20]

To exercise sovereignty and develop the virtues of autonomy-as-a-condition, individuals need autonomous capacities. These are the psychological capacities such as consciousness, understanding, and reasoning used in critical self-reflection, deliberation, and decision making.[21] For the sake of clarity, I reserve "autonomy" for the comprehensive value embracing all senses in which the term is used. I use "autonomous virtues" for autonomy-as-a-condition, referring to autonomy-as-a-right as "sovereignty" and to autonomy-as-capacity as "autonomous capacities."

Autonomous capacities serve as a necessary condition for autonomous virtues and for sovereignty in that one who lacks sufficient autonomous capacities cannot develop the corresponding autonomous virtues and does not qualify for sovereignty. Increased capacities beyond the threshold required to qualify for sovereignty can improve one's ability to exercise this right, but they cannot increase the degree to which one is sovereign because sovereignty as discretionary control does not admit of degrees. Either the individual possesses complete authority within the identified domain of self-regarding decisions, or others retain some authority to intervene. If others retain such authority, the individual lacks discretionary control and (thus) does not enjoy sovereignty. Individuals manifest autonomous virtues in various degrees, however, and the extent to which they develop these virtues depends in part on the degree of autonomous capacities they possess.[22]

C. Competence, Autonomy, and Well-Being

Autonomous acts must involve the exercise of autonomous capacities. The right to informed consent reflects this requirement in that the provider must supply the patient with the relevant information, and the patient must make the treatment decisions. Furthermore, the patient must do so voluntarily and must understand important relevant information and exercise unimpaired reasoning. By granting informed consent

---

[18] FEINBERG, *supra* note 15, at 52–56.

[19] *Id.* at 31–44.

[20] GERALD DWORKIN, THE THEORY AND PRACTICE OF AUTONOMY 24–33, 110–11 (1988) [hereinafter THEORY AND PRACTICE]; Gerald Dworkin, *The Concept of Autonomy, in* THE INNER CITADEL 54 (John Christman ed., 1988) [hereinafter *The Concept of Autonomy*].

[21] FEINBERG, *supra* note 15, at 28–31; THEORY AND PRACTICE *supra* note 20, at 13–20; *The Concept of Autonomy, supra* note 20, at 54.

[22] FEINBERG, *supra* note 15, at 28–31.

for health care, a competent individual exercises autonomous capacities within the domain of sovereignty, authorizing treatment and accepting responsibility for the decision.[23]

In ordinary circumstances, the requirement of informed consent promotes well-being as well as sovereignty. Some theorists identify individual well-being with some form of preference satisfaction, whereas others endorse an objective criterion of well-being such as happiness or self-fulfillment. According to either type of theory, people have welfare interests in certain states of affairs, which allow them to pursue their ultimate good. An interest qualifies as a welfare interest to the extent that virtually all persons must attain it to some minimal degree in order to be able to effectively pursue the other aspects of their well-being. These welfare interests include some minimal level of tangible goods, health, psychological functioning, and freedom to act as they see fit. Attainment of most plausible conceptions of individual well-being will be very difficult or impossible unless these welfare interests are met.[24] The right to informed consent ordinarily allows patients the opportunity to make health care decisions in light of the likely effects of that care on their welfare interests and on their ultimate good.

Certain patients, however, do not make health care decisions likely to maximize their well-being. Some of these patients fail to make decisions in their own best interest because they lack the minimal capacities required to render them competent to manage their own health care. Others possess ordinary psychological capacities but decide in a manner inconsistent with their own long-term interests because of fear, anger, stubbornness, miscalculation, or failure to consider some of the interests involved.

Incompetent patients suffer impairment of the autonomous capacities, which serve as a necessary condition for sovereignty and autonomous virtues. A thorough discussion of incompetence would require careful examination of traditionally difficult legal, psychological, and philosophic issues, including competing theories of cognition, decision making, responsibility, moral agency, and free will.[25] It is sufficient for the purpose of this analysis to say that certain types of psychological dysfunction undermine the autonomous capacities required to meet the threshold for sovereignty because they prevent the individual from engaging in a minimally adequate process of practical reasoning regarding matters that fall within the domain of individual discretion. A legal standard of competence that deprives these individuals of the right to informed consent and the concomitant right to refuse treatment does not violate the principle of autonomy because these individuals lack the autonomous capacities needed to qualify for sovereignty. Throughout the *parens patriae* portions of this book, I use "incompetent" to refer to those who suffer psychological dysfunction sufficient to prevent them from qualifying for sovereignty.[26]

---

[23] BEAUCHAMP & CHILDRESS, *supra* note 14, at 74–79; BUCHANAN & BROCK, *supra* note 14, at 36–40; FADEN & BEAUCHAMP, *supra* note 14, at 235–87; THEORY AND PRACTICE, *supra* note 20, at 101–20.

[24] BUCHANAN & BROCK, *supra* note 14, at 29–36; JOEL FEINBERG, HARM TO OTHERS 31–64 (1984).

[25] *See e.g.*, BUCHANAN & BROCK, *supra* note 14, at 1–86; FADEN & BEAUCHAMP, *supra* note 14, at 274–97; HARRY G. FRANKFURT, THE IMPORTANCE OF WHAT WE CARE ABOUT 11–25 (1988); Elyn R. Saks, *Competency to Refuse Treatment*, 69 N.C. L. REV. 945 (1991); ROBERT F. SCHOPP, AUTOMATISM, INSANITY, AND THE PSYCHOLOGY OF CRIMINAL RESPONSIBILITY 219–51 (1991).

[26] I set aside two related issues. First, I do not attempt to give an account of the types and degrees

Well-being assumes additional importance for these incompetent individuals. Some severely impaired patients lack both the capacities required to qualify for sovereignty and the potential to develop further their autonomous capacities and virtues. In such cases surrogate decision makers and health care providers adhering to the patient-centered approach can only maximize other aspects of well-being. Romeo, the severely retarded resident of a state institution in *Youngberg v. Romeo*,[27] for example, lacked the capacity to significantly improve his cognitive functions. He sustained many injuries as a result of his aggressive conduct in the institution. The staff frequently placed him in physical restraints in order to prevent him from further injuring himself or others. The Supreme Court found a state obligation to provide minimally adequate training to promote safety and freedom from undue restraint. Romeo's lack of potential to significantly improve his autonomous capacities limited providers to promoting other aspects of his well-being by training him in a manner intended to reduce his violent behavior, decreasing the probability of injury and increasing freedom from restraint.

Most incompetent individuals possess autonomous capacities and autonomous virtues to some degree, however, and most have the potential to further develop these traits. Surrogate decision makers and health care providers treat these incompetent individuals in a manner intended to promote their well-being and to improve their ability to exercise autonomous capacities. Frequently, these goals converge in that treatment promotes well-being and facilitates autonomous capacities. In some circumstances, however, these goals conflict and decision makers encounter difficult choices between maximizing autonomous capacities and promoting other aspects of well-being. In order to make and justify these difficult choices, decision makers must clearly distinguish among autonomy, sovereignty, liberty, and freedom.

D. *Autonomy, Sovereignty, Liberty, and Freedom*

Courts and commentators ordinarily address civil commitment, the right to refuse treatment, and other intransigent issues in mental health law as difficult cases involving conflicts between the need for effective treatment and other important considerations such as autonomy or liberty.[28] Autonomy, sovereignty, liberty, and freedom are closely related (but not identical) notions. Although discussions of mental health law often blur the distinctions among these four notions, these distinctions carry significance for the analysis of the defensible limits of *parens patriae* interventions. Freedom is the presence of open options. People have open options when they lack external personal constraints that would prevent them from performing an action or refraining from performing it as they choose. The more options people have open, the more freedom they have. Liberty is the absence of rule-imposed limits on freedom of action within a political system.[29] Thus, liberty is a narrower concept

---

of psychological impairment that should render one incompetent and ineligible for sovereignty. Second, I do not address the evidentiary issue regarding the type of evidence that would be sufficient to show that an individual suffered such impairment.

[27] Youngberg v. Romeo, 102 S.Ct. 2452, 2455–56, 2460 (1982).

[28] *See e.g.*, sources cited *supra* note 8.

[29] FEINBERG, *supra* note 15, at 62–68.

than freedom: Liberty involves only a lack of legal constraints, but freedom requires the absence of any constraints from personal sources.

In certain circumstances, people might be at liberty to perform certain acts but not free to do so, or they might be free to engage in conduct they are not at liberty to perform. People are at liberty to engage in activity but not free to do so when some personal source of constraint other than a political rule prevents them from performing the activity. In principle, one cannot be free to engage in conduct that one is not at liberty to perform because a constraint on liberty constitutes one type of constraint on freedom. In some circumstances, however, *de jure* and *de facto* liberty diverge because laws prohibiting certain types of conduct are not consistently enforced. In such circumstances, one might lack *de jure* liberty to engage in certain conduct yet remain effectively free to do so. In practice, therefore, people can be free to engage in activity they are not at *de jure* liberty to pursue when the political rules forbidding such conduct are not enforced.[30] Suppose, for example, the law in a particular jurisdiction grants civilly committed patients a right to refuse medication absent an emergency or a judicial determination of incompetence.[31] Suppose also, however, that the legal system fails to enforce this law despite routine violations in the public institutions. Committed patients in this jurisdiction would be at *de jure* liberty to refuse treatment, but they would not be free to do so effectively. The staff of the public institution would be free to administer treatment without consent, although they would not be at *de jure* liberty to do so.

Sovereignty is a moral right that constitutes part of the moral value of autonomy. A legal system representing an underlying political philosophy vesting primary significance in this value must protect liberty regarding actions falling within the sphere of sovereignty because legal rules restricting such liberty would violate the individual's standing as sovereign. A corresponding degree of freedom is necessary to give this sphere of sovereignty and liberty practical effect. One could endorse various liberties for reasons other than respect for autonomy. Those who vest value in efficiency or productivity, for example, might support liberty to contract for one's labor or to participate in the marketplace as likely to maximize these values. Individual autonomy is widely recognized, however, as an important value underlying the right to informed consent regarding health care.[32]

Although some patients lack the capacities required to qualify for sovereignty, autonomy remains an important value for those who possess some degree of autonomous capacities or virtues or the potential to develop these traits. A comprehensive respect for the value of autonomy demands both deontic and consequentialist components.[33] The deontic value of autonomy requires respect for competent self-regarding choice as an exercise of sovereignty, although it allows temporary intervention to ascertain the competent, informed, and voluntary status of the choice.[34] This aspect of the value is deontic in that it vests significance in the intrinsic nature of the choice as an exercise of sovereignty by a competent moral agent, rather than in any expectations regarding its consequences.

---

[30] *Id.* at 63.

[31] *See, e.g.*, Rogers v. Com'r of Dept. of Mental Health, 458 N.E.2d 308, 314–15, 321–23 (1983).

[32] BEAUCHAMP & CHILDRESS, *supra* note 14, at 67–74; BUCHANAN & BROCK, *supra* note 14, at 36–40.

[33] BEAUCHAMP & CHILDRESS, *supra* note 14, at 25–26.

[34] FEINBERG, *supra* note 15, at 12–14.

The consequentialist aspect of the value, in contrast, emphasizes the expected consequences of any decision or action on the development of autonomous capacities and virtues. Those who recognize the consequentialist value of autonomy attribute positive normative force to an act insofar as it promotes development of these traits and negative normative force insofar as it undermines them. Acts that encourage development of autonomous capacities and virtues also increase the probability that certain individuals will qualify for sovereignty.

The consequentialist aspect of the value for autonomy commands weight both in itself and as an aspect of the patient's well-being. Recognizing the principle of autonomy commits one to promoting development of autonomous capacities and virtues because they constitute aspects of the comprehensive value for autonomy. Concern for patients' well-being demands concern for development of their autonomous capacities because patients retain welfare interests in these psychological capacities that enable them to effectively pursue their ultimate interests. Finally, self-fulfillment in the form of development of the autonomous virtues constitutes at least part of a person's well-being in a political system vesting value in autonomy. The next section applies this patient-centered approach to difficult cases of *parens patriae* interventions through the mental health system.

IV. Difficult *Parens Patriae* Cases for Mental Health Law

A. *Priorities Between Autonomy and Well-Being*

Autonomy and well-being converge in ordinary circumstances when competent patients exercise the right to informed consent in a manner calculated to promote their most important interests. In some cases involving incompetent patients, autonomy and well-being converge in that surrogate decision makers and health care providers treat these patients in a manner intended to promote well-being as well as the consequentialist aspect of autonomy. These *parens patriae* interventions promote the consequentialist value for autonomy without violating sovereignty because the patient in question lacks the capacities necessary to qualify for sovereignty. Treating grossly impaired and assaultive patients without their consent, for example, may improve their cognitive functioning and reduce assaultive behavior, thereby allowing more freedom from restraint, decreasing risk of injury, and improving autonomous capacities.

In *Washington v. Harper*, the Court allowed involuntary treatment with antipsychotic drugs of seriously mentally ill prisoners who are dangerous to themselves or others when the treatment is in their medical interests.[35] If the criterion of "serious mental illness" is interpreted as limited to psychological impairment sufficient to undermine the capacities necessary to qualify for sovereignty, the *Harper* rule allows treatment to enhance well-being and the consequentialist aspects of autonomy with-

---

[35] *Harper*, 110 S.Ct. at 1028, 1039–40. Although the Court's opinion focused heavily on procedural issues, I am only concerned here with the substantive standard. The Court did not explicate "serious mental illness." I discuss it here as a hypothetical example of a case in which autonomy and well-being would converge if the Court limited "serious mental illness" to impairment sufficient to undermine sovereignty.

out violating the deontic component of that value. Such treatment would be expected to improve well-being by increasing safety from injury, freedom of motion, and autonomous capacities. If the treatment improved these capacities sufficiently to restore these patients to competence, it would enable them to qualify for sovereignty within the limited domain of discretion retained by prisoners. Although this treatment would advance well-being at the expense of the patient's freedom to choose, it would not violate the principle of autonomy. Rather, it would enhance the consequentialist aspect of autonomy in circumstances in which the deontic aspect did not apply because the patient failed to qualify for sovereignty. Thus, involuntary treatment in these circumstances would infringe upon ordinarily protected liberty, but the underlying values of autonomy and well-being would converge.

Any plausible legal system must allow some constraints on individual liberty in order to prevent harm to others or harm to self by clearly incompetent individuals such as infants. To the extent that specific liberties rest on the more abstract moral principle of autonomy, *parens patriae* limitations on liberty that do not violate autonomy do not violate the principles of political morality underlying mental health law. In some cases it may be possible to promote an incompetent patient's well-being through several methods, each of which will improve different aspects of his or her well-being, requiring a choice regarding the most important components of well-being to pursue. For example, medication might reduce severely disturbed patients' injurious behavior by sedating them in a manner that further reduces their already impaired alertness and capacity to comprehend and make conscious choices, thus undermining their already impoverished autonomous capacities. A strictly applied behavioral program involving both positive and aversive consequences for behavior, in contrast, might spare them the reduced autonomous capacities at the cost of inflicting the aversive consequences.

Decision makers who encounter difficult cases must establish priorities between autonomy and well-being as well as among various components of these basic values. Some writers advocate a categorical priority for sovereignty over well-being, rejecting any paternalistic intervention into competent self-regarding decisions. Others balance sovereignty against well-being in each case.[36] Theorists from both schools can accept intervention contrary to incompetent choices when doing so is necessary to promote well-being, but they may differ regarding which aspect of well-being to emphasize. A comprehensive priority for all aspects of autonomy would preclude any intervention that sacrifices either the deontic or consequentialist components of this value in order to promote well-being. Such a comprehensive priority would require that decision makers maximize autonomous virtues and capacities at the expense of other components of well-being. In contrast, those who balance autonomy and well-being as well as some who advocate a priority for sovereignty balance the consequentialist value for autonomous virtues and capacities against other aspects of well-being. Thus, some theorists might consistently endorse the priority of sovereignty over well-being but balance the consequentialist aspects of autonomy against other components of well-being.

Consider, for example, the following cases. George is an elderly widower with serious, chronic, coronary disease. He has received consistent medical advice indi-

---

[36] *Compare* FEINBERG, *supra* note 15, at 57–62 (endorsing priority) *with* BUCHANAN & BROCK, *supra* note 14, at 40–47 (balancing values).

cating that smoking and drinking markedly increase the danger of a fatal heart attack. Although he understands and believes this advice, he continues to smoke regularly, and he meets with three old friends to share a bottle of bourbon twice a week. When asked why he continues to smoke and drink despite the medical advice, he explains that he does so because these activities provide the primary enjoyment in his life.

Heidi is a moderately retarded adult who suffers a painful form of cancer. The only effective treatment for the pain is medication that significantly sedates her, decreasing her alertness and mental acuity, reducing her already impaired autonomous capacities and virtues. Because Heidi is incompetent, a surrogate must decide either to administer the medication, reducing the pain and her already impoverished autonomous capacities and virtues, or to withhold the treatment, maximizing her autonomous capacities and virtues but leaving the pain unabated. In summary, the surrogate must grant priority either to the physical comfort that constitutes one aspect of the Heidi's well-being or to the autonomous capacities and virtues that constitute the consequentialist aspect of autonomy and another component of her well-being.

Ordinary practice and contemporary law would respect George's sovereign choice but call upon a surrogate to decide for Heidi. Some readers would probably share the intuitive judgments that George's sovereignty ought to prevail over his well-being as evaluated from an external perspective and that the surrogate ought to opt for the medication, weighing Heidi's physical comfort more heavily than the resulting cost to her autonomous capacities and virtues. Can one consistently advocate a priority for the deontic aspect of the value of autonomy over well-being by endorsing respect for George's sovereignty, yet sacrifice the consequentialist aspect of the value for autonomy to other aspects of Heidi's well-being? What justifies a priority for the deontic aspect of the value for autonomy but allows balancing of the consequentialist aspect?

Those who vest value in autonomy can recognize human well-being as an additional important value, but they cannot balance well-being against the deontic aspect of autonomy when the two conflict. Those who accept a conception of autonomy that includes individual sovereignty as a right to exercise discretionary control over a specific domain of decisions must grant priority to that right over well-being for two reasons. The first is conceptual. When sovereignty is understood as discretionary control within a domain of essentially self-regarding issues, any institutional authority to paternalistically intervene in decisions within that domain violates sovereignty.

A legal institution claiming authority to prevent George from acting on unreasonable or self-defeating decisions, for example, would undermine an attribution of sovereignty to him. A social structure that grants such authority to override George's competent choice within his domain of "sovereignty" undermines his status as sovereign. George cannot enjoy discretionary control over any decision regarding which any other person or institution holds the authority to intervene because this external authority renders incoherent the claim of discretionary control. The other party's authority recasts his putative right to self-determination as a privilege, revocable at the judgment of those wielding that authority. Thus, the mere fact that others hold this authority undermines his claim to sovereignty, regardless of whether they choose to exercise it.

The second argument for the priority of sovereignty involves the relationship between that right and the well-being of a competent adult. By exercising sovereignty, each competent person defines and pursues those aspects of well-being that are central to the life he or she has chosen. If the state claimed the authority to monitor and supervise all aspects of each person's life, leaving no domain of individual discretion within which that person independently defined his or her own projects and made his or her own decisions, it would dilute the credit and responsibility individuals could claim for their own lives. Individuals merit praise or blame and define their lives and the principles by which they live through the exercise of sovereign discretion. They create their own lives as extended projects that are uniquely their own by exercising sovereign discretion regarding the central self-defining choices.

Certain interests, including food, shelter, and safety, form part of virtually everyone's well-being. These interests, however, are common to all people and, indeed, to nonhuman animals. These interests contribute to one's good as a sentient being, but they do not in themselves constitute well-being unique to humans generally or to any person specifically. Neither do they reflect the defining characteristics of moral agency or of this particular person. Only by exercising sovereignty can one define one's life and embrace certain interests as one's own well-being.[37] Thus, others can act to promote various states of affairs that would be good for George, but only by exercising sovereignty can George render them part of his uniquely personal good. Sovereignty takes priority because it enables him to define his own life and embrace various aspects of well-being as his well-being.

The priority for sovereignty supports both the principle of autonomy and the principle of beneficence insofar as the latter principle addresses the uniquely human well-being this person has adopted as his or her own. Absent the individual exercise of and social respect for sovereignty, those who act on the principle of beneficence can promote only the relatively impoverished notion of well-being common to all people and perhaps to other sentient beings. Those who promote well-being within the context of respect for sovereignty, in contrast, can promote the well-being that this person has defined as central to the life he or she has chosen. Thus, respect for sovereignty enriches the value of well-being for the competent person.

These arguments for the priority of sovereignty extend to improvements in autonomous capacities sufficient to qualify an individual for sovereignty. Such increases take priority over other aspects of well-being because they provide persons with the opportunity to exercise sovereignty by defining their lives and their well-being. Merely incremental increases in autonomous capacities below the threshold that qualifies one for sovereignty lack this effect. Thus, one can coherently advocate a priority for sovereignty and for increasing autonomous capacities that qualify one for sovereignty yet balance the consequentialist value of increases in autonomous capacities that fall below the threshold for sovereignty against other components of the individual's well-being. This approach represents a consistent integration of these values because the latter lack the special significance of the former in enabling the individual to define his or her life. For these reasons, one can coherently embrace the intuitive judgment that we ought to respect George's sovereign choice even as we conclude that reducing Heidi's pain makes a contribution to her well-being sufficient to compensate for the marginal loss in her autonomous capacities.

---

[37] THEORY AND PRACTICE, *supra* note 20, at 13–33, 110–14; FEINBERG, *supra* note 15, at 57–62; James Rachels & William Ruddick, *Lives and Liberty*, *in* THE INNER CITADEL 221 (John Christman ed., 1988).

B. Priorities Within Autonomy

Other cases require choices between the deontic and consequentialist aspects of autonomy. Irene is chronically moderately depressed, but she suffers no major cognitive dysfunction. She remains civilly competent and she understands her condition, its pattern of periodic exacerbation and partial remission, and the proposed treatments. Irene endangers neither her own life nor others' well-being, but she does not develop her talents, pursue any interests or projects, enrich her life, or voluntarily accept treatment. Her history of responsiveness to structured treatment and her fear of civil commitment suggest that threats to initiate commitment proceedings would probably motivate her participation in an outpatient program that would likely improve her well-being, including her autonomous capacities and virtues. When a competent patient refuses treatment likely to improve well-being in a manner that promotes autonomous capacities or virtues, the deontic value for autonomy conflicts with the consequentialist aspect of the same value.

The reasoning that supports the priority for sovereignty over well-being but allows balancing of the consequentialist aspect of autonomy against other components of well-being also supports the priority for the deontic value of autonomy over the consequentialist aspect. The conceptual argument that precludes balancing sovereignty against well-being also precludes balancing sovereignty against the consequentialist aspects of autonomy that constitute components of well-being. Recognizing the state's authority to intervene in sovereign choice in order to promote autonomous capacities or virtues would undermine the individual's sovereignty, even if the state never exercised this authority. Thus, one cannot consistently vest nonderivative value in a conception of autonomy that includes sovereignty yet recognize the state's authority to balance sovereignty against well-being, including those components of well-being that also constitute the consequentialist aspect of autonomy.

The second argument addressing the relationship between autonomy and a person's well-being also applies. To promote Irene's good is to promote the human good that she chooses, pursues, and endorses as her own.[38] Violating her sovereignty, and thus the deontic value of autonomy, in favor of any aspect of her well-being alienates that good from this person, undermining both the values for autonomy and for well-being. Such interventions sever this component of well-being from the person, rendering it no longer fully hers. Paternalistic interventions, such as initiating commitment proceedings or threatening to do so, may improve her well-being, including her autonomous capacities and virtues, but they do so at the expense of rendering that well-being less uniquely and personally hers. This component of Irene's well-being becomes alienated from her because its attainment can no longer be attributed to her.[39]

Some theorists might deny any nonderivative value for sovereignty. Some utilitarians, for example, might reject the patient-centered approach to health care in favor of the paternalistic model, or they might support the patient's right to informed consent as a general rule subject to being overridden when paternalistic intervention

---

[38] FRANKFURT, *supra* note 25, at 88–94.

[39] This discussion addresses only hard paternalism. For a discussion of the distinction between hard and soft paternalism, *see* FEINBERG, *supra* note 15, at 12–16.

would maximize happiness.[40] This book does not attempt to resolve fundamental questions of moral philosophy such as the relative merit of utilitarian and autonomy based theories. The arguments presented above suggest, however, that those who vest nonderivative value in autonomy cannot endorse a balancing approach to cases in which sovereignty conflicts with well-being, including those components of well-being that also constitute the consequentialist aspect of autonomy.

Legal institutions, including those representing a political morality vesting non-derivative value in autonomy, must address circumstances of uncertainty through the efforts of fallible agents. For this reason they must be designed with an eye toward error preference as well as moral principle. Any legal institution that allows intervention into incompetent choices or temporary intervention into questionable choices in order to evaluate decisions for competence risks inaccurate evaluation, resulting in unjustified interference with sovereignty. Yet, institutions that do not allow such intervention allow unjustifiable harm to well-being as a result of incompetent decisions.

Although those who endorse a nonderivative value for autonomy as a fundamental value must reject balancing of sovereignty and well-being in principle, they can accept legal institutions that risk occasional infringements of sovereignty to protect well-being in practice. Legal institutions address practical problems and they express societal value structures. Although institutions that allow intervention in incompetent choices risk occasional violations of sovereignty for well-being in practice, they do not accept balancing in principle because they explicitly repudiate any such infringement as an error, recognizing the aggrieved party's claim to legal remedy. By doing so, these institutions retain the principled priority of sovereignty as a right to self-determination within the identified domain. Thus, they express a value structure rejecting interference with individual sovereignty.

This analysis presents a coherent foundation in widely accepted principles of health care delivery for those components of mental health law that address *parens patriae* interventions. It does not address police power interventions, however, nor does it demonstrate that this approach to such interventions coheres with a defensible foundation for a more comprehensive set of legal institutions. A satisfactory normative framework for an integrated body of mental health law must demonstrate that this approach to the justification of *parens patriae* interventions coheres with the principles of political morality underlying the broader set of legal institutions in a liberal society and that these principles accommodate a compatible approach to the police power components of mental health law. The remaining sections of this chapter provide a skeletal account of the principles of political morality represented by the legal institutions of a liberal society. These sections demonstrate that *parens patriae* interventions reflecting the patient-centered approach to health care delivery are consistent with these political principles underlying the broader set of legal institutions. These more general principles of political morality provide a common foundation for the *parens patriae* interventions discussed in this part of the book and the police power interventions discussed in part III.

---

[40] For the purpose of this discussion, we can describe utilitarianism roughly as the moral theory that identifies happiness as the good and considers right the conduct that maximizes the good. *See e.g.*, J.J.C. SMART & BERNARD WILLIAMS, UTILITARIANISM (1973).

V. *Parens Patriae* Interventions and the Legal Institutions
of a Liberal Society

A. *Liberal Societies*

The *parens patriae* and police powers represent traditional sources of authority for government intrusion into individual action and limitation on individual liberty. As such, they presuppose a legal system reflecting general principles of political morality that support some relatively broad range of individual liberty. A theory of political morality that vested primary value in the maximization of the king's wealth, social productivity, the collective welfare, human happiness, or social harmony, for example, would not recognize a presumption in favor of individual liberty unless there were some reason to believe that such a presumption would promote the outcome valued. In societies reflecting these political principles, either specific individual liberties or government limitation of such liberties would require justification by appeal to the outcome vested with value in that society. In contrast, the *parens patriae* and police powers play a critical role in justifying civil commitment statutes in the United States precisely because the broader legal structures in the United States and other liberal societies institutionalize liberal principles of political morality that support a broad range of individual liberty that includes liberty from physical confinement and unwanted treatment. Thus, state intervention in the form of civil commitment or involuntary treatment requires specific justification.

As a formal principle of justice in constitutional adjudication, the reasonable relationship principle requires that the type, duration, and conditions of intrusion into protected liberties bear a reasonable relationship to principles that justify those intrusions according to the political morality embodied in this legal system.[41] The *parens patriae* and police powers represent certain well-established exceptions to a broad presumption of individual liberty in the liberal society. In order to articulate the appropriate parameters of these exceptions and the corresponding conceptions of incompetence, mental illness, dangerousness, or other criteria that would render mental health intervention consistent with these exceptions, one must interpret them in context of the underlying principles of liberal political morality.

Theorists who advance variants of liberal political theory differ regarding both their precise theoretical formulations and the structure of political institutions they endorse.[42] I do not attempt to resolve central debates in political philosophy; I only provide a skeletal framework of structural political liberalism in order to provide the minimal foundation necessary to interpret the parameters of legitimate mental health intervention in a liberal society.[43]

Structural political liberalism describes and defends basic institutions of political justice that provide a structure for a fair system of social cooperation among individuals who endorse a variety of comprehensive moral doctrines. These comprehensive moral doctrines include a wide array of moral and religious beliefs and principles

---

[41] *See* chapter 2, section III.

[42] *See generally,* WILL KYMLICKA, LIBERALISM, COMMUNITY, AND CULTURE (1989).

[43] Robert F. Schopp, *Verdicts of Conscience: Nullification and Necessity as Jury Responses to Crimes of Conscience,* 69 S. CAL. L. REV. 2039, 2065–79 (1996) (providing a more detailed discussion of this normative structure).

as well as the personal commitments and projects through which individuals order their lives and create meaning in those lives. Those who endorse various comprehensive moral doctrines can differ with one another regarding a number of important moral issues, principles, and obligations yet converge on certain principles of political morality such that they can support mutually compatible liberal political institutions.[44] These institutions establish and protect public and nonpublic domains of jurisdiction. The public jurisdiction includes those areas of life that a particular society defines as appropriate for public regulation through legal institutions. The nonpublic domain includes those aspects of life that the society reserves for personal discretion beyond the reach of public regulation through law. Citizens participate in and influence the public domain through democratic political institutions that instantiate the shared principles of political morality and protect the individual's discretion to pursue a broad range of life plans within the nonpublic domain.[45]

This political structure protects individual self-determination in each domain. Democratic political institutions respect individual self-determination in the public sphere by allowing each competent adult equal standing in the political process by which citizens collectively determine the limits of their own liberty and the boundaries of the public jurisdiction. This equality of standing in political institutions provides the basis for mutual respect among citizens and for self-respect as a member of the political process by each.[46] Although theorists articulate the requirements of equal standing in somewhat different terms, they converge on the central notion that persons qualify for equal standing in the political domain by possessing at least a minimal set of psychological capacities that enables them to participate in the political process of the public domain and exercise self-determination in light of their comprehensive doctrines in the nonpublic domain.[47] To adequately perform these two functions, individuals must have the capacities needed to engage in a process of practical reasoning at the minimal level of competence required for independent functioning by an adult in ordinary circumstances. Minimally competent practical reasoners must possess a set of psychological capacities that enable them to achieve adequate understanding of the rules, circumstances, and their own preferences and to deliberate on this understanding in order to reason to a plan of action in light of the likely consequences.[48]

Liberal societies differ regarding the precise boundaries of the public domain, but each maintains some substantial sphere of nonpublic life beyond the reach of government jurisdiction. This nonpublic sphere allows each person the opportunity to develop and pursue a conception of the good consistent with that person's comprehensive moral doctrine through individual decisions and voluntary relationships with others. Thus, competent adults define their lives through the manner in which

---

[44] JOHN RAWLS, POLITICAL LIBERALISM LECT. I, §§1–3 (1994). Rawls refers to religious, moral, or philosophical comprehensive doctrines. I refer to all of these as moral doctrines in order to include those systems or aspects of systems that people rely on to address moral questions regarding how we ought to live.

[45] Id. at Lect. I, §6.

[46] Id. at Lect. V, §7, Lect. VI, §6.

[47] Id. at Lect. I; FEINBERG, supra note 15 at 27–51.

[48] SCHOPP, supra note 25, at §§4.3, 6.5, 7.4.

they exercise sovereign discretion in the nonpublic sphere and participate as equal citizens in the public domain.[49]

Some structural liberals endorse comprehensive doctrines that include a fundamental value for sovereignty, whereas others might respect sovereignty as a derivative value. All structural liberals must respect sovereignty as categorical, however, in order to maintain the shared liberal political structure. Sovereignty is categorical in the sense that discretionary authority within the domain of sovereignty is not subject to review, compromise, or limitation by government. Conceptually, any claim of authority by the government to review and approve decisions within the protected domain would violate sovereignty, regardless of whether that authority was ever exercised.[50]

Beyond the conceptual argument, structural liberals must recognize sovereignty as categorical because any intrusion into an individual's nonpublic domain undermines the central distinction between public and nonpublic morality that enables structural liberals to converge on common principles of political morality despite differences in their comprehensive doctrines. Any attempt to justify political intrusion into an individual's domain of sovereignty would have to appeal to some moral principle or social goals as sufficient to override the shared principles of political justice. Thus, the shared principles of political morality provide good reasons to maintain distinct public and nonpublic domains. Any justification for transgressing that boundary by subjecting an individual's nonpublic domain to political intrusion must appeal to some other source of morally relevant reasons as outweighing those shared principles. This appeal would effectively endorse that alternate source of morally relevant reasons as superior to the shared principles and to any other moral principles that were not accepted as sufficient to override the shared principles. Acceptance of such reasons as sufficient to justify violation of sovereignty would effectively undermine the distinction between the public and nonpublic domains, and it would undermine equality in the public domain by elevating some comprehensive doctrines above those that were not found sufficient to override sovereignty.

Each liberal society establishes political institutions that embody the principles of political morality endorsed in that society and that protect the sovereignty of each competent adult within the nonpublic domain required by those principles.[51] At this fundamental level, self-determination and equality converge because government must treat persons with respect as beings capable of directing their own lives. It does so by according to each competent individual equal citizenship and participation in the political process as well as a sphere of personal sovereignty that equals that enjoyed by other members of the community and that identifies the person as a member in full standing of that community.[52] Specific variations of structural liberalism share at least the following important commitments: (a) They endorse liberal political principles and institutions as morally valuable, rather than merely as political compromise; (b) they maintain distinct public and nonpublic domains; and (c) they protect the equal standing of competent adults in the public jurisdiction as well as the sovereign control of each competent citizen within the nonpublic domain.

---

[49] RAWLS, *supra* note 44, at Lect. I, §§5, 6.

[50] FEINBERG, *supra* note 15, at 54–55.

[51] *Id.* at 52–57; RAWLS, *supra* note 44 at Lect. V, VIII; JOHN RAWLS, A THEORY OF JUSTICE 243–51, 440–46, 544–46 (1971).

[52] RONALD DWORKIN, TAKING RIGHTS SERIOUSLY 272–74 (1968).

B.   Parens Patriae *Intervention in a Liberal Society*

The patient-centered approach to health care addresses issues regarding informed consent and the right to refuse treatment in a manner that conforms to the broader principles of political morality in a liberal society. *Parens patriae* interventions into the ordinarily protected nonpublic domain remain consistent with the patient-centered approach and with liberal principles of political morality insofar as they are predicated upon a finding of incompetence for person. Psychological impairment sufficient to render the individual incompetent for person renders the individual ineligible for sovereignty in the nonpublic domain of the liberal society. *Parens patriae* interventions into matters that ordinarily fall within the protected nonpublic domain are justified when the individual manifests impairment that prevents that person from exercising discretion within that domain through the exercise of the capacities that qualify competent adults for equal standing in the liberal society.

Ellen and George illustrate the consistency between patient-centered health care and the principles underlying a liberal society. Ellen is subject to *parens patriae* intervention in the form of involuntary health care for her diabetes because her delusional disorder renders her ineligible for equal standing as a competent participant in the liberal society. George differs from Ellen in that he makes the decisions that endanger his health through the exercise of ordinarily competent processes of practical reasoning. *Parens patriae* interventions into George's decision would violate the statute addressing competence, the patient-centered approach to health care, and the underlying principles of the liberal legal institutions because George possesses the capacities required to qualify for sovereignty in the nonpublic domain.

VI.   Conclusion

Legal institutions of a liberal society provide an institutional structure representing underlying principles of liberal political morality. Those principles explain and justify the right to informed consent with the concomitant right to refuse treatment for competent adults who have the capacities needed to qualify for sovereignty in the nonpublic domain. These principles also explain and justify *parens patriae* interventions into the ordinarily protected nonpublic domain when the individual lacks the capacities required to exercise discretion in that domain through the exercise of competent practical reasoning. Statutes authorizing adjudication of competence and guardianship provide legal institutions for the application of these principles to difficult circumstances such as those presented by Ellen, George, and Heidi.

This analysis generates two important questions regarding involuntary civil commitment under the *parens patriae* authority. First, what legitimate role remains for *parens patriae* civil commitment beyond that of the incompetence and guardianship provisions? If these statutes regarding incompetence and guardianship provide a legal mechanism for *parens patriae* interventions involving surrogate decision making regarding care and treatment for those who lack the capacities required to decide for themselves, what independent function remains for *parens patriae* commitment? The lack of an incompetence requirement in most civil commitment statutes suggests that these statutes are intended to protect and treat those who remain competent but need such protection and treatment for their own benefit. This response raises the second question, however, because the central role of incompetence in justifying *parens patriae* interventions raises serious doubt about the justification for civil commitment as a *parens patriae* intervention for those who remain competent. It appears that *parens patriae* civil commitment of those who remain competent constitutes state intrusion into self-regarding decisions made by those who retain the capacities needed to qualify for sovereignty in the nonpublic domain. Framed succinctly: Absent a determination of incompetence, what justifies *parens patriae* interventions, including civil commitment?

Chapter 5
INCOMPETENCE AND COMMITMENT

This chapter reviews *parens patriae* civil commitment and competence and guardianship provisions as common forms of *parens patriae* intervention. The analysis demonstrates that appropriately drafted competence and guardianship provisions provide a form of intervention that effectively integrates the normative foundations for *parens patriae* interventions discussed in chapter 4 with the formal conception of legal mental illness developed in chapter 3. This discussion indicates that many difficulties encountered in the attempt to formulate satisfactory civil commitment statutes reflect the tendency of these provisions to depart from the criterion of incompetence required by the normative structure. Insofar as *parens patriae* civil commitment provisions rectify these deficiencies, they become redundant with the appropriately drafted competence and guardianship provisions.

I. Ellen, Competence, and Commitment

The *parens patriae* rationale supported the extension of Ellen's commitment at the 90-day review because her delusional disorder prevented her from responding adaptively to her diabetic condition. Had Ellen's jurisdiction lacked a civil commitment statute or had one that allowed only police power commitments, authorities could have exercised *parens patriae* control over her at the 90-day review under the authority of common provisions providing for a finding of incompetence for person regarding health care decisions. Ellen's delusional disorder prevented her from understanding that her diabetes threatened her well-being: It prevented her from realistically evaluating the accuracy of the diagnosis she received from the providers she viewed as conspiring to kill her, and her delusional belief in her power to heal led her to unrealistically overestimate her own abilities. This delusional belief also prevented her from realistically understanding the various treatment alternatives and making a reasoned choice. Any alternative treatment strategy involving diet or medication seemed unnecessarily risky and tedious in comparison to her readily available capacity to heal herself through her divine touch. On the basis of these findings, a court could determine that Ellen was incompetent for person, appoint a guardian to make appropriate health care decisions for her, and if necessary, order a protective placement intended to prevent her from suffering harm as a result of her failure to maintain necessary nourishment and treatment for the diabetes.

Ellen's case raises the questions identified at the end of chapter 4 regarding the relationship between *parens patriae* civil commitment and incompetence for person. Prior to the reforms in civil commitment that occurred in the 1970s, civil commitment resulted in explicit or implicit presumptions of incompetence. Commentators, courts, and legislatures then realized that some people could fulfill the criteria of commitment without suffering impairment that rendered them unable to make and communicate reasoned decisions regarding their health care or other aspects of their well-being. As part of the 1970s reforms, the presumption of incompetence for those subject to commitment was explicitly rejected. Thus, civil commitment no longer carries the implication of incompetence.[1]

Rather than resolving questions regarding the most appropriate relationship between incompetence for person and *parens patriae* civil commitment, these developments simply reframe those questions. If the criteria for *parens patriae* civil commitment do not entail incompetence for person, what justifies *parens patriae* intervention in the form of civil commitment? A satisfactory answer to this question must comport with the principles of political morality underlying the broader set of legal institutions in which commitment provisions are embedded. Such an answer must justify the state in engaging in *parens patriae* intrusion into the ordinarily protected nonpublic domain of individuals who possess the capacities of competent practical reasoning that ordinarily qualify competent adults to excercise discretion in that domain as citizens with equal standing.

Absent criteria of commitment that entail incompetence for person, no putative justification for *parens patriae* civil commitment coheres with the broader set of principles underlying the legal institutions of a liberal society, including the law and ethics of health care delivery. Commentators, courts, and legislators accurately recognized that the criteria for *parens patriae* commitment under ordinary civil commitment statutes do not require incompetence for person, but they drew precisely the wrong conclusion. Rather than explicitly severing the previous relationship between civil commitment and incompetence for person, legal institutions should reaffirm this relationship by requiring a judicial determination of incompetence for person as a prerequisite for *parens patriae* intrusion into the ordinarily protected nonpublic domain. To institutionalize *parens patriae* interventions in a form that coheres with the principles underlying liberal legal systems, states should abolish *parens patriae* civil commitment as an independent legal institution; they should address involuntary admission to mental health facilities under the authority of *parens patriae* only as a dispositional issue following a judicial determination of incompetence for person.

II.   Incompetence for Person and *Parens Patriae* Commitment

A.   *Civil Incompetence for Person*

State statutes that address competence and guardianship for person vary significantly. Some variations would accommodate cases such as Ellen's more effectively than would others. This chapter discusses provisions modeled generally after the Uniform Probate Code; some of the discussion does not apply to some state statutes as currently written.[2] This discussion examines the manner in which appropriately written provisions can accommodate cases such as Ellen's, but it does not contend that all

---

[1] SAMUEL J. BRAKEL, JOHN PARRY, & BARBARA A. WEINER, THE MENTALLY DISABLED AND THE LAW 375 (1985); BARBARA A. WEINER & ROBERT M. WETTSTEIN, LEGAL ISSUES IN MENTAL HEALTH CARE 86–87 (1993).

[2] UNIFORM PROBATE CODE §§ 5-101-04, 5-301-12, 8 U.L.A. 321 (1998).

current provisions could do so effectively or in the manner discussed here. Thus, this chapter presents a conceptual and prescriptive analysis regarding a general category of statutes, rather than a descriptive analysis of any particular current provision.

In applying these statutes, courts address competence as the threshold question in that they do not address the appointment of guardians, the authority and duties of the guardians, or substantive decisions such as placements or specific health care procedures unless they have determined that the subjects of the hearings lack competence.[3] The court adjudicates a person incapacitated if it finds that the person "is impaired by reason of mental illness, mental deficiency . . . to the extent of lacking sufficient understanding or capacity to make or communicate responsible decisions."[4] If the court determines that an individual is incapacitated, it appoints a guardian for that individual. The guardian is generally responsible for the care, custody, and control of the incapacitated person unless the court limits the guardian's powers.[5]

The court can limit the guardian's authority negatively by excluding certain matters from the scope of that authority, or it can do so positively by allocating to the guardian only the authority to address specific decisions or issues that extend beyond the individual's competence. Some statutes specifically define certain health care decisions, such as those authorizing psychosurgery, electroconvulsive therapy, or inpatient commitment, as beyond the authority of the guardian. Under these statutes, the court must make these decisions directly. Regardless of these specific statutory exclusions, the court can define and limit the guardian's authority by excluding certain matters in the court order or by narrowly defining the scope of guardianship.[6] The court delegates the decision-making authority to the guardian and retains jurisdiction over the case. Thus, the court can modify the court order; make certain decisions directly; and supervise, discipline, or remove the guardian.[7]

In Ellen's case, for example, her refusal of food and diabetes treatment could provide the impetus for a petition raising the question of her competence for person. This pattern of conduct could support such a petition independently of her presence on the inpatient ward pursuant to the prior commitment. Had she made the same decisions regarding food and health care while living in the community, for example, any interested person, such as a family member, social worker, or visiting nurse, could initiate the petition.[8] The court could order an evaluation of her psychological condition and appoint a visitor who would visit Ellen in her home in order to evaluate her ability to manage her affairs in her living situation.[9] On the basis of this investigation, the court could decide that Ellen's impairment prevents her from compre-

---

[3] UNIFORM PROBATE CODE §§ 5-101-04, 5-301-12, 8 U.L.A. 321 (1998); BRAKEL et. al., *supra* note 1, at 370; WEINER & WETTSTEIN, *supra* note 1, at 287–92.

[4] UNIFORM PROBATE CODE § 5-103(7), 8 U.L.A. 327 (1998).

[5] UNIFORM PROBATE CODE §§ 5-306(c), 5-309, 8 U.L.A. 365, 370 (1998).

[6] The recent trend in the statutes is toward narrower guardianship, allowing the ward to retain as much discretion as possible, but practical limitations may lead courts to rely more heavily on general guardianship orders. UNIFORM PROBATE CODE §§ 5-306(a), (c), 5-407(a), 8 U.L.A. 365, 386 (1998); BRAKEL et al., *supra* note 1, at 284–88; WEINER & WETTSTEIN, *supra* note 1, at 287–90.

[7] UNIFORM PROBATE CODE §§ 5-306(c), 5-311(a), 8 U.L.A. 365, 375 (1998); BRAKEL et al., *supra* note 1, at 386–88; WEINER & WETTSTEIN, *supra* note 1, at 287.

[8] UNIFORM PROBATE CODE § 5-303(a), 8 U.L.A 357 (1998); BRAKEL et al., *supra* note 1 at 379–80; WEINER & WETTSTEIN, *supra* note 1, at 282.

[9] UNIFORM PROBATE CODE § 5-303(b), 8 U.L.A. 357 (1998); BRAKEL et al., *supra* note 1, at 382–83; WEINER & WETTSTEIN, *supra* note 1, at 283–84.

hending her current physical health and making reasoned decisions about that matter. It could then declare her incompetent for person and appoint a guardian, either for person generally or more narrowly for decisions regarding health care related to her diabetic condition. The court could order placement in an inpatient facility if it concluded that such a restriction was necessary to protect Ellen, or it could define the guardian's authority in a manner that allowed the guardian to initiate that admission if it became necessary. Thus, the state could exercise *parens patriae* authority regarding the danger to Ellen's health in the absence of any civil commitment statute.

B.   Parens Patriae *Commitment*

The incapacitated person suffers impairment of the capacity to make and communicate responsible decisions for a variety of reasons, including mental illness.[10] The Uniform Probate Code offers no definition of legal mental illness for this purpose, except insofar as one infers from the definition of an incapacitated person that it refers to any functional impairment that renders the individual unable to make and communicate responsible decisions. By defining the criteria of incapacity in terms of the individual's inability to make and communicate responsible decisions, and by defining the duties of the guardian as care, custody, and control, the Code identifies incapacitated persons as those who suffer impairment such that they require the supervision of a guardian in order to avoid suffering some injury to their interests as a result of their inability to make and communicate responsible decisions.[11]

Similarly, *parens patriae* civil commitment requires mental illness and dangerousness to one's self. Some statutes supplement the dangerousness to self criterion with an alternative articulated in terms such as "grave disability." Individuals usually qualify as gravely disabled if they suffer impairment that renders them unable to provide for their own basic needs such as safety and nourishment. Jurisdictions that include a separate grave disability criterion tend to interpret the dangerousness criterion relatively narrowly to include only active threats to one's well-being, whereas those that do not include a separate grave disability criterion tend to interpret the dangerousness criterion relatively broadly to include either active threats or the passive inability to provide for one's basic needs. Thus, either type of statute can accommodate those who suffer impairment that renders them unable to provide for their basic needs.[12]

In summary, those who endanger themselves as a result of impairment that undermines their abilities to make and communicate responsible decisions regarding their own welfare qualify for *parens patriae* intervention through either the civil commitment statutes or the provisions directed toward competence and guardianship. Although it is widely accepted that civil commitment does not entail incompetence, it is difficult to articulate any clear distinction between two categories of individuals: (a) those who are incompetent for person because their impairment renders them unable to make and communicate responsible decisions regarding their own well-being and (b) those, like Ellen, who are subject to *parens patriae* civil commitment

---

[10] UNIFORM PROBATE CODE § 5-103(7), 8 U.L.A. 327 (1998).

[11] UNIFORM PROBATE CODE § 5-309, 8 U.L.A. 370 (1998).

[12] BRAKEL et al., *supra* note 1, at 32–37; John Parry, *Involuntary Civil Commitment in the 90s: A Constitutional Perspective*, 18 MENTAL & PHYSICAL DISABILITY L. REP. 320 (1994).

because they endanger themselves (i.e., their mental illness involves an impairment that prevents them from comprehending and adequately addressing their basic needs).

Although Ellen represents a threat to her own well-being because she is unable to make reasoned decisions regarding her health care, some individuals pose a more active threat to their own well-being because their psychological functioning is substantially impaired. Consider, for example an individual who suffers chronic depression and has made a number of suicidal threats and gestures. Arguably, some suicides are rational because, for example, they provide the only means available to terminate the intolerable suffering associated with a terminal illness. It is at least plausible to argue that such rational suicides fall within the nonpublic domain of individual discretion for competent persons and thus, that coercive intervention intended to prevent such suicides falls beyond the scope of state authority. This book does not purport to resolve these issues or to define the parameters of rational suicide, if some suicides qualify as rational.

It is analytic in the concept of *parens patriae* authority, however, that if the state can legitimately intervene to prevent suicide under the *parens patriae* authority, then the individual must suffer impairment that undermines the capacities needed to make reasoned decisions regarding the contemplated suicide.[13] Thus, *parens patriae* civil commitment intended to prevent a person from committing suicide comports with the principles underlying the legal institutions of a liberal society only if it is predicated upon some impairment that undermines that person's ability to make a reasoned decision regarding the contemplated suicide. In summary, *parens patriae* civil commitment intended to prevent active danger to one's self or to prevent harm caused by grave disability requires psychological impairment that resembles that required for civil incompetence for person in that it must prevent the person from directing important self-regarding aspects of his or her life through minimally competent processes of practical reasoning. When Ellen endangers herself because her psychological impairment distorts her comprehension and reasoning, therefore, the civil commitment statute and the provisions addressing competence and guardianship provide two alternative procedures for *parens patriae* intervention.

Although the state can address circumstances such as Ellen's either through competence and guardianship provisions or through ordinary civil commitment statutes, these two types of state intervention differ in ways that are potentially important for the establishment of a coherent and defensible body of mental health law. When applying competence provisions, the court initially addresses the question of competence, rather than admission. Thus, the structure of the statute directs the court's attention initially to the individual's ability to decide regarding her own health care and well-being, rather than to the advisability of admission or treatment. The statutes and the procedures frame the question of competence in terms of the functional capacity to make responsible decisions regarding one's own person, rather than as one of the presence of some vaguely articulated mental illness. This approach seems likely to encourage courts and clinical experts to consider the individual's functional impairment of psychological processes as it affects the capacities needed to manage the relevant decisions, rather than to ask whether that person suffers some diagnos-

---

[13] *See* chapter 1, section IV and chapter 4, section V. This book does not address alternative rationales for legal proscription of suicide, such as those grounded in legal moralism or extended harm to others.

able disorder appropriate for treatment.[14] If the court declares the individual to be incompetent for person or for some subset of decisions regarding person, it appoints a guardian for that domain and charges the guardian with making relevant decisions to promote the individual's well-being. Thus, the declaration does not lead to inpatient admission unless the court or the guardian finds good reason to believe that the inpatient placement appears likely to promote the ward's interests.

In summary, the central focus of the statutes and procedures addressing competence and guardianship differs significantly from that of civil commitment statutes. Most civil commitment statutes frame the question as essentially about intervention, encouraging the courts and clinical experts to consider mental illness as a condition that might warrant inpatient admission as an appropriate modality of treatment and obscuring the significance of mental illness as impairment undermining the ability to decide for oneself regarding admission, treatment, or other self-regarding matters.[15] In contrast, incompetence and guardianship provisions frame the question initially in terms of the person's ability to make reasoned, responsible decisions about these matters, secondarily as about the steps likely to promote his or her well-being, and only as one consideration relevant to that second question, as about the advisability of inpatient admission or alternative placement.

The structure of incompetence and guardianship provisions renders them compatible with the principles articulated in chapter 4 and with the conception of legal mental illness discussed in chapter 3. The threshold requirement of incompetence limits the set of individuals subject to state intrusion into the ordinarily protected nonpublic domain to those individuals who lack the capacities needed to exercise sovereignty through minimally competent practical reasoning. The sequence of inquiry by the court promotes interpretation of the initial question as one regarding functional capacities rather than diagnostic category and treatment selection. This approach to interpretation facilitates application in a manner consistent with the normative structure developed in chapter 4 in that the court considers *parens patriae* intervention only if the initial inquiry reveals impairment rendering the individual unable to exercise the capacities needed to qualify for sovereign discretion in the nonpublic domain. If the court determines that the individual is competent, the state refrains from further intrusion. If the court determines that the individual lacks the capacities that qualify one for sovereignty within the nonpublic domain, it issues an order of guardianship crafted in a manner intended to protect the individual's best interests and to promote recovery of the capacities needed to regain sovereignty, if that is a viable option. If attainment of equal standing and sovereignty is not a plausible alternative, the court and guardian structure the guardianship in a manner intended to promote the individual's well-being while allowing that individual as much discretion as possible.[16]

Although *parens patriae* intrusion violates the ordinary boundaries of protected liberty in a liberal society, it violates neither the respect for autonomy underlying widely accepted ethical principles of health care delivery nor the liberal political

---

[14] WEINER & WETTSTEIN, *supra* note 1, at 276–80 (discussing the clinician's functional assessment for the purpose of competence).

[15] Parry, *supra* note 12, at 322. Some commitment statutes at least allow for outpatient commitment, but inpatient admission is often the only available disposition or the only one seriously considered.

[16] *See* chapter 4, sections IV and V.

principles underlying the broader legal institutions, on the condition that such intrusions are limited to individuals who lack the capacities required to qualify for sovereignty in the nonpublic domain. A determination of incompetence represents the legal application of the underlying principles that require autonomous capacities as a necessary condition for sovereign discretion in the nonpublic domain. Thus, *parens patriae* intervention into the decisions and actions of an incompetent person intrudes upon the ordinarily protected range of individual liberty, but it does not violate the underlying principles of political morality.[17]

If an individual lacks the capacities necessary to qualify for sovereignty in the nonpublic domain, various forms of intervention might be justified by the complex set of values protected in the liberal society, including individual and public well-being, possible increases in the individual's autonomous capacities, and the potential return to equal standing with its domain of sovereignty. The previous discussion of George, Heidi, and Irene provides the basic structure of the analysis that courts should perform in order to determine the appropriate priorities among these values in specific circumstances. The general pattern of that analysis is roughly the following. *Parens patriae* interventions into the decisions of incompetent individuals do not violate sovereignty or the liberal principles of political morality, but the nature and extent of the intrusion must conform to those principles. Courts conform to those principles by giving priority to interventions likely to improve the individual's capacities to the extent that these interventions would enable that individual to regain competence. Circumstances that do not allow for the recovery of competence call for balancing increased capacities, other components of individual well-being, and the public interest, although these interests often converge.[18] These priorities remain consistent for any legal institution that comports with the underlying principles. Thus, *parens patriae* civil commitment either requires impairment that renders the individual incompetent for person (and therefore replicates state authority available through appropriately drafted provisions addressing incompetence, guardianship, and protective placement), or it violates the principles supporting the legal system in a liberal society.

In practice, such provisions probably do both. Certain persons committed under these provisions, such as Ellen, suffer impairment that renders them incompetent and appropriate for state supervision regarding their health care. Others probably remain competent and should be immune from *parens patriae* intrusion, but in the absence of clear criteria of legal mental illness for this purpose, courts commit them because they suffer some psychological disorder that seems appropriate for hospital treatment, and they make self-regarding decisions that appear misguided to others.[19]

The local trial court must apply a statute that authorizes commitment on the basis of a vague requirement of mental illness and an equally vague criterion of

---

[17] *See* chapter 4; JOEL FEINBERG, HARM TO SELF 12–16 (1986) (discussing hard and soft paternalism; only hard paternalism violates the liberal principles).

[18] *See* chapter 4, section IV.

[19] Grant H. Morris, *Judging Judgment: Assessing the Competence of Mental Patients to Refuse Treatment*, 32 SAN DIEGO L. REV. 343, 384–435 (1995) (discussing a parallel process in which patients who are competent to refuse treatment are sometimes viewed and treated as incompetent by clinicians who do not understand or apply the legal criteria of competence); Stephen J. Morse, *A Preference for Liberty: The Case Against Involuntary Commitment of the Mentally Disordered*, 70 CALIF. L. REV. 54, 67–79 (1982) (discussing overuse of commitment).

dangerousness that may be stated in a manner that includes something like grave disability or the need for treatment to prevent deterioration or distress. When that trial court encounters an individual who appears to suffer some impairment, clinical expert testimony that includes a clinical diagnosis, and additional expert testimony or other evidence suggesting that the subject of the hearing is suffering some distress and might benefit from treatment, it appears reasonable to conclude that this person is mentally ill and dangerous to himself or herself, at least in the sense that his or her failure to participate in treatment causes unnecessary distress and suffering. Self-regarding decisions that appear misguided to others increase the probability that a trial court might conclude that such a person fulfills the mental illness and dangerousness criteria, although he or she does not demonstrate impairment undermining competence for self-regarding decisions.

Recall, for example, George, who continues to drink and smoke despite medical advice that such conduct markedly increases his risk of a fatal heart attack. George suffers no impairment of his comprehension, reasoning, or reality testing. He has simply made the judgment that the possible benefits of extended life do not warrant the sacrifice of the activities that provide the primary pleasures he experiences in that life. Suppose, however, that clinical evaluation reveals that George manifests depressive symptoms such as dysphoric mood and a sense of hopelessness associated with his serious and chronic medical condition and thus, that he qualifies for the clinical diagnosis of adjustment disorder with depressed mood.[20] Should someone initiate a civil commitment petition regarding George, clinical testimony would accurately represent George as qualifying for a recognized clinical diagnosis and as engaging in conduct that increases the risk of death. Neither the expert nor the court would be likely to address the question of George's competence to make self-regarding decisions because the commitment statute would not require incompetence. Although George's impairment does not undermine his competence for self-regarding decisions, and the increased risk to his health is a product of a competent decision regarding the value he attaches to extending life and to the risky activities, a trial court might reasonably conclude that George qualifies for civil commitment because he is mentally ill and dangerous to himself.

In such circumstances, the court would authorize a *parens patriae* intrusion into central liberties that should fall within George's nonpublic domain of discretionary control, despite the lack of any impairment sufficient to undermine George's competence for sovereign discretion in the nonpublic domain. Such an outcome might occur despite the best efforts of the court and the clinical experts to fulfill their responsibilities under the statutes because many civil commitment provisions provide no meaningful guidance regarding the types of impairment that should qualify as mental illness for the purpose of *parens patriae* civil commitment. Thus, the court and the expert might reasonably conclude that impairment that fulfills the criteria for a clinical diagnostic category constitutes legal mental illness for this purpose. We should not be surprised to find that local decision makers and expert witnesses are unlikely to correct the inadequacies of a vague statute by appealing to underlying principles that do not appear in the statute.

Courts might identify more accurately those appropriate for *parens patriae* in-

---

[20] AMERICAN PSYCHIATRIC ASSOCIATION, DIAGNOSTIC AND STATISTICAL MANUAL OF MENTAL DISORDERS 623–27 (4th ed. 1994) [hereinafter DSM–IV].

tervention because their impairment renders them incompetent for person if these people were brought before the courts only under provisions that explicitly addressed this issue and identified the applicable criteria of incompetence. Thus, the poorly articulated *parens patriae* function of civil commitment statutes may generate frequent unnecessary and unjustifiable commitments.[21] These statutes might also prevent some incompetent persons from getting needed assistance or care. Some individuals might suffer serious impairment that renders them incapable of making competent self-regarding decisions but does not render them dangerous. These persons might live lives of marginal subsistence because they are unable to make effective use of available resources. Insofar as these individuals are addressed through *parens patriae* civil commitment provisions, rather than through determinations of incompetence and limited guardianship, they might avoid civil commitment because they are not dangerous and thereby fail to receive the potential benefits of noncustodial care and assistance from a guardian with limited authority.

In summary, *parens patriae* civil commitment in a liberal society conforms with the political principles that justify the institution of civil commitment and the larger legal system only if it is redundant. That is, these principles justify involuntary civil commitment only of individuals who would qualify for findings of incompetence and for therapeutic or protective interventions through statutes that address competence, guardianship, and protective placement. Furthermore, the common design of civil commitment statutes may reduce the probability that *parens patriae* interventions take the form most appropriate to the particular incompetent individual.

III.   Incompetence Within Civil Commitment

Some proposals recognize the importance of demonstrating impaired ability to decide about health care in order to justify *parens patriae* commitment.[22] One approach to this issue adds a criterion of commitment requiring incompetence for health care or something very similar to incompetence. These proposals retain the basic structure of contemporary hybrid police power–*parens patriae* commitment statutes in that they propose a single provision intended to accommodate both types of commitment. These proposals stand in marked contrast to the approach advanced in this book in that rather than abolishing *parens patriae* commitment in favor of an incompetence and guardianship approach, they attempt to increase the emphasis on the *parens patriae* function within the structure of the hybrid commitment statute. These proposals encounter several difficulties.

The proposed statutes require impaired capacity to make an informed decision regarding treatment. These proposals define this requirement in a manner that closely resembles common descriptions of incompetence for person. One proposal requires, for example, that "1. the person is suffering from a severe mental disorder, and

---

[21] Morris, *supra* note 19 (suggesting that clinicians testifying in hearings regarding competence to refuse treatment often fail to apply the legal criteria but that a legal decision maker with clear criteria can correct for that departure from the legal standard); Morse, *supra* note 19.

[22] American Psychiatric Association, *Guidelines for Legislation on the Psychiatric Hospitalization of Adults*, 140 AMER. J. PSYCHIATRY 672, 674 (1983); Clifford D. Stromberg & Alan A. Stone, *A Model State Law on Civil Commitment of the Mentally Ill*, 20 HARV. J. ON LEGIS. 275, 330 (1983).

... 4. the person lacks capacity to make an informed decision concerning treatment."[23] It is not entirely clear whether this condition is intended to incorporate a requirement of incompetence as required by civil competence and guardianship statutes.[24]

As presented in this book, competence for person requires that one possesses the capacities required to make self-regarding decisions, including health care decisions, through a minimally competent process of practical reasoning. Severely impaired individuals might be incompetent for virtually all such matters, whereas others might be competent for some decisions but not for others. Equal standing entails sovereignty regarding all matters that fall within the nonpublic domain for unimpaired adults, requiring competence for the full range of that domain. Commitment provisions requiring that the person lacks the capacity to make an informed decision concerning treatment apparently address only one aspect of this domain, but an individual who lacks competence for any part of this domain fails to qualify for full standing as a citizen. Modern statutes appropriately provide for limited findings of incompetence and limited guardianship. Even narrowly defined court orders of incompetence and guardianship deny sovereignty and equal standing, however, because they authorize state intrusion into ordinarily protected matters, marking the individual as one who commands a domain of self-determination that is less extensive than that of a fully competent adult.

According to this reading, these proposals require incompetence for a specific type of decision regarding person. If they do not require incompetence for person, they require something very similar to that notion without clarifying the intended difference. Thus, they raise the likelihood that courts will encounter a problem similar to that currently manifested with the vague "mental illness" criterion. In the absence of clear criteria or guidelines that differentiate persons appropriately committed under this commitment statute from those appropriately adjudicated under the civil competence provision the courts may seek guidance from clinical experts. These experts in turn are likely to attempt to clarify a legal criterion by resorting to clinical notions and to their personal common-sense interpretations of the legal significance of clinical diagnosis.

Alternately, if the proposed statutes are intended to require incompetence as required by statutes addressing competence, guardianship, and protective placement, they are redundant, but they are also inadequate, because they do not provide a complete statutory framework designed to implement the protections and responsibilities associated with such a finding. According to one source of this proposal, the proposed criterion requires impaired capacity to understand and reason about the nature and consequences of the proposed hospitalization or treatment, but it does not address the ability to consider available alternatives.[25] One might interpret the ability to understand and reason about proposed treatment as implying the corresponding abilities to understand and reason about alternatives, however, because one arguably cannot reason effectively about one form of treatment unless one can realistically

---

[23] American Psychiatric Association, *supra* note 22; Stromberg & Stone, *supra* note 22, at 330.

[24] American Psychiatric Association, *supra* note 22, at 673; Stromberg & Stone, *supra* note 22, at 334.

[25] American Psychiatric Association, *supra* note 22, at 673; *cf.* ALLEN BUCHANAN & DAN BROCK, DECIDING FOR OTHERS, 23–25, 51–57 (1989); Morris, *supra* note 19, at 401.

compare it to the alternatives. According to this interpretation, the proposed requirement apparently constitutes the conventional notion of incompetence, but other aspects of the proposal do not accommodate that requirement. For example, no specific individual is assigned the fiduciary responsibility of a guardian who is charged to protect the interests of the individual and who is answerable to a court for failing to discharge that responsibility.[26]

The other commitment criteria do not compensate because some, like "severe mental disorder," lack clear meaning specified in terms of relevant functional impairment, and they are designed to provide access to treatment, rather than to set criteria of competence in order to determine whether this individual or others will make treatment decisions for this person.[27] Most important, the same criterion of severe mental disorder applies to *parens patriae* and police power commitments under these hybrid statutes. Thus, it appears unlikely that this notion can be interpreted to require incompetence for person without creating circumstances in which some individuals manifest impairment of a type that generates danger to others and supports police power civil commitment but would not qualify for commitment under these hybrid provisions because they remain competent for person. The inability to accommodate such individuals would not represent a deficit in a legal institution designed strictly to address *parens patriae* interventions, but it creates serious questions regarding the adequacy of hybrid civil commitment statutes.[28]

Because these proposals retain the undifferentiated combination of police power and *parens patriae* functions of current commitment statutes, they require both dangerousness and inability to decide regarding treatment. Although these proposals frame the dangerousness criterion broadly to include the likelihood of substantial mental or physical deterioration, they do not address those who are unable to competently decide about health care that could substantially improve their lives, but who are maintaining a chronically impaired level of functioning, rather than facing the probability of deterioration or acute distress.[29]

Consider, for example, Jill who resembles Irene in that both are chronically depressed. Irene remains competent for person, however, in that she experiences mild to moderate chronic depression with no impairment of her capacities for comprehension, reasoning, or reality testing. Jill, in contrast, has never attained an ordinarily satisfying or functional adult adjustment because since adolescence she has suffered a chronic serious depression, involving the delusional belief that she has committed terrible sins and therefore deserves to suffer endless torment in order to atone for her and others' sins. She rejects treatment, but she does not contemplate or attempt suicide because she believes that when she dies she will suffer forever in hell. She demonstrates no risk of deterioration or physical harm. Rather, she suffers a chronic, deep but stable depression, and her delusional disorder undermines her competence to make reasoned decisions regarding treatment. Despite her severe disorder and

---

[26] UNIFORM PROBATE CODE §§ 5-308(b), 5-309, 5-311, 8 U.L.A. 369, 370, 375 (1998); BRAKEL et al., *supra* note 1, at 384–90; WEINER & WETTSTEIN, *supra* note 1, at 287–92.

[27] American Psychiatric Association, *supra* note 22, at 673 (severe mental disorder), 672 (legislative purpose).

[28] For further discussion of competence for health care and police power commitments, *see* chapter 11.

[29] American Psychiatric Association, *supra* note 22, at 674; Stromberg & Stone, *supra* note 22, at 330, 335.

impaired capacity to make competent decisions regarding treatment, these proposed statutes would not include Jill among those who are subject to involuntary civil commitment because she does not demonstrate risk of harm or deterioration.

One might respond that the state could provide Jill with involuntary treatment through that state's statute addressing competence and guardianship. This approach might well succeed if that provision is appropriately drafted for people such as Jill. This recourse to that statute demonstrates, however, that the hybrid statutes fail to provide an adequate institution for circumstances that warrant *parens patriae* intervention as a result of incompetence for self-regarding decisions. Furthermore, the presence of such a hybrid statute in the code may well undermine the proper functioning of the incompetence and guardianship provision because having both types of statutes with no clear criteria for selecting one or the other may increase the probability that officials attempt to address individuals like Jill only through the civil commitment statute, rather than through the incompetence provision. If Jill appears to the ordinary person to be mentally ill and in need of hospitalization and the civil commitment statute addresses involuntary hospitalization for those who are mentally ill, public officials as well as Jill's family and friends may well assume that the commitment statute provides the sole available approach or the most appropriate approach.

Just as these hybrid proposals encounter difficulty with some cases arising under the state's *parens patriae* function, the requirement that the person lacks the capacity to make an informed decision regarding health care creates difficulties regarding the appropriate approach to some individuals who raise a central concern for the state's police power. These individuals suffer serious pathology and engage in conduct that is dangerous to others but are competent to decide about their own health care. Suppose, for example, that rather than ineffectively flailing with her umbrella, Francine carried a gun and shot those she believed to be part of the conspiracy to kill her. One could include Francine and others who raise similar concerns in the category of those who lack the capacity to make informed decisions regarding their own health care by stipulating that those whose treatment refusal renders them dangerous or increases the probability of state intervention are not capable of deciding about treatment. Doing so, however, markedly alters the usual conception of competence in order to accommodate a police power function within a hybrid *parens patriae* and police power provision.

Francine raises a complex set of questions regarding the parameters of state intervention under the *parens patriae* and police powers and the interaction between the two. Francine remains competent to make her own health care decisions regarding her diabetic condition because her delusional disorder does not impair her capacity to exercise competent practical reasoning regarding this matter. Ellen, in contrast, is incompetent for the purpose of making health care decisions regarding her diabetes. Both women's competence regarding psychoactive medications for their delusional disorders raise a more complex set of questions involving both the *parens patriae* and police powers. Suppose, for example, that Francine engages in no harmful or threatening conduct toward any other person. She cooperates fully with the treatment plan for her diabetic condition, but she refuses psychoactive treatment for her delusional disorder because this medication decreases the frequency and clarity with which she hears God's voice, leading her to conclude that the medication contains poison from Satan intended to interfere with her ability to carry out her divine mission. Hence, she never takes the medication for a sufficient period to experience substantial improvement of her thought disorder. In these circumstances, her refusal of psychoactive medication raises only a question regarding *parens patriae* justification for involuntary medication.

Alternately, consider circumstances in which Francine takes the psychoactive medication for an extended period of time, attaining remission of her delusional disorder and regaining competence for self-regarding decisions. She evaluates the potential benefits of continued medication in light of evidence indicating that this medication aggravates her diabetic condition and her chronically elevated blood pressure. She decides during her period of remission to terminate the psychoactive medication because she prefers to risk future decompensation into a delusional state, rather than to risk the potential harmful effects on her diabetic condition and blood pressure. Given that she is currently competent for person, that she makes an informed and voluntary decision, and that she has a history of carrying a gun and harming or endangering others during periods of psychosis, her decision to terminate the medication raises only a question regarding a police power justification for involuntary medication.

Finally, consider circumstances in which Francine decides during a period of active psychosis to terminate the psychoactive medication because it interferes with her delusional communications with God, and suppose further that she has a history of harming or endangering others when she decompensates into florid psychosis. These circumstances can raise a complex interaction of *parens patriae* and police power issues if conditions such as the effects of the medication on her diabetic condition or blood pressure suggest that the conclusions of the *parens patriae* and police power analyses might diverge.

In order to satisfactorily address these various scenarios, one must clearly articulate and apply the *parens patriae* and police power justifications and analyze the interactions among them. Insofar as the *parens patriae* and police power functions of the state provide two distinct justifications for state intervention, the type of impairment that constitutes legal mental illness for each may vary in a manner appropriate to these justifications. Furthermore, the type and extent of state intervention appropriate to each justification might vary. Thus, in order to determine whether an individual manifests legal mental illness and in order to define the appropriate parameters of intervention, one must identify the source of justification in the *parens patriae* or police power functions of the state. Rather than clearly articulating and justifying the rationale for and limits of each type of state intervention, the hybrid provisions conflate the two in a manner that renders them more difficult to clearly differentiate, specify, and limit. Because this approach renders it very difficult to clearly articulate the criteria of competence and the conception of legal mental illness relevant to each power, it seems likely to enhance the risk that decision makers will interpret the vague criteria expansively when doing so facilitates commitments that seem appropriate on other grounds.

These hybrid proposals emphasize the health care delivery function of commitment by requiring that there is a reasonable prospect that the individual's disorder is treatable at the facility to which he or she is committed.[30] This emphasis is entirely

---

[30] American Psychiatric Association, *supra* note 22, at 672; Stromberg & Stone, *supra* note 22, at 330, 332, 348–57.

appropriate for those who are found incompetent to decide for themselves and committed under the *parens patriae* function. These proposals become problematic, however, because they pursue that emphasis within the structure of a hybrid *parens patriae* and police power provision that is directed primarily toward disposition in the form of commitment. By compressing two distinct state functions and emphasizing placement in a controlled setting, these provisions dilute their health care delivery focus and render that function more difficult to satisfactorily fulfill for those who lack capacities necessary to qualify for, and discharge the responsibilities of, sovereign discretion in the nonpublic domain. Perhaps most important, hybrid statutes render it very difficult to clearly articulate the justification for commitment under each power and, thus, to clearly identify defensible criteria of legal mental illness and defensible conditions and limits of intrusion for each. By obscuring the justification, criteria, and limits of each form of state intervention, these provisions render it very difficult for courts, attorneys, and experts to discharge their responsibilities.

Abolishing *parens patriae* commitment and replacing it with provisions explicitly designed to address competence, guardianship, and protective placement has several advantages. First, it makes explicit the meaning of "mental illness" for this purpose as impairment rendering one unable to engage in minimally adequate practical reasoning regarding decisions of health care and personal well-being. Second, it requires a formal judicial determination of incompetence in this sense. By combining a functional specification of the relevant conception of mental illness with the explicit allocation of this determination to the court, this approach may decrease the tendencies of courts to defer to clinical experts and of clinical experts to accept this invitation to fulfill a judicial responsibility.[31] Third, it provides for an explicit statement of the scope and limits of incompetence and guardianship, in that these conclusions can be crafted as generally or specifically as the individual's impairment and circumstances require. Fourth, a specific individual assumes the responsibilities of the guardian and stands answerable for these.

Fifth, the process returns the disposition cart to its appropriate place behind the incompetence horse. Commitment statutes directly and primarily address intervention, obscuring the threshold question of functional impairment sufficient to render the person unable to make a decision regarding admission specifically and treatment more generally. Hence, commitment statutes render it difficult to avoid framing the central question in terms of whether the individual needs admission and treatment, rather than in terms of whether the individual is capable of making his or her own decisions regarding these issues. Replacing a *parens patriae* commitment statute with a provision that directly addresses competence provides the opportunity to direct the initial inquiry toward the threshold question of incompetence that justifies the state intrusion. The question of placement only arises if the court determines that the individual is incompetent and that the impairment and circumstances warrant consideration of admission to the hospital or alternative protective placements.

The placement decision reflects the complex set of values of the liberal society including the importance of equal standing and of well-being. The individual's interest in regaining the capacities required to qualify for sovereignty in the nonpublic

---

[31] Morris, *supra* note 19, at 384–435 (demonstrating that clinical and legal issues and roles tend to become conflated and that a legal decision maker with a clear understanding of the legal criteria can ameliorate that problem).

domain takes a strong priority if that is a plausible outcome.[32] The proper placement can vary, however, according to the individual's needs and potential and the resources available to address those needs. Ellen, for example, would not be appropriate for inpatient placement if she could be maintained safely on outpatient treatment and no further resources were available on the inpatient ward. In contrast, if an inpatient placement provided access to additional treatment that could be provided only to inpatients and that offered a reasonable opportunity for return to competence, such a placement would be defensible because the potential restoration of the capacities that qualify Ellen for sovereignty promotes a fundamental value of the underlying principles. Such a placement would promote Ellen's sovereignty and her good, rather than merely that which might be good for Ellen.[33]

Addressing Ellen's situation through a statute that explicitly identifies competence as the threshold question and placement as a derivative question decreases the tendency, promoted by a commitment statute, to frame the issue as a choice between admitting Ellen to the inpatient ward or refraining from intervention. This alternative structure might facilitate therapeutically effective interventions while decreasing inappropriate commitments. By providing a guardian charged with promoting the incompetent person's interests and requiring a separate decision regarding disposition for the purpose of protecting and promoting the incompetent person's well-being, this structure might improve the ability of courts and experts to craft a disposition likely to promote therapeutic effectiveness. By addressing the questions of competence and disposition sequentially, this legal structure might provide courts and experts with the opportunity to develop dispositions likely to increase therapeutic effectiveness without intruding upon the protected sovereignty of competent individuals. Thus, this structure might promote the agenda of Therapeutic Jurisprudence within a liberal society.[34]

IV.   *Parens Patriae* Intervention and Treatment Appropriateness

A.   *Contemporary Proposals*

Some commentators advocate a principle of treatment appropriateness according to which civil commitment would apply only to those who are appropriate for treatment. These proposals reflect the central focus on disposition that characterizes civil commitment statutes in that they require that the individual be appropriate for treatment available at the facility to which that individual is committed.[35] According to one formulation, this principle requires that the individual is appropriate for organic or essentially medical treatment because this is the form of treatment that is ordinarily available and effective at the facilities to which commitments are ordinarily made.[36]

---

[32] *See* chapter 4, sections IV and V.

[33] *See* chapter 4, section V.

[34] DAVID B. WEXLER & BRUCE J. WINICK, LAW IN A THERAPEUTIC KEY (1996).

[35] American Psychiatric Association, *supra* note 22, at 674; Stromberg & Stone, *supra* note 22, at 330, 332; Bruce J. Winick, *Ambiguities in the Legal Meaning and Significance of Mental Illness*, 1 PSYCHOL. PUB. POL'Y, & L. 534, 539, 563–70 (1995).

[36] Bruce J. Winick, *Sex Offender Law in the 1990s: A Therapeutic Jurisprudence Analysis*, 4 PSYCHOL., PUB. POL'Y, & L. 1, 26–32 (1998); Winick, *supra* note 35.

These proposals apparently preclude civil commitment of severely impaired individuals who are not responsive to treatment, including those who pose an immediate danger to themselves or others. These proposals suggest, however, that alternative modes of confinement might accommodate individuals who present a risk of harm but do not qualify for commitment under the proposed criteria. One proposal suggests that the criminal justice system should address those who are dangerous to others but are competent to make reasoned decisions regarding treatment.[37] Another proposal suggests that nursing homes, families, or community housing facilities might provide care and supervision for individuals who are not appropriate for treatment in hospitals.[38]

This emphasis on appropriate placement in a hospital or a similar treatment facility as a criterion for civil commitment reflects the more general dispositional focus of these proposals and of current civil commitment statutes. These provisions tend to frame the issue as one of involuntary admission to some treatment facility. Similarly, the scope of the discussion over a broad range of alternative dispositions including police power confinement under the jurisdiction of the criminal justice system as well as alternative placements with nursing homes, family, or community housing reflects the approach taken by hybrid statutes that do not clearly differentiate police power and *parens patriae* interventions. If the requirement of treatment appropriateness only mandated that some individuals are subject to confinement in alternative facilities, it would not constitute a substantive limitation on the state's power to confine. Indeed, states might satisfy such a principle by merely renaming certain buildings or wings of buildings within the traditional public psychiatric hospital. Proposals that would require treatment appropriateness for commitment raise substantive questions insofar as they force us to explain the significance of treatability for the justification of involuntary intervention into the lives of individuals. The police power and *parens patriae* functions of the state provide two different types of justification for state intervention, and thus, the significance of treatment appropriateness might differ for each. This chapter addresses *parens patriae* interventions, and chapter 8 addresses police power interventions. In order to clarify the significance of treatment appropriateness for either type of intervention, one must clarify the applicable conception of treatment.

B. Treatment, Care, and Incapacitation

Contemporary proposals are not entirely clear regarding the type of treatment that must be appropriate for the committed individual. One proposal indicates that some appropriate treatment must be available at the facility to which the individual is committed, that the treatment need not cure the patient, and that merely preventive confinement should fall within the purview of the criminal justice system.[39] These passages might indicate that any intervention beyond merely preventive confinement and appropriate to the individual's condition would meet the requirement. Interpreted in this manner, however, custodial care would satisfy the requirement, rendering it of little significance. One commentator would limit commitment to those who are

---

[37] Stromberg & Stone, *supra* note 22, at 332.
[38] Winick, *supra* note 35, at 582.
[39] Stromberg & Stone, *supra* note 22, at 332.

appropriate for organic or essentially medical treatment.[40] This formulation would rule out commitment involving only custodial care, but it might also rule out commitment of severely impaired individuals who do not respond to medication but who need the type of custodial care, supervision, and management ordinarily available only in mental health facilities. This formulation may represent a conditional proposal, however, in that it may reflect the premises that only organic or essentially medical treatments are ordinarily available in the hospitals to which most people are committed and that psychotherapy and behavior therapy are unavailable or not effective for involuntarily committed patients.[41] In order to determine the significance of treatment appropriateness for the justification of *parens patriae* interventions into the ordinarily protected nonpublic domain, one must clarify the conception of treatment at issue as well as the relationship between treatment and related notions such as custodial care, behavior management, and incapacitation.

Some court opinions address specific forms of treatment, such as treatment with psychoactive medication.[42] Other cases address the more general category of treatment of those who are hospitalized as mentally ill. The courts that discuss this more general category of treatment use both broad and narrow conceptions of treatment. Some courts refer narrowly to curative treatment as interventions intended to cure or substantially improve the person's disorder, and these opinions distinguish such curative treatment from custodial care.[43] Justice Burger, concurring in *O'Connor v. Donaldson*, explicitly distinguished this narrow conception of treatment from a broader conception that includes custodial care within the category of treatment.[44] These court opinions provide no settled legal conception of treatment that is generally applicable to legal questions.

In ordinary usage, "treatment" can refer broadly to any "application of medical care or attention to a patient."[45] The specification of "medical" care in this definition suggests that "treatment" applies most specifically to attention that involves technical clinical skills, rather than nontechnical custodial care. This interpretation comports with the broader definition of "care" as including serious attention, heed, or protective oversight.[46] Application of technical clinical skills cannot constitute a sufficient condition for treatment, however, because execution through lethal injection involves an application of technical clinical skills. In order to qualify as treatment, the application of technical clinical skills must take a form intended to promote the patient's well-being. This suggests a relatively narrow conception of treatment as the application of specialized clinical skills for the purpose of curing or ameliorating the effect of a disease, disorder, or pathological condition. This narrow conception is consistent with definitions found in clinical and legal sources.[47] These clinical and

---

[40] Winick, *supra* note 36, at 10; Winick, *supra* note 35, at 539, 554–70.

[41] Winick, *supra* note 35, at 539.

[42] Washington v. Harper, 494 U.S. 210 (1990); Mills v. Rogers, 457 U.S. 291 (1982).

[43] Donaldson v. O'Connor, 493 F.2d 507, 518–22 (5th Cir. 1974); Wyatt v. Aderholt, 503 F.2d 1305, 1312–14 (5th Cir. 1974).

[44] O'Connor v. Donaldson, 422 U.S. 563, 580–85 (1975) (Burger, J., concurring).

[45] THE NEW SHORTER OXFORD ENGLISH DICTIONARY 3380 (1993).

[46] *Id.* at 338.

[47] BLACK'S LAW DICTIONARY 1502 (6th ed. 1990); ROBERT J. CAMPBELL, PSYCHIATRIC DICTIONARY 665 (5th ed. 1981); RICHARD SLOANE, THE SLOANE–DORLAND ANNOTATED MEDICAL–LEGAL DICTIONARY 746 (1987).

legal sources also adopt a broad notion of "care" as including watchful attention to the needs of another and a related notion of "custodial care" as care that can be provided by lay persons without skilled nursing services.[48] As an initial approximation, therefore, I use "treatment" in this relatively narrow sense involving the application of clinical skills in order to ameliorate a clinical disorder or its effects and "custodial care" to refer to nontechnical attention to another's basic needs including, for example, food, clothing, shelter, and safety. Finally, I use "care" for the more general category of attention that includes both treatment and custodial care.

These rough initial distinctions require further refinement, however, in order to provide useful categories for the purposes of categorizing controversial applications and examining the justifications for those interventions through mental health institutions under the *parens patriae* and police power functions of the state. Certain interventions fall clearly into each category. Medication and psychotherapy intended to reduce clinical impairment or its effects, for example, constitute forms of treatment. Similarly, providing food, clothing, and shelter falls in the category of custodial care; so too does supervision designed to prevent impaired individuals from injuring themselves by wandering into traffic or out into the cold.

Neither criminal incarceration nor quarantine qualifies under either category of care as these terms are defined here. Criminal incarceration is intended to serve several purposes including retribution, prevention, and an expressive function as an institutional representation of widely accepted standards of public morality.[49] Although the preventive purpose is often discussed in terms of deterrence, the criminal law attempts to prevent infractions through several different modalities including deterrence, reform, rehabilitation, the expression of moral condemnation, and incapacitation. Criminal punishment prevents offenses through incapacitation when it renders the offender permanently or temporarily incapable of committing further crimes. Capital punishment provides a permanent form of incapacitation, and incarceration represents a temporary form of incapacitation through containment.

Quarantine provides a method of incapacitation through containment directed toward those who endanger others by virtue of contagious diseases rather than through the tendency to commit crimes. Quarantine as such constitutes mere incapacitation because it serves no purpose other than isolating the individual in order to render him incapable of communicating the communicable disease. Ordinarily, however, the state also provides custodial care for those subject to quarantine, and it may provide treatment insofar as it is available. Thus, the comprehensive state intervention might include quarantine as a form of incapacitation, treatment, and custodial care, but quarantine as such remains mere incapacitation because it does not serve as treatment or care.

Other interventions designed to render the individual unable or less likely to engage in undesirable behavior without concern for improving that individual's adaptive capacities or fulfilling that individual's needs constitute mere incapacitation. Containment provides one form of incapacitation insofar as it represents an attempt to render the individual unable to engage in the target behavior. Certain forms of containment, such as social isolation, can play a role in a variety of strategies. Solitary confinement in a prison setting, for example, can constitute mere incapacitation,

---

[48] BLACK'S, *supra* note 47, at 213; SLOANE, *supra* note 47, at 115–16.

[49] ROBERT F. SCHOPP, JUSTIFICATION DEFENSES AND JUST CONVICTIONS § 3.3.2 (1998).

or it can represent an attempt to direct behavior through management of incentives as well as incapacitation. In contrast, isolation in the form of seclusion in a separate room on a hospital ward can represent either or both of these strategies, or it can represent a form of treatment when it is used to calm an impaired person who becomes frightened or agitated by proximity to others.

Certain interventions are difficult to categorize as treatment, custodial care, incapacitation, or management of incentives. Consider, for example, behavior modification programs that modify behavior by rewarding acceptable conduct with preferred opportunities or experiences and by dispensing aversive consequences for unacceptable behavior.[50] When such programs take the form of a prison conduct code that dispenses canteen privileges or "good time" for acceptable behavior and solitary confinement or exposure to noxious substances for unacceptable behavior, it seems accurate to say that they constitute neither treatment nor custodial care.[51] Rather, these are simply disciplinary mechanisms similar to the criminal law that provided the basis for the initial incarceration. As such, they represent a combination of mere incapacitation and direction through incentive management. Yet, programs that apply similar procedures and principles to severely impaired individuals in order to reduce their self-injurious behavior, such as head banging or self-biting, seem to fall within the category of treatment.[52] These cases suggest that such programs qualify as treatment when designed to protect and promote the individual's interests but not when designed to modify the individual's behavior for the benefit of others.

Other cases suggest that this distinction will not suffice, however, because some clear cases of treatment protect the interests of others. Consider, for example, the use of antipsychotic medication for the purpose of decreasing paranoid delusions, agitation, and disorganized thinking associated with attacks against others in delusional self-defense. These cases seem clearly to qualify as treatment, although the intervention is intended to alter the individual's behavior in a manner that benefits others. These cases differ from the prison discipline cases in that the intervention promotes the interests of others by ameliorating the individual's impairment that generates the behavior that endangers those others. This suggests that amelioration of impairment plays the central role; that is, in order to qualify as treatment, an intervention must ameliorate the impairment suffered by the individual.

Two sets of cases raise problems for this interpretation. First, severely impaired individuals who engage in self-injurious conduct may benefit from a behavior modification program that does not ameliorate the underlying impairment, such as severe retardation or autism. Second, some similar programs for severely impaired individuals address behavior that endangers others rather than the impaired individual. A behavior modification program might reduce assaultive conduct by a severely impaired person who engages in no self-injurious behavior, for example, without ameliorating that person's impairment or preventing any behavior that injures the subject of the treatment. Such programs might promote the interests of the individual less directly, however, by increasing the opportunity for positive activity and by reducing the need for seclusion or physical restraints.

---

[50] See generally, ALAN S. BELLACK, MICHEL HERSEN, & ALAN E. KAZDIN, INTERNATIONAL HANDBOOK OF BEHAVIOR MODIFICATION AND THERAPY (2nd ed. 1990).

[51] See e.g., Knecht v. Gillman, 488 F2d. 1136 (8th Cir. 1973).

[52] Robert F. Schopp, Punishment as Treatment and the Obligations of Treatment Providers, 7 INT'L J. L. & PSYCHIATRY 197, 200–02 (1984).

These cases suggest that neither ameliorating the impairment nor directly benefiting the person undergoing the intervention constitutes a necessary condition for that intervention to qualify as treatment. Rather, these cases suggest that an intervention qualifies as treatment only if it takes the form of an application of clinical skills and knowledge designed to ameliorate an impairment or to reduce the injurious effects produced by that impairment. This conception of treatment appropriately categorizes the cases previously discussed. It includes medication intended to reduce paranoid delusions or psychotic disorganization, regardless of whether those conditions generate injury to self, others, or no one, because this intervention ameliorates the impairment. It includes behavior modification programs designed to reduce assaultive or self-injurious behavior by impaired individuals, because such programs are designed to reduce the injurious effects of the impairment. Finally, it excludes general prison disciplinary programs because they are designed to reduce injurious behavior that is not the result of any clinical impairment.[53]

Two additional cases suggest the need for further qualification. Consider a prison discipline program involving solitary confinement contingent upon assaults by a generally mean and aggressive prisoner who suffers a learning disability and who attacks people who say anything critical of him, including those who say, "can't you read?" The prisoner's impairment is one causal factor in the injurious conduct that the program is designed to address, but it seems clear that this program would constitute a disciplinary program involving incapacitation and management of incentives, rather than a treatment program. Consider also a plan to reduce assaults by a psychotic individual by surgically severing that person's spinal cord and inducing quadriplegia. This intervention would involve the application of clinical skills in order to decrease the attacks that are injurious effects of the impairment, but it seems clear that it constitutes mere incapacitation rather than treatment.

These interventions differ from the behavioral program for the severely impaired individual who engages in assaultive or self-injurious conduct. Such programs attempt to improve adaptive skills, whereas the disciplinary and surgical interventions reduce the injurious effects of the disorders by altering incentives or decreasing capacities without increasing any adaptive skills. This suggests the following revised conception of treatment. An intervention qualifies as treatment only if it takes the form of an application of clinical skills and knowledge designed to ameliorate a pathological condition or to reduce the injurious effects produced by that condition by increasing the individual's adaptive skills, capacities, or functioning level associated with that condition.[54]

---

[53] This interpretation specifies "general" prison programs because some programs administered in prisons might well address injurious conduct produced by impairment such as psychosis or retardation. The critical question is the source of the injurious behavior in clinically significant impairment, rather than the location of the program.

[54] Consider the aversive conditioning program designed to reduce self-injurious behavior in a severely impaired individual. Ordinarily, such programs combine aversive conditioning with positive reinforcement of incompatible and adaptive behavior, and these programs seem intuitively to fall within the category of treatment. A purely aversive conditioning program would not increase the individual's adaptive skills, capacities, or functioning level, but such a program also seems at least arguably to implement a strategy of incapacitation or manipulation of incentives, rather than a treatment program. That is, to the extent that such programs attempt to promote adaptive functioning, they seem to fit more clearly within the category of treatment, and to the extent that they lack any attempt to promote adaptive

In summary, this analysis suggests the following categories of intervention relevant to the current discussion. The first important distinction differentiates interventions that constitute care from those that do not. Relevant interventions that do not constitute care include incapacitation and management of incentives through programs such as those designed to establish prison discipline. Care includes two important subcategories for the purpose of the current discussion: treatment and custodial care. Throughout the remainder of this book, I use the terms as explicated here.

Notice that applications of certain modes of expertise can represent different types of intervention in different circumstances. Biochemical intervention by a physician, for example, can constitute treatment when it is intended to ameliorate a pathological condition or its injurious effects. It can also constitute incapacitation, however, when used for "chemical restraint" or when applied in the form of a lethal injection for the purpose of execution. Similarly, the systematic application of learning theory by a psychologist can constitute behavior therapy as a form of treatment intended to promote an individual's effective functioning and well-being. Alternately, it can take the form of a disciplinary program intended to direct behavior through incentives, or it can constitute incapacitation in the form of aversive conditioning intended to render the individual unable to engage in certain forms of behavior.

C. Difficult Cases Regarding Treatment Appropriateness

As previously discussed, the precise requirements of the treatment appropriateness principle are not entirely clear, partially because different commentators might contemplate different variations on the approach. This principle might preclude the commitment of very few plausible candidates if "treatment" is interpreted broadly to include all care, for example, but it might preclude many more if that notion is interpreted narrowly to exclude custodial care. Consider the following cases, which raise difficult questions under at least some interpretations of the treatment appropriateness requirement for civil commitment.

Kevin is a typical subject of civil commitment under the sexual predator statutes. He manifests no serious impairment of orientation, comprehension, reasoning, or reality testing. He engages in a series of sexual offenses and carries diagnoses of paraphilia and APD.[55] He denies that he has committed any offenses, including those that have been clearly proven in court. He also denies that he suffers any disorder and refuses to participate in any form of treatment. He has been evaluated for treatment programs in prison and identified as not amenable to treatment because of his denial and refusal.

Larry has established a repetitive pattern of assaultive behavior associated with a cyclical pattern of psychosis. He periodically experiences manic episodes involving elevated mood, grandiose and persecutory delusions, and assaultive behavior associated with those delusions.[56] His mood disorder and delusional process respond to

---

functioning, they seem to fall more accurately within the category of incentive structuring, incapacitation, or disciplinary programs.

[55] DSM–IV, *supra* note 20, at 522–32 (paraphilia), 645–50 (APD).

[56] *Id.* at 350–59 (bipolar I disorder).

regularly administered medication. After a period of hospitalization and consistent medication, he demonstrates no evidence of the delusional process he manifests during his psychotic episodes, and his mood returns to normal limits. He refuses to maintain the medication absent coercive administration, however, explaining that the manic episodes are exciting and that during his stable periods, he misses the expansive, elevated moods.

Mike is grossly psychotic. He speaks in unintelligible words and phrases, and he demonstrates no evidence that he comprehends attempts by others to communicate with him. He sometimes engages in violent flailing and screaming that suggests to observers that he is responding to hallucinations, but no one can communicate with him in order to confirm that impression. He carries a diagnosis of schizophrenia.[57] He sometimes attacks other patients on the ward, eliciting retaliation from them. On some occasions, he apparently attacks in order to secure something the other patient has, such as a candy bar brought by a visitor. On other occasions, he apparently attacks because the other patient is in his way or comes too close to him. Sometimes he attacks for no apparent reason. During some of these exchanges, he has seriously injured others, and he has sustained serious injuries from the retaliation by those others. Medication has no apparent effect on him at doses below levels sufficient to endanger his life.

Nathan was diagnosed in early childhood as suffering from childhood autism, and he currently carries a diagnosis of autistic disorder.[58] At various times in the past he has been diagnosed with schizophrenia and mental retardation.[59] He has never developed effective communication or self-care skills. He develops no relationships with others and has no apparent interests. He manifests repetitive, stereotypic movements and limited echolalic speech that others are not able to understand. He has spent most of his life in state hospitals with brief unsuccessful attempts to live at his parents' home. When agitated, he beats his head with his fist, or he bangs his head against the wall in a repetitive, rhythmic fashion. He sometimes causes serious injury to his head and face, but he persists until staff physically intervene and restrain him. He is nonresponsive to personal intervention or medication, but he does respond to a behavior modification program that involves immediate and consistent reinforcement with sweet edible rewards for keeping his hands in his pockets and for staying away from the walls.

Oliver functioned well through his fifties. He married and held a job until his memory and orientation began to deteriorate in his sixties. He is now 75 years old and demonstrates serious impairment in memory, orientation, communication, and self-care. He carries a diagnosis of dementia.[60] When unsupervised, he sometimes endangers himself by wandering across the street without regard for traffic or by walking outside and getting lost in severe weather without a coat. He is nonresponsive to medication and requires ongoing supervision. He functions somewhat more effectively and independently with a very predictable schedule of simple activities. During the past 5 years, he has spent periods of time in a nursing home and periods in the state hospital. These periods demonstrate a repetitive pattern. Typically, he

---

[57] *Id.* at 274–90.

[58] *Id.* at 66–70.

[59] *Id.* at 39–41 (severe mental retardation), 274–90 (schizophrenia).

[60] *Id.* at 133–43.

demonstrates marginal improvements in self-care and communication across a period of time in the hospital during which he maintains a relatively active and repetitive schedule of organized activities and nursing care. He then moves to a nursing home at which there is a paucity of structured activity, and his self-care and communication skills gradually deteriorate until he returns to the hospital ward and the relatively structured schedule.

Kevin and Larry immediately implicate the police power rather than the *parens patriae* power of the state in that they endanger others, and they are currently competent to make reasoned decisions regarding treatment. Kevin provides the most straightforward case under the approaches advocating treatment appropriateness as a requirement for commitment. He engages in conduct harmful to others, but he is neither appropriate for the available treatment nor incapable of making reasoned decisions regarding his own treatment. Moreover, these characteristics of Kevin are stable over time. Presumably, those who make the proposals including requirements of treatment appropriateness would welcome this result, contending that Kevin belongs in the criminal justice system rather than in the mental health system.[61]

Larry raises somewhat more complex issues. Larry is appropriate for the type of treatment that is available in the facilities at which individuals are ordinarily civilly committed, and he has received and benefited from that treatment. He is also currently competent to decide for himself, however, and he currently refuses to continue the treatment on a voluntary basis. Larry raises a different type of treatment appropriateness concern than that directly addressed in the proposals. Larry is currently appropriate for a form of treatment that can be administered on an outpatient basis, but because he refuses to cooperate with the prescribed treatment plan, he will not receive the appropriate treatment unless he remains on the inpatient ward and receives it involuntarily. Furthermore, both proposals that include treatment appropriateness criterion also require serious impairment of the applicable decision-making capacities.[62] Larry currently lacks such impairment, but he manifests it during his periods of psychosis. Thus, he raises a complex set of concerns regarding the appropriate approach to someone who is currently competent to decide regarding his own treatment but whose decision is one that is reasonably expected to generate circumstances in which he will endanger others and in which he will be neither criminally responsible nor competent to decide regarding his own treatment. Because Kevin and Larry raise concerns that include considerations that fall under the police power, I postpone further discussion of their cases until chapter 9.

Mike also raises complex issues involving both the *parens patriae* and police powers, but in contrast to Larry, he presently endangers others. Furthermore, he lacks capacity to make reasoned decisions regarding his own treatment, and he is not a candidate for treatment through medication. Thus, Mike's impairment and dangerousness render him an appropriate candidate for state intervention under both the *parens patriae* and police powers, but the treatability requirement might preclude commitment. If one interprets this requirement as requiring amenability to organic treatment, Mike is apparently not eligible for commitment. If one interprets the re-

---

[61] Stromberg & Stone, *supra* note 22, at 330–35 and n201; Winick, *supra* note 36, at 16–26.

[62] Stromberg & Stone, *supra* note 22, at 330 (severe mental disorder and lacks the capacity to make informed decisions concerning treatment); Winick, *supra* note 35, at 563 (impaired ability to engage in rational decision making or to control harmful behavior).

quirement broadly to include those who are appropriate for custodial care and management, then Mike would qualify, but the criteria seems to lose significance with this interpretation. Mike, like Kevin and Larry, raises complex concerns regarding either the police power or both the *parens patriae* and police powers; I discuss all three cases together (see chapter 11).

Nathan and Oliver fall squarely within the scope of *parens patriae* intervention. Both suffer serious impairment of the capacities needed to make reasoned decisions regarding their person, including health care. Both cause injury or risk of injury only to themselves. Both are subject to state intrusion into ordinarily protected decisions regarding their well-being only because they lack the capacities needed to make these decisions competently. Both are appropriate candidates for treatment if that notion is interpreted broadly to include custodial care, although interpreted in that manner, the requirement of treatment appropriateness apparently carries little significance. No treatment that would cure or substantially ameliorate the underlying pathology is available for either Nathan or Oliver.

Nathan actively injures himself and he needs treatment that is neither organic nor ordinarily considered to fall within the category of essentially medical intervention. The needed behavior therapy does involve the application of technical knowledge, however, and it is intended to reduce the injurious effects of his condition by improving his adaptive skills in an area of maladaptive functioning associated with that condition. Nathan would qualify as appropriate for treatment under the formulation that requires that the individual is treatable at the facility to which he is committed, although he would not qualify under the formulation that requires organic or essentially medical treatment.[63]

Structured behavior therapy programs are most often available in mental health treatment facilities or in nonmedical structured care and training facilities for those with developmental disabilities. They are less likely to be available in nursing homes or in the less intensive community residence settings. Thus, Nathan needs care including supervision, custodial care, and treatment in the form of structured and closely monitored behavior therapy. He is unable to make a competent decision or provide effective consent for his own care.

Oliver differs from Nathan in that he does not actively injure himself, but his remaining self-care and communication skills deteriorate without a consistent structured schedule. Like Nathan, he needs more than minimal custodial care, but unlike Nathan, his additional needs do not require technical clinical knowledge. Nursing staff or conscientious volunteers could establish the repetitive pattern of structured activities Oliver needs in a nursing home or other supervised living situation, although these facilities frequently would not provide such programs. Arguably, Oliver needs care rather than treatment, but this care would take a more structured and intensive form than that which is usually considered minimal custodial care. If such structured programming does not enable Oliver to maximize his remaining capacities,

---

[63] Stromberg & Stone, *supra* note 22, at 330; Winick, *supra* note 35, at 554–70. Recall that Winick's discussion of organic treatment may reflect the premise that only organic treatment is ordinarily available. In his discussion of *Hendricks*, Winick seems to accept treatability with cognitive–behavior therapy as sufficient. Winick, *supra* note 36, at 29. The central point here is that Nathan would be treatable in the sense in which this term is interpreted in this book, although that treatment would not be organic or essentially medical in nature.

then he would require only supervision and custodial care designed to fulfill his basic needs and protect him from harm.

The incompetence and guardianship approach to *parens patriae* interventions advanced in this chapter would address Nathan and Oliver in the following manner. The initial step would involve clinical evaluations and court hearings leading to judicial determinations of incompetence. Following the determinations of incompetence for person, the court would appoint guardians and charge those guardians with the responsibility to make decisions regarding the care needed to protect Nathan and Oliver from harm and to promote their well-being. Either the court or the guardian would select a protective placement to the available facility most appropriate for the particular needs of each ward.

The most appropriate placement for both Nathan and Oliver should provide custodial care and supervision. Nathan should also receive treatment in the form of a program of behavior therapy designed to prevent his self-injurious behavior and to increase his adaptive functioning to the extent possible. Oliver does not require behavior therapy, but his care should involve the repetitive structured format that enables him to slow the decline in his already substantially diminished capacities for self-care and communication. The most appropriate placement for each would depend on the facilities available. The state hospital to which people are currently committed under the civil commitment statute might provide the most appropriate and available placement for both Nathan and Oliver. Alternately, a training school for those with developmental disabilities might best serve Nathan's needs, and a heavily programmed nursing home or residential care facility might provide optimal care for Oliver. Under this approach, the distinctions among treatment, training, custodial care, and supervision would not play a controlling role in determining who is subject to intervention or in selecting the most appropriate placement. The court or guardian would select the placement functionally by identifying the available alternative best suited to promote the well-being of the incompetent individual.

Regarding *parens patriae* interventions, the central insight of the proposed treatment appropriateness requirement consists of the recognition that any intervention justified by the *parens patriae* function of the state must protect and promote the interests of the incompetent individual. Limiting civil commitment to those who are appropriate for treatment in an identified treatment facility seems appropriate when the commitment statute frames the question as one that is primarily about involuntary admission to a treatment facility. Limiting civil commitment to those who are amenable to organic or essentially medical treatment seems appropriate when the treatment facility in question provides only organic or essentially medical treatment modalities. Furthermore, some form of the treatment appropriateness principle may be appropriate in circumstances in which we must work within the framework of contemporary civil commitment statutes and the hospitals to which we commit provide only a relatively narrow range of treatment.

In this manner, the proposals requiring treatment appropriateness for civil commitment reveal the fundamental defect in contemporary civil commitment as a structure for *parens patriae* intervention. That is, these statutes conflate the decisions regarding intervention and disposition or placement into a single question about involuntary admission. The structure of civil commitment statutes encourages decision makers to ask whether admission to the hospital is appropriate for the individual, rather than asking whether that individual is competent to make that decision. Under the *parens patriae* function of the state, the question of treatment or placement appropriateness ought not arise until the court has made a determination that the individual lacks competence to decide that matter. If the court determines that the individual lacks competence regarding person, including health care, then the *parens patriae* function of the state authorizes the state to seek the alternative that best protects and promotes that individual's well-being.

In this context, one might appropriately rename the "treatment appropriateness" requirement as the "care appropriateness" or "dispositional appropriateness" requirement in order to make it clear that legitimate *parens patriae* intervention must take a form appropriate to the needs of the incompetent individual. Framing the issue as one of treatment appropriateness limits the inquiry to only a subset of the questions state actors must address in order to discharge the state's responsibilities under the *parens patriae* function. Civil commitment statutes encourage us to ask only that limited subset of the proper questions because these provisions direct our attention to the issue of involuntary admission to the hospital and away from the two central questions. First, does this individual have the capacity to make these decisions competently for himself or herself? Second, if the individual lacks this capacity, what state intervention best protects his or her well-being? In addressing this second question, the decision maker must address care or dispositional appropriateness, rather than the narrower question of treatment appropriateness. The care needed constitutes the dispositive issue because appropriate disposition depends on correspondence between the care needed and the type of care available with each potential disposition. Therefore, I refer to this revised version of the treatment appropriateness principle as the *care appropriateness principle*.

The incompetence and guardianship approach arguably provides a preferable institution, as compared to civil commitment, with which to apply the principle of care appropriateness under the *parens patriae* function because it frames the initial question as one addressing the individual's ability to make reasoned decisions regarding his or her well-being. In addressing this question, the court inquires into the individual's functional capacities and impairment. This inquiry produces a description of the individual's abilities and functional impairment. If the court concludes that the subject of the hearing is not competent to make reasoned decisions regarding his or her own well-being, this approach then frames the second question as one addressing the type of care most appropriate to the incompetent person's well-being in light of that description of the person's functional impairment. Thus, the principle of care appropriateness does not arise regarding the first question, which is appropriately limited to the ability of the individual to exercise a competent process of practical reasoning in the nonpublic domain. This principle plays a central role in addressing the second question, however, because the *parens patriae* function of the state authorizes the court and the guardian to make decisions expected to provide for the incompetent individual's needs.

Civil commitment statutes, in contrast, tend to conflate these two steps in a manner that obscures the core of each question. These provisions encourage decision makers to interpret the central question as one that asks whether the individual is appropriate for involuntary admission to the mental health facility. This question frames the inquiry in a manner that neither elicits a full description of the individual's broad array of functional capacities and impairments, nor encourages the interpretation of legal mental illness for this purpose as impairment undermining competence for self-regarding decisions. Thus, it obscures the initial matter regarding the individual's ability to make a competent decision. Furthermore, it limits the available information regarding the incompetent person's needs, and it artificially narrows the second question regarding the particular placement most appropriate for those needs.

The competence and guardianship approach provides a more adaptive structure for executing *parens patriae* interventions than does the civil commitment approach partially because it converges with the underlying justification for such interventions. The justification for such intrusions in a liberal society rests upon the presence of legal mental illness in the form of impairment that renders the individual unable to competently exercise discretion in the nonpublic domain. Under the condition of incompetence, the state can intervene in the ordinarily protected nonpublic domain without violating either the principle of autonomy that protects self-determination in health care or the boundary between the public and nonpublic jurisdictions in the liberal society.

When impaired competence justifies *parens patriae* intervention, the state takes on the responsibility to protect the incompetent individual's well-being and not merely the responsibility to decide whether that individual qualifies for civil commitment. Recall the interpretation of the *Jackson* reasonable relationship principle as a formal principle of justice in constitutional adjudication that requires a reasonable relationship between state intervention into protected liberty and the justification for that intervention.[64] The *parens patriae* power justifies state intervention into ordinarily protected liberties because the individual lacks the capacities to protect and advance his or her own interests and therefore fails to qualify for sovereignty in the nonpublic domain. The incompetence and guardianship approach provides for interventions that stand in a reasonable relationship to that state purpose because it limits such interventions to those who lack the relevant capacities, and it requires interventions designed to protect the interests the individual lacks competence to protect.

Any interventions that are not reasonably tailored to protect those interests or that extend into ordinarily protected liberties that the individual remains competent to exercise fail to bear the required reasonable relationship to the justification for *parens patriae* intervention. Thus, such interventions represent arbitrary limitations on liberty that violate the *Jackson* principle. The conventional civil commitment approach violates this principle: It violates the boundary between the public and nonpublic domains by authorizing *parens patriae* interventions absent a determination that the individual lacks the capacities needed to qualify for sovereign discretion in the nonpublic domain, and it fails to tailor the intervention to serve the legitimate state purpose.

V   Conclusion

Although the approach advocated here might provide a series of advantages over the current hybrid civil commitment statutes, it certainly would not provide a panacea for all that ails the state exercise of the *parens patriae* power through civil commitment or through competence and guardianship determinations. No reform of substantive law is likely to resolve difficulties arising from the lack of resources such

---

[64] *See* chapter 2, section III.

as conscientious and competent guardians, placement alternatives to the inpatient ward, or adequate treatment staff. A civil commitment statute that endorses the least restrictive alternative does not create outpatient treatment programs where none are available. Similarly, a statutory preference for limited incompetence and guardianship does not create the judicial resources that would allow courts to carefully tailor and monitor such limited interventions.

Insofar as inadequate resources limit the proper application of either type of statute, however, the competence and guardianship approach may provide conscientious judges with a better opportunity to tailor judicial decisions in a manner designed to ameliorate the harmful effects of those inadequacies. Contemporary competence and guardianship provisions authorize limited guardianship orders through which judges can attempt to tailor the responsibilities of the guardian in a manner expected to serve the interests of the incompetent individual in light of that individual's condition and the specific circumstances the individual encounters, including the limitations of treatment resources. Although the limitations in resources and the abilities of judges to adjust to those limitations will vary widely, competence and guardianship provisions provide the opportunity to adjust judicial orders to these limitations, but commitment statutes tend to encourage dichotomous decisions to commit or to refrain from committing.

Appropriate placement constitutes an important component of the proper exercise of the state's *parens patriae* authority, but placement does not exhaust the range of such decisions. A satisfactory approach to *parens patriae* intervention must also address the scope and limits of the right to informed consent and of the concomitant right to refuse treatment. Cases and commentary address the right to refuse in terms that seem to blur the distinction between the police power and *parens patriae* functions. *Harper*, for example, addressed a case involving a prisoner confined under the police power, but the Court framed a substantive standard that included considerations of dangerousness to self or others and the individual's medical interests.[65] The right to refuse treatment and its underlying foundation arguably implicate different principles and limits when addressed in police power and *parens patriae* contexts. For this reason, chapter 6 addresses the right to refuse under the *parens patriae* function of the state.

---

[65] Washington v. Harper, 494 U.S. 210 (1990).

Chapter 6
THE RIGHT TO REFUSE CARE

Parens patriae commitment and the right of committed individuals to refuse treatment constitute central concerns regarding *parens patriae* intervention through the mental health system. Legal doctrine that fails to address these two issues in a consistent manner can reveal flaws in the reasoning underlying the doctrine, and it can create serious practical problems. Chapter 6 advances an interpretation of the right to refuse treatment by individuals who are subject to *parens patriae* intervention. This analysis demonstrates that one can develop a consistent approach to involuntary admission and treatment under the *parens patriae* authority. Furthermore, this approach coheres with the normative framework discussed in chapter 4 and the formal conception of legal mental illness discussed in chapter 3. It also provides intuitively plausible and theoretically consistent dispositions for a number of difficult cases.

I. Contemporary Civil Commitment and the Right to Refuse

The hypothetical cases discussed in prior chapters give rise to a rather puzzling state of affairs. Ellen, Nathan, and Oliver remain subject to ongoing civil commitment because they suffer serious impairment and endanger themselves. Yet, all three individuals might retain the right to refuse treatment intended to ameliorate either the disorder that renders them subject to the *parens patriae* intervention or the injurious effects of that disorder. Thus, these individuals seem to suffer impairment that justifies the state in limiting their liberty in order to protect their well-being but does not authorize the state to attempt to promote their well-being.

As commitment statutes are currently written and interpreted, commitment neither requires a determination of incompetence nor provides a legal basis for treating the individual as incompetent, and many commitment statutes contain provisions explicitly rejecting an inference of incompetence from commitment.[1] These statutes generate the apparently paradoxical state of affairs in which the state civilly commits certain individuals to mental health facilities under the state's *parens patriae* function, but those individuals retain the right to decide for themselves to accept or to refuse treatment expected to promote their well-being. The apparent paradox arises because the *parens patriae* authority applies to those who are unable to make competent decisions regarding their own well-being, yet commitment under this authority does not require or entail the judgment that the committed individuals lack such competence. *Parens patriae* commitment with a right to refuse treatment apparently

---

[1] BARBARA A. WEINER & ROBERT M. WETTSTEIN, LEGAL ISSUES IN MENTAL HEALTH CARE 86–87 (1993); BRUCE WINICK, THE RIGHT TO REFUSE MENTAL HEALTH TREATMENT 289–91 (1997).

represents the judgments that the state has and has not established that these individuals lack the capacity to make competent decisions regarding their person.

One might argue that this apparent paradox actually reflects a legitimate distinction between competence to decide for oneself regarding admission and competence to decide for oneself regarding treatment in the facility. According to this reasoning, competence requires the capacity to make a reasoned decision regarding the specific question at issue; therefore, individuals might retain the capacity to make reasoned decisions regarding treatment in the facility, although they suffer impairment that renders them incompetent to make reasoned decisions regarding admission. This argument encounters two difficulties. First, the mental illness requirement for civil commitment ordinarily does not specify that the mental illness must take a form that renders the individual unable to make reasoned decisions regarding admission. Thus, the mere fact that individuals fulfill the requirement of mental illness for civil commitment does not establish that they lack capacity to make competent decisions regarding admission. This difficulty permeates *parens patriae* civil commitment in that it undermines the attempt to justify *parens patriae* civil commitment by appeal to the broader justification for the state's *parens patriae* function.

The second difficulty arises from the applicable conception of competence to make reasoned decisions regarding proposed interventions. As ordinarily understood, competence to decide for oneself regarding proposed interventions requires the ability to understand the potential benefits and costs of these proposed interventions and to exercise minimally adequate reasoning regarding these benefits and costs in light of the available alternatives.[2] Hospitalization represents one of a variety of interventions that may occur in various combinations. The ability to reason adequately about each intervention or combination of interventions requires the ability to reason adequately about the alternatives, including those that involve hospitalization. Thus, competence to decide about specific treatment alternatives ordinarily requires competence to decide about the complete array, including hospitalization.

The claim here is not that judicial determinations of competence for person must take the form of a single determination that an individual is either generically competent or generically incompetent for person. Conceptually, competence requires the capacities needed to make and communicate reasoned decisions regarding the matter at hand, and a determination of incompetence for a particular purpose requires a finding that the individual suffers impairment that prevents him or her from making or from communicating reasoned decisions regarding that matter. It remains possible, therefore, that an individual might have the capacities needed to reason competently about one primarily self-regarding decision but not to reason competently about another. Ellen, for example, has a delusional disorder yet remains competent to make reasoned decisions about her own well-being when those decisions involve matters such as crossing streets or dressing warmly in cold weather.

It remains logically possible to encounter circumstances in which an individual would suffer impairment undermining competence to decide regarding admission while remaining competent to decide regarding treatment alternatives after admission. Some individuals might suffer impairment that distorts their capacity to reason competently about particular considerations that apply to one of these decisions, such as admission to a mental health facility, but not to other decisions, such as those

---

[2] ALLEN E. BUCHANAN & DAN W. BROCK, DECIDING FOR OTHERS 23 (1989).

involving treatment alternatives on a ward. The claim here is only that competence for the purpose of selecting among clinical interventions requires the ability to competently reason about the relative costs and benefits of alternative treatment options. For this reason, impairment that renders one unable to competently evaluate one or more modalities is highly likely to undermine one's capacity to choose competently among the complete set of alternatives. It remains difficult to explain, therefore, how those who suffer impairment undermining their ability to make self-regarding decisions about admission to a mental health facility remain competent to make self-regarding decisions about treatment in that facility.

The apparent paradox generated by *parens patriae* civil commitment with a right to refuse treatment in the mental health facility elicits two competing lines of criticism. These criticisms address both the right to refuse treatment and the appropriate roles of clinicians. Those who criticize the right to refuse treatment contend that it undermines the legitimate functions of the mental health facilities and of the providers. These critics contend that allowing committed patients to refuse treatment results in prolonged confinement of impaired people who do not improve because they do not participate in potentially ameliorative treatment. This undermines the well-being of the patients in question and the proper functioning of the facility more generally. If some committed patients remain on the ward without treatment, they occupy beds and staff time that could be devoted to active treatment of other patients. If they are aggressive or disruptive, they endanger other patients or interfere with the treatment program for other patients. Finally, this practice distorts the proper role of clinicians who are unable to provide clinical services to these patients and are forced to fulfill the role of thinly disguised custodians or jailers; they are required to confine and manage these individuals rather than provide the treatment that falls within the proper scope of their expertise and responsibility.[3]

Other critics contend that the manner in which the right to refuse treatment has been interpreted and administered eviscerates the right, violates liberty without due process, and vests unwarranted authority in clinical staff. These critics contend that judicial opinions recognizing the presumptive validity of professional judgment regarding the right to refuse treatment have reduced the right to a hollow right to a second opinion regarding treatment.[4] According to this criticism, judicial decisions that accord presumptive validity to clinical judgment regarding the need for treatment effectively cede judicial authority to clinicians because they allow clinicians to circumvent the requirement of a judicial determination of incompetence. By applying this standard, the cases allow violation of individual liberty without due process of law, undermine the authority of the courts by abdicating judicial responsibilities, and place clinicians in the position of making legal determinations regarding the limits of rights and the justifications for intruding upon individual liberty.[5]

In order to evaluate these competing criticisms and delineate a defensible approach to the rights of committed patients to make decisions regarding their own treatment, one must examine the cases addressing the right to refuse treatment and

---

[3] SAMUEL J. BRAKEL, JOHN PARRY, & BARBARA A. WEINER, THE MENTALLY DISABLED AND THE LAW 341–342 (1985); WINICK, *supra* note 1, at 5 and n17, 18.

[4] Alexander D. Brooks, *The Right to Refuse Antipsychotic Medications: Law and Policy*, 39 RUTGERS L. REV. 339 (1987).

[5] Susan Stefan, *Leaving Civil Rights to the "Experts": From Deference to Abdication Under the Professional Judgment Standard*, 102 YALE L. J. 639 (1992).

the cases applying the PJS to this issue. This project also requires interpretation of these cases in light of the justifications for state intrusion under the *parens patriae* and police power functions. This chapter addresses only the appropriate scope of the right to refuse treatment for those committed under the *parens patriae* function. Chapter 9 addresses the right to refuse for those committed under the police power. The next two sections of this chapter examine a series of cases addressing the right to refuse treatment and application of the PJS to the interpretation and administration of this right. Later sections of this chapter integrate the right to refuse treatment with *parens patriae* civil commitment in a manner that coheres with the justification for *parens patriae* intervention.

II.   The Right to Refuse Treatment

A.   Supreme Court Cases

The Supreme Court has provided relatively sparse guidance regarding the right to refuse treatment, and the most recent cases by the Court have emphasized police power applications. *Riggins v. Nevada* implicated the police power in that it involved the involuntary administration of psychotropic medication to a defendant during his criminal trial.[6] Although the trial court ordered the medication in order to maintain the defendant's competence to stand trial, that court made no findings that the medication was necessary for that purpose or for any other legitimate state purpose, and equivocal expert testimony regarding this matter suggested that the medication might not have been essential to maintaining the defendant's competence.[7] The Supreme Court reversed and remanded, and the Court's reasoning emphasized the defendant's right to a fair trial. The Court recognized the possibility that the medication might have influenced the defendant's appearance, testimony, ability to follow the trial proceedings, or ability to communicate effectively with his attorney.[8] These potential infringements of the defendant's right to a fair trial rendered the medication an unreasonable intrusion because the trial court had made no finding that the medication was necessary for any legitimate state purpose.

The Court's opinion recognizes that some legitimate state purposes would justify involuntary medication. The state might be able to demonstrate that the involuntary medication satisfies due process if it can show that the medication is necessary in order to complete adjudication of the criminal charge. The opinion states that involuntary medication would satisfy due process if that medication were medically appropriate and necessary for the safety of the medicated prisoner or of others.[9] This latter rationale departs somewhat from the general focus of the case on the police power insofar as it includes an apparent *parens patriae* element in the form of the requirement of medical appropriateness. The Court did not elaborate on this requirement that it had announced in its earlier opinion in *Washington v. Harper*.[10]

---

[6] 504 U.S. 127 (1992).
[7] *Id.* at 129–31.
[8] *Id.* at 137.
[9] *Id.* at 135.
[10] 494 U.S. 210 (1990).

Harper addressed substantive and procedural questions involving the involuntary administration of psychotropic medication to a prisoner in a state prison. The case emphasized procedural questions regarding the adequacy of a state statutory procedure for the institutional review of decisions to administer medication involuntarily. The Court addressed substantive and procedural issues sequentially. In its discussion of the substantive standard, it clearly recognized a liberty interest under the Fourteenth Amendment Due Process Clause in avoiding the unwanted administration of antipsychotic drugs.[11] The Court held that "given the requirements of the prison environment, the Due Process Clause permits the State to treat a prison inmate who has a serious mental illness with antipsychotic drugs against his will, if the inmate is dangerous to himself or others and the treatment is in the inmate's medical interests."[12]

Two aspects of this holding merit notice for the present purposes. First, the Court specifically references the holding to the prison environment. The reasoning in the opinion explicitly referred to the special need for management of risk in the prison setting, to the traditional deference of the judiciary to the executive branch in managing prisons, and to the established standard of review for prison regulations that requires courts to establish only that prison regulations are "reasonably related to legitimate penological interests."[13] Thus, the application of *Harper* to nonpenal mental health facilities and patients remains uncertain.

Second, by including the criteria of dangerousness to self or others and of medical appropriateness, the Court seems to address cases that include both police power and *parens patriae* concerns. The case involved circumstances in which the medication was considered by the state to be necessary for the purpose of preventing the prisoner from harming others and expected to promote his clinical interests. Thus, the police power and *parens patriae* functions of the state apparently converged in this case in that the state acted to protect others from harm and to promote the clinical interests of an impaired prisoner. Much of the Court's reasoning supports the interpretation that this administration of involuntary medication was acceptable because it served both the prisoner's medical interests and the state's police power interest in preventing harm.[14]

It is not clear, however, that the Court's opinion requires the convergence of interests for the justification of involuntary medication in the prison setting. The Court addressed circumstances in which this convergence occurred because the medication administered was intended to prevent the prisoner from harming others by improving his clinical condition. Thus, the Court did not encounter circumstances that would require it to decide whether the state could involuntarily administer drugs expected to serve only its police power interests in preventing harm or only the prisoner's medical interests. In summary, *Harper* provides a very limited holding in that it specifically applies to the special concerns of the prison setting, and it addresses circumstances in which the involuntary administration of medication serves the individual clinical interests of the prisoner and is necessary to prevent that prisoner from causing harm. Thus, it does not address cases that arise in mental health facilities or those that appeal only to the state's *parens patriae* function.

---

[11] *Id.* at 221–27.

[12] *Id.* at 227.

[13] *Id.* at 223.

[14] *Id.* at 222–33.

The Court addressed involuntary treatment in two earlier cases, but these opinions provide little further guidance because the Court provided no substantive analysis in remanding to circuit courts in light of other decisions. In *Rennie v. Klein*, the Court remanded a Third Circuit case addressing the right to refuse treatment for reconsideration in light of its decision in *Youngberg v. Romeo*.[15] In *Mills v. Rogers*, the Court remanded a First Circuit case addressing the right to refuse treatment for reconsideration on the basis of state law claims because prior decisions of the supreme court of Massachusetts suggested that state law might provide substantive rights that exceeded those grounded in the United States Constitution.[16]

B.   The Rogers *Series*

The first series of cases addressed the right to refuse medication under Massachusetts state law. In 1980, the First Circuit decided *Rogers v. Okin*, in which it distinguished the police power and *parens patriae* rationales and considered the parameters of the right to refuse treatment under each.[17] The court recognized a Fourteenth Amendment liberty interest in freedom from unwanted drugs and invoked the police power to address cases in which the state administered medication involuntarily in order to prevent the individual from causing harm to himself or to others. The court required that decision makers consider less restrictive alternatives in balancing the individual's liberty interest in freedom from unwanted medication against the state's interest in preventing harm. The court identified the physicians as the decision makers who engaged in the initial balancing with the courts setting procedures to assure that the balancing occurs.[18]

The court explicitly identified the *parens patriae* function of the state in providing care for those who are unable to care for themselves. It included protection and curative treatment within this function. The court reasoned that state authority to treat incompetent patients is inherent in the *parens patriae* function. The state civil commitment statute does not adequately identify incompetent patients, however, because it authorizes commitment on the basis of mental illness and dangerousness to self or others as well as on the basis of grave disability. Only the third criterion suggests incompetence for person, but the commitment process provides no clear way to identify those committed under this third criterion. The statute requires mental illness for commitment, but mental illness does not imply incompetence, and the state statutes provide a separate process for the determination of incompetence. Furthermore, the commitment statute allows committed patients to refuse certain treatments, indicating that the statute does not contemplate incompetence for all committed patients. The court remanded to the district court for consideration of procedures for the determination of incompetence and for providing a substitute judgment regarding the proposed medication after the determination of incompetence.[19]

The U.S. Supreme Court remanded to the First Circuit for reconsideration in

---

[15] Rennie v. Klein, 458 U.S. 1119 (1982); Youngberg v. Romeo, 457 U.S. 307 (1982).

[16] *Rogers*, 457 U.S. at 291.

[17] Rogers v. Okin, 634 F.2d 650 (1st Circ. 1980).

[18] *Id*. at 653–57.

[19] *Id*. at 657–61.

light of possible state law claims, but it provided no substantive analysis.[20] The First Circuit certified a series of questions regarding state law to the supreme court of Massachusetts. The Massachusetts supreme court found that the police power authorizes involuntary medication without prior court approval only when necessary to prevent the patient from causing imminent harm. In administering the medication, the state must consider less restrictive alternatives and follow statutory rules for the use of restraints.[21] Civil commitment under the Massachusetts statute does not establish incompetence for person. Therefore, the *parens patriae* function does not authorize involuntary medication for committed patients unless they have been adjudicated incompetent and had a substituted judgment made for them by the court.[22] The court allowed emergency medication without consent under the *parens patriae* function only if it is necessary to avoid "immediate, substantial, and irreversible deterioration of a serious mental illness," and it required a judicial determination of incompetence and a judicial substitute judgment if that emergency medication is to continue.[23]

In contrast to the Supreme Court's substantive holding in *Harper*, this opinion discusses the *parens patriae* and police power cases as if they are completely distinct. It does not discuss the possibility that the two interact in some important manner when the medication is intended to protect others from the patient by improving the patient's clinical condition. Thus, the court addressed the requirements of involuntary medication under the police power and *parens patriae* functions separately. I postpone discussion of the police power until chapter 9. The Court's analysis of the *parens patriae* function requires a judicial determination of incompetence and a substitute judgment because the Court recognizes that the *parens patriae* authority applies to those who lack the capacity to care for themselves, and it recognizes that commitment under the state statute does not establish this lack of capacity. The Court does not ask, however, why this failure to require incompetence for *parens patriae* commitment does not invalidate such commitments.

The First Circuit accepted the opinion of the Massachusetts supreme court regarding state law and found that this state law gives rise to substantive rights that receive procedural protection under the Fourteenth Amendment.[24] Specifically, Massachusetts law provides protection from involuntary medication because absent an emergency it requires a judicial determination of incompetence and a substitute judgment prior to the involuntary administration of such medication. The United States Constitution as interpreted by the Supreme Court, in contrast, may allow involuntary medication on the basis of the professional judgment of treatment providers. The First Circuit remanded to the district court for a declaration consistent with the findings of the First Circuit and of the Massachusetts supreme court.[25] This series reveals but does not address the need to reconcile the requirement of incompetence for involuntary medication under the *parens patriae* function with the widely adopted contemporary civil commitment statutes that allow commitment under the *parens*

---

[20] *Rogers*, 457 U.S. at 291.

[21] Rogers v. Com'r of Dept. of Mental Health, 458 N.E.2d 308, 321–22 (Mass. 1983).

[22] *Id.* at 312–19.

[23] *Id.* at 322.

[24] Rogers v. Okin, 738 F.2d 1, 5–7 (1st Circ. 1984).

[25] *Id.* at 5–8.

patriae function without a finding of incompetence and with explicit provisions indicating that commitment does not establish incompetence.

C. The Rennie *Series*

The second series of cases occurred approximately contemporaneously with the *Rogers* series, and it addressed the adequacy of the procedures established by a New Jersey statute for review of involuntary medication of committed patients. The initial opinion of the Third Circuit in *Rennie v. Klein* resembled the First Circuit's opinion in *Rogers* insofar as the Third Circuit also recognized a Fourteenth Amendment liberty interest in refusing unwanted psychotropic medication and found that civil commitment does not establish incompetence for the purpose of health care decisions.[26] The court accepted the state's police power and *parens patriae* functions as sufficient to override the individual's liberty interest in some circumstances. It also acknowledged that these two state functions can overlap in that medication can affect some patients in a manner that reduces their symptoms, shortens the duration of confinement, and renders them less dangerous to others.[27] Although the court recognized that the police power and *parens patriae* functions can overlap, it provided no detailed analysis of the manner in which courts should address cases in which both interests apply, as opposed to those in which only one applies.

The court's opinion relied heavily on the least restrictive alternative principle in defining the parameters of the right to refuse and in evaluating the procedures provided by the New Jersey statute. The court related the least restrictive alternative analysis to the reasonable relationship principle from *Jackson*.[28] Although it did not provide a clear analysis integrating the two, it suggested that intrusions into protected liberty that exceed the least restrictive alternative needed to fulfill the legitimate state purpose are not reasonably related to the state interest that justifies the intrusion.[29] The court accepted as consistent with due process the statutory procedures mandating institutional review by mental health professionals of decisions to administer involuntary medication.[30]

Two concurring opinions joined in the court's opinion regarding the liberty interest in a right to refuse medication and regarding the adequacy of the statutory procedures. They differed from the opinion of the court in that they did not accept the least restrictive alternative analysis as the proper basis for the findings. One concurring opinion contended that the least restrictive alternative analysis does not apply to procedures and advocated an analysis using the PJS. This opinion would require that professionals exercise professional judgment regarding the decision to administer medication involuntarily, and it would charge the courts with the responsibility to assure that professionals do so.[31]

The second concurring opinion advocated an analysis that applied the traditional

---

[26] Rennie v. Klein, 653 F2d. 836, 838, 843–44, 847 (liberty interest), 846 (civil commitment does not establish incompetence) (3rd Circ. 1981).

[27] *Id*. at 845.

[28] Jackson v. Indiana, 406 U.S. 715 (1972)

[29] Rennie, at 653 F2d at 845–47.

[30] *Id*. at 848–51.

[31] *Id*. at 854–55 (Seitz, J., concurring).

police power and *parens patriae* principles to the three legitimate purposes of civil commitment. That is, the state's involuntary administration of medication requires justification involving the state's interests in preventing harm to the patient or others or in providing treatment and care for the patient. This analysis would limit the involuntary administration of medication to circumstances in which that involuntary administration was reasonably related to advancing those legitimate state interests. It would authorize the involuntary administration of medication for the purpose of serving the *parens patriae* function of protecting the patients' interests only in those cases in which patients lacked competence to decide for themselves. Involuntarily administered medication beyond these circumstances would not bear the necessary reasonable relationship to the legitimate state interests that justify such intrusion.[32] This opinion rejected the least restrictive alternative analysis as applicable only to discrete legislative enactments, rather than to application of law. The opinion also called into question the legal force of that analysis in light of recent cases.[33]

The court's opinion converged with the concurring opinions insofar as all recognized the liberty interest in refusing involuntary medication; all agreed that civil commitment does not establish incompetence for health care decisions; and all accepted the adequacy of the statutory procedures. They differed regarding the appropriate legal analysis underlying these findings, but they did not clearly address the relationships among the forms of legal analysis they applied, including the least restrictive alternative analysis, the PJS, and the traditional balancing of the individual liberty interest against the state's police power and *parens patriae* functions. The majority and the second concurrence articulated different approaches to the analyses, with the majority emphasizing the least restrictive alternative analysis and the concurrence rejecting that approach. Despite this explicit disagreement, however, they share certain common principles. The court's opinion presented the least restrictive alternative analysis as an application of the underlying reasonable relationship principle in that intrusions beyond the least restrictive were seen as lacking a reasonable relationship to the police power and *parens patriae* functions that provide the legitimate state interests that justify the intrusions. Similarly, the concurrence balances the state's police power and *parens patriae* interests against the individual liberty interest in order to determine whether the involuntary administration of medication is reasonably related to legitimate state interests that justify the intrusion.

The Supreme Court remanded the Third Circuit's decision for reconsideration in light of the Supreme Court's decision in *Youngberg v. Romeo*.[34] On remand, the Third Circuit reaffirmed the judgment from its earlier opinion, but it revised the analysis.[35] The later opinion replaced the earlier least restrictive alternative analysis with the PJS, and it approved the statutory procedures as providing adequate review of the professional judgment exercised by the treatment providers, specifying that such judgment must include consideration of matters such as dangerousness to self or others and the side effects of the medication.[36] This opinion and the three concurrences again call into question the precise relationship between the PJS and the least

---

[32] *Id.* at 856–58 (Garth, J., concurring).
[33] *Id.* at 861–63 (Garth, J., concurring).
[34] Rennie v. Klein, 458 U.S. 1119 (1982); *Romeo*, 457 U.S. at 307.
[35] Rennie v. Klein, 720 F.2d 266 (3rd Circ. 1983).
[36] *Id.* at 267–70.

restrictive alternative analyses as alternative applications of the reasonable relationship principle.

The first concurrence specified that the PJS requires that the professionals consult
with other professionals and consider dangerousness to self or others, potential alternatives to the medication, and side effects.[37] The second concurrence specified
that the exercise of professional judgment must include consideration of the welfare
of the patient, society's interests, alternatives, and side effects. This opinion also
required that medication must constitute part of an effort to treat the disorder that
warrants confinement or to control violent outbreaks and that it cannot merely serve
economic or administrative purposes.[38] The third concurrence advocated the continued application of the least restrictive alternative analysis, contending that *Romeo*
did not reject that analysis for this purpose. This opinion also stated that an adequate
exercise of professional judgment regarding the right to refuse medication must include consideration of less restrictive alternatives.[39]

Collectively, the court's opinion and the various concurring opinions in the case
reaffirm the judgment from the 1981 case, including the recognition of the liberty
interest and the statutory procedures. All of these opinions accept the PJS, although
the third concurrence advocates retention of the less restrictive alternatives analysis
and contends that the adequate exercise of professional judgment must include that
analysis. The opinions specify that the exercise of professional judgment must include consideration of traditional police power and *parens patriae* concerns regarding
dangerousness and individual welfare, alternatives to the unwanted medication, and
side effects. Insofar as professional judgment must address these considerations, it
becomes difficult to explain precisely in what manner the PJS differs substantially
from the least restrictive alternative analysis or the traditional balancing of state
interests under the police power and *parens patriae* functions against the individual
liberty interests. Arguably, these standards differ primarily regarding the distribution
of responsibility in that the courts would directly perform the analyses under the
latter approaches, but the courts would review the exercise of professional judgment
by treatment providers regarding these concerns under the PJS.

D.   Case Synthesis

The Supreme Court cases provide very little clear guidance regarding the right to
refuse medication, particularly in *parens patriae* cases. *Riggins* and *Harper* address
issues that fall primarily within the police power, and each case involves legally
important concerns that distinguish these cases from those that raise relatively pure
questions regarding the committed individual's right to refuse medication. The
Court's reasoning in *Riggins* emphasizes the right to a fair trial in a criminal case,
and the reasoning in *Harper* reflects concerns specific to the prison environment and
the traditional deference of the judiciary to the executive branch regarding prison
regulation. The Court's two earlier cases that addressed the right to refuse treatment
with relatively few complicating issues resulted in remands with little or no substantive analysis.

---

[37] *Id.* at 270–72 (Adams, J., concurring).
[38] *Id.* at 272–74 (Seitz, J., concurring).
[39] *Id.* at 274–77 (Weis, J., concurring).

The *Rogers* series of cases directly addressed a right to refuse treatment for those who were civilly committed under the state's *parens patriae* function. These opinions recognize a right to refuse medication grounded in state law and the Fourteenth Amendment, and they adopt a traditional approach to *parens patriae* interventions in that absent an emergency they require a prior judicial determination of incompetence and a substitute judgment. These opinions reveal but do not address the perplexing question about the relationship between *parens patriae* civil commitment and involuntary medication under the *parens patriae* function. They explicitly require a judicial determination of incompetence prior to *parens patriae* intervention, yet they explicitly acknowledge that *parens patriae* intervention in the form of civil commitment does not require incompetence.

The *Rennie* series of cases resembles the *Rogers* series insofar as they recognize a Fourteenth Amendment liberty interest in freedom from unwanted medication, and they apply the traditional police power and *parens patriae* rationales in order to define the limits of the right to refuse. In contrast to the *Rogers* opinions, the *Rennie* opinions accept professional judgment according to statutory procedures as sufficient procedural protection. The opinions shifted from a least restrictive alternative analysis to a PJS, but the relationship between these two approaches remains unclear. Both approaches appear to be grounded in the reasonable relationship principle from *Jackson* and the traditional police power and *parens patriae* functions of the state. As articulated by the opinions of the court and of the concurrences on remand, the PJS apparently requires consideration of less restrictive alternatives that might fulfill the legitimate state purposes that justify intrusion into a protected liberty. Thus, it appears that the PJS requires consideration of the same factors that the court would consider in balancing the individual liberty interest against the legitimate state interests that justify intrusion under the police power or the *parens patriae* function.

Arguably, two important factors differentiate the PJS approach adopted in the *Rennie* series of opinions from the traditional requirement of a judicial determination of incompetence for *parens patriae* intervention adopted in the *Rogers* series of opinions. The first involves the formal determination of incompetence required by the *Rogers* opinions. The *Rennie* opinions included some language indicating that *parens patriae* intervention applies only to those who lack the capacities needed to provide for their own care. Furthermore, given the nature of the state's *parens patriae* function as the responsibility to provide care for those who lack the capacities to care for themselves, it is not clear that one can coherently speak of *parens patriae* intervention regarding those who remain competent. Yet, the *Rennie* opinions do not require a formal finding of incompetence. The second difference may explain the first in that it involves the distribution of responsibilities to judicial and clinical decision makers. The *Rogers* opinions require a judicial determination of incompetence and a judicial substitute judgment. The PJS endorsed in the *Rennie* opinions apparently requires consideration of factors very similar to those that a judge would consider in applying the least restrictive alternative analysis, but the PJS places the initial decision making in the hands of treatment providers and charges the courts with assuring that these clinicians exercise professional judgment. Thus, the PJS approach cannot require a formal adjudication of incompetence because clinicians rather than courts make the primary decisions.

This reliance upon clinicians to make the primary decisions regarding involuntary medication under the PJS generates two additional questions. First, what judgments are clinicians charged with making under the PJS? Second, is it reasonable to expect that clinicians are prepared to make these judgments?

III. PJS

The Supreme Court has provided controversial precedent regarding the legal signif-icance of professional judgment in circumstances involving the treatment of com-mitted patients and treatment refusal by these patients. The Third Circuit adopted the PJS regarding the right to refuse treatment in response to the Supreme Court's remand in *Rennie* with instructions to reconsider in light of its decision in *Youngberg v. Romeo*.[40] In that case, the Court addressed a claim by a severely retarded resident of a state facility that he had a right to treatment in the facility. That resident had engaged in an extended pattern of assaultive and self-injurious behavior in the in-stitution; consequently, he was frequently injured and physically restrained.[41] The Court recognized a limited right to treatment required "to ensure safety and freedom from undue restraint."[42] The Court also articulated the PJS:

> [i]n determining what is "reasonable"—in this and any case presenting a claim for training by a State—we emphasize that courts must show deference to the judgment exercised by a qualified professional . . . the decision if made by a professional, is presumptively valid; liability may be imposed only when the decision by the profes-sional is such a substantial departure from accepted professional judgment, practice, or standards as to demonstrate that the person responsible actually did not base the decision on such a judgment.[43]

Although the Court articulated the PJS regarding Romeo's assertion of a right to training, some courts have applied it to the right to refuse treatment, and these decisions have been seriously criticized.[44] Commentators contend that the PJS re-duces the right to refuse treatment to a right to a second opinion and that by applying the PJS in this manner, courts forfeit judicial responsibility to clinical professionals who confront a variety of institutional pressures other than the patients' rights or interests.[45] These critics tend to criticize the PJS standard without clearly articulating an interpretation of the range of the standard. The general tone of the criticisms sometimes suggests that the critics read the PJS as broadly authorizing professionals to do what they think is best.[46] This broad reading seems inconsistent with the Third Circuit's discussion of the PJS in *Rennie* on remand from the Supreme Court. In that discussion, the majority and concurring opinions apparently contemplated profes-sional judgment addressing a series of specific considerations such as dangerousness,

---

[40] 457 U.S. 307 (1982).

[41] *Id.* at 309–11.

[42] *Id.* at 319.

[43] *Id.* at 322–23.

[44] U.S. v. Charters, 863 F.2d 302 (4th Cir. 1988); Rennie v. Klein, 720 F.2d 266 (3rd Cir. 1983); Brooks, *supra* note 4; Stefan, *supra* note 5, at 670–72.

[45] Brooks, *supra* note 4, at 354–61; Stefan, *supra* note 5, at 646–85.

[46] Brooks, *supra* note 4, at 355, 360–61; Stefan, *supra* note 5, at 646–55; WINICK, *supra* note 1, at 281–83. Winick provides a comprehensive analysis of the legal right to refuse mental health treatment. This chapter addresses only the application of the PJS to that issue.

side effects, and alternatives less restrictive of constitutionally protected liberty.[47] In contrast to the *Rennie* opinions, however, the *Romeo* opinion fails to clearly specify the subject and limits of professional judgment. Some courts and commentators might interpret it broadly to authorize clinicians in exercising professional judgment regarding the clinically optimum treatment, or regarding the patient's best interests, all things considered.[48]

These broad interpretations seem to render substantive holdings superfluous. Regarding the right to treatment recognized in *Romeo*, for example, if professionals are authorized to do what they think best, then the substantive holding that appears to define the content and limits of the right seems illusory in that professionals might think it preferable to pursue alternative treatment goals rather than freedom from bodily injury or undue restraint. At least one commentator advocates the approach taken in *Harper* as a superior alternative to the PJS.[49] The *Harper* Court applied legal precedent regarding the state's interests in maintaining safety and security in the prison environment as the basis for deriving a substantive standard for the involuntary administration of antipsychotic medication to a state prison inmate. Substantively, the Court held that the state may do so "if the inmate is dangerous to himself or others and the treatment is in the inmate's medical interests."[50] The Court approved a state statutory procedure for institutional review of involuntarily administered medication. This procedure provides for notice, a hearing before a board, and the rights to be present and to cross-examine witnesses. It does not provide for legal counsel or for a judicial decision maker, however, as clinical personal constitute the review board and serve as nonlegal advisor to the prisoner.[51]

In *Harper*, the Court's substantive holding sets a constitutional standard for involuntary treatment in the prison context, and the state statute sets the procedure for professional review of professional judgment regarding involuntary treatment decisions. If one interprets the statutory review procedure as directed only toward ensuring that the involuntarily administered treatment served the prisoner's clinical interests, the procedural holding apparently contradicts the substantive holding. It does so because the latter limits involuntary medication to cases meeting the criteria of dangerousness and medical interests, but the former would allow involuntary treatment as approved by a procedure that addressed only the prisoner's clinical interests, regardless of dangerousness. The case remains coherent, however, if one interprets the review process as one in which professionals review the judgments of other professionals in order to determine whether those judgments fall within the range of acceptable professional judgments regarding treatment intended to fulfill the purposes and limits set by the Court's substantive criteria. Thus, in circumstances controlled by *Harper*, the professional review must determine whether the treatment decision meets professional standards for treatment intended to reduce the risk of harm to self or others in a manner that serves the prisoner's medical interests.

Although the Court did not frame its opinion in *Harper* in terms of the PJS, one can interpret this case as an application of the PJS parallel to *Romeo*. Both decisions

---

[47] *See* section III.

[48] U.S. v. Charters, 863 F.2d 302, 309–11 (4th Cir. 1988); Brooks, *supra* note 4, at 355, 360–61; Stefan, *supra* note5, at 646–55; WINICK, *supra* note 1, at 281–83.

[49] *Harper*, 494 U.S. at 210; Stefan, *supra* note 5, at 681–85.

[50] *Harper*, 494 U.S. at 227.

[51] *Id.* at 228–36.

articulate substantive standards addressing constitutionally appropriate criteria for treatment, and both recognize the responsibility of clinical professionals to prescribe and deliver treatment. Both decisions accept professional judgment regarding the adequacy of these prescriptions, although *Harper* accepted a statutory procedure through which clinicians review the professional judgment of other clinicians regarding involuntary treatment, and *Romeo* articulated a standard of court review regarding professional judgment by clinicians. Thus, both decisions recognize the exercise of professional judgment by clinicians as a constitutionally acceptable basis for the administration of clinical treatment in certain circumstances. Neither decision accepts unconstrained professional discretion, however, because each articulates a substantive legal holding providing the criteria regarding which professionals must exercise judgment.

According to this analysis, the PJS provides the standard of practice that clinicians must meet in selecting treatment intended to comport with the legal substantive standard. The *Harper* Court articulated a substantive standard setting boundaries on the exercise of professional judgment in that it authorized involuntary medication when that medication is in the prisoner's interest and the prisoner is dangerous to himself or others.[52] That is, professional judgment controls the prescription and review processes in the *Harper* approach, but the Court's substantive standard sets legal criteria for involuntary treatment in prison. These criteria limit the legitimate range of professional judgment to the selection of treatment modalities expected to reduce danger and promote the prisoner's medical interests.

Romeo, like *Harper*, provides a substantive standard that articulates the criteria defining the limits within which professionals are authorized to exercise judgment. Just as the *Harper* Court's substantive standard specifically limits involuntary treatment to that which is in the medical interests of dangerous prisoners, the *Romeo* Court's substantive standard specifically requires treatment intended to provide safety from bodily injury and freedom from undue restraint.[53] Just as *Harper's* substantive standard limits professional judgment to the range of treatment modalities appropriate to the concerns identified in that substantive standard, *Romeo's* substantive standard specifies the parameters of professional judgment. That standard requires that professionals exercise judgment for the purpose of selecting treatment modalities intended to protect the constitutional liberty interests in reducing bodily injury and undue restraint. In this manner, *Romeo* and *Harper* adopt a common form; the Court sets the substantive criteria according to the constitutional analysis, and clinical professionals exercise professional judgment regarding treatment intended to address the clinical concerns identified by the legal substantive standard.

This interpretation renders the decisions internally coherent and consistent with one another, but it remains problematic because it requires that the professionals are aware of and understand the Court's substantive criteria and that they are prepared to make professional judgments in the context of those criteria. The Third Circuit's application on remand of the PJS to the right to refuse treatment raises similar concerns. The *Rennie* opinions contemplate the exercise of professional judgment that considers a variety of specific factors including side effects, the patient's welfare, and alternative treatment modalities. Ordinary clinical practice would include con-

[52] *Id.* at 227.
[53] *Romeo*, 457 U.S. at 307, 319.

sideration of these factors. The *Rennie* opinions also called for consideration of certain factors, such as societal interests and the less restrictive alternatives principle, that seem to fall in the category of legal rather than clinical considerations.[54]

Consider the Court's decision in *Parham v. J.R. et al.*[55] In this case, the Court accepted professional review as sufficient procedural protection for voluntary admissions of minors to mental health facilities by their parents or guardians. The Court upheld a clinical review of the admission by a neutral fact finder, including a staff physician, providing that "he or she is free to evaluate independently the child's mental and emotional condition and the need for treatment."[56] *Parham* resembles *Harper* in that the Court did not phrase the holding in terms of the PJS, but it resembles both *Romeo* and *Harper* in that the Court accepted the exercise of professional judgment by clinicians as an appropriate form of procedural protection regarding state action that intrudes on ordinarily protected interests.

The Court's reasoning frames the substantive question as one addressing the balance between the child's liberty interest in freedom from unnecessary confinement for treatment and the legitimate interests of the parents and the state. The parents' interests include the right and the duty to exercise their legitimate authority over their minor children, including their authority to seek and follow medical advice. The Court's opinion accepts a rebuttable presumption that parents ordinarily act in their children's best interests. Furthermore, it recognizes a state interest in limiting costly inpatient services to instances of genuine need. The Court concludes that an independent clinical evaluation of the child's mental and emotional condition and need for treatment provides an appropriate procedure for addressing the combined interests of the child, the parents, and the state.[57]

Although the Court presents the analysis as one of balancing competing interests, this articulation of the interests involved actually interprets them as converging rather than competing. That is, admission serves the interests articulated by the Court for the child, the parents, and the state if but only if the child's clinical condition warrants admission for treatment. Clinical evaluation serves these combined purposes by evaluating the child's mental and emotional condition and need for treatment in order to confirm that the child is clinically appropriate for admission to the facility. Having framed the substantive concerns as the child's mental and emotional condition and the need for admission in order to serve the child's best interests in light of that condition, the Court had defined the substantive question as one that falls at the center of clinical expertise. Thus, a clinical evaluation provides the procedure appropriately tailored to implement the substantive standard.

One can legitimately question whether the Court should have framed the substantive question in this manner and whether the characterization of a staff physician as a "neutral fact finder" is accurate.[58] Given the substantive question as the Court framed it, however, a clinical review of the child's condition and of admission as a treatment intervention appropriate to that condition falls within the expertise of the clinical professions and addresses the substantive legal criteria. Thus, clinical pro-

---

[54] *See* section III.
[55] 442 U.S. 584 (1979).
[56] *Id.* at 607.
[57] *Id.* at 601–08.
[58] *Id.* at 606–07.

fessionals can fulfill the legal purpose of the review by exercising professional judgment in the practice of the clinical professions precisely because the Court has defined the substantive issue in terms compatible with the substance of the clinical professions.

Romeo and *Harper*, in contrast to *Parham*, address substantive issues that do not fall neatly within the scope of the clinician's professional judgment. The substantive standard in *Romeo* recognizes a limited right to treatment needed to protect identified constitutional liberty interests in bodily safety and freedom from unnecessary restraint.[59] The substantive standard in *Harper* defines danger to the prisoner or others and the prisoner's medical interests as the criteria for involuntary antipsychotic medication in a prison setting.[60] Both cases raise significant concerns regarding the likelihood that clinicians exercising their professional judgment will be aware of the substantive standards and will interpret them in a manner consistent with a court's interpretation. Perhaps more important, however, both cases raise an additional significant question regarding the competence of clinicians to exercise professional judgment regarding substantive standards defined in terms of dangerousness or constitutional interests because these notions contain normative or legal components. Thus, neither substantive standard converges with the ordinary basis for clinical judgment to the same degree as the substantive standard in *Parham*. The *Rennie* opinions by the Third Circuit on remand raise similar concerns because they discuss the PJS in a manner that calls upon clinicians to exercise judgment regarding a series of factors that include normative or legal components as well as clinical ones. These include, for example, dangerousness, legitimate state interests, and alternatives less restrictive of constitutionally protected liberty.[61]

Clinicians exercising professional judgment in the process of clinical evaluation for treatment through admission to a particular facility can fulfill their responsibilities as contemplated by the *Parham* decision without being aware of the substantive standard in that case precisely because that substantive standard converges with clinicians' clinical responsibilities. Clinicians' awareness of the substantive standards in *Harper, Romeo,* and *Rennie* represents a more serious concern because these standards do not converge as smoothly with ordinary clinical practice. It seems plausible to suppose, however, that experienced clinicians in prisons or mental health facilities that treat severely impaired and involuntarily committed persons might be required to become familiar with these standards and to consult legal counsel. Thus, clinicians' awareness of the standards remains a serious concern, but it might reasonably be seen as manageable through appropriate consultation.

The second question regarding the competence and authority of clinicians to apply substantive standards with legal or normative components raises a more perplexing issue. The ordinary clinical criteria for professional judgment regarding treatment should include concern for avoiding bodily injury and physical restraint as well as for treatment in the person's clinical interests. Clinicians ordinarily address such concerns as part of a comprehensive approach to treatment planning, however, and this process ordinarily emphasizes the importance of promoting the well-being of the patient. Clinicians can exercise professional judgment regarding descriptive di-

---

[59] *Romeo*, 457 U.S. at 307, 319.
[60] *Harper*, 494 U.S. at 210, 227.
[61] *See* section III.

agnosis, prognosis, risk analysis, and treatment planning through the application of ordinary care and competence in their professions.

Insofar as certain substantive legal criteria (such as the requirement of dangerousness in *Harper,* the notion of undue restraint in *Romeo*, or consideration of alternatives less restrictive of constitutionally protected liberty in *Rennie*) involve normative components, clinicians cannot address them solely through the exercise of professional judgment. Clinicians who attempt to interpret and apply these legal substantive standards that include normative components must extend beyond the scope of professional judgment in the clinical professions. In applying the *Harper* criterion of dangerousness, for example, clinicians must decide whether the risk of harm is sufficient to justify the intrusion into a constitutionally protected liberty interest through the involuntary administration of antipsychotic medication.[62] Similarly, in considering less restrictive alternatives as contemplated by the *Rennie* opinion, clinicians must decide which treatment alternatives constitute greater or lesser intrusions into constitutionally protected liberty. This judgment requires, for example, weighing the Fourteenth Amendment liberty interest in freedom from bodily constraint implicated by the use of physical restraints against the First Amendment liberty interest in freedom of thought implicated by the unwanted administration of psychotropic medication. These determinations necessarily require interpretations of constitutional values that fall beyond the scope of clinical expertise and authority.

This integrated analysis of *Romeo, Harper*, and *Parham* produces an interpretation of the PJS as a standard by which clinicians exercise judgment regarding the approaches to clinical care that are appropriate to the goals and limits set by the substantive legal standards in the cases. According to this interpretation, the PJS provides a workable form of procedural protection for the relevant legally protected interests in cases such as *Parham* in which the Court articulates substantive standards that call for judgment regarding matters that fall within clinical expertise. Court opinions in cases such as *Romeo, Harper*, and *Rennie* call for professional judgment regarding matters that include legal or normative concerns beyond the scope of clinical expertise, however, and these cases raise important concerns regarding clinicians' expertise and authority. The remaining sections of this chapter advance an integrated approach to the PJS, the right to refuse treatment in the context of civil commitment under the *parens patriae* function, and the approach to *parens patriae* intervention developed in chapter 5. This integrated analysis provides a coherent and defensible approach to *parens patriae* interventions, and it addresses the concerns regarding expertise and authority.

IV. *Parens Patriae* Interventions: Admission and Treatment

A. The Central Concerns Revealed by the Rogers and Rennie Series

A satisfactory set of legal institutions for *parens patriae* intervention through the mental health system would address the central concern raised by the review of the *Rogers* and *Rennie* series of opinions. These legal institutions would meet at least the following requirements. First, *parens patriae* intervention must take a form that

---

[62] *See* chapter 10, section V.

coheres with the principles that justify such interventions. Thus, it must apply only to those who lack competence to make and communicate reasoned decisions regarding their interaction with the mental health system. Second, the various *parens patriae* legal institutions must cohere with each other in a consistent set. Third, intervention must conform to the *Jackson* reasonable relationship principle by advancing the state interest that justifies the intervention. Fourth, mental health facilities and providers must function within the bounds of their legitimate purposes and expertise. Finally, applicable doctrines such as the PJS and the least restrictive alternative standard must be interpreted and applied in a manner that appropriately allocates authority and responsibility to the various legal, clinical, and private participants.

B. Integrating Parens Patriae *Admissions and Treatment*

The normative framework discussed in chapter 4 and the approach to *parens patriae* commitment advanced in chapter 5 distinguish police power and *parens patriae* commitment as two distinct forms of state intervention requiring two distinct types of justification. This approach would abolish *parens patriae* civil commitment as an independent institution but retain involuntary hospitalization as one possible disposition following a judicial determination of incompetence and the appointment of a guardian. This approach restores the connection between incompetence and *parens patriae* interventions through the mental health system by requiring a determination of incompetence for person as a prerequisite for any such intervention.

Restoring the connection between incompetence and *parens patriae* interventions has both normative and practical advantages. Normatively, this approach produces institutions of *parens patriae* intervention that cohere internally and with the underlying normative framework that justifies such interventions. Practically, it provides the opportunity to separate legal and clinical judgments in a manner that appropriately distributes responsibility for these judgments to judges and clinicians respectively. Consider first the normative point. This approach promotes normative consistency by authorizing *parens patriae* intervention only when such intrusion does not violate the underlying principles of political morality. This requirement of incompetence protects self-determination in the nonpublic domain for all those who qualify for sovereignty within that domain, and it allows state action intended to protect and promote well-being for those who fail to so qualify.[63]

This approach also resolves the incoherence involving *parens patriae* civil commitment with a right to refuse treatment revealed but not addressed in the *Rogers* series of opinions.[64] That incoherence arises because the state's authority to intervene under the *parens patriae* function rests upon the incompetence of the individual, yet contemporary civil commitment statutes authorize commitment, purportedly justified as an exercise of the state's *parens patriae* function, according to criteria that neither require nor entail incompetence. Thus, contemporary civil commitment statutes generate circumstances in which individuals both qualify and fail to qualify for state intervention under the *parens patriae* function.

The proposed approach precludes these circumstances from arising because it

---

[63] *See* chapter 4, section V.
[64] *See* chapter 6, section II.

requires a determination of incompetence as the initial step in any *parens patriae* intervention by the state. The question of appropriate disposition arises only after the state has demonstrated that these individuals lack the capacities needed to make reasoned decisions regarding their own well-being. The reasonable relationship principle then governs the nature of the intervention. The *parens patriae* intervention must take a form reasonably related to the impairment and the related risk to well-being that render each individual subject to such intervention. Rather than committing the individual without a finding of incompetence and then confronting the question of involuntary treatment, this approach authorizes involuntary admission only if admission provides an appropriate means of providing needed care or treatment of an individual who has been found incompetent for person and in need of such intervention.

The approach advanced here complies with the interpretation of the reasonable relationship principle in *Jackson* as a formal principle of justice in constitutional adjudication. It allows interventions designed to advance the legitimate state interest in protecting and promoting the well-being of those who are ineligible for sovereignty in the nonpublic domain because they lack the ability to make reasoned decisions regarding their own well-being. The requirement of incompetence precludes similar intrusions into the protected liberties of competent individuals. Thus, state interventions designed to promote the well-being of incompetent individuals bear a reasonable relationship to the legitimate state interest in fulfilling its *parens patriae* responsibilities without violating the right of competent individuals to make their own decisions regarding health care, including admission to health care facilities.

This approach justifies involuntary inpatient admission only if that form of intervention provides care or treatment that bears a reasonable relationship to the impairment and need for protection that justifies the prior finding of incompetence. Involuntary inpatient admission would not bear a reasonable relationship to the legitimate state interest that justifies the intrusion, for example, unless the inpatient confinement provided some form of inpatient care that would address the impairment and risk that justifies *parens patriae* intervention. This approach precludes *parens patriae* commitment for care of a person who retains the right to refuse that care. If the court finds the individual incompetent, the state and the guardian can admit and treat in a manner that bears a reasonable relationship to the impairment that justifies intervention. If the court finds the individual competent, the state can neither admit nor treat without consent.

Understood in this manner, the reasonable relationship principle provides guidance in developing defensible interpretations of the least restrictive alternative doctrine as applied to *parens patriae* interventions and of the principle of care appropriateness discussed previously in chapter 5. Judicial opinions and commentary have questioned the continued vitality of the least restrictive alternative doctrine as applied to mental health law.[65] Furthermore, commentators have demonstrated the difficulty that occurs when scholars or treatment providers attempt to estimate the relative restrictiveness of various clinical interventions, particularly when attempting to evaluate the comparative restrictiveness of several treatment modalities, such as re-

---

[65] Rennie v. Klein, 720 F.2d 266, 269–70 (3rd. Circ. 1983); Thomas G. Gutheil, Paul S. Appelbaum, & David B. Wexler, *The Inappropriateness of the "Least Restrictive Alternative" Analysis for Involuntary Procedures With the Institutionalized Mentally Ill*, 11 J. PSYCHIATRY & L. 7, 16 (1984).

straints, seclusion, or involuntary medication.[66] Yet, the Supreme Court apparently referred to that doctrine, or some similar doctrine, in its discussion of involuntary medication in *Riggins v. Nevada*.[67] Several of the concurring opinions in *Rennie* either endorsed the continuing applicability of the doctrine to the right to refuse medication or discussed the PJS in terms that included side effects and alternatives in a manner that suggested consideration of less restrictive alternatives.[68]

The judicial opinion usually understood as applying the least restrictive alternative doctrine to mental health law addressed a case in which the court reviewed the commitment of a woman who suffered early senescent decline resulting in an inability to care for herself and in risk to herself through disoriented wandering. The court reasoned that "[d]eprivations of liberty solely because of dangers to the ill persons themselves should not go beyond what is necessary for their protection."[69] This passage indicates that in selecting interventions intended solely to advance the state interest in protecting those who endanger themselves, decision makers should not select interventions that limit liberty in a manner that is not necessary to serve that single purpose. The passage does not address cases in which the intervention is intended to serve the police power function of preventing the individual from harming others or to serve both police power and *parens patriae* functions.

The opinion does not prescribe the manner in which decision makers should chose from among several alternative interventions of similar restrictiveness. That is, rather than mandating the least restrictive alternative, it prohibits interventions that are more intrusive than necessary. If one assumes that decision makers select from among an array of intrusions ranked in order of increasing restrictiveness, then the proper intervention is the one that serves the state purpose with the least restriction of liberty. Any alternative that falls below the proper one is insufficient to fulfill the legitimate state purpose that justifies the intervention, and any alternative that falls above the proper one limits liberty beyond the degree needed to serve that purpose. On this assumption, the directive that decision makers must select the alternative that does not involve unnecessary restrictions on liberty constitutes the directive that they must select the least restrictive alternative.

If the available alternatives do not distribute neatly along a continuum of lesser to greater restrictiveness, however, the directive to refrain from selecting an unnecessarily restrictive alternative is not the equivalent of a directive to select the least restrictive alternative. Rather, it constitutes the directive to select from among the set of alternatives regarding which no other is both clearly less restrictive and adequate to serve the legitimate state purpose that justifies the intervention. Given the lack of a clearly identifiable hierarchy of restrictiveness among clinical treatment modalities, decision makers satisfy this directive when they select any placement or treatment modality from the array of alternatives that (a) are expected to serve the legitimate state purpose and (b) fall within the general category of alternatives regarding which no other is clearly less restrictive. If decision makers select an intervention that is more restrictive than those that fall within this array, they engage in

---

[66] Gutheil et al., *supra* note 65, at 9–15.

[67] *Riggins*, 504 U.S. at 127, 135.

[68] Rennie v. Klein, 720 F.2d at 269–70 (side effects), 270–72 (Adams, J., concurring) (alternatives and side effects), 272–74 (Seitz, J., concurring) (side effects and alternatives), 274–77 (Weis, J., concurring) (advocating retention of the least restrictive alternative analysis).

[69] Lake v. Cameron, 364 F.2d 657, 660 (D.C. Circ. 1966).

arbitrary limitation of liberty because the excessive restrictiveness does not serve the legitimate state purpose that justifies the intervention.

According to this interpretation, the variation of the least restrictive alternative analysis that is applicable to the selection of involuntary placement and treatment modalities constitutes an application of the reasonable relationship principle. Decision makers who select from among the set of arguably least restrictive alternatives expected to serve the legitimate state purpose select an intervention that bears a reasonable relationship to the state interest that justifies the intrusion. Those who select placements or treatments that are more restrictive than those that fall within this set violate the reasonable relationship principle because intrusion beyond that expected to serve the legitimate state purpose represents an arbitrary limitation on liberty. When various interventions expected to serve the state purpose that justifies the intrusion are not amenable to a clear rank ordering on a scale of restrictiveness, the principle underlying the least restrictive alternative approach enjoins decision makers from engaging in arbitrary restrictions of liberty. Decision makers engage in such arbitrary restrictions when they select placements or treatment modalities that are not among the set of arguably least restrictive alternatives expected to fulfill the legitimate state purpose.

Similarly, the previously discussed principle of care appropriateness represents an application of the reasonable relationship principle. When impaired capacities justify intervention by the state in its *parens patriae* function, the state assumes a responsibility to protect the well-being of the incompetent person. In order to discharge that responsibility, the state must intervene in a manner reasonably related to the impairment and risk that provide the basis for the *parens patriae* intervention. It does so by providing protection, placement, and care reasonably expected to protect and promote the interests that the incompetent individuals lack the capacities to manage through reasoned decision. Thus, both this formulation of the principle of care appropriateness and the variation of the least restrictive alternative analysis applicable to clinical interventions represent applications of the reasonable relationship principle to the state's responsibilities under the *parens patriae* function.

Although cases and commentary tend to present the least restrictive alternative analysis and the PJS as competing approaches to the selection of involuntary treatment modalities, the two converge with care appropriateness as applications of the reasonable relationship principle when they are interpreted and applied in the context of the approach advanced here. The least restrictive alternative analysis and the PJS differ in that the former ordinarily involves direct evaluation of state interventions by the courts but the latter involves deference to the decisions made by professionals.[70] Some judicial opinions discuss the least restrictive alternative analysis in the context of professional decision making regarding treatment, however, raising difficult questions regarding the ability and authority of clinicians to make judgments about the degree to which various treatment modalities restrict constitutionally protected liberties.[71]

The approach endorsed here may minimize the degree to which the PJS involves clinicians in making decisions that exceed their expertise or authority. Contemporary competence and guardianship statutes provide a legal institution with the potential

---

[70] *Romeo*, 457 U.S. at 307, 321–23.
[71] Rennie v. Klein, 720 F.2d 266, 274–77 (3rd Circ. 1983) (Weis, J., concurring); *see* section III.

to properly distribute responsibility for legal and clinical judgments to legal and clinical actors respectively. These statutes provide for guardianship orders that define either broad or narrow powers of guardianship and that can explicitly rule out certain alternatives.[72] The order might rule out, for example, psychosurgery, electroshock treatment, or inpatient confinement in a mental health facility. Under these statutes, the court makes an initial determination of incompetence and appoints a guardian with the responsibility to make decisions intended to promote the individual's well-being within the limits defined by the guardianship order. In making that determination of incompetence and defining the range of the guardian's powers, the court makes the primary normative judgment authorizing *parens patriae* interventions for the purpose of promoting the individual's well-being within the range of decisions permitted by the guardianship order.

Insofar as the individual's impairment, the available alternatives, and legally relevant considerations provide the basis to rule out certain interventions as excessively restrictive in light of the legitimate state interest, the court can make these determinations in crafting the guardianship order. In doing so, however, the court ordinarily will not select the least restrictive alternative because ordinarily no single alternative unambiguously qualifies as the least restrictive alternative that fulfills the legitimate state purpose that justifies the intervention. Rather, the court rules out any form of intervention that clearly falls beyond the range of intrusiveness justified by the legitimate state interest and the circumstances. By setting certain boundaries on the acceptable range of placements and treatment modalities, the court defines the range of interventions that fall within the set of arguably least restrictive alternatives from which guardians and clinicians select in order to promote the incompetent individual's well-being.

Courts may well encounter many cases in which they can identify no principled basis for defining the legally appropriate limits on placement or on clinical interventions. In such cases, however, clinicians certainly cannot do so through the exercise of clinical judgment. Thus, it remains proper for clinicians to exercise clinical judgment in selecting from among the available alternatives on the basis of clinical criteria. Clinicians fulfill their responsibilities when they evaluate, prescribe, and treat in a manner intended to promote the patient's clinical interests with the guardian's consent and within the scope of the guardianship order. Clinicians must exercise clinical judgment, but the range of those judgments falls largely within clinical expertise because the determination of incompetence, the guardianship order, and the consent of the guardian define the purpose of the intervention as providing for the clinical well-being of the patient and place any appropriate limits on the form that intervention can take.

The proposed approach distributes responsibility appropriately among individuals, courts, guardians, and clinicians. Competent individuals decide for themselves regarding proposed health care, including the decision regarding admission to the mental health facility. Courts address the normative questions, including the determination of competence or incompetence, the appointment and supervision of a guardian, and the appropriate limits of the guardianship. Guardians exercise surrogate judgement for the incompetent individual within the limits set by the guardianship order and in light of clinical advice. Clinicians exercise professional judgment re-

---

[72] UNIFORM PROBATE CODE § 5–306(c) U.L.A. 365 (1998).

garding clinical questions by evaluating the individual as well as by prescribing and delivering treatment intended to promote the individual's clinical interests with the consent of the guardian and within the range authorized by the guardianship order. I do not contend that all current competence and guardianship statutes provide appropriate vehicles for this approach or that courts consistently apply current statutes in this manner; I contend only that appropriately crafted competence and guardianship statutes provide an existing legal institution that is amenable to interpretation and application in a manner consistent with this proposal.

V.   Applications

Under the approach advanced here, the state would not simply extend Ellen's initial police power commitment into an ongoing *parens patriae* commitment. Rather, when Ellen no longer qualified for police power commitment because she no longer endangered others, the state would either release her from confinement or bring her to a competency hearing. The court would make a determination of incompetence for person because her delusional disorder prevents her from making reasoned decisions regarding her diet and health care. Following the determination of incompetence, the court would appoint a guardian with authority to make decisions regarding treatment and placement as necessary to protect Ellen's well-being. Independent living with regular visits from a visiting nurse or a supervised group home might suffice if Ellen is willing to comply with the necessary diet and blood sugar monitoring in these contexts. Alternately, if she refuses to comply in these settings, protection of her health may require placement on a locked ward comparable to that to which she would be committed under a civil commitment statute.

The court must determine whether the guardian takes only the limited powers to secure the treatment and conditions needed to address her diabetic condition or general authority to make decisions regarding her health care. The range of guardian powers depends on the range of Ellen's incompetence. It is possible in principle that her disorder might distort her reasoning about certain aspects of her treatment without distorting her reasoning about other aspects. Recall that Francine makes reasoned judgments about the treatment plan for her diabetic condition, although her delusional disorder distorts her reasoning regarding the legal process and her psychological condition that constitutes an important consideration relevant to her decisions regarding psychotropic medication.

It is difficult to describe circumstances in which a person who suffers from a delusional disorder remains competent to make reasoned decisions regarding treatment for that delusional disorder. One might reject the treatment for good reasons, including unpleasant or detrimental side effects. A competent choice requires that one balance these reasons to refuse the treatment against the applicable reasons to accept the treatment, however, and this process of reasoning appears to require the ability to comprehend and make reasoned decisions about the importance of improving one's delusional thought processes. It is not clear how one can accurately comprehend the delusional nature of one's delusional beliefs and thought processes or the potential benefits of improving one's delusional disorder. Rather it seems inherent in the notion of a delusional disorder that one is unable to accurately comprehend and reason effectively about that disorder.

It seems likely, therefore, that Ellen lacks competence to make reasoned decisions about her mental health care as well as about her diabetic condition. Therefore, her guardian must make decisions regarding both types of treatment in light of relevant clinical advice. Although her diabetic and delusional disorders may warrant inpatient care, outpatient care or partial hospitalization may provide viable alternatives if the appropriate resources are available and Ellen will cooperate. Clinicians should exercise clinical judgment in prescribing and delivering health care from among the available alternatives that fall within the range of the guardianship order.

In some ways, Nathan and Oliver present easier cases because their initial commitments would fall within the category often referred to as grave disability under some contemporary civil commitment statutes.[73] Both qualify for findings of incompetence and guardianship under the applicable statutes because they are unable to safely care for their basic needs. Oliver suffers dementia and sometimes endangers himself by wandering into traffic or out into the cold without sufficient clothing. Oliver's already diminished capacities for self-care and communication deteriorate more quickly when he lacks a structured schedule of activities. He functions more effectively when involved in a repetitive and predictable schedule. In the absence of any viable treatment that will restore Oliver's capacities, his guardian and the clinicians would seek a placement and treatment plan that provides the supervision that will protect him from injury and the schedule of repetitive activities that tends to maximize his capacities. These resources might be most available at a nursing home or in the state hospital. No obvious issues of lesser or greater restrictiveness arise because any viable option must provide the level of confinement and supervision needed to protect him from harm.

In certain circumstances, the guardian might be forced to balance various interests. Suppose, for example, that one local nursing home offered a relatively rich schedule of activities but lacked secure grounds. This placement would require that Oliver spend most of the day locked in a single building. A different nursing home might provide larger fenced grounds that would allow him to walk outside, but that facility lacks the structured activities. Finally, the state hospital can provide a schedule of activities and fenced in grounds, but the distance from his home would prevent frequent family visits. These circumstances would require that the clinicians advise and the guardian select in a manner that balances various interests. The clinicians would advise on the basis of the clinical judgment regarding the likely clinical benefits and costs of each alternative, however, rather than upon any attempt to apply a least restrictive alternative analysis. On the approach advanced here, the court would have the responsibility to define any limits based on legal considerations in the guardianship order, and the clinicians would have the responsibility to exercise clinical judgment regarding the treatment plan expected to promote Oliver's well-being. Similarly, the guardian would have the responsibility to make decisions expected to promote Oliver's interests.

Nathan resembles Oliver in that he is clearly incompetent for person and in need of protective placement and care. Because of his autistic disorder and self-injurious behavior, he needs custodial care as well as an active treatment plan designed to reduce the frequency and severity of the self-inflicted injuries. Clinical review might suggest that physical restraint, sedation, or behavior therapy including aversive con-

---

[73] *See* chapter 5, section IV for descriptions of Nathan and Oliver.

ditioning would reduce that self-injurious behavior. All three modalities might have some promise and some significant costs. The physical restraint might be expected to prevent the injuries at the cost of substantial loss of freedom. The medication might be expected to reduce the injuries at the cost of sedation that would markedly reduce his general functioning level. The behavior therapy might be expected to reduce the injuries at the cost of experiencing the aversive stimuli. According to the approach advanced here, the court would make the initial determination of incompetence, appoint a guardian, and define any legal limits on the guardian's authority. The clinicians would exercise clinical judgment regarding the treatment recommendations expected to maximize Nathan's clinical interests, and the guardian would select from among the available options in order to promote Nathan's well-being. Neither the guardian nor the clinicians would attempt to evaluate the alternatives in terms of restrictiveness of constitutionally protected liberties.

Recall Irene, who suffers chronic moderate depression that involves dysphoric mood, loss of energy and satisfaction with life's activities, and failure to develop her talents or interests. Irene's depression does not involve delusions, hallucinations, or impairment of reality testing, however, and she accurately understands that she is depressed.[74] She endangers neither others nor herself, but she refuses to participate in any regular treatment program, although she has benefited from treatment in the past. Under the approach advanced here, the state would have no authority to intervene under the *parens patriae* function because she would not qualify for the determination of incompetence that serves as the threshold requirement for *parens patriae* intervention. Clinicians would remain free to advise, to attempt to persuade her to accept the advice, and to provide treatment insofar as Irene consents to participate. Absent a judicial determination of incompetence, however, neither involuntary admission nor involuntary treatment would fall within the state's authority.

VI. Conclusion

The approach to *parens patriae* intervention through the mental health system advanced in chapters 5 and 6 is internally coherent and consistent with the normative structure articulated in chapter 4. It applies the formal conception of legal mental illness developed in chapter 3 and the broad principles revealed by court decisions regarding civil commitment and the right to refuse treatment. I do not claim that the approach discussed here represents the only possible set of institutions that meet these conditions. Rather, I offer an approach that builds upon currently available competence and guardianship provisions in order to illustrate the manner in which a coherent and justifiable set of institutions could be developed.

An important step in developing this approach to *parens patriae* intervention involves disentangling these institutions from those designed to implement the police power function of the mental health system. An integrated framework for mental health law must address both functions, however, and it must do so in a consistent manner. The next three chapters develop an approach to the police power function of mental health law that is consistent with but distinct from the approach advocated for the *parens patriae* function.

---

[74] *See* chapter 4, section IV.

Part III

Police Power Intervention

Chapter 7
NORMATIVE STRUCTURE II:
The Police Power

Clearly distinguishing *parens patriae* and police power interventions facilitates careful analysis of the justification for each. This chapter begins the analysis of police power interventions. Sexual predator statutes provide a particularly cogent focal point for such an analysis because they authorize police power intervention through the mental health system immediately following conviction and punishment in the criminal justice system. This chapter makes use of these statutes in formulating a normative framework for a conceptually consistent and defensible set of institutions for the exercise of the police power. This framework provides the foundation for an interpretation of police power civil commitment as an institution that complements the criminal justice system by providing an alternative form of coercive social control for those who do not qualify as responsible subjects of the criminal justice system. This framework also coheres with that advanced for *parens patriae* intervention in that both reflect the underlying principles of political morality discussed in chapter 4.

I. Police Power Commitment and the Sexual Predator Statutes

Commitment following an insanity acquittal ordinarily provides a clear case of police power intervention. In *Jones v. United States*, the Supreme Court upheld statutes authorizing automatic commitment following an insanity acquittal on the rationale that the insanity verdict establishes mental illness and dangerousness.[1] That case has been criticized because it would allow commitment on the basis of criminal conduct that would not ordinarily establish dangerousness at a civil commitment hearing, because of either the nature of the offense or the passage of time.[2] Jones, for example, was initially arrested on a misdemeanor charge for attempting to steal a coat from a store. The case provides no evidence to suggest that he engaged in violent or threatening behavior during that incident or at any other time.[3] Thus, he might not qualify for commitment under general civil commitment provisions that require dangerousness to persons as evidenced by threats or dangerous behavior. Soon after the arrest, Jones was committed to a hospital for evaluation of his competency to stand trial. Approximately 6 months later, he was found competent to stand trial, acquitted by reason of insanity, and committed pursuant to the postinsanity acquittal provision.[4] Even if one accepts that the insanity verdict establishes mental illness and danger-

---

[1] 463 U.S. 354, 363–66 (1983).

[2] Christopher Slobogin, *Dangerousness as a Criterion in the Criminal Process* in LAW, MENTAL HEALTH, AND MENTAL DISORDER 360, 375 (Bruce D. Sales & Daniel W. Shuman eds., 1996).

[3] *Jones*, 463 U.S. at 359.

[4] *Id.* at 359–600.

ousness at the time of the offense, that verdict addressed Jones's conduct and condition 6 months prior to the acquittal. Thus, it remains plausible that his impairment and dangerousness at the time of the acquittal and postacquittal commitment might differ significantly from his impairment and dangerousness at the time of the crime. The concern that the individual's impairment and dangerousness at the time of the acquittal might differ significantly from those properties at the time of the offense increases as the duration of hospitalization and treatment pursuant to a finding of incompetence to proceed increases.

Although criticism of the *Jones* decision tends to emphasize the issue of dangerousness, *Jones* also failed to provide any analysis supporting its conclusion that legal mental illness for the purpose of the insanity defense establishes legal mental illness for the purpose of commitment. This is particularly significant in light of the Court's discussion of the release criteria. The Court indicated that an insanity acquittee would qualify for release when he was no longer mentally ill or no longer dangerous to himself or to society.[5] These criteria, addressing danger to self or society, suggest that the court accepts continued commitment of those like Ellen who are initially committed under the police power pursuant to a postinsanity acquittal commitment provision, but whose continued commitment rests on a *parens patriae* rationale. Nothing in the opinion suggests that the type of impairment required for continued commitment under a *parens patriae* rationale differs from that required for the insanity acquittal and postacquittal commitment. Thus, the opinion seems to suggest that an insanity acquittal establishes that the individual suffers a type of impairment that supports civil commitment under either the police power or *parens patriae* rationales.

Chapters 4 and 5 argue that *parens patriae* interventions should require incompetence for person. Accepting these arguments raises questions regarding the notion that impairment sufficient to support an insanity acquittal necessarily supports continuing commitment on a *parens patriae* rationale. The cases of Ellen and Francine suggest that impairment establishing legal mental illness for the insanity defense does not necessarily establish it for *parens patriae* intervention. Both Ellen and Francine were legally mentally ill for the purpose of police power intervention, yet Ellen is legally mentally ill for the purpose of *parens patriae* civil commitment at the 90-day review, whereas Francine is not, and this difference does not reflect differential response to treatment or diminution of pathology during the 90-day commitment. Both remain delusional but not grossly disorganized or assaultive.

Although Ellen and Francine remain similar insofar as they continue to manifest similar impairment, Ellen's impairment leads her to make decisions that endanger her, but Francine's does not. One might argue, therefore, that dangerousness, rather than impairment, constitutes the critical factor in differentiating those who are appropriate for *parens patriae* commitment, those who are appropriate for police power commitment, and those for whom neither type of commitment is appropriate. According to this interpretation, any form of psychological impairment can establish legal mental illness for commitment if it causes dangerousness. The type of dangerousness determines the type of commitment in that dangerousness to self supports *parens patriae* commitment and dangerousness to others supports police power commitment.

---

[5] *Id.* at 370.

This interpretation fails for two reasons. First (and as argued in chapters 4 and 5), defensible *parens patriae* commitment in a liberal society requires impairment that renders one incompetent for person. Thus, impairment that produces a danger to one's self does not necessarily qualify as legal mental illness for the purpose of *parens patriae* commitment in a legal system representing coherent principles of liberal political morality. Second, impairment that causes danger to others does not necessarily support police power civil commitment in such a society. Consider, for example, an individual who is chronically angry and mildly depressed. Because of his chronic depression, he finds it difficult to get out of bed in the morning, and because of his chronic anger, he resents the demand that he do so in order to hold a job. Rather than holding a job, he resorts to armed robbery in order to support himself. He qualifies for the diagnostic category of dysthymic disorder, and this impairment plays a causal role in his criminal conduct that endangers others, but it seems clear that he is appropriate for police power intervention through the criminal justice system, rather than through civil commitment to the mental health system.[6]

Similarly, consider a different individual who is mean and aggressive and has a learning disability that renders it difficult for him to read. Since adolescence, he has engaged in a pattern of criminal behavior, including assaults on persons who anger or inconvenience him. When he asks a ticket agent which bus goes uptown, the agent responds "check the signs over the windshields." He assaults the ticket agent because he gets angry when people tell him to read signs he is unable to read. This individual qualifies for the diagnostic categories of reading disorder and APD, and the psychological characteristics that fulfill the diagnostic criteria for these disorders play a causal role in his assaultive conduct that endangers others.[7] It seems clear, however, that he is appropriate for police power intervention through the criminal justice system, rather than through civil commitment to the mental health system. Indeed, various sources indicate that a large portion of prisoners in correctional facilities qualify for the category of APD because the diagnostic criteria for that category depend heavily on a history of antisocial behavior.[8] Yet, these individuals engage in criminal conduct in circumstances in which they qualify as criminally responsible, and the presence of large numbers of individuals with APD in the prisons reflects the societal judgment that they qualify for police power intervention through the criminal justice system.

These cases suggest that police power commitment resembles *parens patriae* commitment insofar as each requires not only impairment of some form but impairment of a type that justifies involuntary intervention through the mental health system specifically. Impairment that renders the individual incompetent for person justifies such intervention under the *parens patriae* function. Cases involving seriously impaired offenders, such as Ellen and Francine, seem to suggest that impairment qualifies as legal mental illness for the purpose of the police power when it renders the person not criminally responsible and, thus, not appropriate to the criminal justice system as the primary institution of police power enforcement. The sexual predator

---

[6] AMERICAN PSYCHIATRIC ASSOCIATION, DIAGNOSTIC AND STATISTICAL MANUAL OF MENTAL DISORDERS 345–49 (4th ed. 1994) [hereinafter DSM–IV].

[7] *Id.* at 48–50 (reading disorder), 645–50 (APD).

[8] DSM–IV, *supra* note 6, at 648; Mark D. Cunningham & Thomas J. Reidy, *Antisocial Personality Disorder and Psychopathy: Diagnostic Dilemmas in Classifying Patterns of Antisocial Behavior in Sentencing Evaluations*, 16 BEHAV. SCI. & L. 333, 341 (1998).

statutes call this interpretation into question, however, because they authorize civil commitment of those who have been held criminally responsible for the criminal conduct that provides the basis for police power commitment under these provisions. These statutes seem to indicate that certain mental abnormalities or personality disorders render one appropriate for police power civil commitment without undermining one's status as criminally responsible for the conduct that supports the criminal convictions, the civil commitment, and the diagnoses.

II.   Sexual Predator Statutes, Criminal Incarceration, and Civil Commitment

The sexual predator statutes instantiate pure police power commitment. They also provide an opportunity to examine closely the appropriate conception of legal mental illness for the purpose of police power intervention as well as the defensible relationship between the criminal justice system and the mental health system as institutions of coercive social control under the police power. These statutes authorize pure police power intervention in that they address those who endanger others, authorize commitment for the purpose of protecting the public from these individuals, and include no requirement that these individuals suffer any impairment that renders them incompetent to make reasoned decisions about their own health care. By authorizing ostensibly *civil* commitment on the basis of disorders defined largely in terms of the tendency to engage in criminal conduct, they pointedly raise important questions regarding the appropriate conception of legal mental illness for this purpose and regarding the justification for resorting to commitment rather than relying on the criminal justice system.

Although the Kansas and Washington statutes differ in some respects, they share several key provisions that illustrate important factors relevant to the two previously identified questions. These concerns permeate civil commitment generally, but the sexual predator statutes raise them more explicitly. Both statutes provide for indefinite civil commitment of sexually violent predators.[9] Both statutes define the category of sexually violent predators as "any person who has been convicted of or charged with a crime of sexual violence and who suffers from a mental abnormality or personality disorder which makes the person likely to engage in the predatory acts of sexual violence if not confined in a secure facility."[10] Both statutes include individuals who have been found incompetent to stand trial regarding sexually violent offenses and those who have been found NGRI for sexually violent offenses within the category of those charged with a crime of sexual violence.[11]

These statutes resemble more general civil commitment statutes insofar as the requirements of a mental abnormality or personality disorder that makes the individual likely to engage in sexual violence are analogous to the more general civil

---

[9] KAN. STAT. ANN. § 59-29a07 (Supp. 1997); WASH. REV. CODE ANN. § 71.09.060 (Supp. 1998).

[10] KAN. STAT. ANN. § 59-29a02a (Supp. 1997); WASH. REV. CODE ANN. § 71.09.020(1) (Supp. 1998).

[11] KAN. STAT. ANN. § 59-29a03(2), (3) (Supp. 1997); WASH. REV. CODE ANN. § 71.09.030 (Supp. 1998).

commitment criteria of mental illness and dangerousness.[12] Insofar as these provisions are applied to offenders who suffer severe impairment, they are redundant with general civil commitment statutes and with specialized provisions providing for commitment pursuant to findings of incompetence to proceed or of NGRI. Either these specialized provisions, the general civil commitment statutes, or the sexual predator statutes could provide for the commitment of individuals who commit relevant offenses while suffering severe impairment that supports the findings (a) that they are incompetent to stand trial for those offenses, or (b) that they are NGRI for those offenses.

The legislative findings make it clear, however, that these sexual predator statutes are not intended to address offenders who suffer severe impairment. Rather, they provide for commitment of dangerous offenders who do not manifest impairment of a type that renders them appropriate for commitment under general commitment statutes.[13] Both statutes define a mental abnormality as "a congenital or acquired condition affecting the emotional or volitional capacity which predisposes the person to the commission of criminal sexual acts in a degree constituting such person a menace to the health and safety of others."[14] Although neither statute provides a definition of "personality disorder," the Washington supreme court interpreted this statutory term with reference to the category of Personality Disorders as defined in the American Psychiatric Association's *Diagnostic and Statistical Manual of Mental Disorders.*[15]

Sexual predator statutes invite controversy partially because they authorize commitment of individuals who manifest only these statutory mental abnormalities or personality disorders rather than severe impairment of a type that would ordinarily support civil commitment. Furthermore, they authorize commitment of offenders who have served criminal sentences for their sexually violent offenses and who demonstrate no evidence of deterioration in their psychological capacities since they were convicted of these offenses. Cases brought under these statutes frequently demonstrate this pattern. The subjects of the petitions for commitment in these cases had recently completed, or were approaching completion of, sentences for repetitive violent sexual offenses. None of these offenders carried diagnoses that indicated serious impairment of orientation, consciousness, comprehension, reasoning, or reality testing. They carried diagnoses (including APD and the paraphilias) that can be based heavily upon the demonstrated propensity to commit such offenses. Although the appellate opinions provide only partial reference to the expert testimony, these references indicate that this testimony emphasized the pattern of criminal conduct that generated the conviction and sentences.[16]

The legislative findings indicate that the purpose and justification of the distinct

---

[12] John Parry, *Involuntary Civil Commitment in the 90s: A Constitutional Perspective*, 18 MENTAL & PHYSICAL DISABILITY L. REP. 320 (1994).

[13] KAN. STAT. ANN. § 59-29a01 (1994); WASH. REV. CODE ANN. § 71.09.010 (Supp. 1998).

[14] KAN. STAT. ANN. § 59-29a02(b) (Supp. 1997); WASH. REV. CODE ANN. § 71.09.020(2) (Supp. 1998).

[15] In Re Young, 857 P2d 989, 1002–03 (Wash. 1993); DSM–IV, *supra* note 6, at 629–34. The court referred the then current third revised edition.

[16] In Re Hendricks, 912 P.2d 129, 131, 137–38 (Kan. 1996); State v. Carpenter, 541 N.W.2d 105, 108–09 (Wis. 1995); In Re Linehan, 557 N.W.2d 171, 175–79 (Min. 1996); State v. Post, 541 N.W.2d 115, 119 (Wis. 1995); In Re Young, 857 P.2d at 989, 994–96.

sexual predator commitment provisions rest on the premise that the general commitment statutes do not apply to these individuals who do not suffer severe impairment and whose proclivity to commit sexual offenses has not diminished following the completion of their criminal sentences.[17] The sexual predator statutes allow commitment partially on the basis of prior criminal acts, requiring no more recent overt act indicating dangerousness for those who have been confined during the period since those criminal offenses.[18] This omission reflects the tacit assumption that the characteristics of these offenders that led to the perpetration of the sex offenses that resulted in their initial criminal convictions endure through the time of their mandatory release dates. Furthermore, the cases implementing these statutes justify continued confinement by reference to the criminal conduct for which these individuals have been criminally convicted and punished. In this respect, these provisions depart from statutes that authorize commitment of sex offenders as an alternative to criminal incarceration.[19]

These cases and statutes force us to confront the previously identified questions regarding the appropriate relationship between the criminal justice and mental health systems as instruments of coercive social control. The criminal justice system and police power civil commitment serve as two alternate legal institutions for the exercise of the police power. As ordinarily understood, the state exercises coercive social control over adults primarily through the criminal justice system, but police power civil commitment provides an alternative institution more appropriate to those who endanger others as a result of serious mental illness. According to this interpretation, the two seem to provide complementary institutions, with the criminal justice system providing the primary institution of coercive social control for most competent adults, and civil commitment providing an alternative for the small minority of adults who require police power intervention but suffer psychological impairment that renders them inappropriate for conviction and punishment through the criminal justice system.[20]

The sexual predator statutes appear inconsistent with this interpretation because they subject some individuals to both criminal incarceration and police power civil commitment in the absence of any reason to think that their psychological condition has changed. The *Hendricks* majority implicitly recognizes the justificatory concerns raised by this sequential conviction, incarceration, and civil commitment. The majority opinion suggests a line of reasoning intended to address these concerns when it concludes that the substantive criteria for commitment contained in the Kansas statute's definition of a sexual predator satisfy the requirements of due process. The reasoning supporting this conclusion relies heavily on the contention that these criteria limit confinement to "those who are unable to control their dangerousness."[21] The majority opinion strongly suggests that this putative inability to control is central to the constitutional adequacy of the statute at issue in *Hendricks*.[22]

The majority opinion explicitly recognizes freedom from physical restraint as

---

[17] KAN. STAT. ANN. § 59-29a01 (Supp. 1997); WASH. REV. CODE ANN. § 71.09.010 (Supp. 1998).

[18] WASH. REV. CODE ANN. § 71.09.060 (Supp. 1998).

[19] Allen v. Illinois, 478 U.S. 364 (1986).

[20] Eric S. Janus, *Preventing Sexual Violence: Setting Principled Constitutional Boundaries on Sex Offender Commitments*, 72 IND. L.J. 157 (1996).

[21] Kansas v. Hendricks, 117 S.Ct. 2072, 2080 (1997).

[22] *Id.* at 2079–81.

central to the liberty protected by the Due Process Clause of the Fourteenth Amendment, but it also recognizes legitimate exceptions from this protection for the civil detainment of those who endanger others because they are unable to control their behavior. The opinion draws an analogy between these civil detainment statutes and the sexual predator statute at issue in *Hendricks*. The majority opinion emphasizes Hendricks's diagnosis as a pedophile and his claim that he is unable to control his urge to molest children in its analysis of his pedophilia as a mental abnormality that makes him likely to engage in acts of sexual violence as required by the statute, and it refers to this apparent volitional impairment in differentiating him from those who are more properly addressed through the criminal justice system.[23] The majority concludes: "[t]his admitted lack of volitional control, coupled with a prediction of future dangerousness, adequately distinguishes Hendricks from other dangerous persons who are perhaps more properly dealt with exclusively through criminal proceedings.[24]

The *Hendricks* Court did not explicitly hold that the Kansas statute was constitutional only if it was interpreted as incorporating the requirement that those committed under it must be unable to control their conduct. This notion of volitional impairment or inability to control plays a central role in the majority's interpretation of the statute as consistent with due process, however, and the majority opinion provides no alternative criterion that would distinguish those subject to commitment from those appropriate to coercive social control only through the criminal justice system. Unfortunately, the *Hendricks* majority provides neither a satisfactory account of this purported inability to control behavior nor any explanation regarding its justificatory significance. The opinion advances no reason to believe that Hendricks was unable to control his criminal conduct. The majority merely repeats his unsubstantiated and unexplained assertion that he was unable to control his extended pattern of planned, organized, goal-directed, and secretive behavior. The opinion provides neither an explanation regarding what this claim means nor any account of the type of evidence that would support a claim that a particular individual either was or was not able to control the apparently deliberate and organized patterns of conduct at issue in these cases. Finally, the court supplies no analysis that would reconcile this putative inability to control the criminal conduct with the prior finding of criminal responsibility.[25]

In summary, the sexual predator statutes and the Court's opinion in *Hendricks* reveal but fail to address a series of important questions regarding the relationship between the criminal justice and mental health systems as legal institutions through which the state exercises the police power. This series includes at least the following questions. First, what specific conception of legal mental illness justifies treating some people differently than most competent adults by exercising coercive social control over them through the mental health system, rather than or in addition to the criminal justice system? Second, in what manner does this conception of legal mental illness justify the state in treating people who are mentally ill in this sense differently

---

[23] *Id.*

[24] *Id.* at 2081.

[25] Stephen J. Morse, *Culpability and Control*, 142 U. Pa. L. Rev. 1587 (1994); Robert F. Schopp, Automatism, Insanity, and the Psychology of Criminal Responsibility: A Philosophical Inquiry § 6.3 (1991).

than it treats most people who violate the criminal law? Third, what type of impairment could render Hendricks legally mentally ill in this sense that subjects him to civil commitment because he was unable to control his sexual conduct but not prevent him from fulfilling the well-established voluntary act requirement for criminal responsibility regarding that conduct?[26]

III.   Coercive Social Control in the Public Domain

A.   Parens Patriae *and Police Power in the Liberal Society*

Chapter 4 sketches a normative structure for a liberal society that accords equal respect to competent adults in the form of equal standing in the public jurisdiction and sovereign discretion in the nonpublic domain. The justification for state intervention under the police power differs fundamentally from the justification for *parens patriae* interventions, but these justifications cohere in legal institutions reflecting this common normative structure. Although the state's *parens patriae* function involves interventions into the ordinarily protected nonpublic domain, the state exercises the police power in regulating the public domain. The police power regulates the public domain through legal institutions that protect individuals from illegal intrusions by others and that provide those individuals with the opportunity to avoid state intervention by directing their conduct in accordance with law. The criminal justice and mental health systems provide institutions of coercive police power intervention. These institutions can cohere with each other and with the underlying normative framework if they adopt appropriate conceptions of legal mental illness for this purpose.

B.   The Criminal Justice System

The criminal justice system protects individual self-determination and equal standing by proscribing, preventing, and punishing actions by some citizens that violate the rights and interests of others. Thus, the criminal law not only maintains the widely accepted standards of public morality that order cooperative social interaction in the public domain, it also articulates certain contours of each individual's protected domain of individual discretion by proscribing specified types of intrusions as crimes.[27] When a liberal state enforces the core rules of the criminal law, it not only strives to maintain the public order and safety through deterrence and restraint, it also vindicates the equal standing of the victims by punishing and condemning conduct that violates their right to direct their own lives within the limits set by law.

    The criminal law proscribes certain types of conduct and prescribes punishment

---

[26] AMERICAN LAW INSTITUTE, MODEL PENAL CODE AND COMMENTARIES § 2.01 (final code and revised commentaries 1985) [hereinafter MPC].

[27] Some types of activity might be criminalized for other reasons. Perjury, for example, is proscribed in order to promote the effectiveness of the legal system, and securities regulations are designed to promote effective functioning of the economy. Crimes such as those against person and property, however, partially define the individual's sphere of sovereignty by forbidding others from intruding into those areas.

for those who are convicted of engaging in those types of conduct under conditions of culpability as defined by the code. By doing so, the criminal law guides social behavior through several different mechanisms. Most obviously, it is intended to prevent criminal conduct through incapacitation and deterrence.[28] Perhaps more important, however, it serves as an official representation of an important part of the widely accepted standards of public morality. As such, it articulates boundaries of socially acceptable behavior in the public jurisdiction, providing guidelines for voluntary compliance by those who accept a responsibility to conform to those standards. To the extent that the criminal law converges with standards widely held among citizens, it is likely to be accepted by the majority as representative of the public morality, thus reinforcing those standards and helping to shape them.

Insofar as it represents, reinforces, and shapes the accepted public morality, the expressive function of the criminal law may influence behavior more effectively than does the attempt to direct conduct through enforcement.[29] Although legal institutions maintain a variety of incentives intended to influence behavior, criminal punishment differs markedly from alternative means of altering incentives through law such as those involving fees, taxes, or civil compensatory damages. In contrast to these alternative methods, criminal punishment carries expressive significance that serves unique functions for the widely accepted public morality. Joel Feinberg argues that moral condemnation inheres in the concept of punishment and that this expression of condemnation differentiates criminal punishment from alternative forms of incentive such as those mentioned above. Condemnation in this sense includes both reprobation, as a stern message of disapproval, and resentment, as angry or vengeful attitudes.[30]

The core rules of the criminal law proscribe violations of person and property, expressing widely accepted moral standards within the society.[31] By setting minimally acceptable standards of morally relevant social behavior that correspond at least roughly with widely accepted moral standards and by prescribing punishment for violations of these standards, the criminal law provides an official representation of an important component of the accepted standards of public morality. The forms of punishment ordinarily prescribed for those who culpably engage in the proscribed conduct become socially acknowledged symbols of moral condemnation. Execution and imprisonment, for example, take on special significance as symbols of moral condemnation in a society that relies primarily upon these modes of punishment for serious crimes.

The expressive significance of these modes of punishment and of criminal prohibition becomes reciprocally reinforcing. That is, criminal prohibition communicates an expression of condemnation partially by prescribing these paradigmatic forms of

---

[28] WAYNE R. LaFave & AUSTIN W. SCOTT, JR., SUBSTANTIVE CRIMINAL LAW § 1.5 (1986).

[29] H. L. A. HART, A CONCEPT OF LAW 38–39, 193–98 (1961). The enforcement process serves both as a direct tool of coercive behavior control and as a means of communicating the expressive function. Thus, to a certain extent, enforcement constitutes one means of expression. JOEL FEINBERG, DOING AND DESERVING 95–118 (1970). For recent work examining the relationship between criminal law and informally held views of relevant aspects of the public morality, see NORMAN J. FINKEL, COMMONSENSE JUSTICE (1995); PAUL H. ROBINSON & JOHN M. DARLEY, JUSTICE, LIABILITY, AND BLAME (1995).

[30] FEINBERG, supra note 29, at 95–118.

[31] MPC, supra note 26, at Part II; HERBERT MORRIS, ON GUILT AND INNOCENCE 33 (1976).

punishment, and these forms of punishment communicate condemnation partially because they are reserved for serious crimes that violate the widely accepted public morality. For this reason, some penalties that do not carry the same traditional expressive significance can express condemnation if the court applies them in the context of criminal conviction. Probation, fines, or house arrest, for example, can express condemnation within limits if they are associated with criminal conviction. Similarly, people may cease to view certain offenses as criminal if the courts consistently apply only relatively ambiguous forms of penalty, such as fines. Thus, courts sometimes resort to imprisonment in circumstances that do not require it for incapacitation because the courts understand that only with a sentence of incarceration can they unambiguously condemn the conduct.[32]

Paradigmatic cases involving conviction and punishment of fully culpable defendants for committing criminal offenses that violate widely accepted moral standards express condemnation of five different types at two levels of analysis. First, criminal offense definitions condemn categories of conduct at the institutional level by proscribing those types of behavior and prescribing punishment. The court or the jury expresses the second through fourth types of condemnation at the level of specific application by convicting a defendant of a crime. Conviction expresses the second type of condemnation by ratifying the institutional condemnation of the general category of behavior proscribed by the offense definition, and it expresses the third type of condemnation by conveying the jury's condemnation of this particular instance of the prohibited type. Fourth, conviction in any system that requires culpability for conviction condemns the defendant as one who violated the criminal law under conditions of culpability by systemic standards. Fifth, conviction condemns the defendant as morally blameworthy by systemic standards for wrongful behavior.[33]

Certain cases fail to qualify for all five types of condemnation, but the first and fourth types inhere in criminal punishment in criminal justice systems such as those in the United States and many other countries.[34] The fourth type is particularly significant for the purpose of this chapter. Criminal justice systems such as those in the United States adopt systemic criteria of culpability that limit criminal responsibility to those who deserve punishment by virtue of violating an offense definition while meeting these criteria. These include, for example, the requirements of a voluntary act and a specified mental state such as purpose, knowledge, or recklessness, as well as the lack of any impairment that would ground an excuse.[35]

Many legal theorists limit the justified application of punishment to individuals who meet the systemic criteria of culpability by requiring that the person knowingly and voluntarily committed an offense. These theorists argue that distribution of punishment to individuals on the basis of the retributive principles of guilt and desert restricts justified punishment to those who violate the law despite a fair opportunity to conform and maintains the criminal justice system of a liberal society as a choos-

---

[32] United States v. Bergman, 416 F. Supp. 496 (S.D.N.Y. 1976).

[33] ROBERT F. SCHOPP, JUSTIFICATION DEFENSES AND JUST CONVICTIONS §§ 2.3.1, 2.3.2 (1998) (providing a more detailed discussion of the condemnation inherent in punishment).

[34] Id. at § 2.3.2.

[35] MPC, supra note 26, at §§ 2.01, 2.02, 4.01. Minimally retributive theories and institutions are those that require desert by systemic standards as a necessary condition for the justification of punishment. Some might argue that these systems are, or ought to be, retributive in a stronger sense. For the purpose of this book I take no position on that issue.

ing system for persons who direct their lives through the exercise of reasoned choice.[36] By limiting punishment to knowing and voluntary offenders, criminal justice systems express respect for persons as beings who possess the capacity to direct their lives through the exercise of reason. These theorists identify rule-based criminal justice systems as providing a method of behavior guidance uniquely appropriate to those who possess this capacity. Liberal states respect the standing of competent adults by establishing rule-based criminal justice systems as the form of coercive behavior control that is uniquely appropriate to them. Thus, they limit criminal punishment to those who possess the capacities required to qualify for this status, and they recognize rule-based criminal justice systems with appropriate criteria of culpability as the only legitimate form of coercive state behavior guidance for these persons.[37]

These approaches to the justification of criminal punishment recognize the preventive purpose of the criminal justice system. They also pursue a retributive purpose through the application of retributive principles in the distribution of punishment. By limiting the manner in which the state pursues the retributive goal, retributive institutions of punishment express respect for responsible agents and constitute part of a social structure that enables people to function as rational agents.

This view of the criminal justice system as a social behavior-guiding mechanism designed to prevent offenses while maintaining a choosing system that respects persons through the application of retributive principles is consistent with contemporary American law. Current penal codes define offenses according to a structure of offense elements, including the requirement of a voluntary act and a specified mental state such as purpose, knowledge, or recklessness.[38] Additional defenses exculpate defendants who satisfy the offense definitions under conditions that prevent them from directing their conduct through reasoned choice in a manner that supports attribution of culpability.[39] Finally, general civil commitment statutes are ordinarily written, interpreted, and applied in a manner that limits confinement for protection and involuntary therapy to those who suffer some major mental illness that prevents them from directing their lives through reasoned choice.[40] These statutes serve both to exclude responsible agents from coercive therapy and to provide an alternative method of behavior control for those who are not rational agents, thus preserving the criminal justice system as uniquely applicable to those who qualify as responsible persons.

Condemnation of the defendant as a culpable transgressor carries particular significance for understanding the relationship between criminal incarceration and police power civil commitment in a liberal society. This expression of condemnation inherent in criminal conviction and punishment in a minimally retributivist criminal justice system reaffirms the standing of the defendant as one who qualifies for equal

---

[36] H. L. A. HART, PUNISHMENT AND RESPONSIBILITY 22–24, 44–49 (1968).

[37] SCHOPP, *supra* note 25, at § 7.4.

[38] MPC, *supra* note 26, at §§ 2.01, 2.02.

[39] *Id.* at § 4.01 (insanity), 2.09 (duress); PAUL H. ROBINSON, CRIMINAL LAW DEFENSES §§ 25(a), 161(a)(2) (1984). These excuses exculpate defendants who performed offenses under conditions such that they were not responsible (liability responsibility) for their conduct.

[40] SAMUEL J. BRAKEL, JOHN PARRY, & BARBARA A. WEINER, THE MENTALLY DISABLED AND THE LAW 24–25 (1985). The claim here is that the legal institutions are designed in this manner, not that they always function according to design.

standing in the public domain. It serves this function because the requirements of criminal responsibility limit criminal liability to those who violate the criminal law while possessing the capacities necessary to direct their conduct in compliance with a rule based legal system through a process of competent practical reasoning. Thus, by trying and convicting the defendant in the retributive criminal justice system rather than resorting, for example, to civil commitment to the mental health system, legal institutions treat the defendant as a citizen who possesses the capacities required for equal standing in the public jurisdiction.

Interpreted in this manner, these requirements of criminal responsibility consti-tute criteria of retributive competence in the sense that those who possess the ca-pacities required for criminal responsibility are competent to participate in the min-imally retributive criminal justice system as the primary legal institution of coercive social control in the public jurisdiction. By retaining the minimally retributive crim-inal justice system as the primary institution for the exercise of the police power, the liberal society directs the conduct of those who are retributively competent in a manner that provides these individuals with the opportunity to direct their own lives within the bounds set by enacted law through the exercise of the capacities they possess as unimpaired adults. Thus, the liberal society promotes the opportunity for self-determination in the public jurisdiction by setting the bounds on individual choice through a democratic legislative process in which competent adults are eli-gible to participate and by enforcing those bounds through the minimally retributive criminal justice system.

Police power intervention through the mental health system provides an alter-native means of police power intervention for those who lack the capacities of retributive competence that render one eligible to participate in the criminal justice system that provides the primary institution of coercive social control. Those who suffer impairment that renders them not criminally responsible lack the capacities required to participate fully in the public jurisdiction. These individuals qualify as legally mentally ill for the purpose of participation as responsible subjects of the minimally retributive criminal justice system. Civil commitment provides an alter-native form of coercive intervention appropriate to those who lack retributive com-petence. To maintain a defensible and coherent set of legal institutions of coercive social control, a liberal society needs a conception of legal mental illness for the purpose of criminal responsibility that accurately identifies those who are appropriate for alternative police power interventions because they lack the retributive compe-tence that would render them appropriately subject to social control through the criminal justice system.

IV.   Legal Mental Illness: Criminal Responsibility and Retributive Competence

A.   *Legal Mental Illness as Lack of Competence*

Properly interpreted, competence can provide a unifying concept that generates in-stitutions of police power intervention that cohere with each other and with the *parens patriae* institutions. As applied to determinations of legal competence re-garding various domains of decision making, competence ordinarily requires the capacities needed to engage in reasoned choice regarding decisions within that domain.[41] As interpreted in chapters 3 to 4, impairment that renders individuals incompetent to make reasoned decisions regarding their well-being constitutes legal mental illness for state *parens patriae* functions. This conception of legal mental illness coheres with the principles underlying the legal institutions of a liberal society because it allows state intervention to promote well-being within the limits set by the value for self-determination. It also conforms to the principles of patient-centered health care delivery because it protects sovereign discretion regarding self-regarding decisions but allows intervention to protect the well-being of those who lack the relevant capacities.

Consider the possibility that an analogous conception of retributive competence can provide a defensible notion of legal mental illness that generates integrated institutions of police power intervention. According to this interpretation of the legal significance of psychological impairment, competence for particular functions provides a common core to the meaning of legal mental illness for police power and *parens patriae* intervention. The same abstract conception of competence as the capacities needed to perform a particular task in the circumstances applies to both functions. Both apply the same formal conception of legal mental illness as functional impairment rendering the individual incapable of adequately performing the psychological operations specified in the criteria of eligibility for the legal status at issue. Incompetence for person constitutes the threshold criterion for *parens patriae* intervention. Courts address involuntary admission and treatment as dispositional options following such determinations of incompetence. A parallel analysis supports the contention that police power interventions through the mental health component of the institution of social control should apply only to those who suffer impairment rendering them incapable of performing the operations necessary to qualify as competent to participate in the retributive criminal justice system of social control. The requirements of criminal responsibility implicitly articulate standards of competence to direct one's conduct in compliance with a rule-based system through the process of practical reasoning, and thus, to participate in a retributive system of criminal justice in the capacity of a responsible agent. Individuals who meet this standard are retributively competent in the sense that they possess the capacities required to participate with equal standing in the criminal justice system that orders the public domain.

The capacities needed to engage in a minimally adequate process of practical reasoning constitute retributive competence because those who possess these capacities have an opportunity to participate in the public jurisdiction in a manner that is unique to unimpaired adult human beings.[42] These capacities include the ability to form accurate beliefs about their own priorities, wants, and circumstances, including the legal limits on their conduct; an associative process that enables them to call the relevant wants and beliefs to awareness; and the ability to reason accurately about the relationships among the relevant wants, beliefs, and legal consequences. Those who possess these capacities have the opportunity to pursue the projects and values

---

[41] ALLEN E. BUCHANAN & DAN W. BROCK, DECIDING FOR OTHERS 18–25, 48–51(1989).

[42] By "unimpaired adults" I do not mean those who suffer no impairment of any kind. Rather, I exclude only those who suffer serious impairment that renders them unable to engage in the minimal level of deliberation and decision making required for criminal responsibility in the public jurisdiction. The determination regarding the level of impairment required to undermine this status unavoidably includes normative judgments.

by which they define their lives in such a manner as to participate in the public jurisdiction according to the contingencies set by the criminal law without directly experiencing the aversive consequences prescribed by the criminal justice system. Thus, they have the opportunity to exercise the capacities of practical reasoning in order to pursue their lives without subjecting themselves to the aversive consequences prescribed for those who violate the criminal law while fulfilling systemic criteria of culpability.[43]

Conviction and punishment in the retributive criminal justice system entails condemnation of the person convicted as one who has violated an offense definition under conditions of culpability by systemic standards.[44] Some individuals lack the capacities necessary to justify such condemnation. When these individuals engage in behavior that otherwise would warrant societal intervention through the criminal justice system for the purpose of social control, society must exercise that control through an alternative institution that neither expresses condemnation of the individual as culpable nor requires retributive competence as a criterion of eligibility. Police power civil commitment provides one such alternative institution.

The conception of retributive competence discussed here differs significantly from the familiar notion of competence to proceed in the criminal process. Competence to proceed involves the capacities needed to participate in the criminal proceedings, including, for example, the criminal trial or sentencing hearing. Competence to proceed ordinarily requires the capacities to comprehend the proceedings and communicate with an attorney in order to participate in one's own defense.[45] Retributive competence, in contrast, addresses the individual's capacities at the time of the offense, rather than at the time of the trial or sentencing proceeding. Retributive competence requires the capacities needed to fulfill the requirements of criminal responsibility regarding the conduct that violates an offense definition. Those who qualify as retributively competent have the capacities needed to direct their conduct in the public domain through the exercise of reasoned choice in light of the limits set by the criminal justice system.

This conception of retributive competence converges with the traditional analysis of criminal responsibility. Theorists identify four senses of "responsibility": role responsibility, causal responsibility, liability responsibility, and capacity responsibility. The last two senses are central to attributions of criminal responsibility. An individual is responsible for his crimes in the sense of liability responsibility if he is appropriately held liable to criminal conviction and punishment for those crimes. In order to qualify for liability responsibility, that individual must meet all criteria for criminal liability under the criminal justice system. "Capacity responsibility" refers to one important set of these criteria, involving the psychological capacities, such as comprehension, reality testing, and reasoning, that are necessary to fulfill the conditions of culpability required by the criminal law.[46] Capacity responsibility constitutes a necessary but not sufficient condition for liability responsibility for most serious crimes in a minimally retributive criminal justice system.[47]

---

[43] SCHOPP, *supra note* 25, at §§ 4.3, 6.5, 7.4.

[44] *See* section III.

[45] LaFave & Scott, *supra note* 28, at § 4.4.

[46] HART, *supra note* 36, at 211–22.

[47] *See* section III.

One might say that one person is appropriately held responsible for his criminal behavior but the second is not because the first is a responsible adult but the second is not. The apparent ambiguity in this statement is resolved when one understands that the first use of "responsible" refers to liability responsibility, but the second use of that term refers to capacity responsibility. Thus, the statement asserts that the first person is appropriately held liable to conviction and punishment but the second is not because the first has the psychological capacities necessary to fulfill the required conditions of culpability, but the second does not. Ordinarily, statements of the form "X is a responsible adult" attribute capacity responsibility, but statements of the form "X should be held responsible for that conduct" prescribe liability responsibility.

Most important for the purpose of this chapter, this traditional analysis of criminal responsibility coheres with an interpretation of criminal responsibility as requiring retributive competence. The capacities that constitute capacity responsibility qualify an individual as retributively competent because they enable that individual to adequately fulfill the role of a competent participant in the rule-based criminal justice system. Although these capacities qualify individuals as retributively competent, retributive competence is not sufficient to establish criminal responsibility as that notion is usually applied. Most adults are retributively competent, but they are not criminally responsible unless they engage in criminal behavior without justification while meeting the systemic requirements of culpability. Thus, retributive competence is the legal status for which individuals qualify by possessing the capacities that allow them to fulfill the requirements of criminal responsibility regarding specific behavior when they engage in that behavior in circumstances that provide the opportunity to bring those capacities to bear on that behavior.

The capacities of retributive competence enable the individual to participate in the public jurisdiction as a subject of a minimally retributive criminal justice system. The criteria of criminal responsibility for a particular system define the requirements of retributive competence in that system, and impairment that renders one unable to fulfill those requirements constitutes legal mental illness that renders one ineligible for the status of retributive competence. Legal mental illness of this type undermines eligibility for participation in the criminal justice system that orders the public jurisdiction of the liberal society, and it renders one appropriate for alternative forms of social control under the police power. An exhaustive review of the mainstream requirements of criminal responsibility would extend beyond the scope of this book. The following sections of this chapter demonstrate that this interpretation is consistent with several widely accepted standards.[48]

B.   Cognitive Standards

Cognitive deficits can undermine criminal responsibility for a particular crime by preventing the individual from fulfilling the mental state required by the offense definition. Recklessness, for example, requires conscious disregard of a substantial and unjustifiable risk that one's conduct will cause the harm prohibited by an offense definition.[49] A defendant with serious mental retardation might fail to fulfill this

---

[48] For a more complete analysis, *see* SCHOPP, *supra* note 25.

[49] MPC, *supra* note 26, at § 2.02(2)(c).

offense element because this defendant does not consciously perceive and disregard a risk that a person of ordinary intelligence would recognize. In this manner, this defendant might not fulfill the offense elements for reckless homicide, for example, despite engaging in conduct that causes a death and that most people would recognize as creating a substantial and unjustified risk of death.[50]

Impaired capacities are not necessary to this defense claim, however, because misleading circumstances rather than impaired capacities can support unambiguous applications. Consider the following case: An unimpaired defendant turns off the heat to the garage in the winter, unaware that an inebriated homeless person is hiding there; the homeless person subsequently dies of exposure. The defendant might fail to meet the mental state requirement for reckless homicide because he or she did not know that anyone was seeking refuge in the garage. Defense claims of this type frequently would not take a form conducive to interpretation in terms of retributive competence because they rely on claims about misleading circumstances rather than impaired capacities or lack of criminal responsibility. Indeed, some jurisdictions reject expert evidence regarding psychological impairment when that evidence is offered as relevant to a "diminished capacity" or "diminished responsibility" defense regarding the mental element required by the offense definition.[51]

The most common formulations of the insanity defense include cognitive standards consistent with an interpretation of this excuse in terms of retributive competence. Consider, for example, the traditional *M'Naghten* test and the recent federal variation of that standard. The traditional *M'Naghten* standard exculpates a defendant who commits an offense while "labouring under such a defect of reason, from disease of the mind, as to not know the nature and quality of the act he was doing; or, if he did know it, that he did not know that he was doing what was wrong."[52] Similarly, the federal variation exculpates a defendant who "as a result of severe mental disease or defect, was unable to appreciate the nature and quality or the wrongfulness of his acts."[53] Although the latter standard adopts "appreciate" rather than "know," it is difficult to advance a plausible interpretation that differentiates these standards. Furthermore, the courts tend to interpret the nature and quality disjuncts narrowly. Thus, both standards address most plausible cases as involving questions regarding knowledge of wrongfulness.[54]

Although these provisions are often referred to as ignorance standards, they differ from claims of ignorance regarding the requirements of knowledge or recklessness in the offense definitions in that knowledge of wrongfulness is not an offense element for the vast majority of offenses. Furthermore, these standards exculpate on the basis of ignorance only if the defendant suffers impairment that produces that ignorance. The traditional formulation requires a defect of reason from disease of the mind, and the federal provision requires a mental disease or defect that renders the defendant unable to appreciate the wrongfulness. The precise meaning of these terms remains controversial, but neither standard exculpates on the basis of a mere failure of knowledge.[55] Rather, both require impairment that renders the individual unable to perform

---

[50] *Id.* at § 210.3(1)(a).

[51] LaFave & Scott, *supra* note 28, at § 4.7.

[52] M'Naghten's Case, 8 Eng. Rep. 718, 722 (1843).

[53] 18 U.S.C. § 17(a) (1986).

[54] Schopp, *supra* note 25, at § 2.1.

[55] *Id.* at §§ 2.1, 3.2.

the psychological operations needed to accurately recognize the wrongfulness of the conduct that fulfills the objective elements of the offense definitions.

Although these standards are less than fully satisfactory in a number of ways, they represent standards of criminal responsibility consistent with the interpretation of criminal responsibility as requiring retributive competence and with the interpretation of legal mental illness for this purpose as impairment that renders one unable to engage in the operations needed to qualify for retributive competence. They define the criteria of eligibility for the status of criminally responsible in terms of the ability to perform the psychological operations necessary to accurately identify the wrongfulness of conduct. Psychological impairment that renders one unable to perform these psychological operations constitutes legal mental illness for this purpose. Those who suffer legal mental illness of this type lack the capacities required to qualify as criminally responsible and to justify the condemnation inherent in conviction and punishment. Thus, they lack the capacities required for retributive competence.

C. Volitional Standards

The most common contemporary version of an insanity defense that includes a volitional clause exculpates an offender if "as a result of mental disease or defect he lacks substantial capacity . . . to conform his conduct to the requirements of the law."[56] Volitional standards have been widely criticized. This criticism frequently suggests that the problem is primarily evidentiary. Critics contend that neither experts nor the courts have the ability to accurately differentiate those who are unable to conform to the requirements of law from those who simply fail to do so.[57] These standards encounter a more severe problem than this criticism would suggest, however, because neither courts nor scholars have presented any clear account of the meaning of the putative inability to control or of what would count as evidence that any particular defendant suffered this form of impaired capacity.[58] Furthermore, to the extent that it refers to some inability to direct one's bodily movement through ordinary psychological processes, this standard appears redundant with the voluntary act provisions that require as an offense element that the conduct constituting the offense includes a voluntary act.[59]

Arguably, the volitional clause in the insanity defense differs from the voluntary act requirement in that it requires impaired psychological process. The "mental disease or defect" phrase applies to both the ignorance and the volitional excusing conditions, indicating that exculpation under either standard requires some impairment of psychological capacity, although the two may arise from different types of impairment. For the purpose of this chapter, it is not necessary to pursue any further the inquiry as to what if any type of impairment would support the volitional clause. The most important point for the immediate purpose is that this volitional clause, like the ignorance criterion, requires impaired capacity that renders one unable to perform certain psychological operations, the ability to perform which constitutes

---

[56] MPC, *supra* note 26, at § 4.01.

[57] *See e.g.*, Richard Bonnie, *The Moral Basis of the Insanity Defense*, 69 A.B.A.J. 194 (1983).

[58] *See* chapter 8, section IV.

[59] MPC, *supra* note 26, at § 2.01; SCHOPP, *supra* note 25, at § 6.3.

the criteria of eligibility for criminal responsibility. Thus, any impairment that renders an individual unable to conform would constitute legal mental illness that renders that person retributively incompetent.

D. Process Standards

I have argued elsewhere that both ignorance and volitional formulations of the insanity standard misconstrue the significance of serious psychopathology for criminal responsibility. According to an alternative interpretation of the psychology of criminal responsibility, certain forms of psychopathology undermine criminal responsibility because they involve impairment of the psychological processes that enable the individual to direct his or her conduct through intact processes of practical reasoning in light of the limits established by the criminal law. Impairment of these capacities prevents one from deliberating effectively. The significance of such impairment rests not on belief content or some vaguely defined volitional impairment, but rather on the individual's inability to direct his or her conduct through a process of competent practical reasoning that enables the unimpaired adult to participate with at least minimal adequacy in the retributive criminal justice system.[60]

This process approach integrates the defining characteristics of severe psychopathology with the normative framework that supports the criminal justice system of the liberal society. Severe psychopathology of the types most clearly relevant to criminal responsibility involves impairment in the psychological capacities that enable one to function as a minimally competent participant in the criminal justice system. These include, for example, impairment of consciousness, comprehension, reasoning, and reality testing.[61] Such impairment undermines the justification for punishment because individuals who suffer such impairment lack the opportunity to avoid punishment by engaging in a minimally adequate process of practical reasoning regarding conduct prohibited by the criminal law. Such impairment renders inappropriate the condemnation inherent in criminal punishment because it undermines the fourth type of condemnation of the offender as one who has violated the law while meeting systemic criteria of culpability. Impairment of this type constitutes legal mental illness for the purpose of criminal responsibility, and it renders the individually retributively incompetent.

V. Conclusion

Whether one accepts the process interpretation of the psychology of criminal responsibility or the more traditional ignorance and volitional standards, psychological impairment that undermines criminal responsibility does so because it renders the individual retributively incompetent. This interpretation provides a conception of legal mental illness that serves the discriminative and justificatory functions discussed in chapter 3. It serves the discriminative function by directing the courts to

---

[60] SCHOPP, *supra* note 25, at §§ 6.4–6.7.

[61] *Id.* at §§ 5.2, 5.3, 6.4, 6.5; DSM–IV, *supra* note 6, at 123–63 (delirium and dementia), 273–315 (schizophrenia and other psychotic disorders), 317–82 (mood disorders with severe features).

identify those who engage in criminal conduct without the capacity to perform the psychological operations required by the applicable standard. Some standards, such as the traditional volitional standards, create special difficulties regarding the discriminative function because neither the statutes nor the cases provide any clear conception of volitional impairment. Thus, trial courts must attempt to identify defendants who suffer such impairments without any helpful guidance regarding the proper interpretation of the criterion. Insofar as clinicians provide clear descriptions and explanations of the impairment suffered by the offenders they evaluate, courts must make the normative determination that such impairment does or does not qualify as sufficient to render the person not responsible. The court has no algorithm it can mechanically apply in order to make this decision, but the decision is a normative one that falls within the responsibility of the court or jury.

This interpretation serves the justificatory function because it defines the parameters of police power intervention in a manner that conforms to the justification of punishment through legal institutions representing liberal principles of political morality. This approach precludes criminal punishment of those who do not deserve the condemnation inherent in such punishment because they lack the capacities needed to function competently as subjects of the criminal justice system. Although this approach precludes criminal punishment of those who lack retributive competence, it addresses these individuals through an alternative institution of social control in the form of police power intervention through the mental health system.

By requiring legal mental illness that undermines retributive competence as a criterion of police power civil commitment, this approach limits police power intrusion into the lives of retributively competent individuals to that which occurs through the criminal justice system. Thus, it precludes unwarranted police power intrusions through the mental health system into the lives of those who qualify for equal standing as responsible agents in the public jurisdiction.[62] This approach provides the basis for coherent institutions of police power intervention by integrating the police power institutions of the criminal justice and mental health systems.

This approach addresses the three questions identified at the end of section II as raised but not addressed by the sexual predator statutes and the *Hendricks* opinion. First, impairment that renders individuals unable to function competently as subjects of the criminal justice system of the public jurisdiction through the exercise of the capacities required for retributive competence constitutes legal mental illness that renders those individuals appropriate for coercive social control through the mental health system when they require such intervention. Second, legal mental illness of this type justifies the state in exercising the police power through the mental health system rather than through the criminal justice system because it undermines retributive competence and the justification for criminal conviction and punishment. The third question asks what kind of impairment could render Hendricks legally mentally ill for the purpose of civil commitment without undermining his criminal responsibility for the conduct that provides the basis for his criminal convictions and for the commitment. This analysis provides no good answer to this question. Chapter 8 explains further why it should not.

Some readers might contend that the approach advanced here creates dangerous

---

[62] *See generally,* Janus, *supra* note 20 (discussing the priority of the criminal justice system as the primary legal institution for the exercise of the police power).

circumstances because it relegates a class of citizens to reduced standing. These readers might suggest an alternative approach that rests upon the importance of state interests. This alternative approach would resemble the approach endorsed here insofar as it recognizes the criminal justice system as the primary institution for the exercise of the police power. It would allow exercise of the police power through civil commitment only when justified by a heightened state interest that occurs when certain individuals create danger to persons in circumstances that do not allow social control through the criminal justice system.[63]

The approach advanced in this book converges with this alternative proposal in certain respects. Both identify the criminal justice system as the primary legal institution through which the state must exercise the police power. Both authorize police power civil commitment only as an alternative to the criminal justice system in circumstances that justify police power intervention but preclude criminal conviction and punishment because of the individual's psychological impairment.[64] These two approaches diverge insofar as the approach advanced in this book identifies certain individuals as appropriate for police power intervention through the mental health system because they fail to qualify for full standing in the public jurisdiction, but the alternative proposal rejects this attribution of lesser standing in order to avoid the dangers inherent in identifying a class of people as enjoying less than full standing in the public domain.[65]

Clearly, however, the alternative does not recognize every heightened state interest as sufficient to justify intervention through the mental health system. The heightened state interest in reducing the elevated crime rate among poor young males, for example, would not justify civil commitment of individual members of that category of citizens. The alternative proposal apparently endorses police power civil commitment through the mental health system only for those individuals regarding whom the state has a heightened interest in exercising alternative means of social control because these individuals create danger that warrants police power intervention but are not susceptible to police power control through the criminal justice system because of mental illness. Understood in this manner, however, the heightened state interest is an interest in exercising alternative forms of police power control over a certain class of individuals because they manifest psychological impairment that renders them ineligible to participate as fully responsible subjects of the retributive criminal justice system. This impairment relegates them to reduced standing by virtue of its significance in rendering them retributively incompetent and therefore subject to an alternative form of social control. That is, identifying individuals as appropriate for police power intervention through the mental health system, rather than through the criminal justice system as the primary institution of coercive social control, constitutes an attribution of reduced standing to those individuals.

In summary, the approach advanced in this book does not differ from the alternative proposal by virtue of identifying a class of individuals with reduced standing.

---

[63] Eric S. Janus, *Toward a Conceptual Framework for Assessing Police Power Commitment Legislation: A Critique of Schopp's and Winick's Explications of Legal Mental Illness*, 76 NEB. L. REV. 1, 6, 47–49 (1997); Janus, *supra* note 20, at 208–12.

[64] Janus, *supra* note 63, at 47; Janus, *supra* note 20, at 208–12.

[65] Janus, *supra* note 63, at 47–48.

Rather, it differs insofar as it does so explicitly, articulates a relatively specific conception of legal mental illness that grounds such reduced standing, and advances a justification for that reduced standing. By explicitly recognizing and justifying the criteria for such reduced standing, the approach advanced here attempts to establish relatively clear, enforceable, and defensible limits on this category.

Although impairment undermining retributive competence justifies the state in exercising the police power through the mental health system rather than through the criminal justice system, the mere presence of such impairment is not sufficient to justify police power intervention generally or civil commitment specifically. The parameters of police power intervention depend upon the purpose and justification of such interventions. Chapter 8 advances a proposal for integrated institutions of police power intervention that rests upon those purposes and justifications, and it evaluates the role of sexual predator statutes in that context.

Chapter 8
SEXUAL PREDATOR STATUTES AND
THE POLICE POWER

This chapter describes and defends an integrated approach to police power intervention reflecting the normative structure discussed in chapter 7. This proposal does not purport to represent a fully developed set of model statutes. Rather, it provides a general structure for institutions of police power intervention that cohere with the underlying normative structure, the legal conception of mental illness, and the *parens patriae* institutions previously discussed. This proposed approach reveals and rectifies the defects that pervade civil commitment generally and sexual predator commitment specifically. Finally, this proposal addresses a series of problematic cases introduced in prior chapters.

I. Preventive Intervention Under the Police Power

Although the analysis presented in this book applies the same abstract conceptions of competence and legal mental illness to *parens patriae* and police power interventions, the criteria of competence and of legal mental illness do not necessarily coincide. Francine, for example, was legally mentally ill for the police power function, but she was not legally mentally ill for the *parens patriae* function. The criteria of legal mental illness for the *parens patriae* function identify those who lack the capacity to engage in competent practical reasoning regarding their own well-being. In contrast, the criteria of legal mental illness for the police power function distribute individuals to either the criminal justice or the mental health components of the institutions for social control. These criteria identify those who suffer impairment that renders them incompetent for the role of responsible agent in the retributive criminal justice system.

This analysis suggests that police power civil commitment, like *parens patriae* commitment, is redundant and can be eliminated as an independent legal institution. The legal system might abolish police power commitment statutes and accommodate the appropriate cases of police power commitment through postacquittal commitment for those who are acquitted because of insanity, diminished capacity, or automatism, and through a police power commitment hearing for those deemed permanently incompetent to stand trial. According to this interpretation, *parens patriae* and police power civil commitment collapse into civil incompetence and criminal justice provisions respectively, and no legitimate function remains for an independent institution of civil commitment.

Consider, however, the case of Peter, who demonstrates pathology similar to that manifested by Ellen and Francine in that he suffers chronic delusional process and auditory hallucinations with persecutory, grandiose, and religious content. The religious content takes the form of delusional beliefs that he is the reincarnation of various biblical figures. He hears a voice that he interprets as God's voice telling him that he is the reincarnation of these figures and that each has been brought back in his body because each in some way failed to complete a divine charge from God during that person's first incarnation. During one period, Peter believed he was Joseph, wore a homemade robe of many colors, and accosted people on the street because he took them to be his brothers. He annoyed but never harmed these "brothers" as he attempted to reconcile with them and convert them because he understood his sin in his prior incarnation as one of pride that led to his failure to convert his brothers to God's way.

Later, Peter began called himself John and attempted to baptize all the members of various Jewish temples because he understood his sin in the prior incarnation as the failure to discharge his mission from God to baptize as Christians the entire Jewish population. He first came to the attention of the police and the mental health system during that period because he was arrested for sprinkling water on people leaving the temples after services. The behavior was considered too trivial for criminal charges, however, and he was not committed at a civil commitment hearing because the sprinkling was considered annoying rather than dangerous. He has had intermittent contact with the outpatient clinic since that hearing, when the social worker has been able to persuade him to attend.

Recently, Peter has begun calling himself Abraham and spending time at the playground where the neighborhood children play. He has addressed several of the young boys as Isaac and spoken in a vague and disorganized manner of the need for sacrifice being greater now than ever before. Should we await conduct by Peter precipitating an insanity acquittal or a finding of incompetence to stand trial, or do we need a distinct institution of police power intervention for Peter?

II.   Police Power Intervention Absent a Criminal Charge

Recall that chapter 5 reinterprets *parens patriae* commitment as a dispositional alternative following a determination of incompetence for person. According to this approach, the initial inquiry addresses the individual's competence to make decisions regarding personal well-being, including health care. Placement is a secondary issue that arises only if the initial inquiry concludes that the subject of the hearing lacks competence for this purpose. The placement selected reflects the complex set of social values contained in the underlying principles of political morality as well as the subject's needs and assets and the available resources. Similarly, according to the framework advanced in chapter 7, the insanity verdict or other acquittal because of legal mental illness establishes the defendant's incompetence to participate as a responsible agent in the retributive criminal justice system. The secondary questions regarding placement or alternative forms of social control arise following this initial finding of incompetence in the relevant sense.

Ordinary civil commitment hearings reverse this priority in that they frame the inquiry in a manner that addresses placement as the central issue. Most commitment statutes provide at best a vague conception of legal mental illness, and they do not specify the appropriate relationship between the relevant conceptions of mental illness and of competence for a particular purpose. Furthermore, these statutes and hearings conflate the *parens patriae* and police power functions, obscuring the different criteria of competence and of legal mental illness appropriate to justify intervention under each of these distinct functions. Finally, and perhaps most important, ordinary civil commitment hearings frame the question as being about the placement, with questions of mental illness addressed as instrumental to this primary question.

Consider the possibility that we should abolish police power civil commitment and replace it with an institutional structure for making a determination of retributive competence for participation in the public jurisdiction as a responsible subject of the criminal justice system. The statute and practices involved in such an institution would resemble those providing for determinations of civil competence, guardianship, and protective placement insofar as a determination of competence would constitute the initial step. Conduct raising questions regarding retributive competence and the need for social control would lead to a hearing that would address competence to participate in the retributive criminal justice system as the primary question. If the hearing determined that the individual possessed the capacities needed to qualify as retributively competent, the individual would remain subject to criminal prosecution for any conduct violating an offense definition, but the state would not subject him to any alternative form of police power intervention following the hearing. Thus, the individual would retain full standing in the public domain. If the hearing determined that the individual lacked retributive competence, the court would assign that person to the mental health system as the institution through which the state exercises the police power regarding those who lack retributive competence.

Just as conduct raising questions regarding civil competence can lead to a petition and hearing addressing that issue, some conduct indicative of the need for social control and raising a colorable question regarding retributive competence would trigger the process for a petition and hearing addressing competence in the retributive sense. Ordinarily, this conduct would violate an offense definition and the question of competence would arise within the conventional criminal process. The assaults committed by Ellen and Francine, for example, led to criminal charges and raised the questions regarding competence to stand trial and insanity. In these circumstances, the determination of retributive competence would occur as a conventional step in the process of adjudicating the criminal case, and the disposition would be appropriate to the criminal case.[1]

Absent criminal conduct leading to a criminal trial, a petition by the county attorney might trigger a hearing regarding retributive competence according to a procedure similar to that which currently initiates a civil commitment hearing or a civil competence proceeding. For example, Peter's previous behavior involving the coat of many colors and the sprinkling of water in combination with his recent behavior at the playground suggests that he is delusional, that he has previously acted according to his delusional process, and that conduct reflecting his current delusional process might be severely harmful. This evidence could raise the questions

---

[1] Strictly speaking, a determination of incompetence to stand trial would not establish retributive incompetence because it would address competence to participate in the adjudicative process rather than competence to participate in society as a citizen subject to the rule-based criminal justice system. Thus, for individuals found incompetent to stand trial, the determination of retributive competence would occur at trial after they had regained competence to proceed or at commitment hearings when it had been determined that they were incompetent to proceed and were not expected to regain competence. Jackson v. Indiana, 406 U.S. 715 (1972).

of retributive competence and of the possible need for alternative forms of social control. The hearing would determine whether the individual suffers functional impairment that constitutes legal mental illness rendering him incompetent to participate in the retributive institution of social control. Such a hearing would not determine whether the person was guilty of the conduct in question. Indeed, the conduct ordinarily would not constitute a violation of an offense definition for which one could be found guilty. If it did, the question of retributive competence would ordinarily arise in the context of the criminal adjudication.

Rather than determining guilt, the hearing would determine whether the individual engaged in the conduct raising the question of retributive competence with the capacities of practical reasoning needed to qualify that individual as competent to participate as a responsible agent in the retributive criminal justice system. Although the conduct in question might be relevant to an estimate of risk that the individual will harm others, this determination of retributive competence addresses a fundamentally different question than that of risk. Retributive competence requires that the individual possess the psychological capacities that enable him or her to participate as an equal in the public jurisdiction as a subject of the retributive criminal justice system. Retributive competence in this sense differs significantly from competence to proceed. It requires the capacities necessary to direct one's conduct through a process of competent practical reasoning in light of the rule-based criminal law and the likely consequences of one's actions.[2] Impairment sufficient to render the person retributively incompetent constitutes legal mental illness for this purpose, and it relegates this person to the alternative institution of social control.

Although this book advances a relatively abstract conceptual and normative framework rather than a model statute, it must address at least three questions regarding the proposed determinations of retributive competence in order to support the proposal as amenable to interpretation and application. First, what types of conduct suffice to trigger such a hearing? Second, insofar as retributive competence requires the capacities needed for criminal responsibility by systemic standards, and these standards address accountability for a particular act that violates an offense definition, in what sense can one meaningfully attribute retributive competence or incompetence regarding an act that does not constitute an offense? Third, does a determination of retributive competence or incompetence assign some global status of the person regarding all conduct, or can this person be retributively competent for some conduct but not for other conduct?

Peter's hearing is triggered by the pattern of recent behavior regarding children at the park, including frequenting the park, addressing the boys as Isaac, speaking of the need for sacrifice, and the other overt manifestations of his delusional identity as Abraham. Peter's history of approaching people on the street in his identity as Joseph and of sprinkling people with water outside the temples in his identity as John also supports the inference that a hearing is appropriate. This pattern of recent and remote conduct triggers the hearing by providing a prima facie case for two propositions the county attorney must establish at such a hearing. First, Peter suffers serious pathology that undermines the capacities of perception, comprehension, rea-

---

[2] ROBERT F. SCHOPP, AUTOMATISM, INSANITY, AND THE PSYCHOLOGY OF CRIMINAL RESPONSIBILITY (1991) (providing a detailed argument for the interpretation of the psychology of criminal responsibility in terms of competent practical reasoning).

soning, and reality relatedness required for competent participation in the public jurisdiction though a minimally adequate system of deliberation and practical reasoning.[3] Second, Peter's conduct signals a risk of harm sufficient to justify at least minimal state intrusion through an alternative form of social control, appropriate to his impairment.

Some civil commitment standards require an overt act or threat as part of the basis for establishing dangerousness.[4] If one interprets these standards as requiring dangerous conduct, Peter's behavior does not qualify. If these provisions require overt conduct or threats that provide evidence of dangerousness, however, Peter's behavior qualifies because the pattern of recent and remote conduct demonstrates that Peter acts on his delusional process, and the evidence regarding his current delusional process provides good reason to expect that action representing the current delusional process would harm others. Thus, the complete body of evidence regarding Peter's psychopathology and conduct supports the two propositions the county attorney must establish in order to demonstrate retributive incompetence and justify at least minimal intrusion. According to this interpretation, the county must establish that Peter has engaged in some conduct that provides evidence of risk, but not necessarily that Peter has engaged in risky conduct. Rather, the county attorney must provide evidence of conduct and impairment that together establish both that Peter represents a current risk of sufficient gravity to establish the need for some police power intervention and that he is retributively incompetent regarding that conduct.[5]

The evidence establishing risk would not necessarily suffice for criminal conviction because the conduct might not constitute a crime. It might support civil commitment under some current statutes, depending on the precise content and local interpretation of provisions regarding dangerousness and overt conduct.[6] The significance of this showing differs substantially, however, between civil commitment and retributive competence hearings. In the former, the showing of mental illness and dangerousness fulfills the criteria for involuntary confinement. In the latter, in contrast, the evidence demonstrating serious psychopathology and the tendency to engage in risky conduct associated with that pathology would establish the need for police power intervention, and the evidence demonstrating the impaired process of practical reasoning regarding the decision to engage in that conduct would establish retributive incompetence. The court would then select the appropriate form of police power intervention. Although this intervention might take the form of involuntary confinement, that extreme form of intrusion under the proposed approach constitutes the ordinary form of intrusion under current commitment statutes, and the structure of the retributive incompetence provision would allow and might encourage less drastic interventions.

The finding of retributive incompetence establishes the need for police power intervention through institutions other than the criminal justice system, but it does not establish the precise form of such intervention. Recall the interpretation of the *Jackson* reasonable relationship principle as a formal principle of justice in constitutional adjudication that requires a reasonable relationship between a state intrusion

---

[3] *Id.* at §§ 4.3, 6.5, 7.4.

[4] MICHAEL L. PERLIN, LAW AND MENTAL DISABILITY § 1.05 (1994).

[5] For a discussion of risk and of dangerousness as a statutory criterion, *see* chapter 10.

[6] PERLIN, *supra* note 4, at §§ 1.03–1.05.

into individual liberty and a legitimate state interest sufficient to justify that intrusion.[7] As applied to *parens patriae* interventions, this principle prohibits as arbitrary restrictions of liberty any interventions that are more restrictive than those in the set of arguably least restrictive alternatives that fulfill the justifying state interest.[8]

Similarly, the *Jackson* reasonable relationship principle, rather than the retributive principles of culpability, desert, and proportion, defines the limits on police power intervention through the mental health system. As applied to these interventions, this principle limits the state to methods selected from among the set of arguably least restrictive alternatives that adequately serve the legitimate state interest in protecting the public from harm by those who lack retributive competence. Any intrusion beyond that necessary to serve this legitimate state interest in protecting the public from harm caused by retributively incompetent individuals would violate the reasonable relationship principle as an arbitrary limitation on liberty.

As with *parens patriae* interventions, potential police power interventions rarely fall into a clear hierarchy of restrictiveness such that a court can clearly identify each as more or less restrictive than the alternatives. One might reasonably argue, for example, that involuntary injections of psychotropic medication on an outpatient basis are either more or less restrictive of liberty than involuntary confinement on a locked ward without involuntary medication. As applied to police power intervention through the mental health system, the reasonable relationship principle serves a purpose analogous to the purpose it serves regarding the state's exercise of its *parens patriae* function. That is, it forbids as arbitrary limitations on liberty interventions that are more restrictive than those in the set of arguably least restrictive alternatives that adequately serve the justifying state interest in protecting the public from harm caused by retributively incompetent individuals. Section III explores the application of this approach to the four offenders identified in chapter 1, section I, and chapter 9 addresses the right to refuse treatment in the context of police power intervention.

The second question regarding the proposed approach to police power intervention based on a determination of retributive incompetence calls for clarification of the sense in which one can understand an attribution of retributive incompetence for conduct that does not constitute an offense. Ordinarily, an acquittal under the defense of insanity or automatism, for example, represents the conclusion that the individual was not criminally responsible for this particular criminal conduct. Understood as findings of retributive incompetence, these acquittals represent the determinations that the defendants lacked the ability to apply the capacities of retributive competence to their decisions to engage in the criminal conduct for which they were acquitted. Important components of retributive competence include the capacities needed to comprehend the nature and likely consequences of one's conduct in the context of the criminal law and to engage in a process of competent practical reasoning regarding that conduct in light of that understanding. Ellen and Francine, for example, lacked retributive competence regarding their assaults because their delusional processes prevented them from understanding that the conduct was harmful and unjustified and from reasoning clearly regarding that conduct.[9]

Regarding Peter, in contrast, the determination of retributive competence ad-

---

[7] *See* chapter 2, section III.
[8] *See* chapter 6, section IV.
[9] *See* chapter 4, section I.

dresses conduct that is neither harmful nor criminally proscribed. Thus, the conduct in question does not stand in the same relationship to the criminal law. The court cannot ask whether Peter violated the law as a result of an applicable type of impairment because Peter did not act contrary to law. The court can inquire, however, into the psychological process of decision making Peter used in deciding to engage in the conduct at issue, and it can determine whether this process demonstrates impairment of a type that undermines Peter's ability to participate fully in the public jurisdiction as a subject of the retributive criminal justice system. That is, does the conduct that raises a concern regarding the need for social control reveal a pattern of impaired practical reasoning that would undermine criminal responsibility if Peter engaged in illegal conduct generated by a similar process? A positive response to this question constitutes a determination of retributive incompetence regarding the conduct at issue, although that conduct does not constitute an offense.

The court might determine that Peter lacks retributive competence regarding the conduct in question, for example, by considering testimony regarding Peter's conduct and the impaired process that contributed to it. Ordinary testimony from witnesses to his conduct would establish that he wore the coat of many colors; took the names of Joseph, John, and Abraham; sprinkled the water; frequented the park; addressed the boys as Isaac; and so on. Expert testimony by clinicians could describe and explain the clinical evidence of psychotic impairment including auditory hallucinations; delusional thought process; and inability to reason clearly about the relationships among his conduct, the circumstances, the requirements of law, and his own moral standards, as well as the standards of public morality represented by law. If these witnesses were persuasive, the court might reasonably conclude that Peter's conduct reflects psychological impairment that would preclude criminal responsibility for criminal conduct generated by similar processes and, therefore, that the entire body of evidence establishes that Peter lacks retributive competence.

Although a court might interpret this testimony as fulfilling a common insanity standard framed in terms of the inability to know or appreciate wrongfulness, the interpretation advanced in this chapter makes explicit the significance of impaired psychological process, rather than belief content, for criminal responsibility. By recognizing the significance of retributive competence for criminal conviction and of an impaired process of practical reasoning for retributive incompetence, this approach demonstrates the need for standards of criminal responsibility framed in terms of impaired process, rather than belief content.

Space precludes a detailed interpretation of the role of impaired process in criminal responsibility. I present here only a minimal sketch of the central ideas that I have discussed in detail elsewhere.[10] Consider, for example, the insanity defense. Traditional standards for the insanity defense exculpate defendants who commit crimes while suffering psychological impairment that prevents them from knowing the nature and quality of their conduct or that it is wrongful.[11] These standards address the significance of serious psychopathology for criminal responsibility as if it were primarily a matter of inaccurate belief content rather than a matter of impaired process. Yet, the major psychological disorders that provide the most plausible bases

---

[10] For a more detailed discussion, *see* SCHOPP, *supra* note 2, at § 6.4; *see* chapter 7, section II for a brief discussion of this issue.

[11] *See* chapter 7, section IV; SCHOPP, *supra* note 2, at § 2.1.

for exculpation under the insanity defense are characterized by distortion of psychological process and specifically of cognitive process. Although distorted cognitive process often produces inaccurate belief content, legal standards that define criteria of insanity in terms of belief content misconstrue the nature of the primary dysfunction involved in major psychopathology, and they misrepresent the exculpatory significance of this dysfunction in a manner that suggests that the insanity defense is essentially a matter of mistake.[12]

Some insanity statutes augment the cognitive standard with a volitional provision that exculpates those who lack the capacity to conform to law. Yet, neither the courts nor the commentators have provided any interpretation of this provision that applies to plausible candidates for the insanity defense, and no one has explained what would serve as probative evidence for the claim that defendants who engage in organized, goal-directed behavior suffer such impairment.[13] The majority and dissenting opinions in *Hendricks* extend this pattern of asserting claims of volitional disorder without explanation or evidence from the insanity defense to police power commitment. Both opinions accepted without question Hendricks's unsupported assertion that he lacked the capacity to control his sexual conduct, and both opinions accepted without explanation the claim that this putative inability establishes a mental abnormality for the purpose of commitment under the Kansas sexual predator statute.[14] Thus, neither the common formulations of the insanity defense nor the sexual predator statutes and cases have articulated relevant conceptions of legal mental illness for their respective functions.

The notion of retributive competence explicitly identifies the significance of impaired capacity to engage in certain psychological processes as the condition that explains the significance of serious psychological impairment for the individual's standing in the public jurisdiction and for the appropriate exercise of the police power. Retributive competence distributes individuals to either the criminal justice or the mental health institutions of social control under the police power. Thus, the court's determination regarding retributive competence involves the evaluation of the individual's capacity to participate as an equal in the criminal justice system rather than a judgment that the individual is guilty or not guilty of a specific offense. Criminal or noncriminal conduct can raise the question of retributive competence, provide relevant evidence of the presence or lack of that competence, and provide relevant evidence of the appropriate disposition for those who are adjudicated retributively incompetent.

This book does not purport to provide the complete body of substantive and procedural law that would implement this approach, nor does it address all of the practical problems that would arise in its implementation. As with any other body of law, problems involving evidence, the potential for abuse, error preference, and limited resources would influence the manner in which such law should be drafted. The analysis presented in this book supports the contention, however, that retributive competence represents the conceptual and normative key to an integrated structure

---

[12] SCHOPP, *supra* note 2, at § 6.4. Some standards rephrase the knowledge requirement such as to require that the defendant was unable to appreciate the wrongfulness of the conduct, but no one has advanced an interpretation of "appreciate" that differs significantly from the requirement of knowledge and remains plausible. *Id.* at § 2.1.1.

[13] *Id.* at § 6.3.

[14] Kansas v. Hendricks, 117 S.Ct. 2072, 2081, 2088–89 (1997).

for the criminal justice and mental health institutions for the exercise of the police power in a liberal society.

In response to the third question identified above regarding the scope of a determination of retributive incompetence for police power intervention, this determination does not constitute a prospective determination that Peter is not criminally responsible for any future conduct, because future conduct might reflect different decision-making processes. Some individuals demonstrate a pervasive pattern of grossly disorganized thought processes that apparently influences much of their behavior, whereas others manifest an encapsulated delusional process that apparently influences only narrow areas of their lives.[15] Pathology of the former type might support the conclusion that the person would lack retributive competence for most conduct, but pathology of the latter type might support only the inference that the individual would lack retributive competence for conduct that fell within the scope of that narrowly circumscribed area of dysfunction. Either pattern would reveal a type of impairment that would render the individual retributively incompetent regarding some sphere of conduct, supporting a judgment that this person lacks the capacities for retributive competence required for full standing in the public jurisdiction. Thus, the mere determination of retributive incompetence would not represent a global status of nonresponsibility, but it would establish some deviation from equal standing in the public jurisdiction.

The determination of retributive competence or incompetence identifies the appropriate institution through which society exercises social control in the public domain. If the hearing determines that the subject is retributively competent, any social control must occur through the criminal justice system. If the hearing determines that the subject engaged in the conduct that triggered the hearing while lacking the capacities required for retributive competence, the court moves on to the secondary question of disposition. In a manner parallel to the civil competence process, the finding of incompetence raises the question of disposition, but it does not necessarily generate commitment. Rather, the individual becomes subject to public supervision under the police power for the purpose of preventing that person from causing harm to others. Ordinarily, a specific person should be appointed as supervisor, analogous to a guardian for the subject of a determination of civil incompetence. The court's protective order, analogous to a court order defining guardianship responsibilities pursuant to a finding of civil incompetence, can define the conditions of social control under the police power along a continuum of restrictiveness, ranging from very specific to very general.[16] Protective confinement similar to that available under contemporary police power civil commitment provisions might be warranted in certain cases on the basis of the complex set of social values contained in the principles underlying the liberal society.

The finding of retributive incompetence provides the threshold condition for the protective order for social control because it establishes that the subject lacks the capacities that would qualify him to participate as a responsible agent in the criminal justice system that orders the public jurisdiction.[17] Thus, the subject of the order

---

[15] AMERICAN PSYCHIATRIC ASSOCIATION, DIAGNOSTIC AND STATISTICAL MANUAL OF MENTAL DISORDERS 296–301 (4th ed. 1994) [hereinafter DSM–IV] (describing Delusional Disorder as involving narrowly encapsulated delusional process).

[16] See chapter 1, section V.

[17] See chapter 3, sections III and IV.

takes on a status of less than equal standing in the public domain, but this does not deprive him of all claims. Rather, he takes on a status somewhat analogous to that of an individual who has been found civilly incompetent in that he retains a variety of legitimate interests and relevant capacities. Contemporary guardianship statutes encourage limited guardianship designed to maximize the independence of incapacitated persons.[18] Although courts may tend to appoint general guardians under current provisions, substantive and procedural law could define the dispositional criteria and procedures following a finding of retributive incompetence in such a manner as to require interventions from the set of arguably least restrictive alternatives. Formulating these provisions in such a manner would render them more consistent with the *Jackson* reasonable relationship principle.

Liberal societies can differ significantly in the legal rules and social policies they adopt in the public jurisdiction, but any plausible liberal society will vest substantial weight in the individual and collective well-being of its citizens. Individual well-being includes welfare interests in maintaining the liberty, opportunities, and capacities required to pursue one's specific interests. Thus, individuals who are subjects of findings of retributive incompetence and protective orders retain strong interests in maximizing their degree of liberty, as a general good and as necessary to the pursuit of their other interests, and in maximizing their autonomous capacities in order to attain increased liberty and equal standing, or at least to increase their ability to pursue lives of their own.

Society's interests include, but are not limited to, a strong interest in protecting the public from the risk presented by the retributively incompetent person. Because liberal societies rely heavily on voluntary compliance with law, they have an interest in maximizing each person's capacities to live a self-reliant life, ideally including attainment of retributive competence and equal standing. Thus, social interests tend to converge with the interests of the retributively incompetent individual insofar as both include increasing that individual's autonomous capacities and promoting attainment of equal standing, if possible. Society's interests also converge with those of the incompetent individual insofar as both include promoting the individual's well-being, including the general interest in liberty to pursue one's own life as fully as possible.

This complex set of interests requires a balancing approach to the protective order for the retributively incompetent individual. Although that person has an interest in increasing liberty, he has no right to the full range of liberty accorded retributively competent adults because he lacks the capacities needed to qualify for equal standing in the public jurisdiction. Therefore, society does not wrong that individual or violate his standing merely by balancing his liberty interests against the social interest in protecting the public or by recognizing a lesser range of liberty than would be recognized for an individual who possesses the capacities of retributive competence.[19] Nothing in this analysis reduces the difficulty inherent in estimating the risk of social harm presented by a particular individual.[20] Thus, in developing the appropriate degree and conditions of intrusion authorized by a court order for public supervision following a finding of retributive incompetence, the court

---

[18] UNIFORM PROBATE CODE § 5-306, 8 U.L.A. 365 (1998).

[19] *See* chapter 7, sections III and IV.

[20] JOHN MONAHAN & HENRY STEADMAN, VIOLENCE AND MENTAL DISORDER: DEVELOPMENTS IN RISK ASSESSMENT (1994).

should seek conditions of supervision that minimize restraint and maximize the potential for increasing autonomous capacities and individual liberty in light of the evidence of risk.

The ideal disposition would place the individual in a treatment setting that would provide the minimum constraints required for public safety and the therapeutic assets likely to maximize development of the person's capacities for safe and independent functioning. Such a disposition would promote both social and individual interests. No plausible system will produce such ideal dispositions for all retributively incompetent individuals. Current systems can only strive for some reasonable approximation of a safe and therapeutic disposition. A statutory structure designed according to the analysis presented here might promote some progress toward the ideal in two ways. First, by making explicit the underlying principles of political morality, the relevant conception of legal mental illness, and the manner in which social and individual interests converge or diverge, it might enhance the ability of courts and clinicians to select the most defensible and therapeutically effective dispositions from those available. Second, it might generate testable hypotheses regarding alternative dispositions expected to promote therapeutic effectiveness within the bounds defined by the underlying principles of political morality. Thus, this approach might encourage development of the Therapeutic Jurisprudence research agenda in a manner that gradually informs the legal system's ability to improve dispositional decisions.[21]

Some critics might object that this formulation is too abstract to provide the constraints on state intrusion needed to avoid overuse.[22] Such critics would be correct in recognizing that the conceptual and normative proposal contained in this book does not provide an adequate statutory formulation for practical application. Furthermore, a statutory structure reflecting this proposal could not provide a mechanical procedure for defining the appropriate degree of intrusion. Although a statutory structure based upon this proposal cannot reasonably be expected to eliminate unjustified extensions of commitment, several factors might discourage overuse of such a procedure more effectively than we have been able to prevent overuse of ordinary civil commitment provisions. First, by clearly differentiating *parens patriae* and police power interventions, this approach might decrease the tendency to dilute the criteria of involuntary intervention under the police power that results from the perception that the individual needs treatment and, therefore, that commitment would be "for his own good." Police power intervention, as distinct from *parens patriae* intervention, would require an explicit finding of retributive incompetence prior to the consideration of any disposition. Thus, the meaning and significance of legal mental illness as impairment that renders the individual unable to participate in the retributive criminal justice system as a responsible agent would be clarified and made explicit.

Second, the court and experts might find it less difficult to identify and conform to their respective responsibilities regarding the determination of retributive incompetence as a judicial decision, because the hearing would explicitly address eligibility for a specified legal status. In this manner, this approach might encourage courts to recognize and discharge their judicial responsibility to make a legal determination of eligibility to participate in the criminal justice system, rather than deferring to

---

[21] See generally, DAVID B. WEXLER & BRUCE J. WINICK, LAW IN A THERAPEUTIC KEY (1996).

[22] See, e.g., Stephen J. Morse, A Preference for Liberty: The Case Against Involuntary Commitment of the Mentally Ill, 70 CALIF. L. REV. 54, 67–79 (1982).

clinicians regarding this matter. Similarly, this approach might encourage clinicians to provide descriptive and explanatory testimony within the range of clinical expertise, rather than extending into judgments regarding competence or disposition that properly fall within the scope of judicial responsibility.

Third, explicit consideration of disposition as an independent question following a determination of retributive incompetence might encourage decision makers to pursue more effectively the public interest in avoiding excessive reliance on intrusive and expensive inpatient confinement. A properly formulated statute could encourage this tendency by requiring dispositions selected from the set of arguably least restrictive alternatives and by defining the types of interventions considered most intrusive. A statute might require, for example, a separate finding by the court in order to authorize inpatient confinement or involuntary medication. Fourth, the development of a specific disposition plan following a determination of incompetence and the appointment of a specific supervisor analogous to a guardian might encourage personal responsibility in the monitoring process.

Fifth, the determination that a person lacks retributive competence would establish a record supporting a future claim by that person that his impairment renders him not criminally responsible for some future conduct. The prospect of establishing such a record would provide a strong incentive for county attorneys to pursue such determinations sparingly, in order to avoid undermining any future criminal prosecutions. The finding of retributive incompetence would constitute a determination that the individual engaged in the conduct raising the question of retributive competence while suffering impairment of the capacities needed to fulfill the criteria of eligibility for participation as an accountable agent in the criminal justice system. Although it would create a record supporting a future claim of nonresponsibility for criminal behavior, it would not conclusively establish that claim. The nature and degree of psychopathology can change over time, and impairment that remains constant over time máy or may not influence different behavior in different ways. Thus, an individual's psychopathology might play a central role in some conduct but little or none in other conduct. Furthermore, clinical intervention following a finding of retributive incompetence might significantly alter the individual's capacities. In summary, a finding of retributive incompetence for the purpose of police power intervention would support but not conclusively establish a future claim by that individual that he lacked criminal responsibility regarding some future conduct.

The range of possible dispositions alleviates to some degree the severity of the harm caused by the chronic difficulty with making accurate judgments of dangerousness. Although some commitment statutes allow for outpatient commitment, conventional civil commitment hearings ordinarily frame the question as one about involuntary admission to a mental health facility. This formulation of the issue generates a stark dilemma for decision makers in conditions of marked uncertainty. If they decide that the subject of the hearing is not dangerous in a manner that justifies inpatient confinement, they release that person from all supervision. If he later harms an innocent victim, they will have exposed that victim to harm and themselves to severe criticism by others and by themselves. Alternately, if they decide that the person is dangerous, they rarely have practical alternatives to inpatient confinement. The approach suggested here calls for an initial determination of retributive incompetence. If such a determination is made, it allows a broad range of monitoring and supervision analogous to the broad range of specific or general guardianship orders available to the court. Hence, it might reduce the tendency toward relying upon involuntary confinement.

Most important, crafting an order for public supervision after an explicit finding of retributive incompetence constitutes a fundamentally different type of intrusion than civil commitment of one who has *not* been subject to such a determination. The latter involves not only limitation of the person's liberty and opportunity to direct his own life, but also a denial of his equal standing, absent an explicit determination that he lacks the capacities needed to qualify for that standing. The former does not infringe on the person's full standing as an accountable agent in the public jurisdiction because it occurs only after it has been established that he does not qualify for that status. The approach proposed here requires a very difficult balancing of individual and public interests that the court should pursue very cautiously and with proper regard for the potential harm to the individual under conditions of marked uncertainty regarding risk. In contrast to the current practice of civil commitment, however, it does not involve an infringement of individual standing because it requires a prior determination that the individual suffers impairment that precludes him from qualifying for full standing as an accountable agent in the criminal justice system that orders the public domain.[23]

Although many people found retributively incompetent would probably demonstrate pathology sufficiently severe to raise questions about competence for health care, a finding of retributive incompetence would not entail incompetence to decide about treatment. The finding of retributive incompetence would allow state intervention for the purpose of social control, but it would not allow involuntary treatment solely for the individual's benefit absent the additional finding of incompetence for that purpose. The individual's participation in appropriate treatment would, however, constitute one relevant factor for the court to consider in determining the necessary type and degree of state intervention. When the need for social control arises directly from the nature of the pathology, treatment reducing the nature of that pathology might reduce the severity of the intervention required. If Peter refuses treatment, for example, and retains his psychotic identity as Abraham, this decision might necessitate a more intrusive form of state control, such as involuntary confinement, than would be required if he participated in outpatient treatment and monitoring. Chapter 9 addresses the issue of involuntary treatment under the police power.

III.   Applying the Police Power to Sex Offenders

Recall the four offenders described in the first section of chapter 1. Anderson, Baker, Cook, and Davis illustrate four types of offenders who qualify for commitment under

---

[23] Recent discussion of preventive detention suggests that some approaches to that question would support this approach. *See, e.g.*, Michael Louis Corrado, *Punishment and the Wild Beast of Prey: The Problem of Preventive Detention*, 86 J. CRIM. L. & CRIMINOLOGY 778, 789 (1996) (recognizing involuntary commitment as legitimate nonpunitive detention, but without supporting analysis); Stephen J. Morse, *Blame and Danger: An Essay on Preventive Detention* 76 BOS. U. L. REV. 113, 122–34 (1996) (suggesting that narrow police power commitment of those who are excused from criminal liability due to their psychological impairment might be acceptable); Christopher Slobogin, *Dangerousness as a Criterion in the Criminal Process* in LAW, MENTAL HEALTH, AND MENTAL DISORDER 360, 368–70 (Bruce D. Sales & Daniel W. Shuman eds. 1996) (recognizing an "incapacity" exception to a general conclusion that the state ought not intervene in individual liberty on the basis of judgments of dangerousness).

the sexual predator statutes, although they differ significantly regarding their standing in the criminal justice system and in the mental health system as represented by conventional commitment statutes. Cook provides a relatively clear case of an offender who lacks the capacities of retributive competence. His moderate retardation does not prevent him from fulfilling the mental state required by the offense definition. He purposefully seeks and engages in sexual activity with children.[24] Although he is found incompetent to stand trial and committed to a mental health facility, his retardation also provides the basis for a strong argument for exculpation under ordinary formulations of the insanity defense.

Some insanity standards include clauses exculpating those whose impairment prevents them from understanding the nature and quality of their conduct, and courts have interpreted these conditions narrowly to refer to the physical characteristics of their conduct and that it is harmful.[25] Cook is aware of the physical characteristics of his conduct, but he does not understand that it might be harmful. He engages in that conduct because he likes to do so, and he elicits but does not coerce cooperation from children who willingly participate. He causes no observable physical harm or suffering, and he lacks the capacity to understand the risk of relatively subtle or distant harms such as distorted psychological development. Similarly, he lacks knowledge of wrongfulness in any meaningful sense. The sense of wrongfulness at issue under these standards remains ambiguous in that courts have interpreted it as involving illegality, social moral standards, and individual moral standards, but none of these interpretations provides a satisfactory standard.[26] When confronted with his behavior, Cook admits it is wrong, but when asked what he means by that, he responds "mama will yell." As Cook understands his offense, it is wrong in the same sense in which it is wrong to eat cookies before dinner or to track mud into the house on his shoes. Regardless of the interpretation of the wrongfulness clauses one adopts, it is difficult to explain Cook's level of understanding as sufficient to ground criminal culpability and retributive competence.

Cook also lacks criminal responsibility under the process standard discussed in chapter 7 (see section IV). Cook not only lacks any meaningful conception of abstract moral and legal notions such as wrongfulness, he also lacks the ability to apply those legal and moral standards to particular conduct in order to draw any but the most simple inferences regarding that conduct. Thus, he is unable to engage in the process of deliberation through which people with ordinary intelligence direct their conduct by prospectively applying moral or prudential reasons for refraining from certain behavior in order to conform to moral standards or to the penal code. In summary, he lacks retributive competence because he lacks the capacities needed to function as a competent practical reasoner in the public jurisdiction as ordered by the criminal law.

The state properly exercises police power intervention through the mental health system as the alternative institution of coercive control for those who are not eligible to participate in the criminal justice system because they lack retributive competence.

---

[24] MODEL PENAL CODE AND COMMENTARIES §§ 2.02 (culpability elements), 213.3(1)(a) (defining an offense involving sexual intercourse with minors) (Official Draft and Revised Comments 1985) [hereinafter MPC].

[25] SCHOPP, *supra* note 2, at § 2.1.

[26] *Id.* at § 2.1.2.

According to the reasonable relationship principle, the appropriate intervention regarding Cook might include any of several modalities drawn from among the set of arguably least restrictive alternatives. These might include, for example, structured living arrangements involving supervised group homes and sheltered workshops, placement in locations remote from schools or playgrounds, or monitoring of time away from the supervised group homes and workshops. If necessary to protect children, Cook might require placement in a locked facility. Such a placement would require justification in the form of the need to protect the public from harm, however, because Cook lacks the capacities of retributive competence that would enable him to fulfill the requirements of guilt and desert that justify confinement through the criminal justice system.

Davis also qualifies for police power intervention through the mental health system, but his impairment complicates this matter somewhat because his functioning level varies across time. As previously described, Davis consistently experiences sexual fantasies and urges involving young children, but he acts on them only during his periods of psychosis. In contrast to Cook, he experiences periods of remission during which he possesses the capacities of retributive competence. He would be subject to police power intervention through the criminal justice system regarding criminal offenses committed during those periods. Providing that he continues to engage in sexual conduct with children only during the periods in which he suffers serious thought disorder, he lacks retributive competence regarding the decisions to engage in that criminal conduct.

During the periods of psychosis, he suffers serious thought disorder that interferes with his ability to engage in a competent process of practical reasoning regarding his criminal conduct. This impairment does not prevent him from fulfilling the mental state required by the offense definition because he purposefully engages in sexual conduct with children. He knows what he is doing in that he understands that he is engaging in sexual intercourse with children. It may seem tempting to say that he does not realize what he is doing because he believes he is fulfilling a divine mission, but this belief provides an account of his reason for engaging in conduct that he knows to be sexual conduct with children. It is not at all clear, however, that he understands the quality of his conduct insofar as that requirement involves the knowledge that the conduct is harmful. Davis understands that society considers this conduct harmful, but he believes that God commands it and may think that God's command prevents harm. A similar problem arises regarding the knowledge of wrongfulness provision in that he knows that law and social moral standards forbid this conduct, but he may believe that it is not only right but morally required in light of God's directives. Davis, like Cook, illustrates some of the unsatisfactory aspects of ignorance standards in that none of the various interpretations of these standards seem to adequately address Cook, Davis, and the full array of potential candidates.

Davis clearly lacks retributive competence under the process standard. His impaired reality testing and delusional thought disorder undermines his capacity to accurately comprehend and evaluate the circumstances and his own conduct. His impairment disrupts the ordinary process of practical reasoning by which unimpaired adults draw inferences and make use of their own moral standards as well as the likely legal consequences in order to direct their conduct. During his periods of remission, Davis demonstrates the ability to engage in this type of process in order to refrain from performing the criminal conduct. During these periods, he experiences the fantasies and urges, but he refrains from acting on them by thinking about the legal ramifications, condemning such behavior as wrongful, and intensifying his religious activity. During his periods of psychosis, however, his thought disorder and misinterpretation of reality distort his reasoning about this conduct and prevent him from functioning as a competent practical reasoner in the public jurisdiction.

Davis qualifies as an appropriate subject of police power intervention through the mental health system because his impairment renders him retributively incompetent and, thus, ineligible to participate in the criminal justice system. He engages in criminal conduct during periods of psychosis, suggesting that if treatment brings his psychotic disorder into remission, outpatient treatment and monitoring might provide police power intervention sufficient to serve the justifying state interest. If such an intervention fulfills that function, then any more restrictive intervention would violate the reasonable relationship principle as an arbitrary limitation on liberty. As discussed previously, the set of arguably least restrictive alternatives might contain several combinations of monitoring, supervision, treatment, and confinement. The reasonable relationship principle would not mandate selection of any specific alternative from among this set, but it would preclude the involuntary imposition of an intervention that was more restrictive of liberty than those within that set. If, however, he refuses treatment sufficient to prevent deterioration into the psychotic state associated with his criminal behavior, or if he decompensates despite treatment, inpatient confinement might represent the only form of police power intervention sufficient to fulfill the legitimate state interest in protecting the public that justifies the exercise of the police power.

Anderson and Baker, like Cook and Davis, initially appear to present clear cases. Neither suffers any impairment that prevents him from fulfilling the mental state required by the offense definition, and both purposefully engage in the conduct that violates the offense definition. Both understand the nature and quality of their conduct in that both understand the physical characteristics of their behavior and that it is harmful. Baker simply has no interest in the harm he causes. Anderson might rationalize his behavior, but he understands that the results can include distress and trauma, and he knows that such conduct is considered harmful according to the social standard represented by the law. Furthermore, both fully understand that the conduct is criminal and wrongful according to the generally accepted public morality. Baker may dismiss all talk of morality as hypocrisy, and Anderson might attempt to rationalize his conduct by arguing that the public morality is misguided. Both understand that the conduct violates the widely endorsed public morality, however, and both make efforts to avoid discovery of their crimes.

Although most readers would probably agree that Anderson and Baker know that their conduct is harmful and wrongful in a sense that Cook and Davis do not, it becomes very difficult to provide a clear explication of this difference because all four are aware that the law and conventional moral standards prohibit their behavior. The process approach, in contrast, clearly differentiates Anderson and Baker from Cook and Davis. The latter two offenders manifest serious impairment in their capacities for abstraction, comprehension, reasoning, and reality relatedness, but the former two defendants suffer no such impairment. Anderson and Baker possess unimpaired capacities of practical reasoning that allow them to comprehend legal constraints, prospectively apply those constraints to their conduct through a process of deliberation, and direct their conduct through a process of practical reasoning in light of this deliberation. They carefully plan their illegal conduct in order to avoid discovery and conviction, and they often succeed in this effort. In summary, they clearly possess the capacities of retributive competence that render them eligible to participate in the public jurisdiction as subjects of the criminal justice system.

It seems, therefore, that Anderson and Baker differ from Cook and Davis in that the former two offenders clearly qualify for police power intervention through the criminal justice system rather than through the alternative mental health system. Both qualify for diagnoses under the most common diagnostic nomenclature, and mental health treatment might provide some assistance in reducing the probability of recidivism, particularly for Anderson.[27] Impairment sufficient for clinical diagnosis does not necessarily undermine retributive competence, however, and some retributively competent individuals might also benefit from treatment.

Although Anderson and Baker apparently provide clear cases of offenders who commit criminal offenses under conditions that justify the exercise of the police power through the criminal justice system rather than through the alternative mental health system, both qualify for civil commitment under the sexual predator statutes. Both fulfill the diagnostic criteria for diagnoses, including paraphilia and APD, that have been recognized in prior cases as mental abnormalities or personality disorders that fulfill the commitment criteria under these provisions.[28] Both qualify for criminal conviction and punishment under the criminal justice system and for ostensibly civil confinement under statutes that purport to authorize commitment within the alternative mental health system. Neither Anderson nor Baker presents evidence that their psychological condition has changed between their offense and their commitment. Furthermore, the conduct constituting the offenses provides the primary bases for their diagnoses and for the commitment. By authorizing commitment of Anderson and Baker under these conditions, the sexual predator statues apparently simultaneously endorse conflicting premises: that these two offenders are retributively competent and that they are not and that they suffer legal mental illness and that they do not.

IV.   The Sexual Predator Statutes as Police Power Intervention

A.   Sexual Predators and Legal Mental Illness

Sexual predator statutes dramatically demonstrate the defects that more subtly pervade general civil commitment statutes. Because these statutes lack any clear conception of legal mental illness, they distort the criteria of equal standing in the public jurisdiction and undermine the legal structure that provides institutional limits on the manner in which the state can exercise the police power. The central cases addressing the sexual predator statutes and related provisions include the *Young* and *Hendricks* opinions that directly addressed sexual predator statutes as well as the *Blodgett* and *Linehan* cases that addressed related Minnesota statutes.[29] The statutes addressed in

---

[27] *See* chapter 11, section II (discussing the recent empirical evidence regarding treatment and recidivism).

[28] *See* chapter 7, section II.

[29] *Hendricks*, 117 S.Ct. at 2072; Matter of Linehan, 557 N.W.2d 171 (Minn. 1996); In Re Blodgett, 510 N.W.2d 910 (Minn. 1994); In Re Young, 857 P.2d 989 (Wash. 1993).

these cases differ from each other in some respects, but they converge insofar as they provide for civil commitment of convicted offenders after those offenders have served their criminal sentences. Furthermore, they authorize commitment of offenders on the bases of diagnostic categories and of determinations of dangerousness that rely heavily upon the pattern of criminal conduct for which the offenders have been convicted and served sentences.

B.   Early Cases

The *Young* and *Blodgett* cases occurred roughly contemporaneously and addressed challenges regarding the lack of any clear or substantive requirement of mental illness in a sexual predator statute and in a related provision. The petitioners in both cases challenged their commitments under the respective statutes, contending that their commitments to mental health facilities were illegitimate because they did not suffer from, and the statutes did not require, mental illness. The petitioners contended that commitment despite the lack of any medically recognized mental illness violated the Supreme Court's ruling in *Foucha*.[30] Both courts rejected these claims, concluding that these petitioners suffered mental illness of the type required by the respective statutes and sufficient to satisfy *Foucha*. Both courts reviewed statutory language, expert testimony, and passages from the *DSM* in reasoning to the conclusion that the petitioners suffered mental illness appropriate for commitment. The courts reviewed several purported categories of mental illness, including psychopathy, personality disorders, "mental abnormality," and paraphilia.

The Minnesota Psychopathic Personality Control Act challenged in *Blodgett* specifically applies the state's general civil commitment statute to psychopathic individuals. The petitioner challenged this statute under which he was committed upon completing his sentence for criminal sexual conduct. He claimed that *Foucha* precluded commitment because he suffered no mental illness. The expert witnesses agreed that the petitioner was properly diagnosed as manifesting APD and that he met the statutory definition of a psychopathic personality.[31]

The majority concluded that the petitioner was mentally ill and upheld the commitment. As the majority interpreted the statute and the facts, the petitioner suffered mental illness that rendered him dangerous to the public because he had a volitional disorder involving uncontrollable sexual urges. As the court interpreted the statute, this disorder is a limited form of APD in that it is limited to those who engage in sexually assaultive behavior. The majority characterized psychopathic personality disorder for the purpose of the statute as a "violent sexually deviant condition or disorder."[32] In determining whether an individual manifests this disorder, the court considers the nature and frequency of the assaults, the degree of violence involved, the offender's attitude and mood, and other factors that bear on the predatory sex impulse and the lack of power to control it. In summary, the court inferred the purported inability to control the violent conduct and the purported disorder from the properties of the conduct constituting the offenses. The court interpreted the

---

[30] Foucha v. Louisiana, 112 S.Ct. 1780 (1992); In Re Blodgett, 510 N.W.2d at 910, 914–16; In Re Young, 857 P.2d at 989, 1001–04.

[31] In Re Blodgett, 510 N.W.2d at 912.

[32] *Id.* at 915.

statute as identifying a class of offenders that victimizes women and children in a particular manner. The court concluded that Minnesota confines these sexual predators with uncontrollable sex drive in state hospitals after the completion of their prison sentences.[33]

This vague claim of mental illness leading to dangerousness as a result of volitional disorder is common to *Blodgett* and *Young*. *Young* involved two petitioners who were subject to commitment under Washington's sexual predator law following completion of their prison sentences. Both had histories of repetitive violent sexual offenses. They were diagnosed as manifesting APD and paraphilia.[34]

The *Young* majority explicitly recognized mental abnormality as a legislative category rather than a clinical disorder or category of clinical disorders. It reasoned that the *DSM* is not dispositive regarding inclusion within this legislative category. Despite this reasoning, the majority then supported its conclusion that the petitioners were mentally ill by explaining that their diagnoses are recognized by the *DSM* or consistent with diagnoses recognized by it.[35] The court differentiated the petitioners from the petitioner in *Foucha* by reasoning that Foucha was described by the expert as an antisocial personality, whereas the instant case involved APD. The court explicitly relied on the *DSM*'s categorization of the latter as a disorder and of the former as merely a "V" code, which the *DSM* applies to those who do not suffer clinical disorders.[36] In summary, the court rejected the *DSM* as authoritative but relied almost entirely upon it in supporting the conclusion that these defendants suffered mental illness.

Although the *Young* majority recognized that the statute requires mental illness that makes the petitioner likely to engage in predatory sexual violence, it provided no clear description of the kind of psychological impairment present in these defendants or of the manner in which it makes them likely to engage in predatory violence. Rather, it supported the claim that the petitioners suffered mental disorder by showing that the *DSM* recognizes their diagnoses or some categories that resemble these diagnoses, and it supported the claim of dangerousness by reference to past behavior and expert testimony.

The Minnesota and Washington courts adopted similar approaches to the analysis of legal mental illness for the purpose of postsentence commitment in *Blodgett* and *Young*. Both courts recognized that the key statutory terms referring to mental illness, including "mental abnormality," "personality disorder," and "psychopathic personality," represent legislative categories rather than clinical psychological disorders. Furthermore, neither court accepted clinical notions or the *DSM* as dispositive regarding inclusion within these categories, and the *Young* court explicitly rejected the *DSM* as dispositive.[37] Recall the three senses of "mental illness" as functional impairment of psychological process ("psychological impairment"), clinically recognized patterns of psychological impairment recognized by clinical nomenclatures ("diagnostic categories"), and legally significant patterns of psychological impairment that render a person incapable of meeting some legally relevant standard of

---

[33] *Id.* 915–17.

[34] In Re Young, 857 P.2d at 992–96.

[35] In Re Young, 857 P.2d at 1001–03.

[36] *Id.* at 1005–08 and n12.

[37] In Re Blodgett, 510 N.W.2d at 914–16; In Re Young, 857 P.2d at 1001–02 and n5.

adequate functioning ("legal mental illness").[38] In these terms, both courts recognized that the *DSM* and related clinical notions address patterns of psychological impairment that are sufficiently frequent and clinically significant to warrant recognition as diagnostic categories for clinical purposes of diagnosis and treatment. They also recognized, however, that these clinical sources are not dispositive for adjudication under statutes that require legal mental illness.

Despite recognizing this distinction, neither court fulfilled its responsibility to articulate the legal criteria of competence and legal mental illness for this statutory purpose. Neither identified the types of psychological impairment that would undermine the petitioners' standing as competent in the relevant sense and therefore qualify as a legal mental illness. Both courts suggested that the petitioners suffered mental illness of a volitional type, but neither provided any evidence of volitional impairment, any account of what could count as evidence for such impairment, or any explanation of what "volitional disorder" or "uncontrollable impulse" means.

The courts are correct in stating that the notion of mental illness relevant to the statutes is a legal one rather than a clinical one and in denying that clinical categories are authoritative. Although courts often appeal to the *DSM* to establish that a psychological disorder qualifies as a "real" mental illness, inclusion of a disorder in the current edition of the *DSM* is neither necessary nor sufficient to establish that it qualifies as legal mental illness for statutory purposes; it simply identifies the pattern of impairment as one that has been recognized as a psychological disorder for clinical purposes. Such inclusion might be indirectly relevant in that it suggests that the pattern of impairment is one that occurs with sufficient frequency to elicit recognition. This might increase the court's confidence that this person actually suffers the apparent impairment. That is, it might decrease suspicion of misdiagnosis or of malingering.

The directly relevant question is whether the person manifests a pattern of psychological impairment that constitutes a legal mental illness, that is, one that undermines the individual's status as competent in the legally relevant sense. For the purpose of these statutes, persons are mentally ill if they suffer impairment that renders them appropriate for the mental health system's institutions of social control by undermining their eligibility to participate in the criminal justice system or by satisfying some alternative justification that neither the statutes nor the courts articulate. None of the categories of psychological disorder discussed in these cases include any impairment of process such as comprehension, consciousness, orientation, perception, reasoning, or reality relatedness that would ordinarily suggest impaired capacity to participate in the rule-based criminal justice system as competent practical reasoners.

Minnesota's statutory definition of a psychopathic personality requires no impairment of processes that would undermine the individual's status as a competent practical reasoner. The statute addresses conditions of emotion, impulsiveness, or judgment that render the person irresponsible regarding sexual matters.[39] Certain individuals, such as Cook and Davis, might exercise poor judgment regarding sexual

---

[38] *See* chapter 3, section III.

[39] MINN. STAT. § 526.9 (1975). The statute also includes a failure to appreciate, but it provides no account of what this means. *See* SCHOPP, *supra* note 2, at § 2.1.1 (discussing the lack of any helpful interpretation of this term).

matters because the capacities required for practical reasoning are severely impaired, but nothing in the statutes requires that irresponsible conduct result from such impairment.[40] Some writers have discussed disturbances of ideation or unusual coping mechanisms in some persons who might fall within the scope of this statute; however, they neither discuss severe impairment of reality testing, comprehension, or reasoning that would ordinarily render a person incompetent to participate in the criminal justice system, nor do they impute these traits to all who would qualify under the statute.[41] The *Blodgett* opinion provided no evidence of such impairment in the petitioner.

Neither the statute nor the *Blodgett* opinion provide any account of the disorders referred to as disordered emotion, desire, or impulse that suggests that these "disorders" consist of anything other than desire to engage in criminal conduct and willingness to act on that desire. Any voluntary conduct suggests the presence of some motivation to engage in such conduct, but the mere presence of desire or impulse provides no suggestion of exculpatory or incapacitating significance. Those who are greedy experience a strong desire for wealth, but greed neither exculpates those who commit theft nor suggests that they suffer disorder that renders them unable to control their acquisitive conduct or incompetent for any legal purpose.

Perhaps a volitional disorder that rendered one unable to direct one's conduct related to desires or impulses would be significant for these purposes. Although *Blodgett* alludes to a volitional disorder or inability to control violent sexual impulses, the opinion gives no explanation of what that might mean or of what might count as evidence of such a disorder.[42] The defendant's conduct was directed, organized, and planned, bearing no resemblance to movement such as that involved in a seizure or reflex that occurs without the conscious direction of the psychological decision-making processes. Neither the court, the statute, nor any other source provides any account of noncognitive volitional disorders that apply to organized, directed behavior.[43]

The court listed several factors that indicate the presence of such a volitional disorder: the nature and frequency of the assaults, the degree of violence involved, the relationship of the offender and the victim, the offender's attitude and mood, the medical and family history, the results of psychological evaluation, and other factors that bear on the predatory sex impulse and the lack of power to control it.[44] Although the court identified these factors as indicative of inability to control violent conduct, it provided no explanation of the putative significance of these factors as indicia of any impairment of volitional capacities. Most of these factors are ordinarily reviewed as sentencing factors that are understood in other criminal contexts as bearing on culpability and blameworthiness.[45] The court provides no reason to think that these

---

[40] *See* chapter 1, section I for descriptions of Cook and Davis.

[41] Margit C. Henderson & Seth C. Kalitchman, *Sexually Deviant Behavior and Schizotypy: A Theoretical Perspective With Supportive Data*, 61 PSYCHIATRIC Q. 273 (1990); James R. P. Ogloff & Stephen Wong, *Electrodermal and Cardiovascular Evidence of a Coping Response to Psychopaths*, 17 CRIM JUST. & BEHAV. 231 (1990).

[42] In Re Blodgett, 510 N.W.2d 910, 915 (Minn. 1994).

[43] Stephen J. Morse, *Culpability and Control*, 142 U. PA. L. REV. 1587 (1994); SCHOPP, *supra* note 2, at § 6.3. Both sources explain that claims of noncognitive impairment rendering persons unable to control their conduct are usually metaphorical at best.

[44] In Re Blodgett, 510 N.W.2d at 915.

[45] MPC, *supra* note 24, at § 7.03 (criteria for extended term of imprisonment for felonies include

factors indicate culpability for other defendants but volitional impairment for these petitioners.

The court correctly identified these petitioners as belonging to a class of predatory offenders whose conduct reveals aggravating characteristics relevant to sentencing.[46] The confusion arises because after identifying a series of properties of criminal conduct ordinarily considered supportive of extended sentencing, the court characterizes this pattern as revealing uncontrollable impulses, these individuals as lacking power to control their conduct, and the court's responsibility as identifying those who suffer a certain kind of personality disorder. Initially, it seems odd that the supreme court of Minnesota would call upon trial courts to diagnose personality disorders because the terminology suggests that personality disorders are clinical psychological disorders. The trial courts' role seems more appropriate, however, when one realizes that in charging trial courts with the responsibility to identify those who manifest the volitional or personality disorder at issue in these cases, the supreme court of Minnesota directs those trial courts to identify those offenders who demonstrate a tendency to engage in criminal conduct marked by a pattern of aggravating sentencing factors that support prolonged incarceration. The incoherence, then, lies not in charging the trial court with making the determination, but in prescribing confinement in the form of commitment rather than in the form of extended sentencing as justified by aggravating sentencing factors.

The *Blodgett* court explicitly characterized psychopathic personality as a limited form of the *DSM*'s APD, involving antisocial conduct of a violent sexual nature. As defined in the manual referred to by the court, however, APD does not consist primarily of some pattern of impaired psychological process that causes antisocial conduct; rather, the pattern of antisocial conduct provides the primary diagnostic criteria for the disorder. The manual defines APD primarily as a personal history demonstrating a pattern of antisocial conduct beginning in adolescence, and it specifically excludes those whose antisocial conduct is associated with major psychological impairment in the form of schizophrenic or manic disorder.[47] Thus, the presence of APD as defined in the manual to which the court referred does not suggest impaired psychological process that might meet the criteria of legal mental illness rendering the subject incompetent to participate as a competent practical reasoner in the criminal justice system that orders the public jurisdiction.

Other diagnostic nomenclatures might provide different conceptions of APD, psychopathy, or sociopathy that require some specified impairment as the cause of the antisocial behavior. Some individuals who qualify for such diagnoses might also meet the criteria of legal mental illness for the purpose of identifying those appropriate to the exercise of the police power through the mental health system. The *Blodgett* court, however, explicitly referred to the conception of APD in the edition of the *DSM* that was current at that time. The possibility of alternative conceptions demonstrates the importance of the point made previously; the critical inquiry for legal purposes is the relationship between the pattern of psychological impairment

---

repeat offenses, dangerous mental abnormality, danger to others); ARTHUR W. CAMPBELL, THE LAW OF SENTENCING § 10.1 (2d ed. 1991) (discussing the broad range of sentencing factors including the details of the crime, offender, and the victim impact).

[46] In Re Blodgett, 510 N.W.2d at 914–15.

[47] DSM–IV, *supra* note 15, at 649–50. The court referred to the revised third edition.

and the criteria of legal mental illness and *not* whether the offender qualifies for any particular clinical diagnosis or for any diagnosis in a clinical nomenclature.

Both subjects of commitment in *Young* received diagnoses of paraphilia as well as of APD. Paraphilia define patterns of deviant sexual desire that either cause the individual discomfort or are accompanied by functionally or socially maladaptive conduct.[48] These desires can take the form of obsessive or intrusive fantasies and urges, but as with APD or the psychopathic personality, there is no evidence of any inability to control conduct related to these urges, nor is there any account of what would count as such evidence or of what this "inability" means. Most paraphiliac conduct is directed, organized, and carefully planned.[49]

If some individuals experience paraphilia as including intrusive, obsessive fantasies and urges that cause them distress or interfere with their ability to function, it may be reasonable to categorize this pattern of experience as a psychological disorder for clinical purposes because it constitutes a pattern of thinking and feeling that causes these individuals discomfort and impairs their ability to concentrate their mental processes on other subjects or projects that matter to them.[50] Even if we accept paraphilia as a psychological disorder in this sense, however, conduct consistent with these urges does not qualify as a symptom in the strong sense that identifies a symptom as a necessary consequence of the disorder.[51] The diagnosis applies to those who act on these urges and to those who are markedly distressed by them but do not act on them. Nothing in the description of the disorder provides reason to think that the urges of those who act on them are less controllable than are the urges of those who do not. The willingness to act on the urges may result from stress, substance abuse, or antisocial personality traits rather than from any feature of the disorder. Thus, accepting the proposition that individuals cannot control these intrusive urges and fantasies in the sense that they cannot simply decide not to experience such mental events does not entail that they cannot refrain from acting on these mental events.

Some people are greedy, and some may even be greedy in an obsessive sense. That is, they may desire wealth so strongly and single-mindedly that they find themselves obsessed with the idea of increasing their wealth when they would rather concentrate on some other topic. Yet, greed provides a motive for theft rather than an excuse that exculpates theft or a type of impairment that renders one ineligible to participate in the criminal justice system as a competent practical reasoner. If a number of people seek clinical assistance because their obsession with wealth is preventing them from enjoying life or causing them anxiety, it might become useful for clinical purposes to identify this pattern as a specific subtype of obsessive personality disorder or anxiety disorder.[52] The mere fact that this pattern of pathological greed had been recognized as a clinical diagnostic category would not suggest, how-

---

[48] *Id.* at 522–23. The court referred to the revised third edition. I focus on these disorders as described in the DSM because the courts adopted this source. I do not suggest that we should consider the manual to be clinically or legally authoritative.

[49] W. L. Marshall, D. R. Laws, & H. E. Barbaree, *Present Status and Future Directions*, in HANDBOOK OF SEXUAL ASSAULT 390–91 (W. L. Marshall, D. R. Laws, and H. E. Barbaree eds. 1990).

[50] Bernard Gert, *A Sex Caused Inconsistency in DSM–III–R: The Definition of Mental Disorder and the Definition of Paraphilia*, 17 J. L. & MED. 155 (1992).

[51] JOEL FEINBERG, DOING AND DESERVING 259–60 (1970) (three senses of "symptom").

[52] DSM–IV, *supra* note 15, at 673 (personality disorder NOS), 444 (anxiety disorder NOS).

ever, that it should qualify as legal mental illness for any particular legal purpose such as exculpation or commitment.

C. Later Cases

The United States Supreme Court had previously upheld the Minnesota statute at issue in *Blodgett* after the Minnesota supreme court interpreted it as applying to those who were utterly unable to control their sexual impulses.[53] After upholding the same statute in *Blodgett*, the Minnesota supreme court overturned a commitment under it because the court found that evidence at the hearing failed to establish that the subject lacked the capacity to control his conduct.[54] The Minnesota legislature then passed a different statute that authorized commitment of those who engage in a harmful sexual conduct and manifest a disorder indicating the likelihood of further harmful sexual conduct. This later statute differs from the prior provision as interpreted by the supreme court in that it does not require the inability to control sexual conduct.[55]

This later Minnesota statute resembles the sexual predator provisions at issue in *Hendricks* and *Young* insofar as it provides for commitment of convicted offenders who have served criminal sentences, and it fails to provide any substantive conception of legal mental illness that fulfills the discriminative or justificatory functions. The Minnesota supreme court upheld this statute in *Matter of Linehan*,[56] and the court's opinion resembled those upholding the earlier statutes in several respects. First, the court reviewed testimony from the hearing that discussed Linehan's diagnoses as APD and paraphilia. Some experts denied that he fulfilled the diagnostic criteria for these diagnoses, but no expert suggested that Linehan suffered any significant impairment of orientation, comprehension, reasoning, reality testing, or any other function necessary to engage in a competent process of practical reasoning.[57] The trial court applied the diagnostic criteria for APD to Linehan's history of antisocial behavior, and the Minnesota supreme court accepted APD as sufficient to fulfill the requirement of a disorder or dysfunction under the statute.[58]

Second, although the Minnesota supreme court denied that the diagnosis of APD was merely a restatement of Linehan's criminal behavior, the trial court accepted the diagnosis largely by citing to Linehan's past criminal and otherwise antisocial behavior, and the Minnesota supreme court cited to the acceptance of APD by the current edition of the *DSM*.[59] Thus, neither the statute nor the courts provide any account of legal mental illness for this statute that explains what kind of functional impairment is necessary or sufficient for inclusion under the statute. Finally, the conclusion that Linehan's disorder rendered him likely to engage in harmful sexual conduct rested largely upon his past antisocial conduct, including the criminal conduct for which he had been found criminally responsible.[60] In summary, this case

---

[53] Minnesota ex rel. Pearson v. Probate Court, 309 U.S. 270 (1940).

[54] Matter of Linehan, 518 N.W.2d 609 (Minn. 1994).

[55] Matter of Linehan, 557 N.W.2d 171, 179 (Minn. 1996).

[56] 557 N.W.2d 171 (Minn. 1996).

[57] *Id.* at 176–77.

[58] *Id.* at 180–86.

[59] *Id.* at 177, 185.

[60] *Id.* at 190–91.

resembles the earlier cases in that neither the statute nor the court opinions provide any substantive account of legal mental illness for this purpose, and the evidence supporting the statutory criteria of commitment relied heavily upon Linehan's pattern of antisocial conduct, including his past criminal conduct for which he had been convicted and served the sentence.

The Supreme Court's opinion in *Hendricks* continues familiar patterns begun by the state courts in *Young* and *Blodgett*. The *Hendricks* majority denied that clinical diagnoses control legal conceptions of mental illness, and it recognized broad legislative authority to define criteria of mental disorder for statutory purposes. The majority also continued the pattern of these state courts in emphasizing volitional impairment in its discussion of Hendricks' putative inability to control his sexual conduct.[61] Unfortunately, the Court also followed the pattern of the state courts insofar as it provided no account of legal mental illness sufficient to fulfill the vague statutory reference to mental abnormalities or personality disorders, nor did it provide any reason to believe that Hendricks was unable to control his criminal conduct or any guidance regarding what would count as evidence of such an inability. Although the *Hendricks* Court accepted Hendricks's unsupported assertion that he was unable to control his planned, organized, and goal-directed sexual conduct, it provided no interpretation of this putative volitional disorder that would place any limitation on its attribution to any other offender who becomes the subject of a petition for commitment.

The *Hendricks* majority implicitly recognizes the justificatory concerns regarding the use of civil commitment as a police power intervention following a criminal sentence. The Court's reasoning supporting its conclusion that the sexual predator statutes satisfy the requirements of due process relies heavily on the contention that the commitment criteria limit confinement to "those who are unable to control their dangerousness."[62] The majority opinion strongly suggests that this putative inability to control is central to the constitutional adequacy of the statute at issue in *Hendricks*.[63] The majority opinion explicitly recognizes freedom from physical restraint as central to the liberty protected by the Due Process Clause of the Fourteenth Amendment, but it also recognizes legitimate exceptions from this protection for the civil detainment of those who endanger others because they are unable to control their behavior. The opinion draws an analogy between these civil detainment statutes and the sexual predator statute at issue in *Hendricks*. The majority opinion emphasizes Hendricks's diagnosis of pedophilia and his claim that he is unable to control his urge to molest children in its analysis of his pedophilia as a mental abnormality that makes him likely to engage in acts of sexual violence as required by the statute, and it refers to this putative volitional impairment in differentiating him from those who are more properly addressed through the criminal justice system.[64] The majority concludes, "[t]his admitted lack of volitional control, coupled with a prediction of future dangerousness, adequately distinguishes Hendricks from other dangerous persons who are perhaps more properly dealt with exclusively through criminal proceedings."[65]

---

[61] *Hendricks*, 117 S.Ct. at 2072, 2079–81.

[62] *Id.* at 2080.

[63] *Id.* at 2079–81.

[64] *Id.*

[65] *Id.* at 2081.

The *Hendricks* Court did not explicitly hold that the Kansas statute was constitutional only if it was interpreted as incorporating the requirement that those committed under it must be unable to control their conduct. This notion of volitional
impairment or inability to control plays a central role in the majority's interpretation
of the statute as consistent with due process, however, and the majority opinion
provides no clear alternative criterion that would distinguish those subject to commitment from those appropriate to the criminal justice system. The Court's failure
to provide any explication of this putative volitional impairment undermines the
discriminative and justificatory functions of a legal standard of mental illness. The
opinion provides lower courts with no guidance regarding which individuals they
should identify as legally mentally ill in this sense and no justification for subjecting
these individuals to confinement through the mental health system. Finally, the Court
supplies no analysis that would reconcile this putative inability to control the criminal
conduct with the prior finding of criminal responsibility.

Although the *Hendricks* opinion provides no account of the putative inability to
control, it refers to the Minnesota statute upheld in *Blodgett* as an example of a
statute that allows commitment of those who suffer "volitional impairment rendering
them dangerous beyond their control."[66] The *Hendricks* opinion appeals to this Minnesota statute previously upheld in *Pearson* as precedent for civil commitment of
those who are dangerous by virtue of the inability to control their conduct, but neither
that statute nor the cases upholding it provide any explication of this "utter lack of
power to control." In upholding that Minnesota statute, the Supreme Court characterized that provision as requiring "evidence of past conduct pointing to probable
consequences."[67] This reference to past conduct as a basis for inferring probable
consequences suggests an inference of current dangerousness from the past criminal
conduct, raising the same concerns discussed previously regarding the inference from
past criminal conduct to both the purported disorder and the likelihood of reoffending. This reference to *Pearson* provides no elaboration of the still mysterious inability
to control.

The supreme court of Minnesota later overturned the commitment of Dennis
Linehan pursuant to the statute upheld in *Pearson* precisely because the expert testimony had failed to establish that Linehan lacked the ability to control his sexual
conduct.[68] The court reviewed the relevant testimony of four expert witnesses, two
of whom identified Linehan as a psychopathic personality. All four experts described
Linehan's conduct as controlled, planful, and directed, and the court concluded that
the state had failed to establish the required "utter lack of power to control."[69] Two
years later Linehan was committed under the new Minnesota statute that resembles
the sexual predator statutes in Kansas and Washington in that it predicates commitment upon a pattern of harmful sexual conduct and a disorder indicating the likelihood of future harmful sexual conduct.[70] Although the *Hendricks* majority draws an
analogy between the Kansas sexual predator statute and the earlier Minnesota statute
requiring the utter lack of power to control, the later Minnesota statute more closely

---

[66] *Id.* at 2080.
[67] *Pearson*, 309 U.S. at 270, 274.
[68] Matter of Linehan, 518 N.W.2d 609 (Minn. 1994).
[69] *Id.* at 612–13.
[70] Matter of Linehan, 557 N.W.2d 171 (Minn. 1996).

resembles the Kansas and Washington sexual predator statutes. The case of Linehan indicates that the later Minnesota provision differs from the earlier Minnesota statute precisely because the later provision does *not* require the inability to control conduct.

The *Hendricks* majority's emphasis on the putative inability to control sexual conduct in its interpretation of the mental abnormality provision of the sexual predator statute raises perplexing questions in light of the recent trend away from volitional clauses in insanity defense standards, including the federal provision.[71] Those who support this trend appeal at least partially to the apparently widespread belief that neither courts nor clinical experts are able to differentiate those who are unable to control their conduct from those who simply choose not to refrain from that conduct.[72] Some commentators report data that purportedly call into question the claim that clinicians are not able to accurately evaluate volitional impairment.[73] The data reported address interrater reliability in assessing the cognitive and volitional standards, however, rather than the accuracy of the agreed upon assessments. That is, the data support the contentions that clinicians agreed with one another regarding the cognitive and volitional assessments at comparable rates, but they neither demonstrate the accuracy of these assessments nor provide any clear indication of the meaning of volitional impairment for this purpose.[74]

The problem is more fundamental than an inability to accurately measure degrees of volitional impairment. The most central concern is not merely that we have difficulty measuring or identifying volitional impairment or the inability to control. Rather, we have no clear conception of what we are trying to measure or identify. Neither the statutes, the cases, nor the commentary provide any account of the behavior constituting the offenses as produced by impaired processes or capacities that would explain why these individuals were unable to direct their conduct through the same processes that ordinary people use to direct their ordinary behavior. That is, when addressing plausible candidates for the insanity defense or for commitment as a sexual predator, we neither have any clear idea what it could mean to say that they were unable to control their conduct or that they suffered volitional impairment, nor do we have any guidance regarding what would count as evidence of such impairment.[75]

D. Sexual Predator Commitment and Retributive Competence

In summary, if legal institutions are to address these cases appropriately, legislatures and courts must articulate legal standards of retributive competence and the corresponding notions of legal mental illness. Experts must describe the pattern of psychological impairment suffered by any particular defendant. The fact finder must apply the legal standard to the defendant's impairment in order to determine whether this defendant is legally mentally ill for this purpose. None of the categories of clinical psychological disorder discussed in *Blodgett, Young, Linehan,* or *Hendricks* involve impairment that constitutes legal mental illness for the purpose of rendering

[71] 18 United States Code § 17 (a) (1988); SCHOPP, *supra* note 2, at § 2.1.1.

[72] Richard Bonnie, *The Moral Basis of the Insanity Defense*, 69 A.B.A. J. 194 (1983).

[73] *See, e.g.,* Richard Rogers, *APA's Position on the Insanity Defense*, 42 AMER. PSYCHOLOGIST 840 (1987).

[74] *Id.* at 841–42.

[75] Morse, *supra* note 43; SCHOPP, *supra* note 2 at § 6.3.

these individuals appropriate for police power intervention through the mental health system. Rather, these statutes and cases illegitimately shift competent practical reasoners from the appropriate criminal justice institution of police power intervention to the inappropriate mental health component.

Some commentators support sexual predator statutes as legitimate alternatives to preventive detention through the criminal justice system because criminal incarceration of individuals who have already served their sentences and have not been found guilty of additional offenses undermines the moral force of the criminal law.[76] These commentators are correct in claiming that such use of the criminal law would undermine the moral force of the criminal law. It does so by criminally confining those who have not qualified for further incarceration by committing additional criminal offenses under conditions of culpability that justify the condemnation inherent in criminal conviction and punishment.

The sexual predator statutes raise a similar problem, however, in that they undermine the moral force of several related components of the legal institutions through which the state exercises the police power. These statutes undermine the moral force of mental health law by misusing the system to constrain those not properly subject to it and by falsely suggesting that these people suffer impairment of the capacities of practical reasoning that qualify them for retributive competence. They also undermine the moral force of the criminal law by misrepresenting as ineligible to participate in that system those who have already been punished in that system. If criminal responsibility requires retributive competence in the criminal justice system of social control and police power civil commitment provides an alternative institution of social control for those who are not eligible to participate in the criminal justice system because they lack retributive competence, then commitment under these police power provisions explicitly identifies these individuals as not eligible to participate in the criminal justice system in which they have been punished.

The division of the police power institutions into the criminal justice system for those who possess the capacities of retributive competence and the mental health component for those who lack retributive competence allows the consistent normative foundation that justifies both systems. Thus, it is perhaps most insidious that the sexual predator statutes undermine this foundation by violating the underlying principles of political morality and misrepresenting the conditions of competency to participate in the criminal justice component of the comprehensive system of social control.

In cases such as *Blodgett, Young, Linehan,* and *Hendricks,* the criminal law suffers loss of moral force by failing to protect the public by permanently containing offenders who have engaged in a series of offenses such as those committed by these petitioners. The criminal justice system must rectify this failure, but it cannot do so by distorting the police power component of the mental health system, the relationship between this system and the criminal justice system, and the principles of political morality that justify both.

This analysis does not entail the conclusion that any defendant must be both exculpable and committable or neither. Because of the possibility of deteriorating psychological condition over time, a defendant might be retributively competent at the time of the offense but not at the end of the sentence. Alternately, a defendant

---

[76] Paul H. Robinson, *Forward: The Criminal–Civil Distinction and Dangerous Blameless Offenders,* 83 J. Crim. L. & Criminology 693 (1993).

might suffer acute psychopathology such that he does not qualify as retributively competent at the time of the offense but does so qualify at the point of evaluation for commitment. Offenders subject to sexual predator statutes are particularly unlikely to manifest these patterns, however, because these statutes target these individuals for commitment precisely because they are considered dangerous by virtue of the expectation that their psychological processes and behavioral tendencies remain constant throughout the period that includes their prior offenses, their criminal sentences, and the postsentence commitment.

V.   Conclusion: Police Power Intervention and the Normative Structure

Chapters 7 and 8 advance and defend an approach to police power intervention through the criminal justice and mental health systems as complementary institutions of coercive social control in the public jurisdiction. Sexual predator statutes dramatically demonstrate the defects that more subtly pervade the current approach to police power commitment under civil commitment statutes. Some readers might find it difficult to sympathize with the plight of offenders who become subject to indefinite confinement by engaging in patterns of repetitive criminal activity against others. Indeed, many reasonable citizens who read the descriptions of the criminal activity engaged in by the petitioners in these cases might suggest that the anticipated release from custody of these petitioners represented the only injustice apparent in these cases. To appreciate the significance of these statutes and cases, however, one must evaluate their institutional significance.

The incoherence that pervades these statutes and cases violates the principles of political morality underlying a liberal society, and it distorts the parameters of the criminal justice and mental health institutions of social control through which the state exercises the police power. By proceeding under these statutes, the state operates on the premises that these individuals are legally mentally ill and that they are not, that they are retributively competent and that they are not, and that they are eligible for equal standing in the public jurisdiction and that they are not. One need not endorse the entire interpretation of liberal political morality and the significance of retributive competence advanced in this book to accept the insidious effect of this incoherence in these statutes and cases. Strict and clearly articulated legal criteria for criminal conviction and for mental health commitment place meaningful limits on the state exercise of the police power by requiring criminal responsibility or legal mental illness for conviction or commitment, respectively. Each of these requirements limits the manner in which the state can apply these institutions of social control to individuals. Statutes and cases that dilute the boundaries between criminal conviction and civil commitment by adopting vacuous conceptions of legal mental illness and authorizing commitment on the basis of a pattern of criminal activity render more amorphous the limits and requirements of each institution. Thus, they weaken the constraints that each places on the state exercise of the police power. The court opinions in the sexual predator cases approach the insidious conclusions that (a) the state can confine mentally ill people without meeting the usual requirements of criminal conviction, and (b) "mental illness" can mean anything the state says it means.

Chapter 9
THE RIGHT TO REFUSE CARE UNDER
THE POLICE POWER

Legitimate police power interventions through the mental health system occur when those who lack retributive competence create risk to others sufficient to justify the state in exercising its authority to protect the public from harm. These interventions raise questions regarding the limits on the exercise of the police power through the mental health system, including those addressing the state's authority to involuntary administer treatment and the corresponding right of the individual to refuse treatment. This chapter examines that issue, but it neither surveys the various legal doctrines relevant to the right to refuse treatment nor purports to replace such analysis.[1] That approach fulfills an important function by formulating and evaluating the specific legal arguments available under these various legal doctrines. This chapter pursues a different but complementary project in that it develops a more abstract analysis of the right to refuse treatment under the police power that coheres with the normative structure and the accompanying approaches to *parens patriae* and police power interventions discussed in this book. In this manner, it develops a coherent normative framework for the arguments from the various specific legal doctrines. The next section identifies some difficult cases and the central concerns raised by these cases. The following sections begin to address these cases and concerns.

I. Difficult Cases

First, consider Davis, who suffers from paranoid schizophrenia and engages in sexual offenses against children during periods of psychotic dysfunction. His crimes reflect his delusional thought, including his belief that he is charged with a divine mission to create a "sacred family of chosen acolytes."[2] The state intervenes under the police power in order to protect the public. The initial intervention takes the form of a criminal arrest and trial. According to the approach presented in this book, the insanity acquittal establishes that the state properly exercises ongoing social control through the mental health system because Davis lacks retributive competence. His current diagnosis and prior experience indicate that antipsychotic medication provides a promising treatment reasonably expected to ameliorate his delusional disorder, improve his reality testing, and protect the public from the criminal conduct associated with his psychotic disorder. During his psychotic periods, however, he understands his hallucinations, his delusional process, and his criminal conduct as

---

[1] BRUCE J. WINICK, THE RIGHT TO REFUSE MENTAL HEALTH TREATMENT (1997) (providing a recent survey and analysis of the relevant legal doctrine).

[2] *See* chapter 1, section I.

components of his divine mission rather than as a manifestation of his psychopathology. Thus, he refuses treatment.

These circumstances raise important questions regarding Davis's competence to make decisions regarding his treatment and his right to refuse involuntary treatment reasonably expected to decrease the risk he presents to the public. In addition, we must determine whether the right to refuse treatment under the police power varies with his competence for person or with the likelihood that the treatment will promote his clinical interests in addition to the public safety.

Second, recall Anderson and Baker, who commit sexual crimes in the absence of severe impairment of a type that would undermine retributive competence and justify police power intervention under the mental health system, rather than the criminal justice system.[3] Anderson is socially anxious and inadequate, and he qualifies for the clinical diagnoses of pedophilia and avoidant personality disorder. Baker engages in an extended pattern of aggressive and criminal behavior, qualifying for the clinical diagnostic categories of pedophilia, sexual sadism, and APD.

As with Davis, the state intervenes under the police power in order to protect the public, and this intervention takes the form of a criminal arrest and trial. In contrast to Davis, however, Anderson and Baker are convicted, sentenced, and imprisoned. As they approach the end of their criminal sentences, the state initiates commitment proceedings under sexual predator statutes. Although research regarding the success of sex offender treatment programs yields inconclusive results, some available data suggest that cognitive–behavioral treatment might augment self-management skills in a manner expected to decrease the probability of recidivism, especially for Anderson.[4] Other interventions, including aversive conditioning or chemical or surgical castration, might decrease recidivism by decreasing arousal or rendering these offenders unable to commit some offenses.[5]

Both offenders clearly qualify as competent regarding person and as retributively competent. The prospect of administering these treatment modalities to these offenders involuntarily raises questions regarding the competent person's right to refuse treatment intended to protect the public. Furthermore, we must determine whether the justification differs for interventions such as the cognitive–behavioral treatment expected to decrease the probability of recidivism by promoting adaptive skills, as compared to techniques expected to reduce the probability of recidivism by decreasing the motive or the ability to offend, such as aversive conditioning or chemical or surgical castration.

Third, consider Larry, who engages in a series of assaults associated with periodic manic episodes involving grandiose and persecutory delusions.[6] Larry resembles Davis in several important respects. The justification for state intervention regarding both rests on the state's authority to exercise the police power in order to protect the public from harm. Both qualify for police power intervention through the mental

---

[3] *See id.*

[4] *See* chapter 11, section II.

[5] Kirk Heilbrun, Christine Maguth Nezu, Michelle Keeney, Susie Chung, & Adam L. Wasserman, *Sexual Offending: Linking Assessment, Intervention, and Decision Making*, 4 PSYCHOL., PUB. POL'Y & L. 138, 147 (1998); William Winslade, T. Howard Stone, Michele Smith-Bell, & Denise M. Webb, *Castrating Pedophiles Convicted of Sex Offenses Against Children: New Treatment or Old Punishment*, 51 S.M.U. L. REV. 349, 366–76 (1998).

[6] *See* chapter 5, section IV.

health system, rather than criminal conviction and incarceration, because they lack retributive competence at the time of their criminal conduct. Finally, Larry resembles Davis in that his history and current diagnosis suggest that medication for his mood disorder will likely prove effective in reducing his impairment and the resulting danger to the public. Larry presents an additional concern, however, in that he refuses the medication when he is in remission. During these periods, he possesses the capacities of retributive competence and of competence for person, and he refuses the medication because he misses the elevated moods and dislikes the drug effects. Thus, he precipitates decompensation by refusing the medication during periods of competence.

Larry raises questions similar to those raised by Anderson and Baker insofar as all three refuse treatment reasonably expected to reduce the risk they present to the public. Larry differs from Anderson and Baker in one important respect. All three refuse treatment reasonably expected to reduce recidivism, but only Larry refuses treatment expected to maintain retributive competence. Larry, in contrast to Anderson and Baker, would probably not qualify as a retributively competent subject of the criminal justice system at the time of any future offenses. Thus, Larry raises an additional question regarding a competent person's right to refuse treatment reasonably expected to prevent him from rendering himself retributively incompetent and a danger to others.

Mike presents the fourth category of difficult cases discussed here. He is a grossly psychotic resident of a state hospital ward who does not engage in intelligible communication and who attacks others on the ward in a variety of circumstances. On some occasions he injures others, and on some occasions he sustains serious injuries as others retaliate. Mike does not respond to medication in doses below levels that threaten his life.[7] The state intervenes under both the *parens patriae* and police powers because Mike harms others and himself while manifesting severe impairment that clearly renders him incompetent for person and retributively. Because he does not respond therapeutically to medication or to therapeutic interventions that rely on verbal interaction, treatment providers can offer only custodial care and behavioral management intended to reduce the frequency and severity of assaults and injuries. Mike raises questions regarding the involuntary administration of behavior modification and other management or care techniques when these interventions are intended to alter the individual's behavior to serve social purposes but are not expected to ameliorate the impairment suffered by the incompetent individual.

In summary, these cases reveal a series of important factors relevant to the task of defining the boundaries of the right to refuse involuntary treatment in a variety of circumstances. First, involuntary state intervention through the mental health system can occur under police power, the *parens patriae* function, or both. Chapter 6 addresses cases that involve only the *parens patriae* function of the state, and this chapter addresses cases that involve the police power or both the *parens patriae* and police power functions. Second, the issue of involuntary treatment can arise for individuals who qualify as competent for person, retributively, in both domains, or in neither. Anderson and Baker clearly qualify as competent for person and retributively. Mike and Romeo, the severely retarded and assaultive petitioner in *Young-*

---

[7] *See id.*

berg v. Romeo,[8] clearly lack competence in both domains. Davis and Larry lack retributive competence when they perform their criminal conduct, and they present distinct problems regarding competence for person. Davis suffers impairment that calls into question his competence to make reasoned decisions regarding treatment expected to promote his clinical interests and decrease the danger he presents to others. Larry possesses the capacities of competence for person at the time he refuses the treatment, but that treatment refusal is reasonably expected to result in deterioration of his capacities and in increased risk to the public. Third, state and individual interests can converge in some circumstances, but they might diverge in others. Finally, questions regarding the justification for and boundaries of involuntary intervention can arise regarding treatment, custodial care, management, or incapacitation.

II. Judicial Framework

The court cases addressing the right to refuse treatment provided relatively little guidance regarding the parameters of that right for those committed under the police power.[9] The principle Supreme Court cases emphasized the involuntary administration of treatment in circumstances in which state and individual interests converged. These cases did not address circumstances in which the state's police power and *parens patriae* functions diverge, either because treatment intended to serve the state's interests does not serve the individual's interests, or because the individual to be involuntarily medicated in order to protect the public remains competent for person.

The Court's substantive holding in *Harper* authorizes the involuntary administration of antipsychotic medication to a prisoner with serious mental illness "if the inmate is dangerous to himself or others and the treatment is in the inmate's medical interests."[10] The range of application is difficult to discern because the Court's holding and the supporting reasoning specifically address the prison environment. Furthermore, the holding applies to circumstances in which the state and individual interests converge insofar as the medication is expected to serve the state interest in preventing harm by promoting the inmates' medical interests. It does not address circumstances in which these interests diverge because treatment expected to prevent harm does not serve the individual's medical interests. Although the opinion rejects the petitioner's claim that the involuntary administration of antipsychotic medication should require a judicial determination of incompetence, the holding specifically applies to the involuntary administration of antipsychotic medication to prisoners with serious mental illness when that treatment serves the prisoners' medical interests.[11] The Court does not specify that the serious mental illness must impair the individual's ability to make reasoned decisions regarding treatment. By authorizing the involuntary administration of antipsychotic medication to those for whom such treatment would serve their medical interests, however, it addresses a population reasonably expected to suffer serious impairment of the processes of reasoning and

---

[8] Youngberg v. Romeo, 457 U.S. 307 (1982).

[9] *See* chapter 6, section II.

[10] Washington v. Harper, 494 U.S. 210, 227 (1990).

[11] *Id.* at 217, 222, 227.

reality relatedness. The opinion does not limit involuntary treatment to these circumstances; rather, it addresses only the circumstances presented.

The circumstances explicitly addressed by the Court in *Riggins* resulted in a very limited decision in which the Court rejects only the involuntary medication of a defendant during a criminal trial when that medication may prejudice the trial and the trial court makes no finding that such medication is necessary for any essential state purpose.[12] The Court endorses the *Harper* standard allowing involuntary medication that is medically appropriate and necessary to prevent harm to others or to the individual medicated, and it suggests that the need to maintain competence to stand trial might provide a sufficient justification for involuntary medication.[13] As previously discussed, the dangerousness and medical interests criteria address circumstances in which individual and state interests converge in that the treatment is intended to serve the individual's treatment needs in a manner that renders him or her less dangerous. Similarly, circumstances in which involuntary treatment maintains competence to stand trial are likely to involve a severely impaired defendant who may well be incompetent to make reasoned decisions regarding treatment expected to advance the individual's clinical interests in a manner that promotes the state's interest in completing the criminal trial. Thus, the Court provides little guidance regarding the requirements for involuntary treatment under the police power when the state interest in protecting the public and the individual interests diverge or when the individual is clearly competent to make reasoned decisions regarding treatment.

The court opinions in the *Rogers* series discuss police power and *parens patriae* cases as distinct categories. The First Circuit adopted the findings of the Massachusetts supreme court that allowed involuntary medication under the police power without prior court approval only to prevent imminent harm and only in keeping with the applicable rules regarding restraints.[14] The Massachusetts supreme court addressed involuntary medication under the police power only as a form of restraint, with no apparent recognition that in many instances involuntary treatment protects others by decreasing the severity of the impairment that gives rise to the patient's dangerous behavior.[15] Similarly, the court addressed *parens patriae* cases as requiring a finding of incompetence for person and a substituted judgment formulated in light of six factors that addressed the patient's wishes and interests but did not address the possibility of protecting others from the patient.[16] Thus, the court did not explicitly address instances in which the police power and *parens patriae* functions intersect because the treatment in question is expected to ameliorate impairment that renders the individual dangerous to others.

Presumably, the court would authorize such treatment following a finding of incompetence for person in cases in which the impairment that renders individuals dangerous to others also renders them incompetent for person. In these circumstances, the impairment would fulfill the incompetence criteria for *parens patriae* intervention, and the treatment would advance the state's *parens patriae* and police

---

[12] Riggins v. Nevada, 504 U.S. 127, 138 (1992).

[13] *Id.* at 135.

[14] *See* chapter 6, section II.

[15] Rogers v. Com'r of Dept. of Mental Health, 458 N.E.2d 308, 321–22 (Mass. 1983).

[16] *Id.* at 312–19.

power functions. It remains unclear, however, how the court would or should address cases in which the impairment renders the individual dangerous to others but does not undermine competence for person.[17]

The court opinions in the *Rennie* series recognize but do not discuss the potential interaction of the police power and *parens patriae* functions. The *Rennie* opinions differ from the *Rogers* opinions in that the latter but not the former require judicial determinations of incompetence for involuntary treatment under most conditions. The *Rennie* opinions accept statutory procedures that allow clinicians to make and review decisions to administer involuntary treatment. These opinions discuss the parameters of the clinicians' duty in terms that include professional judgment, least restrictive alternatives, and traditional police power and *parens patriae* considerations without clarifying the relationships among these.[18] The complete body of case law addresses the right to refuse treatment in a fragmented manner and leaves at least two particularly difficult situations inadequately addressed. The first involves circumstances in which the treatment would advance the state's interest in protecting the public but the threshold criterion for *parens patriae* intervention is not met because the individual remains competent for person. The second involves circumstances in which the treatment would protect the public without improving clinical impairment suffered by the individual.

This chapter develops a more general framework for the involuntary administration of treatment under the police power. It does so by applying the normative framework developed in prior chapters to the series of difficult circumstances discussed in chapter 9, section I. According to this framework, competence provides the most central criterion for defining the proper form and limits of state intervention. As discussed in chapter 6, purely *parens patriae* interventions provide relatively straightforward applications of this framework because incompetence for person represents the primary criterion for involuntary intervention, and an appropriate *parens patriae* intervention takes a form expected to promote the well-being of the incompetent person. In crafting appropriate interventions under this approach, the least restrictive alternative analysis, the PJS, and the principle of care appropriateness converge as applications of the reasonable relationship principle. This approach distributes responsibilities regarding *parens patriae* interventions appropriately among courts, clinicians, and guardians.[19]

Involuntary treatment under the police power raises more complex questions because retributive incompetence triggers police power intervention through the mental health system. Thus, the determination of incompetence that elicits intervention through the mental health system establishes incompetence to participate in the criminal justice system rather than incompetence to make reasoned decisions regarding treatment. The difficult circumstances described in section I of this chapter provide the opportunity to examine the relationship between retributive incompetence and incompetence for the purpose of involuntary mental health treatment.

---

[17] The court's opinion suggests but does not explicitly state that its discussion of medication as chemical restraint applies to those who are incompetent. *Rogers*, 458 N.E.2d at 321 ("chemical restraint forcibly imposed upon an unwilling individual who, if competent, would refuse such treatment").

[18] *See* chapter 6, section II.C.

[19] *See* chapter 6, section IV.

III. Uniformly Incompetent Offenders

Mike resembles the severely retarded petitioner in *Youngberg v. Romeo* insofar as both cases involve a convergence of central considerations: retributive incompetence, incompetence for person, the state's police power and *parens patriae* functions, and state and individual interests.[20] When severely impaired people endanger themselves, others, or both as a result of their impairment, competence and the relevant interests converge at several levels. Considerations of competence converge in that these actors suffer severe impairment that renders them incompetent for person and retributively. Thus, courts, clinicians, and guardians must make treatment or care decisions expected to protect these individuals and others from the harm they might cause. The state functions also converge in that uniform incompetence and the need for care and control by others supports legitimate state intervention under the police power and *parens patriae* functions. Furthermore, the mental health system provides the appropriate institution for intervention under the police and *parens patriae* functions because these individuals lack competence for person and retributively.

State and individual interests converge in these cases because the incompetent individuals do not qualify for discretionary control in the nonpublic domain, and state interventions designed to promote their well-being (by ameliorating the severity of the impairment or by reducing the harmful behavior associated with that impairment) frequently take a form that is reasonably expected to protect the public from harm. These impaired individuals' interests in avoiding injury, improving functioning level, and increasing freedom all benefit from behavioral training and management programs that maximize their ability to function adaptively within their limited potential. Similarly, these programs designed to promote these individuals' interests are also reasonably expected to promote the state's interest in protecting the public, including the limited subset of the public with whom these individuals interact during confinement in a mental health facility. The claim here is not that any intervention designed to protect the public also promotes the well-being of the subject of that intervention. Rather, involuntary care and treatment plans ordinarily can be designed in a manner intended to serve both legitimate state purposes because insofar as severely impaired persons endanger the public by virtue of their impairment, interventions can seek to improve their functioning level in a manner that reduces the danger they pose to others.

Cases such as those of Mike and Romeo reveal the deficiency in the reasoning through which the supreme court of Massachusetts addressed the use of antipsychotic drugs under the police power.[21] It did so by considering the medication only as a chemical restraint; it did not consider the possible interaction of the state's police power and *parens patriae* functions. Cases such as those of Mike and Romeo require consideration of the potential effects of the involuntarily administered interventions on both state functions. Some circumstances may arise in which involuntary medications serve merely as a form of restraint under the police power with no expectation that they will serve the individuals' therapeutic interests in improved well-being. Such circumstances, however, do not raise issues of involuntary treatment or of the right to refuse treatment. Such use of medication constitutes mere incapacitation

---

[20] *Romeo*, 457 U.S. at 307.
[21] *Rogers*, 458 N.E.2d at 319–22.

rather than treatment. Thus, courts must balance state and individual interests as they would regarding any other state intrusion into ordinarily protected liberty under the police power.[22] Questions arise regarding the right to refuse involuntary treatment under the police power precisely because some interventions intended to protect the public are *not* analogous to restraint as mere incapacitation. Rather, they involve legitimate attempts to protect the public by providing treatment that ameliorates the impairment that gives rise to the risk.

Two additional matters complicate the interpretation of the opinion of the supreme court of Massachusetts as applied to the approach advanced here. First, that court was directly concerned with the procedural issues regarding the proper roles of the clinicians and the courts in authorizing involuntary treatment to competent patients because it addressed a system of civil commitment that authorizes commitment absent any determination of incompetence. This reveals the incoherence discussed in chapter 6, section II. Second, that court endorsed a substituted judgment standard without addressing the serious problems involved in the application of this standard to individuals who have never been competent.

Cases involving uniformly incompetent individuals generate compatible roles for courts, clinicians, and guardians. Severely impaired individuals lack the right to refuse treatment because they lack the capacities of competence for person that would enable them to make reasoned decisions regarding treatment. Under the approach developed in this book, the court makes the determination of incompetence for person and of retributive incompetence and either orders placement in a controlled setting or appoints a guardian with the authority to do so. The court retains supervisory authority in order to assure that the guardian properly fulfills that role.

The guardian exercises informed consent regarding treatment programs designed to promote the ward's interests, and these interventions also serve to protect others from the ward. That is, in circumstances such as those presented by Mike and Romeo, the impaired individual endangers others by virtue of a severely impaired functioning level. Behavioral treatment and management programs designed to maximize their ability to function effectively in interaction with others protect those others from harm and promote the impaired individuals' interests in improved capacities as well as in freedom from restraint or injury. Clinicians promote these individual and public interests by diagnosing, prescribing, and treating in a manner expected to maximize the impaired individuals' functioning level and freedom in light of their available capacities.

Just as competent individuals and treatment providers must agree on treatment plans considered clinically appropriate and in the individual's interests, guardians and clinicians must agree on treatment plans expected to promote the incompetent individuals' clinical interests. If guardians will not consent to treatment plans considered clinically appropriate by clinicians, the courts retain supervisory authority. Recall that Romeo's mother refused to authorize clinicians to apply a behavioral program that the clinicians designed to advance Romeo's functioning level and to decrease the frequency of injury to Romeo and others.[23] In circumstances such as these in which clinicians and guardians cannot agree on mutually acceptable treatment plans, courts must exercise their supervisory authority. Clinicians provide the

---

[22] *See* section IV (discussing this matter in more detail).

[23] *Romeo,* 457 U.S. at 311–12.

courts with evidence regarding the clinical evaluations, and they describe and explain the proposed treatment plans. The guardians present their objections as representatives of the impaired individuals, and the courts make the necessary decisions in light of the wards' interests. The guardians pursue the wards' interests, and in so doing they are pursuing the interests of others because maximizing functioning level can be expected to decrease injuries to the wards and to others while reducing the need for emergency restraint or seclusion of the wards. The courts retain responsibility to balance the interests of the wards and of others if these interests conflict or if guardians and clinicians cannot agree on the best interpretation of the wards' interests in order to agree on treatment plans.

IV. Uniformly Competent Offenders

In contrast to Mike and Romeo, Anderson and Baker clearly possess the capacities of competence, both retributively and for person. Neither suffers any impairment of the capacities, such as consciousness, reality relatedness, comprehension, or reasoning, needed to make reasoned decisions in light of their own interests and the circumstances, including the legal ramifications. Uniformly competent offenders can raise difficult questions regarding involuntary treatment intended to reduce the probability of recidivism. Reviews of the effectiveness of treatment in reducing recidivism differ, but it is at least plausible to think that some programs might reduce recidivism by some offenders.[24] Some reviewers find significant effects with cognitive and behavioral programs, particularly for offenders such as Anderson who do not demonstrate psychopathic traits. Anderson clearly possesses the capacities required to qualify as retributively competent and as competent for person. His disorders involve interpersonal discomfort as well as sexual urges and conduct regarding children, but he suffers no impairment of the capacities needed to direct his conduct through the exercise of practical reasoning in the public jurisdiction or in the context of decisions regarding person.[25] Thus, his disorders provide no basis for *parens patriae* intervention, and the criminal justice system provides the appropriate institution of police power intervention.

Anderson can voluntarily participate in treatment, either in prison or after release. Furthermore, criminal conviction justifies curtailment of liberty, and the state can set conditions of probation or parole that include participation in treatment programs. Should Anderson refuse to participate in the programs required as a candidate for probation or parole, the court or parole board may revoke probation or parole and incarcerate Anderson for the maximum sentence authorized by law. These coercive conditions burden the choice to refuse, but culpable violation of the criminal law justifies the state in exercising coercive intervention.[26] The Constitution limits probation and parole conditions by prohibiting those that violate specific constitutional liberties and those that bear no reasonable relationship to the state purpose in setting

---

[24] *See* chapter 11, section II.

[25] *See* chapter 1, section I.

[26] Arthur W. Campbell, Law of Sentencing §§ 5.1, 5.4 (2nd ed. 1991); Neil P. Cohen & James J. Gobert, The Law of Probation and Parole §§ 1.04, 1.07, 6.61–63 (1983).

those conditions.[27] Within these broad limits legislatures and courts can set a broad range of conditions intended to prevent recidivism or to promote other legitimate state purposes.

The justification for requiring treatment as a condition of probation or parole differs significantly from the justification for police power interventions through the mental health system as an alternative to the criminal justice system. These justificatory differences reflect the significance of competence. Police power interventions regarding retributively incompetent individuals, including Romeo and Mike, provide appropriate alternatives to the criminal justice system because these individuals lack competence to participate in the public jurisdiction as accountable subjects of the criminal law. The mental health system must provide an alternative institution of social control precisely because these individuals fail to qualify as participants in the criminal justice system that provides the primary institution of social control for retributively competent adults in the public jurisdiction of a liberal society.

The state exercises coercive control over retributively competent offenders, including Anderson and Baker, through the criminal justice system. The state may impose a wide variety of conditions on probation or parole precisely because these offenders have culpably committed offenses that justify state intervention under the police power in the form of criminal incarceration. These individuals retain the option of refusing to cooperate with any such conditions, but doing so maintains their alternative status, which consists of criminal incarceration. Treatment programs as conditions of probation or parole do not constitute state intrusions into individual liberty. Rather, they provide culpable offenders with opportunities to exercise some choice regarding the form of that police power intervention. Providing uniformly competent offenders with this opportunity remains consistent with the underlying normative framework because they are uniformly competent. They are subject to the specified criminal sentences because they committed crimes with retributive competence, and they retain the option to choose either to participate in the proffered treatment programs or to complete their criminal sentences because they retain competence for person.

Certain programs such as those involving surgical or chemical castration reduce recidivism by reducing the motivation or ability to perform certain offenses.[28] These modalities might succeed with either Anderson or Baker. Baker's psychopathic traits constitute a lesser impediment to the therapeutic aim of reduced recidivism through chemical or surgical castration than they do with the cognitive–behavioral approaches because the former modalities depend less than do the latter on offender motivation and cooperation with the therapeutic process. They are less dependent on motivation and cooperation precisely because they render the offender less capable of performing the conduct constituting the offenses.

The legal and ethical status of chemical or surgical castration as a condition of probation or parole remains highly controversial.[29] Some commentators distinguish the therapeutic use of chemical agents for the purpose of reducing abnormally high levels of sexual drive and fantasies to normal levels and chemical castration, which

---

[27] CAMPBELL, *supra* note 26, at § 5.5; COHEN & GOBERT, *supra* note 26, at § 5.10.

[28] *See supra*, sources cited at note 5.

[29] Robert D. Miller, *Forced Administration of Sex-Drive Reducing Medications to Sex Offenders: Treatment or Punishment?* 4 PSYCHOL., PUB. POL'Y, & L. 175 (1998).

renders the individual sexually impotent.[30] The discussion in this chapter addresses surgical or chemical castration in the latter sense. Recently passed statutes and currently pending bills in various states require chemical castration as a condition of parole or as part of a criminal sentence.[31] This book does not purport to evaluate the legality of chemical castration under current legal doctrine. Rather, this chapter addresses chemical and surgical castration as examples of police power interventions intended to reduce recidivism, and it examines the manner in which consideration of such interventions might inform our understanding of the right to refuse treatment under the police power.

Compare these modalities to execution or severing of the spinal cord. These interventions also reduce recidivism by rendering the offender less capable of reoffending. Some might endorse these modalities as appropriate forms of state intervention for the purpose of preventing further offenses. Prevention of further criminal offenses by the same offender constitutes one argument sometimes advanced in favor of capital punishment. Few would argue, however, that execution or severing of the spinal cord constitutes treatment. Rather, these interventions incapacitate, and execution effectively prevents recidivism precisely because it incapacitates categorically. Surgical and chemical castration, in contrast, are sometimes discussed as modes of treatment intended to reduce recidivism.[32] In order to understand and evaluate the arguments regarding the justification for the involuntary administration of such interventions and the significance of these arguments for the right to refuse treatment under the police power, one must clarify the classification of these interventions as treatment or as incapacitation.

Recall the definition of treatment derived in chapter 5, section IV. As interpreted there, treatment involves the application of clinical skills and knowledge designed to ameliorate a pathological condition or to reduce the injurious effects produced by that condition by increasing the individual's adaptive skills, capacities, or functioning level associated with that impairment. The cognitive–behavioral programs qualify as treatment because to the extent that they reduce recidivism, they do so by promoting the development of responses, skills, and strategies through which the offenders alter their behavior in such a manner as to avoid repeating their offenses. These might include, for example, developing strategies for avoiding circumstances that precipitate offenses, learning adaptive means to reduce anxiety or arousal, increasing empathy with victims, or cognitively reinterpreting internal or situational factors related to prior offenses.[33] By developing capacities and skills such as these, offenders increase their ability to function effectively in society by refraining from behavior that injures others, violates enacted limits on interpersonal conduct, and elicits police power intervention through the criminal justice system.

Surgical and chemical castration, like execution and severing of the spinal cord, constitute methods of incapacitation rather than treatment. These forms of intervention seek to reduce the injurious effects caused by the offenders' deviant arousal,

---

[30] *Id.* at 181–83.

[31] *Id.* at 188–92; Winslade et al., *supra* note 5, at 376–86. These provisions differ insofar as they authorize chemical or surgical castration as conditions of parole or as part of criminal sentences. Although these provisions may use the term "treatment," the interventions they authorize constitute incapacitation rather than treatment, as explained below.

[32] Heilbrun et al., *supra* note 5, at 146–47; Winslade et al., *supra* note 5, at 365–67.

[33] *See* chapter 11, section II.

anxiety, lack of social skills, or lack of empathy or conscience. They do not, however, seek to accomplish this goal by increasing the offenders' adaptive skills, capacities, or functioning level. Rather, these forms of intervention resemble execution and severing of the spinal cord in that they attempt to reduce recidivism by reducing the functional capacities of the offenders and by rendering them incapable of repeating their offenses. These strategies do not raise questions regarding the justification of coercive treatment or regarding the right to refuse treatment, but they do raise important questions regarding the justification of state intervention in the form of incapacitation, and any justificatory argument must justify them as incapacitation.

Recall the prior discussions of the courts' vague references to a putative volitional impairment or inability to control sexual conduct in the sexual predator cases. The court opinions that upheld the sexual predator statutes supported their decisions heavily by reference to the personality disorders and paraphilias manifested by the subjects of commitment, and they contended that these disorders involved volitional impairment that rendered these individuals unable to control their conduct.[34]

The incapacitating interventions discussed here, including execution, severing of the spinal cord, and surgical or chemical castration, effectively reduce recidivism precisely because they remove the conduct constituting the offenses from the offenders' control. Certain incapacitating interventions, such as execution, render offenders permanently and categorically unable to direct their conduct, whereas others, such as chemical castration, may have temporary, partial, or selective effects. Insofar as they successfully reduce recidivism, however, they do so by rendering offenders unable to control their conduct through the exercise of the ordinary processes of decision making and volition. Contrary to the court opinions, these offenders possess the capacity to control the conduct constituting the offenses until these interventions deprive them of that ability. Any argument purporting to justify incapacitating interventions must justify state intervention designed to render the subjects of those interventions unable to direct their behavior in a specific manner.

In contrast to chemical castration, some chemical interventions are designed to reduce abnormally high rates of sexual arousal and fantasy to ordinary levels. Such treatment is intended to provide relief from intrusive fantasies and urges and to facilitate the development of personally and socially adaptive sexual responses.[35] These interventions qualify as treatment because they are intended to enable the individual to develop adaptive skills that ameliorate the injurious effects of their prior condition. As such, they represent appropriate voluntary treatment programs, and the state might offer such programs as conditions of probation or parole on the same basis that the state would offer other programs involving treatment, education, or occupational training. The competent offender can accept them or choose to forgo probation or parole. Should they refuse, they remain fully accountable for any further crimes they commit after completion of those sentences. In contrast to uniformly competent individuals and uniformly incompetent individuals, some offenders present less clear or consistent patterns of impairment. The next section addresses some of these cases.

---

[34] *See* chapter 8, section IV.
[35] Miller, *supra* note 29, at 181–83.

V. Complex Cases

In contrast to those who qualify as uniformly competent and to those who qualify as uniformly incompetent, some individuals, including Davis, Harper, and Larry, demonstrate serious impairment of the capacities relevant to competence yet retain substantial capacity to recognize and reason about their own interests, at least some of the time. Although these individuals suffer significant impairment, they differ from Romeo and Mike in several relevant respects. The severity and breadth of their impairment are more limited. They are not obviously incompetent for person, although competence remains an open question. Their impairment varies significantly across time, and during their periods of more intact functioning they appear to possess the capacities of competence for person and of retributive competence. They are subject to treatment that significantly ameliorates their underlying impairment, and this treatment may render them competent for person or retributively.

Davis differs from Romeo and Mike in that his general level of comprehension and reasoning is sufficient for competence in the public and nonpublic domains when his psychotic disorder is in remission, and he remains competent for some functions when he is psychotic. He remains competent to stand trial in the public domain, for example, and similarly to Francine, he would probably remain competent to make decisions regarding health care unrelated to his delusional process.[36] If we stipulate that he resembles Francine insofar as he qualifies for exculpation under the insanity defense but remains competent to make certain decisions regarding his health care, such as those addressing treatment for diabetes or other physical conditions, he is retributively incompetent but apparently remains competent for person or for some aspects of person. Thus, competence apparently fails to completely converge across the public and nonpublic domains, raising the question regarding whether the state can administer involuntary treatment to protect the public if the individual remains competent for person or for some decisions regarding person.

Davis's individual interests in improved functioning converge with the state interests in protecting the public because Davis endangers others as a result of his psychosis. Thus, treatment intended to ameliorate his psychotic disorder would be reasonably expected to promote the state interest in protecting the public from harm by promoting his clinical interests in improved functioning. Although he is not generally incompetent for health care, his refusal of treatment reasonably expected to improve his functioning level in a manner that would allow more liberty suggests that his competence for making this particular health care decision should be reviewed carefully. It is important to understand here that the claim is not that making the "wrong" decision renders one incompetent, but rather that the apparently self-defeating nature of this decision provides some reason to doubt his competence and calls for careful inquiry regarding that matter.

Can one be competent to make treatment decisions regarding one's delusional disorder? Because of his disordered thought process, Davis understands his criminal sexual conduct as behavior designed to implement a divine plan and the treatment as Satan's attempt to disrupt that divine plan. His thought disorder renders him unable to make reasoned decisions regarding treatment designed to ameliorate his delusional disorder because it distorts his abilities to realistically comprehend the relevant ben-

---

[36] See chapter 1, section I and chapter 3, section II.

efits and costs of the treatment and to reason effectively about them. Suppose, however, that his reason for refusing the treatment were more mundane, such as his dislike for the realistically unpleasant side effects of the medication. As long as his delusional disorder remains active, he lacks the capacity to comprehend and reason competently about the costs of remaining delusional or about the benefits of improving that delusional disorder.

One can be aware that one suffers some types of impairment of perception and cognition, such as mere perceptual disorders or learning disabilities, because these disorders do not directly undermine one's capacity to comprehend and reflect upon the disorders themselves. One cannot realistically comprehend and reason about one's delusional disorder, however, without rendering oneself no longer delusional. Davis cannot, for example, delusionally believe that his sexual offenses are part of God's plan and simultaneously understand that these beliefs are delusional. If he were to understand that what seemed to be God's plan was actually a product of his delusional thought process, and if he were to reason about that matter through unimpaired cognitive processes, he would then understand that it was not God's plan, and thus, he would no longer be delusional because he would then be reasoning realistically about this matter. That is, delusional impairment necessarily involves distortion of the processes of comprehension and reasoning regarding some aspect of one's life. That one experiences delusional process regarding some aspect of one's experience necessarily distorts the ability to competently understand and reason regarding that aspect of one's experience, including one's beliefs and thought regarding that experience. Similarly, Davis experiences auditory hallucinations involving what he understands to be God's voice instructing him to commit the conduct that constitutes the offenses. If he were to accurately understand that these voices were hallucinations and reason about them as such, they would no longer qualify as hallucinations. Rather, by interpreting these voices as perceptual distortions of reality, he would experience them as mere perceptual aberrations rather than as hallucinations that distort his reality relatedness and his reasoning regarding that aspect of his experience.[37]

Competence to decide for oneself regarding prescribed treatment requires the ability to make reasoned choices about that treatment in light of an accurate understanding of the expected costs and benefits of that treatment and of the available alternatives. Thus, delusional individuals cannot make competent choices about treatment expected to improve their psychotic impairment such as that involving delusions or hallucinations because they cannot comprehend and reason effectively about that psychotic disorder or about the costs or benefits of treatment that ameliorates that disorder. Psychotic impairment necessarily involves distortion of one's understanding of some aspect of that impairment. Therefore, it necessarily undermines one's ability to realistically appraise the costs and benefits of treatment expected to ameliorate that disorder and one's competence to make reasoned decisions regarding that treatment.

The claim here is a limited one; psychotic process precludes competent decision making regarding treatment reasonably expected to ameliorate that process because it precludes accurate comprehension and reasoning about the impairment itself and, thus, about the costs and benefits associated with the alternative of refraining from

---

[37] ROBERT F. SCHOPP, AUTOMATISM, INSANITY, AND THE PSYCHOLOGY OF CRIMINAL RESPONSIBILITY §§ 6.4, 6.5.

treatment. It does not follow either that the psychotic person necessarily lacks competence regarding all treatment decisions or that a psychotic person ought always receive treatment for the psychotic disorder. Recall Francine as an example of a delusional person who remains competent to decide regarding treatment for her diabetes because the treatment decision does not require unimpaired comprehension and reasoning regarding her delusional disorder.[38] Mike provides an example of one who lacks competence as a result of psychotic process but for whom antipsychotic medication carries severe risk. Thus, Mike's impairment renders him incompetent to decide regarding treatment for his psychotic disorder, but the risk to his well-being renders the antipsychotic medication inappropriate for him. The responsibility to decide to withhold such treatment falls to the clinicians and the guardian, with the court retaining authority to resolve disputes among them.

The analysis presented here is not limited to psychosis, although psychotic impairment may provide the type of disorder that most clearly qualifies. This analysis addresses disorders that involve severe impairment that undermines the individual's ability to make reasoned decisions about treatment intended to ameliorate that impairment or its harmful effects. Cook, for example, suffers serious retardation rather than psychosis, but his impairment prevents him from comprehending and reasoning effectively about state interventions in the form of training, behavior management, or placement intended to alter his behavior that constitutes his sexual offenses. It does so because it prevents him from understanding and reasoning effectively about the harmful effects of his offenses or about the legal consequences of engaging in such conduct. As discussed previously, he understands his criminal conduct as comparable to other conduct regarding which "mama will yell."

The Court's opinion in *Harper* arguably provides an analysis consistent with this approach. *Harper* involved a prisoner, rather than a patient in a mental health facility, rendering it difficult to determine the degree to which one can extrapolate to those subject to intervention through the mental health system. Harper reportedly endangered others because he had a psychotic disorder, however, and the Court's substantive holding authorized involuntary treatment with antipsychotic medication for prisoners who endanger themselves or others if the medication is in their medical interests.[39]

If one accepts the premises that he suffered a psychotic disorder, that this disorder caused him to endanger others, and that the treatment in question was reasonably expected to decrease the risk of harm to others by ameliorating the psychotic impairment that caused his assaultive conduct, then *Harper* involves circumstances consistent with the interpretation of Davis provided above in that the impairment undermines the capacities of retributive competence and of competence to make reasoned decisions about treatment expected to ameliorate that impairment. Under these conditions, the state's police power and *parens patriae* functions would converge in that the psychotic impairment undermines retributive competence regarding these assaults and competence for this treatment decision regarding the psychotic disorder that plays a causal role in the assaults. Thus, involuntary treatment expected to ameliorate that psychotic disorder would serve the state's legitimate interests in protecting others from Harper and in advancing Harper's interests in improved well-

---

[38] *See* chapter 3, section II.
[39] *Harper*, 494 U.S. at 210, 213–19, 227.

being in the form of decreased impairment. Such intervention would not violate Harper's right to decide about his own treatment because his psychotic disorder prevents him from qualifying for that right by undermining his capacity to make reasoned decisions regarding treatment expected to ameliorate that disorder.

The court's reasoning in *Harper* emphasized the judicial branch's traditional deference to the executive in prison regulation.[40] Furthermore, this book advances an abstract normative framework intended to provide a coherent foundation for various legal doctrines, rather than an application of one specific doctrine. Thus, I do not claim that the court's reasoning explicitly applies the analysis presented here. I claim only that given the premises stated previously, the *Harper* opinion represents reasoning consistent with this analysis.

Larry resembles Davis insofar as he suffers a psychotic disorder that undermines both retributive competence and competence to make reasoned decisions regarding treatment intended to reduce his dangerousness to others by ameliorating that disorder. He presents an additional complication, however, because he refuses to continue the treatment after he recovers the capacities required for competence. Larry's mood disorder responds well to the appropriate medication. Remission of the psychotic phase renders him retributively competent and competent to make reasoned decisions regarding his own health care. During this period of competence, he decides to terminate the medication because he finds certain effects of the drug to be unpleasant and because he misses the exuberance of the elevated mood states he experiences during manic phases. In summary, during a period of competence he makes a reasoned decision to forgo the treatment that ameliorates his impairment and maintains his competence, increasing the probability that he will experience repeated periods of incompetence during which he will pose an enhanced risk to the public.

Larry's refusal provides no basis for intervention under the state's *parens patriae* function because he possesses the capacities needed to qualify as competent for person when he makes the decision to cease taking the medication. A right to make self-regarding decisions (including the right to refuse treatment) that did not include the right to make decisions that others consider misguided would reduce to the vacuous right to decide in a manner that others approve. Larry's refusal raises issues regarding the right to refuse treatment and regarding the state's authority to intervene under the police power because his history demonstrates that periods of exacerbated impairment endanger others.

Should Larry decompensate into a psychotic state and engage in conduct that harms or endangers others, he would qualify for police power intervention through civil commitment under ordinary commitment statutes. The approach to police power intervention advocated in chapters 7 and 8 would provide for similar intervention through a determination of retributive incompetence. As compared to ordinary civil commitment practices, this approach might allow more flexible and effective intervention in that a finding of retributive incompetence and risk would authorize police power intervention that might take a variety of forms. If necessary, it would allow confinement comparable to inpatient commitment under ordinary civil commitment statutes. Alternately, it could authorize outpatient monitoring and treatment. According to the prior analysis of competence to decide regarding treatment for a condition that includes psychotic impairment, Larry's psychosis would render him incompetent

---

[40] *Id.* at 223–27.

during periods of active psychosis to make reasoned decisions regarding treatment expected to ameliorate that impairment. Thus, the approach advanced here would authorize police power and *parens patriae* interventions through the mental health system when the treatment refusal resulted in decompensation sufficient to undermine retributive competence or competence for person. It might seem, however, that an effective legal structure should authorize intervention when Larry ceases the treatment, rather than after the expected decompensation occurs.

If applied as written, ordinary civil commitment statutes would not apply, because Larry fulfills neither the mental illness nor the dangerousness criteria at the time he discontinues the treatment. If his history of decompensation following cessation of treatment renders the probability of decompensation and harmful conduct sufficiently high, one might argue that he fulfills the dangerousness criterion because he engages in behavior that creates a risk of injury to others in the foreseeable future. He does so in the absence of any significant impairment, however, precluding a finding of mental illness if that criterion is treated as substantive.

Under the approach endorsed in this book, he would not qualify for intervention through the mental health system under either the police power or *parens patriae* functions because he possesses the capacities of retributive competence and of competence for person. Consider, however, the criminal justice system as the appropriate legal institution for the exercise of the police power over a retributively competent individual who endangers the public. If Larry has established a predictable pattern of decompensation and injurious conduct following cessation of treatment, then his refusal to continue treatment constitutes reckless endangerment.[41] That is, by refusing treatment during a period of retributive competence, he knowingly creates a substantial and unjustifiable risk of harm to others.

He might fail to fulfill the offense elements if the full body of evidence fails to support the inference that the probability of harmful behavior is sufficiently likely to establish a substantial risk. Alternately, he might fail to fulfill the offense elements if his history with the treatment demonstrates that the treatment itself causes harmful side effects sufficient to justify the increased risk of decompensation and harmful behavior. Suppose, for example, that Larry has engaged only in occasional minor assaultive behavior and that the treatment sometimes causes very harmful side effects. In these circumstances, Larry would not violate the offense definition for reckless endangerment because the risk created would not qualify as substantial and unjustified, and therefore Larry would not have acted recklessly.[42]

If these conditions obtain, however, Larry does not provide an appropriate candidate for police power intervention through either the criminal justice or mental health systems because the police power does not authorize intrusion for the purpose of preventing speculative or trivial risk. Intervening in the treatment decision of a competent individual through the mental health system, rather than through the criminal justice system, does not render the intrusion into protected liberty less a violation of discretionary control. Furthermore, it adds an additional injury in that it denies

---

[41] AMERICAN LAW INSTITUTE, MODEL PENAL CODE AND COMMENTARIES § 211.2 (Official Draft and Revised Comments 1985) [hereinafter MPC]. For a similar analysis *see* David B. Wexler, *Inducing Therapeutic Compliance Through the Criminal Law*, in ESSAYS IN THERAPEUTIC JURISPRUDENCE 187 (David B. Wexler & Bruce J. Winick eds. 1991).

[42] MPC, *supra* note 41, at § 2.02(2)(c).

the standing of the individual by inaccurately portraying him as one who lacks the capacity to participate in the criminal justice system as the legal institution that regulates the conduct of retributively competent adults in the public jurisdiction.

Given his current lack of impairment sufficient to undermine retributive competence regarding the decision to forgo the treatment, the criminal justice system provides the appropriate institution for the exercise of the police power. If that decision creates a risk sufficient to justify police power intervention, arrest and conviction for reckless endangerment provide an available and appropriate vehicle. If that decision does not create a risk of that magnitude, framing an intervention as an application of the mental health system cannot justify police power intrusion into the decisions of a retributively competent individual. Involuntary intervention through the mental health system in these circumstances would distort the legitimate function of this system by misusing it as a preventive detention system for those who qualify as subjects of the criminal justice system.

If Larry refuses to participate in the prescribed treatment plan under conditions that fulfill the offense elements for reckless endangerment, the state can intervene through the criminal justice system. The state cannot require that he accept the treatment as an involuntary mental health intervention because he remains retributively competent and competent for person at the time of the refusal. Following a conviction for reckless endangerment, however, the court can require participation in such a treatment program as a condition of probation or parole. Insofar as the penal code authorizes the court in setting conditions of probation or parole in lieu of incarceration, the court can require evaluation and treatment as such a condition. Participation in treatment under these conditions would be coercive, but conviction renders any convicted offender subject to coercive probation or parole conditions involving matters that would otherwise qualify as matters of individual discretion.

The analysis of Davis, Harper, and Larry suggests that incompetence for the purposes of the state's police power and *parens patriae* functions may converge more often than first impressions might suggest. If retributive incompetence requires serious impairment of the capacities of comprehension and reasoning, and if competence for health care requires intact capacities of comprehension and reasoning regarding all matters relevant to the treatment decision including the alternative of remaining in the untreated state, then it becomes difficult to describe realistic cases in which an individual remains retributively incompetent but competent to make decisions regarding treatment for the disorder that renders that person retributively incompetent. Furthermore, the state's interests under the police power and *parens patriae* functions tend to converge regarding individuals who endanger others as a result of their serious impairment.

VI. Conclusion

Some readers may find it difficult to accept the argument that the state should not have the authority to involuntarily treat individuals like Larry who refuse treatment while competent despite awareness that refusing increases the probability of deterioration and the risk to the public. Why limit the state to reckless endangerment charges rather than allow it to require involuntary treatment in order to reduce the risk? Limiting the state exercise of coercive social control over retributively competent individuals to the criminal justice system serves several important purposes. First, it requires that the state treat competent individuals in a manner consistent with their standing as determined by their capacities. Second, it requires that the state meet the well-established substantive and procedural demands of the criminal justice system in order to exercise such coercive force. Third, it reinforces a fundamental limitation on state authority by precluding state interference in the psychological processes that qualify persons as competent participants in legal and political institutions of the public jurisdiction. Thus, it serves both to protect individuals from state intrusion into the psychological processes that qualify them as competent to participate as equals in the public jurisdiction and to restrain the range and manner within which the state can exercise power over citizens.

The mental health system provides an alternative institution of coercive social control for those who lack retributive competence. Many retributively incompetent individuals also lack competence to make reasoned decisions regarding treatment intended to ameliorate the disorders that render them retributively incompetent. In order to qualify as retributively incompetent but retain the right to refuse treatment for the disorder that renders one retributively incompetent, one must have the capacities to make reasoned decisions about the very impairment that prevents one from making reasoned decisions about criminal conduct. Furthermore, in order to escape coercive social control through the criminal justice system, that individual must refuse applicable treatment in circumstances that do not fulfill the offense elements for reckless endangerment.

As indicated previously, this analysis does not purport to replace doctrinal analysis of the right to refuse treatment. Rather, it complements that doctrinal analysis by providing an analysis grounded in a more abstract normative framework intended to identify the more general principles of political morality represented by specific legal provisions. Courts and commentators examine and defend a variety of doctrinal arguments compatible with the more abstract framework proposed here. Arguments framed in the First Amendment protection of freedom of thought or in the Fourteenth Amendment right to privacy, for example, protect central aspects of the more abstract right to maintain sovereign discretion in the nonpublic domain.[43] Legal arguments must reflect recognized legal authority, including constitutional provisions, statutes, and case law. Furthermore, legal arguments must take a form amenable to relatively consistent interpretation and application in a variety of specific circumstances.

The analysis presented here advances a more abstract interpretation of general principles that support various legal doctrines relevant to the right to refuse as components in an integrated body of mental health law. Thus, this analysis seeks primarily to portray the relationships among the right to refuse and other related components of mental health law, such as those involving criminal responsibility and civil commitment, rather than to propose interpretations of specific doctrines. Ideally, an enhanced understanding of the normative foundations of an integrated body of mental health law would enable us to understand more clearly the most justifiable formulations of the doctrines and the appropriate roles and responsibilities of various legal and clinical agents in the legal institutions that embody mental health law. The next three chapters examine these roles and responsibilities.

---

[43] WINICK, *supra* note 1, at chapters 10 and 11.

Part IV

Professional Roles, Professional Judgment, and Legal Determinations

Chapter 10
RISK AND DANGEROUSNESS

The first nine chapters of this book advance a conceptually coherent and normatively defensible framework for an integrated body of mental health law. Appropriate application of mental health law requires the development of professional roles and responsibilities for clinical and legal participants. These roles and responsibilities must cohere with the underlying framework, the expertise of the professions, and other related roles. Chapters 10–12 examine the defensible parameters of the exercise of professional judgment by clinicians and social scientists in various roles that arise in the context of commitment under the sexual predator statutes or general civil commitment provisions. These chapters examine the appropriate exercise and limits of professional judgment and the appropriate relationships between the clinical and judicial domains of responsibility. This chapter directs primary attention toward expert testimony involving professional opinions regarding risk and dangerousness in order to develop a general framework for such judgments. Chapter 11 applies this framework to commitment under the sexual predator statutes in order to clarify the manner in which specific statutory formulations and judicial determinations can affect the proper exercise of professional judgment. Chapter 12 extends this analysis to related clinical roles. All three chapters demonstrate that a complex interaction of conceptual, empirical, and normative factors define the proper range of clinical judgment in specific circumstances. An integrated body of mental health law based on the framework developed in the first nine chapters accommodates and informs the development of a complementary set of professional responsibilities.

I. Professional Judgment Within Professional Roles

The application of the PJS to decisions regarding the administration of treatment without the patient's consent elicits strident objections from some commentators who apparently understand that standard as depriving citizens of due process of law by subjecting them to involuntary treatment on the basis of clinical judgment without judicial review.[1] The core of this criticism addresses the proper relationship between clinical and judicial authority and responsibility, rather than simply the proper exercise of professional judgment. Clinicians appropriately exercise professional judgment in many functions that fall within the scope of mental health law, but those who interpret the PJS as allocating broad discretion to clinicians to do what they think best without judicial review criticize the standard because interpreted in this manner, it delegates broad discretion to clinicians regarding certain matters that are properly decided or reviewed by courts. Chapter 6 advances an alternative interpretation of the PJS as one that authorizes professional judgment regarding clinical

---

[1] *See* chapter 6, section III.

decisions expected to serve legally defined purposes within legally established constraints, and it recognizes that effective application of the PJS requires an appropriate fit between the legal parameters and the clinical expertise.[2]

Although the PJS applies to professional roles within which courts allocate relatively broad discretion regarding certain decisions to clinicians, many other professional roles involve the exercise of professional judgment by clinicians. Those components of mental health law that provide for judicial hearings, for example, call upon clinicians to form professional judgments and offer expert opinions regarding the questions at issue. Commitment hearings under sexual predator statutes or general civil commitment provisions often rely heavily upon expert opinions by clinicians regarding the application of the commitment criteria to the subjects of the hearings.[3] As with the PJS, the appropriate allocation of authority and responsibility for rendering opinions and determinations regarding commitment criteria depends partially upon the proper interpretation of the clinical and normative components of these criteria.

Section II discusses the appropriate scope of expert testimony regarding the statutory commitment criterion of mental illness in light of the formal conception of legal mental illness presented in chapter 3. Section III briefly presents the standard view of the clinician's role regarding the prediction of dangerousness, and sections IV and V raise questions regarding this common view and advance an alternative interpretation of the statutory criterion of dangerousness. Sections VI and VII examine the appropriate roles of clinicians and of courts in applying this interpretation. Section VIII concludes the chapter.

II.   Expert Testimony Regarding Legal Mental Illness for Civil Commitment

Clinicians routinely provide expert testimony regarding commitment criteria framed in terms of mental illness, mental abnormality, or some similar phrase. Chapter 3 provides a formal conception of legal mental illness. This formal conception informs the appropriate responsibilities of clinical and legal participants in determining that an individual manifests legal mental illness, and it suggests an analogous approach to the distribution of responsibilities regarding a determination of dangerousness. According to this conception of legal mental illness,

> persons are not eligible for legal status S just in case:
>
> 1. they suffer impairment of psychological capacities
> 2. rendering them unable to competently perform
> 3. psychological operations O

According to this conception, a determination of legal mental illness requires an integrated legal and clinical analysis. Clinicians fulfill their roles as expert witnesses within the constraints of professional expertise by describing and explaining the individual's impairment and the manner in which it affects the ability to perform

---

[2] *Id.*

[3] *See* chapter 3, section V (describing the basis for commitment of sexual predators).

operations O. The court must determine whether that impairment constitutes a legal mental illness rendering the person ineligible for the status at issue. Any plausible legal criteria of competence or culpability must include legal and moral considerations, and thus, a determination that an individual's psychological impairment renders that person legally mentally ill for a particular purpose requires application of those legal and moral considerations to that impairment. Therefore, professional opinions that individuals are (or are not) legally mentally ill necessarily exceed clinical expertise.

Sexual predator statutes and many civil commitment statutes are fundamentally defective precisely because they provide no account of the operations one must be able to perform in order to fulfill the criteria of eligibility for the status at issue and thus, no criteria of legal mental illness for this purpose. Thus, these statutes fulfill neither the discriminative nor the justificatory functions served by provisions with an adequate formulation of legal mental illness. Despite this common pattern, the defensible boundaries of expert testimony regarding legal mental illness for the purpose of civil commitment remain clear in principle. Clinicians can provide relevant descriptive and explanatory testimony regarding the impairment of psychological processes manifested by the individual and regarding the manner in which that impairment influences the individual's capacities and behavior, including those relevant to the civil commitment hearing. Courts must evaluate this testimony according to the legal and moral components of the appropriate conception of legal mental illness for the specific legal purpose. A similar analysis applies to the criterion of dangerousness for general civil commitment and to the likelihood of reoffending for commitment under the sexual predator statutes.

III. A Common View of the Clinician's Role: Predicting Dangerousness

An extensive literature documents the recent research and debate regarding dangerousness among those who suffer psychological disorder.[4] Rather than reviewing that literature, this section summarizes the general parameters of that discussion. Some writers discuss predictions of dangerousness; others address predictions of violence, harm, or dangerous conduct. Some use these phrases interchangeably, whereas others adopt one formulation. Most, however, frame the discussion of dangerousness as one of prediction.[5] Reliance upon clinical evaluation to predict that a particular individual

---

[4] See, e.g., Thomas Grisso & Paul S. Appelbaum, *Is It Unethical to Offer Predictions of Future Violence?*, 16 L. & HUM. BEHAV. 621 (1992); Thomas R. Litwack & Louis B. Schlesinger, *Assessing and Predicting Violence: Research, Law and Applications*, in HANDBOOK OF FORENSIC PSYCHOLOGY 205 (Irving B. Weiner & Allen K. Hess, eds. 1987); John Monahan, *Mental Disorder and Violent Behavior*, 47 AMER. PSYCHOLOGIST 511 (1992); VIOLENCE AND MENTAL DISORDER: DEVELOPMENTS IN RISK ASSESSMENT (John Monahan & Henry J. Steadman, eds. 1994) [hereinafter VIOLENCE AND MENTAL DISORDER].

[5] See e.g., Grisso & Appelbaum, *supra* note 4, at 622–23, 632; Litwack & Schlesinger, *supra* note 4; John Monahan, *The Prediction of Violent Behavior: Toward a Second Generation of Theory and Policy*, 141 AMER. J. PSYCHIATRY 10 (1984); John Monahan & Henry J. Steadman, *Toward a Rejuvenation of Risk Assessment Research*, in VIOLENCE AND MENTAL DISORDER, *supra* note 4, at 1; Randy K. Otto, *Prediction of Dangerous Behavior: A Review and Analysis of "Second-Generation" Research*, 5 FORENSIC REP. 103 (1992); Norman G. Poythress, *Expert Testimony on Violence and Dangerousness:*

will cause harm remains vulnerable to many sources of error including low base rates, a lack of reliable clinical indicators of future violence, and social circumstances that tend to encourage a preference for false positives over false negatives among those responsible for making predictions. As a result of these difficulties, it has become widely accepted that clinicians tend to substantially overpredict violence, with approximately two thirds of such predictions representing false positives.[6] These circumstances lead some commentators to prefer actuarial prediction.[7]

A growing body of research suggests some improvement in actuarial predictions, but accuracy remains problematic for practical application for the purpose of commitment. Recent data suggest, for example, that base rates of violence by sex offenders are significantly higher than sometimes supposed and that current psychosis is associated with increased rates of harmful conduct.[8] Prediction of dangerousness on the basis of any specific diagnosis or type of impairment continues to produce many false positives, however, and some demographic profiles remain better predictors than active psychosis.[9] Some commentators contend that improved data regarding recidivism among sex offenders allows more accurate prediction of dangerousness among past sexual offenders, specifically in the form of recidivism.[10] Indeed, some commentators contend that underprediction, rather than overprediction, represents the more probable error regarding prediction of recidivism by sex offenders.[11] Finally, individual commitment on the basis of actuarial prediction raises serious concern regarding the legal and moral justification of intrusion into individual liberty on the basis of membership in statistical categories.[12] In light of these formidable concerns, some writers advocate abandoning commitment standards involving dangerousness in favor of alternatives addressing various types of functional impairment.[13]

Commentators who have reviewed the literature tend to endorse one of two lines of thought regarding predictions of dangerousness by expert witnesses. Some contend that clinicians should never predict dangerousness because accurate predictions extend beyond the scope of present expertise.[14] Others argue that clinicians should, or at least may, predict in certain circumstances, although those who do so should make

---

Roles for Mental Health Professionals, 5 FORENSIC REP. 135, 142 (1992); VERNON L. QUINSEY, GRANT T. HARRIS, MARNIE E. RICE, & CATHERINE A. CORNIER, VIOLENT OFFENDERS: APPRAISING AND MANAGING RISK (1998).

[6] Dennis M. Doren, *Recidivism Base Rates, Predictions of Sex Offender Recidivism, and the "Sexual Predator" Commitment Laws*, 16 BEHAV. SCI. & L. 97 (1998); Monahan & Steadman, *supra* note 5, at 5.

[7] Litwack & Schlesinger, *supra* note 4, at 207–23; Poythress, *supra* note 5, at 142; QUINSEY et al., *supra* note 5.

[8] Monahan, *supra* note 4, at 514–19 (psychosis associated with violence); QUINSEY et al., *supra* note 5, at 129–32 (base rates higher).

[9] Monahan, *supra* note 4 at 519.

[10] *See* chapter 11, section II.

[11] Doren, *supra* note 6.

[12] *See e.g.*, Marc Miller & Norval Morris, *Predictions of Dangerousness: An Argument for Limited Use*, 3 VICTIMS & VIOLENCE 263, 272–77 (1988).

[13] *See e.g.*, Allen Kirk, *The Prediction of Violent Behavior During Short-Term Civil Commitment*, 17 BULL. AMER. ACAD. PSYCHIATRY & L. 345, 350–52 (1989).

[14] Grisso & Appelbaum, *supra* note 4, at 621–22.

clear the limitations of their predictions.[15] Although commentators sometimes disagree regarding the propriety of making such predictions or regarding the specific level of confidence that is currently warranted regarding such predictions in various circumstances, they agree insofar as almost all participants discuss judgments of dangerousness as predictions of dangerousness, harm, or violence. Although clinicians' ability to make such predictions with an appropriate degree of confidence remains much more controversial than their ability to provide expert testimony regarding mental illness, the courts continue to call on clinicians for professional opinions regarding both requirements.[16]

IV.   Reconsidering Predictions of Dangerousness

Suppose that you read a report regarding current airline safety indicating that commercial airline flights crash at a rate of 1 in 10,000 flights.[17] The report lists all commercial airlines with their crash rates, and almost all fall close to this rate of 1 in 10,000. At the bottom of the list sits Dork Airlines with a crash rate of 1 in 100 flights. Dork catches your attention because its rate of crashes stands out as much worse than any other; the worst rate for any other airline is 1 in 9,000. Dork's rate also catches your attention because you are reading this report while waiting to board Dork Flight 37. Do you still plan to board the plane? My informal survey has yet to identify anyone who professes willingness to board. All agree that Dork is just too dangerous. Yet, do you predict that Dork 37 will crash? Absent any information specific to Dork 37, it seems that your only relevant information is Dork's baseline of 1 crash in 100 flights. Thus, should you not predict with a high degree of confidence that Dork 37 will not crash?

If a judgment of dangerousness constitutes a prediction that a harmful event will occur, then it seems that we must either conclude that Dork 37 is dangerous and predict that it will crash or predict that it will not crash and conclude that it is not dangerous. Yet, most people seem to agree that on the basis of the current information we should predict that Dork 37 will not crash and that we should refuse to board because it is too damn dangerous! These conclusions should lead us to question the notion that judgments of dangerousness constitute predictions that harmful events will occur. The following sections of this chapter suggest that judgments of dangerousness neither constitute nor include predictions. The alternative analysis carries significance for the manner in which we interpret the results of relevant research as well as for the allocation of professional responsibilities among clinicians and judicial decision makers.

The alternative formulation of judgments of dangerousness suggests that the most critical objections to expert predictions of statutory dangerousness do not arise from inadequate rates of accuracy. Predictions of dangerousness are objectionable in

---

[15] Grisso & Appelbaum, *supra* note 4; Litwack & Schlesinger, *supra* note 4.

[16] Alexander D. Brooks, *Defining the Dangerousness of the Mentally Ill: Involuntary Civil Commitment*, in MENTALLY ABNORMAL OFFENDERS 280, 288–95 (Michael Craft & Ann Craft eds., 1984) (discussing the tendency of legislatures and courts to rely on expert testimony rather than defining dangerousness).

[17] I do not suggest that these figures approximate accuracy. I make them up for the purpose of this thought experiment.

principle because determinations of statutory dangerousness do not constitute predictions. Putative predictions of dangerousness distort the law of civil commitment and clinicians' proper function as expert witnesses testifying within the scope of their expertise. Marked improvement in accuracy would not alleviate this distortion. Experts who predict dangerousness for the purpose of civil commitment conflate empirical and normative judgments, and they fuse the roles of witness and decision maker.[18] Such predictions reflect an erroneous distribution of authority and responsibility across expert witness and judicial decision maker, regardless of the attainable level of accuracy.

V.   An Alternative Formulation of Statutory Dangerousness

Consider the current civil commitment statutes in Nebraska and Wisconsin. Nebraska limits commitment to any individual found to be a "mentally ill dangerous person," and it defines such a person as one who is a "mentally ill person . . . who presents: (1) a substantial risk of serious harm" to himself or to others.[19] Wisconsin allows commitment only of an individual who "1. is mentally ill . . . and 2. is dangerous."[20] Both statutes limit commitment to those who are *currently* mentally ill and dangerous. Nebraska requires a finding that the individual *is* a mentally ill person who *presents* a substantial risk. Wisconsin commits only a person who *is* mentally ill and *is* dangerous. Both statutes require both conditions as current properties of the individual in question. Nothing in the language of the statute suggests that dangerousness is a future condition subject to prediction, and nothing supports treating the two requirements differently regarding their temporal relationship to the hearing.

In ordinary language, a person, condition, or event is dangerous if it is "fraught with danger or risk . . . causing or occasioning danger . . . perilous."[21] "Danger" means "liability or exposure to harm or injury."[22] The Nebraska and Wisconsin statutes define dangerousness in a manner consistent with these meanings in ordinary language. Nebraska defines a dangerous person as one who presents a "substantial risk of serious harm."[23] Wisconsin interprets dangerousness as involving a "substantial probability of physical harm."[24] According to the statutes and ordinary language, a dangerous person is one who currently has the property of exposing himself or others to risk or peril of harm or injury.

Although commentators frequently frame the discussion of dangerousness and expert testimony regarding dangerousness in terms of predictive accuracy,[25] danger-

---

[18] I use "empirical" in its ordinary broad sense in which it refers to descriptive claims based on observation and sense experience. Actuarial and clinical descriptions and judgments are both empirical in this sense. "Normative" refers here to prescriptive norms regarding the manner in which we ought to behave, rather than to descriptive standards that measure the manner in which people actually behave.

[19] NEB. REV. STAT. §§ 83–1037 (commitment criteria), 1009 (definition of mentally ill dangerous person) (1987).

[20] WIS. STAT. ANN. § 51.20(1) (West 1997).

[21] I OXFORD ENGLISH DICTIONARY 644 (compact ed. 1977).

[22] *Id.* at 644.

[23] NEB. REV. STAT. §§ 83–1009(1), (2) (1987).

[24] WIS. STAT. ANN. §§ 51.20(2)(a), (b) (West 1997).

[25] *See* section III.

ousness for the purpose of commitment is a current property of the person in the circumstances, and it is incoherent to predict that an individual currently manifests a property. Although it is incoherent to predict the present, one can coherently predict either that the individual will continue to manifest the current property of dangerousness or that the individual will engage in harmful conduct.[26] That is, because dangerousness is the current property of exposing oneself or others to risk of harm, a prediction of dangerousness would not constitute a prediction of future harmful conduct; rather, it would represent the proposition that the individual will in the future have the property of exposing himself or others to the risk of harm. For example, to the extent that actuarial data demonstrate higher risk of violence among poor male adolescents or among those who are actively psychotic, the prediction that the individual will in the future be a poor male adolescent or psychotic constitutes the prediction that the individual will in the future be dangerous. This prediction does not entail, however, the claim that the person will perform harmful conduct. Recent data suggest that psychotic individuals are more likely than the general population to engage in harmful behavior but that the majority do not do so.[27] Thus, it is consistent and accurate to say that psychotic individuals are dangerous but most probably will not perform injurious conduct.

A determination of dangerousness under these statutes requires a finding that the individual currently represents a risk of harm; it does not require a prediction that the individual will engage in injurious conduct at some future time. If the criterion of dangerousness were satisfied by all those who present any risk of harm, all subjects of commitment hearings would be dangerous. Every subject, like the attorneys, the witnesses, the judge, and virtually anyone who is not currently in a permanent vegetative state, presents some risk of harm. To avoid rendering the requirement trivial, it must be understood as referring to some threshold of risk.

Some commentators contend that the dangerousness criterion for civil commitment rests on the assumption that mentally ill people as a class are more dangerous than the general population.[28] Absent data supporting this assumption, these commentators sometimes conclude either that civil commitment ought to be abolished or that the dangerousness criterion ought to be revised.[29]

To evaluate this argument, one must distinguish two senses in which one can speak of those who suffer mental illness "as a class." To speak of the class collectively is to speak of the class as such, that is, to speak of the category rather than of the individuals who fall within the category. The claim that the class of mentally ill persons as a general category is more (or less) dangerous than other general categories of persons is irrelevant to civil commitment, however, because the commitment criteria always apply to some particular mentally ill person who is the

---

[26] The debate tends to emphasize violence, but neither the statutes nor the concept of dangerousness limits the notion to violence. I discuss dangerousness in terms of harmful or injurious behavior including but not limited to violence.

[27] Monahan, *supra* note 4, at 519.

[28] Stephen J. Morse, *A Preference for Liberty: The Case Against the Involuntary Commitment of the Mentally Disordered*, 70 CAL. L. REV. 54, 62–63 (1982); Note, *Developments in the Law—Civil Commitment of the Mentally Ill*, 87 HARV. L. REV. 1190, 1230 (1974).

[29] Morse, *supra* note 28 (abolish or severely restrict); Clifford J. Stromberg & Alan A. Stone, *A Model State Law on Civil Commitment of the Mentally Ill*, 20 HARV. J. ON LEGIS. 275, 280–86 (1983) (emphasizing treatment delivery rather than dangerousness).

subject of the hearing. The contention that a particular mentally ill person ought to be committed because mentally ill persons collectively are more dangerous than the general population (and therefore, that this particular individual is dangerous) embodies the fallacy of division. That is, it predicates an attribute to a member of a class merely on the basis that the attribute applies to the class.[30] Such an argument fails because of fallacious reasoning independently of the relative dangerousness of mentally ill persons as a class.

Alternately, the claim that mentally ill people as a class are more (or less) dangerous than the general population might be intended in the distributive sense. In this sense, it asserts that each and every person in the class is more (or less) dangerous than the general population.[31] If commitment were premised on the claim that every member of the class of mentally ill persons is dangerous, mental illness would be considered sufficient for commitment under the types of statutes we discuss. That is, if mental illness and dangerousness were considered jointly sufficient for commitment, and mentally ill people, taken distributively, were more dangerous than others to a degree sufficient to justify commitment, then mental illness would fulfill both conditions, and the dangerousness requirement would be redundant. It is not; mental illness is necessary, and mental illness and dangerousness are jointly sufficient under these statutes. The dangerousness requirement is substantive only if the statute writers and interpreters assume that mentally ill people as a class, taken distributively, are not sufficiently dangerous to justify commitment.

If virtually all people present some risk, and mentally ill people, taken distributively, are not more dangerous than the general population, what does the dangerousness clause in commitment statutes require? Consider an individual who suffers from paranoid schizophrenia with persecutory delusions. He has experienced several periods of psychosis during the past 10 years. During each of these periods, he has become afraid to leave his room at a boarding house. He has never engaged in any aggressive or dangerous behavior. During the periods of psychosis, he hides in his room until the social worker from the outpatient clinic comes to the boarding house and convinces him to attend the clinic and resume medication. Most clinicians and courts would probably agree that he is not subject to civil commitment under most commitment statutes because he is mentally ill but not dangerous.

Suppose that the court and the experts so agree and that he is released from a commitment hearing without commitment. Shortly thereafter the county attorney schedules another court hearing in order to decide whether the same individual suffers a mental illness that renders him dangerous. At first glance, the hearing seems redundant in that the court and experts have just agreed that he is mentally ill but not dangerous. This hearing, however, does not address civil commitment. Rather, the court must decide whether to revoke his permit to carry a concealed weapon under a state statute that mandates issuance of such permits to all adult citizens who fulfill the statutory application procedures unless they "are dangerous as demonstrated by a history of criminal behavior or mental illness."[32]

---

[30] WESLEY C. SALMON, LOGIC 55–56 (3d ed. 1984). This fallacious pattern of reasoning would generate, for example, the following argument. The members of the United States Senate reside in 50 different states. Jones is member of the United States Senate. Therefore, Jones resides in 50 different states.

[31] Id. at 55.

[32] He has not recently secured the permit during a period of psychosis. Rather, he has held the

Would or should most clinicians agree at this hearing that he is not dangerous? My informal conversations with clinicians, lawyers, and ordinary citizens suggest that many of these individuals, including many who do not categorically oppose concealed weapons permits, consider this individual dangerous for this purpose. Those who share the opinion that one can qualify as dangerous for the purpose of carrying a concealed weapon but not qualify as dangerous for the purpose of civil commitment should consider the possibility that the relevant conception of dangerousness varies with the specific legal purpose. Insofar as the appropriate conception of dangerousness varies with the legal purpose, a judgment of dangerousness ordinarily falls beyond the scope of psychological expertise because the relevant considerations ordinarily include normative components as well as estimates of risk.

Recall the analysis employed by the *Lessard* court.[33] The court recognized civil commitment as a massive limitation of individual liberty, requiring a compelling state interest analysis. Mental illness is not sufficient to provide a compelling state interest, but dangerousness triggers the traditional police power and *parens patriae* rationales for state intrusion.[34] The minimal sense of dangerousness that applies to everyone cannot provide the compelling state interest needed to support commitment, which constitutes an unusual intrusion into the liberty ordinarily recognized as appropriate for most people. If this minimal sense of dangerousness were sufficient to limit liberty, it would support a decreased level of liberty for all, rather than civil commitment as a special limitation on the liberty of a few. The compelling state interest analysis serves to justify intrusions into the liberty available to most people under ordinary circumstances. The *Lessard* court concluded that commitment requires "an extreme likelihood that if the person is not confined he will do immediate harm to himself or others."[35] The court also established an evidentiary requirement that the evidence establishing this dangerousness includes a recent overt act, attempt, or threat to do substantial harm.[36]

This analysis produces a conception of dangerousness for the purpose of civil commitment with two components. First, dangerousness is a current descriptive property of the person. That is, the person must present a risk of harm as demonstrated by some pattern of circumstances and conduct. Second, dangerousness contains a normative component in that this risk must be sufficient to justify the intrusion into liberty inherent in civil commitment.[37] Alternative state interventions, including rev-

---

permit for an extended period because he often works as a night watchman and commutes to work along deserted streets shortly before his midnight to eight shift. I do not suggest that any particular concealed carry statute includes precisely these words. Rather, this hypothetical provision represents conditions common to such statutes.

[33] Lessard v. Schmidt, 349 F.Supp. 1078 (E.D. Wis. 1972).

[34] *Lessard*, 349 F.Supp. at 1093–94.

[35] *Lessard*, 349 F.Supp. at 1093. The court's 1974 order did not contain this precise language but was consistent with it. Lessard v. Schmidt, 379 F.Supp. 1376, 1379 (E.D. Wis. 1974).

[36] *Id.*

[37] Humphrey v. Cady, 405 U.S. 504, 509 (1972) (interpreting a Wisconsin statute in a manner consistent with this principle); Grisso & Appelbaum, *supra* note 4, at 626–28; Miller & Morris, *supra* note 12, at 272–76; Monahan, *supra* note 5, at 14; John Monahan & David B. Wexler, *A Definite Maybe: Proof and Probability in Civil Commitment*, 2 L. & HUM. BEHAV. 37 (1978). Others have recognized this normative aspect of the conception of dangerousness as a criterion of commitment. This chapter pursues the ramifications of that analysis for the roles of clinicians and courts.

ocation of permits to carry concealed weapons, involve different limitations of different liberties. The degree and type of risk sufficient to justify these interventions, and thus sufficient to qualify as dangerousness for these particular legal purposes, might vary. To establish the type and degree of risk that justifies a particular type of intervention, one must examine the normative arguments relevant to the liberty and the intervention at issue. The responsibilities of clinicians and courts in determining dangerousness reflect the descriptive and normative components of the conception.

VI. The Clinician's Role

The clinician's scope of expertise includes the diagnosis of psychological disorder in the broad sense in which diagnosis involves the description and explanation of various types of impairment of psychological process. Clinicians can also evaluate prognosis with and without appropriate treatment. Furthermore, they can prescribe and deliver a variety of treatment modalities. These diagnostic and prognostic skills may be relevant to the descriptive component of dangerousness, but nothing in the clinician's range of expertise addresses the normative component.

The normative determination that a subject is dangerous enough to justify commitment extends beyond the scope of clinical expertise because it includes legal and normative determinations that fall within the responsibility of the court and legislature in a representative democracy. The degree and type of risk necessary to justify various legal interventions varies with the legal purpose and with the intrusion to be justified. The court must weigh the state interest to be protected against the necessary intrusion into individual liberty.[38] Thus, the legal determination that the individual is dangerous means that he or she presents a risk of harm sufficient to justify a particular legal response. The justificatory argument appeals to the principles of political morality embodied in the legal institutions of the society.

For the sake of clarity, this book reserves "dangerousness" for the legal conception of dangerousness that includes both descriptive and normative components. "Risk" refers to the descriptive component of this legal conception of dangerousness. Thus, expert witnesses provide descriptive and explanatory testimony regarding risk as the current likelihood of harmful conduct, and courts consider this evidence in light of the appropriate normative considerations in order to determine whether the individual is dangerous in the sense required by the commitment statute.[39]

The clinician can describe and explain the pattern of impairment demonstrated by the individual, and this testimony can include actuarial information regarding the risk of harm associated with clinical characteristics such as psychosis.[40] The clinician can also explain any apparent relationship between the individual's pathology and

---

[38] Youngberg v. Romeo, 457 U.S. 307, 319–21 (1982); JOHN E. NOWAK & RONALD D. ROTUNDA, CONSTITUTIONAL LAW § 11.4 (4th ed. 1991).

[39] By doing so, I use "risk" when many people in ordinary conversation would use "dangerous." This convention has two advantages. First, it draws attention to the difference between this ordinary notion of dangerousness and the more complex legal conception of statutory dangerousness with the normative component. Second, it is consistent with a current tendency in academic psychology to refer to at least some empirical research programs relevant to dangerousness as "risk assessment." *See, e.g.*, VIOLENCE AND MENTAL DISORDER, *supra* note 4.

[40] Monahan, *supra* note 4, at 516–19 (discussing risk associated with psychosis).

associated risky conduct. The clinician can also testify regarding the probable effects of available treatment. The clinician cannot, however, predict dangerousness or offer a professional opinion that the individual is (or is not) dangerous. The clinician cannot predict dangerousness because statutory dangerousness for the purpose of civil commitment is a current property rather than a future state subject to prediction. The clinician cannot offer an opinion that the individual is (or is not) dangerous because dangerousness for this purpose is a legal notion that includes a normative component that necessarily extends beyond the scope of the clinician's expertise.

Thus, regardless of current rates of accuracy, clinicians should refrain from predicting dangerousness and from offering opinions that individuals are (or are not) dangerous. Clinicians who predict dangerousness or offer such opinions distort the meaning of "dangerousness" in the statute by misrepresenting it as an empirical prediction, obscuring the normative component and misdirecting the temporal focus from the present to the future. They also misrepresent their expertise and responsibility by addressing a normative judgment beyond the scope of their professions. Finally, they preempt part of the court's responsibility. Although the current focus on the clinician's proper role can create the erroneous impression that the difficulty arises solely because clinicians do not recognize their limits, these conclusions also address lawyers and courts. That is, lawyers should not ask expert witnesses for predictions of dangerousness or for opinions that individuals are (or are not) dangerous, and courts should exclude such testimony as beyond the witnesses' expertise. By revising their participation in the process in a compatible manner, clinicians, attorneys, and courts can define and fulfill their respective professional responsibilities.

Although they should not predict dangerousness or offer opinions that individuals are (or are not) dangerous, clinicians can testify in descriptive and explanatory terms regarding risk. Specifically, clinicians can describe and explain the individual's impairment and the possible relationship of that impairment to injurious conduct. The best indicator of risk is past conduct in similar relevant circumstances.[41] Insofar as the individual's current psychological functioning and impairment are related to his or her past risky conduct, clinicians can offer testimony relevant to dangerousness because the pattern of impairment constitutes one type of relevantly similar circumstance.

The *Lessard* court and many statutes, including those in Nebraska and Wisconsin, require some overt conduct as part of the body of evidence establishing dangerousness.[42] Ordinary factual evidence regarding this overt conduct demonstrates risk at the time of that conduct (T1). Insofar as clinical evidence and records are available, clinicians can describe and explain the individual's impairment at T1 and the relationship between the impairment at T1 and the conduct that demonstrates risk at T1. This testimony informs the court's understanding of the association between the individual's risky conduct at T1 and his or her psychopathology at that time.

Legal standards requiring mental illness and dangerousness for commitment sometimes require not only the conjunction of these two conditions, but also that the person is dangerous by virtue of the mental illness. This book addresses nor-

---

[41] JOHN MONAHAN, PREDICTING VIOLENT BEHAVIOR 104–41 (1981);
Alexander D. Brooks, *The Constitutionality and Morality of Civilly Committing Violent Sexual Predators*, 15 UNIV. PUGET SOUND L. REV. 709, 750 (1992).
[42] NEB. REV. STAT. § 83–1009 (1999); WIS. STAT. ANN. § 51.20(1)(2) (West 1997); Lessard v. Schmidt, 349 F.Supp. 1078, 1093 (E.D. Wis. 1972).

mative questions regarding the most defensible substantive standards for commitment in prior chapters. This chapter addresses only the appropriate range of professional and judicial responsibility regarding the applicable criteria. Clinical testimony relevant to dangerousness describes and explains the manner in which the pathology contributes to or is otherwise associated with risk. The relationships among the individual's conduct, impairment, and circumstances render risk within the scope of the clinician's expertise. Thus, regardless of whether the statute authorizes commitment for all who are mentally ill and dangerous, or limits commitment to those who are dangerous by virtue of mental illness, expert testimony can address the manner in which the risk presented by the individual is associated with psychopathology in the circumstances.

Insofar as clinical evidence and the record allow, clinicians can describe and explain the individual's impairment at the time of the commitment hearing (T2) and the relationship between the current impairment at T2 and the impairment at T1, providing the court with information relevant to its evaluation of the probative weight of the risky conduct at T1 for current dangerousness. Thus, clinicians' testimony provides the court with information relevant to its normative judgment regarding whether the individual is dangerous for the purpose of commitment at T2. The court must integrate the full body of evidence in the following manner. The overt conduct at T1 provides evidence of risk at T1. The information regarding the relationships among that conduct at T1, the pathology at T1, and the pathology at T2 provides the court with evidence relevant to its determination of dangerousness at T2. It does so by informing the court regarding the relationship between the conduct providing evidence of risk and the pathology at T1 and regarding whether the pathology at T2 is sufficiently similar to the pathology at T1 to support the inference that the evidence of risk at T1 is indicative of dangerousness at T2; that is, whether pathology is a relevant similar circumstance imputing evidence of risk at T1 to the person at T2.

The court must also consider the similarity of circumstances other than psychological functioning at T1 and T2. Although clinicians may have relevant information regarding these other circumstances, alternative sources may well have more reliable information of this type. If clinicians have any special expertise regarding this category of information, it involves the ability to describe and explain the relationships among these circumstances, the individual's psychological processes, and behavior.

According to this analysis, the requirement of overt conduct at T1 can serve two distinct functions. In some cases, it can establish dangerousness at T1, and in others it serves as part of the comprehensive body of evidence from which to derive a judgment of dangerousness at T2 without establishing dangerousness at T1. In neither case does it serve to increase predictive accuracy, however, because the judgment of dangerousness does not constitute a prediction. On the first alternative, the risky conduct at T1 serves a critical purpose in the court's determination of dangerousness at T2. By determining that the conduct at T1 was sufficiently risky to justify commitment, the court establishes statutory dangerousness as a current property of the person in the circumstances at T1. In order to support a determination of dangerousness at T2, the court must consider the likely role of psychopathology or other circumstances in contributing to that risky conduct at T1 and the similarity of these circumstances across T1 and T2. This analysis of events and circumstances occurring during the period from T1 to T2 takes place at T2, precluding any need for a predictive component in the determination.

By treating the overt conduct as demonstrating dangerousness at T1, the court reformulates the troublesome question regarding the adequacy of verbalizations to fulfill the overt conduct requirement. According to this approach, verbalizations can establish risk sufficient for dangerousness at T1 if they take a form that would justify legal intervention at T1. Certain types of threats, for example, violate criminal statutes prohibiting assault or terrorist threats.[43] Arguably, verbalizations that would constitute criminal offenses against a person establish sufficient risk at T1 to support intervention through civil commitment if the risk represented by that conduct can be imputed to the individual at T2 and the other statutory requirements for commitment are satisfied.

Expert testimony informs the court's determination of dangerousness for the purpose of commitment at T2 to the extent that this testimony provides reason to believe that the individual's dangerous conduct at T1 was associated with pathology and that this pathology at T1 was sufficiently similar to the individual's pathology at T2 to provide good reason for treating the dangerous conduct at T1 as a reliable indicator of dangerousness at T2. The judgment that the harmful conduct at T1 was associated with the individual's psychopathology means only that the pathology and conduct were associated in such a manner as to render the continuation of the pathology reasonable grounds to support the judgment that the risk represented by that conduct remains. It does not require that the pathology was the sole cause of the conduct.[44]

In some circumstances, overt conduct at T1 can support a judgment of dangerousness although that conduct was not dangerous. Recall the case of Peter who delusionally adopted the identity of various biblical figures and began addressing boys in the playground as Isaac during the period in which he adopted the identity of Abraham.[45] His earlier sprinkling of water and wearing a coat of many colors did not establish dangerousness at that earlier time, but it contributed to the entire body of evidence supporting a judgment of dangerousness at the time of the commitment hearing. Circumstances such as these involve the court in a determination of dangerousness at T2 without providing the point of demonstrated dangerousness at T1 that allows evaluation of relevantly similar or dissimilar circumstances in order to infer that the dangerousness established at T1 applies at T2. This lack of demonstrated dangerousness renders the current basis for establishing dangerousness less clear, but it does not transform the determination of a current property into a prediction. The court must evaluate the complete body of available evidence in order to draw an inference that the individual is (or is not) dangerous as a current property of the person in the circumstances.

VII.   Judicial Determinations of Dangerousness as Judgments Rather Than Predictions

At first glance, it might appear that the determination of dangerousness remains a prediction because courts justify the confinement of the individual at T2 on the basis

---

[43] NEB. REV. STAT. §§ 28–310, 311.01 (1995) (third-degree assault and terroristic threats, respectively).

[44] JOEL FEINBERG, DOING AND DESERVING 201–05 (1970) (explaining causal factors and causal citations).

[45] *See* chapter 8, sections I and II.

of the expectation that absent commitment, he or she will cause harm during the period for which commitment is contemplated. Judges, like clinicians, have no special expertise in predicting harmful conduct. Therefore, this interpretation merely shifts the responsibility for making such predictions from clinicians who lack the ability to predict to judges who also lack the ability to do so.

Courts must regularly make such judgments of dangerousness in conditions of uncertainty. Criminal courts, for example, must make decisions regarding pretrial release on bail and suspended sentences or probation in sentencing.[46] That courts make such judgments regularly does not in itself render this practice defensible. By recognizing the determination of dangerousness as a normative judicial decision, however, we avoid the illusion of empirical predictive expertise and subject the practice to normative argument and justification. Furthermore, the thought experiment regarding Dork 37 demonstrates that judgments of dangerousness differ from predictions of harmful events.

The judicial determination of dangerousness in civil commitment hearings is not a prediction of future dangerousness or of harm, but a judgment regarding a current property of the person in the circumstances. The present and the future are two periods of time with substantial duration; the future begins after the completion of the present or current period.[47] From the perspective of the commitment hearing, it seems natural to say that T1 occurred in the past, that T2 occurs in the present, and that the court makes its determination at T2 on the basis of a prediction about some indefinite period in the future. Notice, however, that one could define each of these periods differently for different purposes. Although it seems natural to say that T2 marks the time of the commitment hearing during which the clinician testifies and the court makes a determination regarding the individual's current mental illness and dangerousness, one could further subdivide T2. For example, the clinician evaluates the individual at T2A; the court convenes the hearing at T2B; other witnesses testify regarding the individual's conduct relevant to the overt conduct requirement at T2C; at T2D the expert testifies regarding the results of the evaluation performed at T2A; and the court makes a ruling at T2E. For our purposes, we speak of this extended period as T2, the time of the commitment hearing, and from the perspective of that hearing, the entire sequence occurs in the present.

What is the correct duration of the present; that is, the current period? In a narrow sense, the present is "the immediate, instantaneous, momentary, and transient part of time (or durationless instant) at which any given experience takes place."[48] For some purposes, the present is "conceived as having no duration or small duration."[49] It merely marks the transition from past to future. This is not, however, the sense we ordinarily use for practical purposes. It takes time to utter the phrase "I am presently in charge." The entire phrase apparently refers to the present, but if "presently" is used in the narrow sense, uttering the term "presently" would have been a future event when the speaker began the statement and a past event when

---

[46] WAYNE R. LaFAVE & JEROLD H. ISRAEL, CRIMINAL PROCEDURE §§ 12.1, 12.3 (pretrial release), § 26.1(d) (community release in sentencing) (2d ed. 1992).

[47] The future is "time to come . . . a condition in time to come . . . different from the present." "Present" means "existing at the time of speaking or writing . . . at this time . . . occurring or going on now." I OXFORD ENGLISH DICTIONARY, *supra* note 21, at 1101, 2285.

[48] PETER A. ANGELES, DICTIONARY OF PHILOSOPHY 223 (1981).

[49] DAGOBERT D. RUNES, DICTIONARY OF PHILOSOPHY 249 (1977).

the speaker completed the sentence. When the speaker actually articulated the word, the thought would have been formed and the statement begun in the past. A speaker who utters this statement in practical circumstances probably intends the term "presently" to refer to some finite period. A foreman might understand the present as covering the current 8-hour factory shift. A president might understand the sentence as referring to a 4-year term.[50]

Consider the case of Quincy and Rhonda. Quincy is an assistant professor, and Rhonda is an investment advisor. Usually, Rhonda leaves the house for work at 7:30 a.m., the children board the school bus at about 8:00 a.m., and then Quincy goes to his office. This semester, Quincy must leave by 7:30 because he teaches an 8:00 class. Prior to the first day of class, Quincy and Rhonda discuss the schedule because the children are too young to wait for the bus alone. Quincy says, "For now, I can drop them off at school early on my way to class." Rhonda asks, "Do you still have to work weekends?" Quincy replies, "Yes, for the present, I do." Later, Rhonda adds, "Maybe in the future we can consider buying a house, but currently we must continue building enough savings for a down payment."

As Quincy and Rhonda understand their conversation and circumstances, the present for the purpose of Quincy's dropping the children at school starts tomorrow and continues for 15 weeks until his 8:00 class ends. That is, the current semester constitutes the present. For the purpose of Quincy's working weekends, however, the present began when he accepted his assistant professorship 3 years ago, and it will continue for 3 more years until his tenure review. Finally, for the purpose of accumulating a down payment for a house, the current period began when they married and continues for some indefinite period to be determined by the amount they can save, the state of the economy, and the local housing market. In summary, Quincy and Rhonda, like most ordinary people, understand temporal indicators such as "now," "present," or "current" as referring to periods of time with substantial duration that varies with the specific purpose and circumstances.

The present has no fixed duration independent of purpose and context. It is coherent to speak of the present in terms of hours, days, or longer periods. For some purposes, one might speak of the present decade or century. For legal purposes, the "present time" sometimes takes a sense in which it means "a period of appreciable and generally considerable duration within which certain transactions are to take place."[51] For civil commitment, the court must decide at T2 whether the individual is presently dangerous. The court's determination, like the previously discussed statements by the foreman, the president, Quincy, and Rhonda, refers to some finite period of time, rather than to an indefinite period. The present for this purpose is best understood as the current period of dangerousness (CPD) during which conditions remain relevantly similar. That is, the CPD represents a maximum duration of commitment that extends from the determination of current dangerousness at T2 until a mandatory release or review at T3. The decision to commit at T2 represents the judgments that the individual is currently dangerous and that the relevant circumstances supporting this judgment are sufficiently stable to warrant treating the period from T2 to T3 as the CPD for the purpose of commitment.

---

[50] "Presently" often serves the primary rhetorical function of marking the state of affairs as temporary or continuing only for some fixed period rather than permanent or indefinite. I thank Bob Works for this observation.

[51] BLACK'S LAW DICTIONARY 1148 (6th ed. 1990).

Ideally, the court would calculate an appropriate CPD for each committed person in light of all relevant considerations, including the nature of the individual's impairment and the circumstances. The CPD would vary for each commitment, and it would accurately represent the duration of the risk presented by this person in these circumstances. Our primitive understanding of the manner in which impairment and circumstances interact as well as the need to develop law at some reasonable degree of generality preclude such a fine-grained approach. Ordinarily, commitment statutes provide a very rough approximation of this approach by setting a maximum duration of commitment prior to mandatory review. This period from commitment at T2 to mandatory review at T3 represents a general statutory estimate of the CPD.

The duration of the CPD extends from T2 to T3 as defined partially by a complex set of factors including the length of time we think pathology tends to remain active, the time needed for treatment to take effect, the balance of our values for liberty and well-being, and judicial economy. The duration of confinement we allow before review reflects these considerations. Thus, the duration of the CPD for the purpose of civil commitment is a legal convention involving the integration of empirical and normative considerations. Clinicians can provide descriptive and explanatory testimony relevant to the empirical components, but the normative components and the final determination drawn from the integration of the empirical and normative components extend beyond clinical expertise.

Similarly, the duration of the period T1 to T2 extends for some reasonable period of time defined partially by the length of time we think pathology tends to remain active, the opportunities the individual has had for relevant conduct, the relative stability of the individual's pattern of pathology, and the balance of our values for liberty and well-being. The required recency of behavior for the overt conduct requirement reflects these considerations. For example, violent conduct that occurred a year ago may be appropriately considered as evidence of current dangerousness for an individual who has spent the last year in closely supervised confinement and whose pathology now remains unabated, but not for an individual who responded to aggressive treatment with marked remission and who has been living unsupervised for the last 6 months.[52]

Some critics might object that this discussion of dangerousness as a current property is misleading because the current condition involves a risk of future harm. Thus, these critics might contend, to say that the individual is currently dangerous is just to predict that he or she will cause future harm.

This criticism fails, however, because as demonstrated by the thought experiment regarding Dork 37, neither a determination of dangerousness nor a statement of risk constitutes a prediction of harm. Consider the following cases. As Sue and Terri talk at a tavern, Sue drinks more than usual, becoming quite intoxicated. As they leave, Terri insists that it is dangerous for Sue to drive home, but Sue refuses to ride with Terri. Sue drives home, weaving across traffic lanes and ignoring traffic signals, but she has no accident because the roads are deserted. The next day, Sue says to Terri,

---

[52] The *Young* court recognizes this difference in its treatment of the recent overt act requirement. In Re Young, 857 P.2d 989, 1008–09 (Wash. 1993). Although the duration of the CPD varies substantially across purposes or situations in principle, law as a practical institution may have to adopt some relatively predictable periods in application. The Nebraska commitment statute, for example, requires reports and reviews every 90 days for 1 year after commitment and every 6 months thereafter, establishing these periods as the presumptive CPD. NEB. REV. STAT. § 83–1045 (1999).

"I told you my driving wasn't dangerous; nothing happened." Sue clearly is wrong in saying that the lack of an accident establishes that her driving was not dangerous. The mere fact that no harm resulted does not undermine Terri's claim that Sue's driving under the influence was dangerous. This remains true whether they used "dangerous" in the comprehensive sense in which it is used in this chapter or in the narrow sense referred to as risk in this chapter.

Urban and Vic live in similar neighborhoods. They both celebrate New Year's Eve by shooting their pistols into the air in their backyards. Urban's bullet falls harmlessly to the ground, but Vic's shatters a neighbor's window. Both are arrested and charged with reckless endangerment.[53] Urban claims as a defense in court that he endangered no one because no harm resulted. Not only does this claim fail to establish a legal defense to the endangerment charge, which requires no injury, but it provides no reason to think that Urban's conduct was less risky than Vic's. Urban and Vic engaged in equally risky conduct because they engaged in similar conduct under similar circumstances. The mere fact that Vic's conduct produced harm whereas Urban's fortuitously did not has no effect on the riskiness of the conduct when each performed it.

If a judgment of dangerousness constituted a prediction of harm, criminal endangerment statutes would be superfluous in the sense that it would never be most appropriate to charge under them. If the defendant's conduct harmed someone, the appropriate charge would be one, such as homicide or assault, that reflected the harm caused. If the conduct did not cause harm, that fact would retrospectively prove that the conduct was not dangerous. That is, the lack of harm would render the endangerment charge a false positive. Urban and Vic are both guilty of reckless endangerment precisely because a judgment of dangerousness does not constitute a prediction of harm. In summary, legal standards and common sense converge in evaluating risk and dangerousness as properties of conduct when it is performed rather than as predictions of harm.

Now, consider the analogous cases of Walter and Xang who are subjects of commitment hearings. Walter is a 19-year-old, poor, and unemployed young man with a diagnosis of paranoid schizophrenia; he is currently psychotic and delusionally believes there is a conspiracy to kill him. Since age 16, he has attacked three other residents of the group homes in which he resided, and in each case, the attack was associated with the same delusional content he currently manifests. The court decides that Walter is mentally ill and dangerous, committing him to a secure inpatient ward. Xang is a 50-year-old middle-class woman with a history of mild to moderate anxiety and depression. She has no history of injurious conduct toward herself or others. The court refuses commitment because of lack of dangerousness. Shortly thereafter, Walter is injured in an accidental fall, becoming quadriplegic and never engaging in any further risky conduct. Xang suffers a psychotic episode associated with accidental ingestion of a toxic substance, and in delusional terror she stabs a neighbor with a kitchen knife.[54]

---

[53] AMERICAN LAW INSTITUTE, MODEL PENAL CODE AND COMMENTARIES § 211.2 (Official Draft and Revised Comments 1985) (defining reckless endangerment as reckless conduct that places or may place another person in danger of death or serious bodily harm).

[54] AMERICAN PSYCHIATRIC ASSOCIATION, DIAGNOSTIC AND STATISTICAL MANUAL OF MENTAL DISORDERS 310–15 (4th ed. 1994).

Did the court err in its determinations that Walter was dangerous but Xang was not? If a judgment of dangerousness constitutes a prediction of future harmful conduct, then the court made erroneous determinations in both cases. Yet, it seems clear that the court made the correct determinations in both cases. At T2, the court correctly determined that at that time, Walter but not Xang manifested the property of representing a sufficient risk of harm to justify commitment. Subsequent events changed circumstances in such a manner as to bring about harmful conduct by Xang rather than Walter, but these events do not alter the accuracy of the estimate of current risk at T2. Rather, these events changed conditions such as to render circumstances after those events no longer sufficiently similar to those at T2 to justify considering T2 and the period following those changes both part of the CPD for the purpose of civil commitment. These changes marked the end of the period appropriately considered the current one from the perspective of T2. In summary, the determination that the individual is dangerous at T2 constitutes the judgment that he or she currently represents a risk of harm sufficient to justify commitment; it does not constitute a prediction that the individual will in the future do such harm.

Thus, the original objection that this interpretation merely shifts the prediction from an unqualified clinician to an equally unqualified court misconstrues the nature of the determination of dangerousness. This interpretation does not shift the prediction problem from the clinician to the court because properly understood, commitment under these standards involves no prediction of harm. The court makes a normative determination that the evidence of current risk is (or is not) sufficient to justify state intervention of a particular type. The nature of the determination of dangerousness as a normative judgment based partially on the evidence of current risk explains why clinicians can provide descriptive and explanatory testimony but cannot offer a professional opinion that an individual is (or is not) dangerous, regardless of any improvements that might occur in the accuracy of risk estimates.

Suppose, for example, that clinicians develop the ability to identify a certain subtype of paranoid schizophrenia with a high degree of accuracy and that a consistent body of data demonstrates that 75% of people with this specific diagnosis commit violence relevant to their delusional content within 30 days. Should clinicians offer an opinion or prediction of dangerousness under these conditions? Suppose the violence rate is 98%?

No; regardless of accuracy regarding estimate of risk, clinicians cannot offer a prediction or an opinion that an individual is (or is not) dangerous. If they have this statistical information regarding risk, they should present it as part of the descriptive testimony. Regardless of accuracy, however, the conclusion that the individual is dangerous under the statute is a determination of legal status based upon a normative judgment regarding a current property of the individual. As such, it remains properly within the authority of the court and beyond the expertise of the expert witness because it requires consideration of normative concerns including the severity of infringement of liberty, the threat to public safety, and the relative importance of liberty and well-being.

VIII. Conclusion

Contrary to common discussion, a determination of dangerousness for a particular legal purpose involves no prediction of dangerousness or of harm. That a person is dangerous under the statute is a normative judgment by the court regarding a current property of the person in the circumstances. Clinicians may have descriptive and explanatory testimony relevant to that normative judgment, but no advance in predictive accuracy can transform that normative judgment regarding a current condition into a description or a prediction within the clinician's expertise.

This delineation of responsibility does not entail the claim that clinicians should never make judgments of dangerousness. Clinicians may encounter situations in which they must make such estimates in order to decide whether to alter treatment plans, initiate emergency detention, or warn third parties. In these circumstances, clinicians act as public safety officers charged with protecting the patient or the public. Just as the police officer's authority to arrest on the basis of probable cause does not entail the expertise or the authority to offer a professional opinion as to guilt or innocence at trial, the clinician's duty to estimate danger in certain circumstances does not entail the expertise or the authority to offer a professional opinion as an expert witness that the individual is (or is not) dangerous under the statute. Chapter 11 applies the framework developed in this chapter to the role of the expert witness in commitment hearings under sexual predator statutes. Chapter 12 uses these statutes as an opportunity to examine the circumstances in which clinicians take on extended duties as public safety officers and the manner in which such roles alter the appropriate interpretation of professional judgment and responsibility.

Chapter 11
EXPERT TESTIMONY AND COMMITMENT AS A SEXUAL PREDATOR

Chapter 10 provides a framework for expert testimony regarding common commitment criteria involving mental illness and dangerousness or similar notions. The sexual predator statutes and cases provide an interesting opportunity to examine the application of that framework. This chapter interprets the defensible range of expert testimony regarding sexual predator commitments. In doing so, it demonstrates that the general framework presented in chapter 10 enables one to define coherent and complementary boundaries for the roles of clinical, social scientific, and legal participants in judicial hearings brought under the statutes. This demonstration exemplifies the pattern of analysis that can be applied to hearings under other provisions.

I. The Subject of the Testimony: The Commitment Criteria

The cases brought under the sexual predator statutes demonstrate that the courts call upon psychologists and other clinicians to testify regarding the presence of a mental abnormality or personality disorder and the statutory requirement that the disorder makes the person likely to offend.[1] The experts called to testify regarding whether Hendricks satisfied the requirement that he manifests a mental abnormality or personality disorder consistently diagnosed him as qualifying for the diagnosis of pedophilia.[2] Appellate reviews of commitments under similar statutes frequently involve subjects who received the diagnoses of paraphilia, APD, or some combination of the two.[3] The patterns of conduct described in the appellate opinions for at least some of these defendants include multiple violent offenses and suggest that some might also qualify for the traditional diagnostic category of psychopathy.[4] Young, for example, had committed at least six violent rapes of adult women during an extended period.[5] The expert for the state diagnosed Young as "(1) a severe personality disorder not otherwise specified, with primarily paranoid and antisocial features, (2) a severe paraphilia, which would be classified as paraphilia sexual sadism or

---

[1]For the sake of convenience, I use the general term "disorder" to refer to the various types of psychological aberration that the statutes and cases recognize under the statutory terms "mental abnormality" and "personality disorder."

[2]Kansas v. Hendricks, 117 S.Ct. 2072, 2078–81 (1997).

[3]State v. Carpenter, 541 N.W.2d 105, 108–09 (Wis. 1995); In Re Linehan, 557N.W.2d 171, 176 (Min. 1996); State v. Post, 541 N.W.2d 115, 119 (Wis. 1995); In Re Young, 857 P.2d 989, 994–96 (Wash. 1993).

[4]In Re Linehan, 557 N.W.2d 171, 175–79 (Min. 1996); In Re Young, 857 P.2d at 989, 994–96; Stephen D. Hart, Robert D. Hare, & Adelle E. Forth, *Psychopathy as a Risk Marker for Violence: Development and Validation of a Screening Version of the Revised Psychopathy Checklist* in VIOLENCE AND MENTAL DISORDER 81 (John Monahan & Henry J. Steadman eds. 1994).

[5]In Re Young, 857 P.2d at 989, 994.

paraphilia not otherwise specified (rape)."[6] Cunningham had accumulated a 10-year history of sexual crimes, including three convictions for rapes of adult women.[7] A psychologist diagnosed Cunningham as "severe paraphilia, not otherwise specified (rape)."[8]

Linehan began a record of sexual misconduct at age 15, including rapes, window peeping, and other offenses, many of which were against young girls. In a telephone conversation with his wife, Linehan said that one of his victims "deserved what she got."[9] One expert testified that Linehan suffered from alcohol dependence (in remission), impulse control disorder, and APD and added that Linehan was very likely to reoffend; his assessment was based on Department of Justice base rate statistics and five violence prediction checklists.[10] A second expert concluded from written records that Linehan met the criteria for APD, paraphilia (not otherwise specified), alcohol dependence (by history), and voyeurism (by history).[11]

A common pattern emerges from these appellate cases. These experts consistently diagnosed these offenders with diagnoses, including paraphilia and personality disorders, and their diagnoses were derived to a substantial degree from the pattern of criminal behavior. They also expressed opinions that these individuals were likely to commit further offenses, and they based these estimates of risk to a substantial degree on the pattern of past offenses. Thus, the pattern of past offenses contributed substantially to the testimony regarding the statutory criteria of commitment including the diagnoses that fulfilled the requirement of a mental abnormality or personality disorder and the opinions that these disorders made the offenders likely to engage in sexual violence.

Interpreted in isolation, the requirement that the disorder makes the person likely to offend is open to discriminative or causal interpretations. According to the discriminative interpretation, this provision requires only that the disorder provide some reasonably reliable indication that the person is likely to reoffend. To say that the disorder makes the person likely to reoffend in this sense is only to say that the disorder is correlated with reoffending and, thus, that the presence of the disorder signals the probability of offending. Such a correlation provides the court with one basis on which to discriminate between those who are more likely to reoffend and those who are less likely to do so, but it entails no causal inference. The causal interpretation, in contrast, requires not only some reasonable probability of reoffending but also some causal connection between the disorder and the probable offenses. To the extent that experts diagnose the disorder primarily on the basis of the pattern of past offenses, they can address the discriminative interpretation insofar as the diagnosis represents the past pattern of conduct, and prior conduct by this person in similar circumstances provides good evidence of the probability of future conduct.[12]

---

[6] *Id*. The state's expert, Dr. Irwin Drieblatt, testified solely on the basis of a review of certain records as opposed to a personal clinical interview. This method of diagnosis resurfaces in the opinions discussed below and is not uncommon or surprising given the alleged sexual predators' disincentives to cooperate with clinicians assigned to assess them.

[7] *Id*. at 995.

[8] *Id*. at 995–96.

[9] Matter of Linehan, 557 N.W.2d at 171, 175.

[10] *Id*. at 176.

[11] *Id*.

[12] JOHN MONAHAN, PREDICTING VIOLENT BEHAVIOR 104–41 (1981); VERNON L. QUINSEY, GRANT

When interpreted in this discriminative manner, testimony that the individual manifests a disorder that makes further offenses likely is merely a convenient way of indicating that this individual has previously demonstrated that he was a person who engaged in this type of conduct and that baring changes, he remains such a person.

When applied to diagnoses that rely heavily upon the pattern of criminal conduct, such as those commonly made in the sexual predator cases, this discriminative interpretation invites two serious objections to the statute and to the expert testimony. First, this approach raises substantive questions regarding the justification for commitments under the statute. When interpreted and applied in this manner, the propensity to offend demonstrated by the pattern of prior criminal behavior constitutes the "disorder," and the grounds for the putative civil commitment consist only of a pattern of recidivism and the expectation of future crimes. These factors strongly suggest that the "civil commitment" is either an *ex post facto* extension of the criminal sentence or simple preventive detention on the expectation of future crimes.[13]

Second, this interpretation undermines the claim that the clinicians' testimony represents expertise in a clinical field. If the "disorder" consists merely or primarily of a propensity to offend demonstrated by a pattern of past offenses as reflected in the criminal history, testimony regarding the diagnosis of such a disorder and the likelihood of further offenses seems to require only an awareness of the criminal history and of the general principle that past conduct by this person in certain circumstances provides a reasonably good indicator of his likely future conduct in similar circumstances. Thus, the diagnosis of the disorder seems to require no expertise in the field of psychology or in any other field beyond the understanding of ordinary people. There is no obvious reason why anyone with access to the criminal history would not be as qualified as a clinician to diagnosis this type of disorder and render this type of opinion.

These objections, as well as the statutory definition of a mental abnormality as a condition that "predisposes" the individual to offend, seem to weigh in favor of the causal interpretation.[14] If one adopts the causal interpretation, however, this seems to require that the mental abnormality or personality disorder consists of some psychological impairment susceptible to description distinct from the conduct constituting the offenses and capable of causing that conduct. Diagnoses that merely identify the person as one who has engaged in the pattern of offenses provide no causal explanation for the offenses and cannot be understood as making the person likely to reoffend in the causal sense. Ideally, the expert would describe impaired psychological processes and explain the manner in which these caused the conduct constituting the target offenses.

This causal interpretation seems to address the two difficulties identified for the discriminative interpretation. Consider these in inverse order. Regarding the difficulty involving expertise, this causal interpretation reveals a role for psychological exper-

---

T. HARRIS, MARNIE E. RICE, & CATHERINE A. CORMIER, VIOLENT OFFENDERS: APPRAISING AND MANAGING RISK 129–32 (1998).

[13] In Re Hendricks, 912 P.2d 129, 131, 137–38 (Kan. 1996); In Re Young, 857 P2d. at 989, 995–96.

[14] KAN. STAT. ANN. § 59-29a02(b) (Supp. 1997); Wash. Rev. Code Ann. § 71.09.020(2) (Supp. 1998).

tise that lies beyond the abilities of the ordinary person. Under the causal interpretation, the state must establish that the individual manifests some impaired psychological processes or capacities distinct from the pattern of criminal conduct, and it must explain the causal role this impairment plays in producing that conduct. Thus, the expert must look beyond the criminal conduct in order to evaluate the offenders' psychological processes, identify the relevant impairments, and explain the connections between the former and the latter. This requirement provides at least a plausible claim that establishing the criteria of commitment requires expertise in the field of psychology or a related discipline that extends beyond the abilities of the ordinary person.

Regarding the first difficulty (i.e., the justificatory function), it suggests a plausible response in that the impaired capacities that cause the conduct constituting the offenses might provide good reasons for the state to exercise social control through commitment to a mental health facility. That is, impaired psychological capacities or processes that cause an individual to commit offenses against persons appear to present the type of impairment that would ordinarily justify the state in invoking civil commitment statutes requiring a demonstration of mental illness and dangerousness. These responses to the two difficulties originally identified for the discriminative interpretation raise important justificatory concerns regarding the causal interpretation. I set these aside, however, because this chapter addresses the appropriate scope of expert testimony rather than the justification for these statutes. The discriminative and causal interpretations both rest at least partially on the abilities of experts to diagnose the relevant disorders and to provide testimony relevant to the probability of reoffending with a degree of accuracy sufficient to represent professional expertise. The next section discusses the empirical evidence regarding these areas of expertise.

II.   Empirical Evidence

A.   Diagnosis

Experts testifying in commitment hearings brought under the sexual predator statutes consistently apply the diagnostic categories of paraphilia and personality disorder to the subjects of those hearings. The record of criminal offenses reported for these offenders suggests that some might qualify for the traditional diagnostic category of psychopathy. This diagnostic pattern is consistent with that found among sex offenders more generally in that psychological assessment of sex offenders ordinarily generates a range of diagnostic categories that resembles the distribution of diagnoses found among the general prison population. The only diagnostic features that consistently characterize most sex offenders involve the illegal conduct that provides the basis for the criminal convictions and the pattern of arousal or illegal conduct that fulfills the criteria for the diagnoses of paraphilia or personality disorder.[15] Some studies of sex offenders document a pattern of comorbidity similar to that found in the sexual predator cases in that sex offenders meet the diagnostic criteria for paraphilia as well as for other diagnostic categories, particularly personality disorder

---

[15] *See* chapter 3, section I.

and substance abuse. Very few of these offenders manifest serious emotional or thought disorders.[16]

The American Psychiatric Association's diagnostic manual defines paraphilias by reference to personally or socially maladaptive patterns of sexual fantasies, urges, or behavior. Pedophilia, for example, involves "over a period of at least six months, recurrent, intense sexually arousing fantasies, sexual urges, *or behaviors* involving sexual activity with a prepubescent child or children (generally age 13 years or younger)."[17] Offenders who engage in a series of offenses over a period lasting at least 6 months meet the behavioral disjunct of these criteria by virtue of the conduct constituting the offenses. The diagnostic criteria for APD, like those for the paraphilias, rest heavily upon patterns of conduct that violate social norms.[18] Thus, the history of conduct giving rise to the criminal charges contributes significantly to these clinical diagnoses.

It may be difficult to differentiate rapists who manifest specific disorders involving sexually disturbed thought and arousal patterns from those who commit rape as part of a more general pattern of criminal conduct. Some researchers report general histories of adjustment difficulties and antisocial behavior among rapists, some of whom also demonstrate extensive histories of deviant sexual activity including a variety of paraphilias as well as related stalking.[19] These reports remain tentative because methodological limitations permeate research in this area. Most studies lack appropriate control groups and representative samples of offenders. Furthermore, many offenders have strong incentives to deny sexually deviant urges or thought patterns.[20] Thus, researchers often must infer diagnostic formulations from the conduct that constitutes the basis for the current legal inquiry as well as from prior criminal history.

Although researchers studying populations of offenders and clinicians evaluating individual offenders frequently must infer disorders from reported criminal conduct, these inferences might well produce diagnoses that are at least as reliable as those made in many other types of legal cases. The diagnostic categories involved in these cases depend to a substantial degree on the patterns of conduct documented during the criminal investigations, trials, and sentencing hearings. These legal investigations, records, and hearings may provide unusually detailed sources of information regarding past behavior relevant to diagnostic criteria formulated to a large extent in terms

---

[16] Vladmir Konecni, Erin Mulcahy, & Ebbe Ebbeson, *Prison or Mental Hospitals: Factors Affecting the Processing of Persons Suspected of Being "Mentally Disordered Sex Offenders"* in NEW DIRECTIONS IN PSYCHOLEGAL RESEARCH 87, 112–15 (Paul Lipsitt & Bruce Sales, eds., 1980); QUINSEY et al., *supra* note 12, at 127–28; Richard M. Yarvis, *Diagnosing Patterns Among Three Violent Offender Types*, 23 BULL. AM. ACAD. PSYCHIATRY & L. 411, 412 (1995).

[17] AMERICAN PSYCHIATRIC ASSOCIATION, DIAGNOSTIC AND STATISTICAL MANUAL OF MENTAL DISORDERS 528 (4th ed. 1994) (emphasis added).

[18] *Id.* at 649–50.

[19] Lita Furby, Mark R. Weinrott, & Lynn Blackshaw, *Sex Offender Recidivism: A Review*, 105 PSYCHOL. BULL. 3, 5 (1989); Robert E. Longo & Nicholas Groth, *Juvenile Sex Offenses in the Histories of Adult Rapists and Child Molesters*, 27 INT'L J. OFFENDER THERAPY & COMP. CRIMINOLOGY 150 (1983); Gordon C. Nagayama Hall & William C. Proctor, *Criminological Predictors of Recidivism in a Sex Offender Population*, 55 J. CONSULTING & CLINICAL PSYCHOL. 111 (1987); QUINSEY et al., *supra* note 12, at 129; RICHARD T. RADA, CLINICAL ASPECTS OF THE RAPIST 77 (1978).

[20] Mack E. Winn, *The Strategic and Systemic Management of Denial in the Cognitive Behavioral Treatment of Sexual Offenders*, 8 SEXUAL ABUSE: A J. RES. & TREATMENT 25 (1996).

of observable behavior. The appellate records regarding several of the sexual predator cases discussed previously, for example, provide relatively detailed accounts of criminal histories that support diagnoses of paraphilia or personality disorder.[21] In summary, the availability of relatively detailed and well-documented histories and the prevalence of diagnoses that rely heavily on overt behavior support the inferences that diagnosticians can offer descriptive and explanatory clinical diagnosis in sexual predator cases with reliability that is at least comparable to that for analogous testimony in other types of cases.

B.   Recidivism

By authorizing commitment of offenders whose mental abnormalities or personality disorders make them likely to commit acts of sexual violence, the sexual predator statutes adopt a criterion of dangerousness that emphasizes recidivism.[22] Thus, actuarial data regarding recidivism provide a directly relevant source of evidence.[23] Methodological limitations (e.g., disproportionate reliance on institutional samples, variations in relapse criteria, limited duration of follow-up periods, and nonrepresentative samples) render it difficult to identify a consistent set of risk factors correlated with recidivism.[24] Consistent with previous inquiries related to risk assessment in general, many studies tend to focus upon historical or criminological factors as indicia of risk.

Offender characteristics related to sex offender recidivism include, for example, age, marital status, and employment status, with younger, single, and unemployed offenders presenting higher risk.[25] A variety of specific offense-related factors are related to recidivism.[26] Child molesters who choose younger victims present higher risk than those who choose older victims.[27] Offenders who are less directly related

---

[21] *See* section I.

[22] KAN. STAT. ANN. § 59–29a02(a) (Supp. 1997); WASH. REV. CODE ANN. § 71.09.020(1) (Supp. 1998).

[23] Eric S. Janus & Paul E. Meehl, *Assessing the Legal Standard for Predictions of Dangerousness in Sex Offender Commitment Proceedings*, 3 PSYCHOL., PUB. POL'Y & L. 33 (1997) (proposing a method for courts to quantify their standards for commitment of sex offenders and to assess the legitimacy of those commitments based on actuarial methods).

[24] Furby et al., *supra* note 19 (institutional samples and relapse criteria); Robert A. Prentky, Austin F. S. Lee, Raymond A. Knight, & David Cerce, *Recidivism Rates Among Child Molesters and Rapists: A Methodological Analysis*, 21 L. & HUM. BEHAV. 635, 642–56 (1997) (follow-up).

[25] Gene G. Abel, Mary Mittelman, Judith V. Becker, Jerry Rathner, & Joanne L. Rouleau, *Predicting Child Molesters' Response to Treatment*, 528 ANNALS N.Y. ACAD. SCI. 223, 230 (1988); R. Karl Hanson, Richard A. Steffy, & Rene Gauthier, *Long-Term Recidivism of Child Molesters*, 61 J. CONSULTING & CLINICAL PSYCHOL. 646, 650 (1993); William L. Marshall & Howard E. Barbaree, *The Long Term Evaluation of a Behavioural Treatment Program for Child Molesters*, 26 BEHAV. RES. & THERAPY 499, 509 (1988); Marnie E. Rice, Vernon L. Quinsey, & Grant T. Harris, *Sexual Recidivism Among Child Molesters Released From a Maximum Security Institution*, 59 J. CONSULTING & CLINICAL PSYCHOL. 381, 385 (1991) (marital status).

[26] Robert J. McGrath, *Sex Offender Risk Assessment and Dispositional Planning: A Review of Empirical and Clinical Findings*, 35 INT'L J. OFFENDER THERAPY & COMP. CRIMINOLOGY 328, 332–43 (1991).

[27] Nagayama Hall & Proctor, *supra* note 19.

to the victims as well as those who exercised physical violence during the offense present greater risk of recidivism.[28]

Victim selection factors, such as sex and age of victim, might indicate deviant arousal patterns related to recidivism. Studies report conflicting results with respect to the significance of victim sex for risk of reoffense. Some but not all evidence suggests that male offenders who have offended against male victims display higher rates of recidivism.[29] Abel and colleagues reported that child molesters who have offended against both sexes are more likely to reoffend than are those who offend against either sex solely.[30] Nagayama Hall and Proctor reported a significant relationship between prior sexual offenses against adults and re-arrests for sexual offenses against adults and a similar but less robust pattern for those who offend against children.[31] Deviant sexual preferences, as measured by plethysmographic assessment,[32] multiple paraphilias,[33] and a history of sexual violence,[34] all increase the probability of recidivism.[35]

Psychopathy and APD are positively correlated with recidivism.[36] Psychopathy and APD overlap in many respects, but they also diverge in significant ways. The current formulation of APD reflects the taxonomic strategy of relying primarily upon observable behavior as specific criteria for diagnosis. To the extent that this strategy fails to capture traditional notions of psychopathy, APD and psychopathy diverge.[37] Despite some degree of divergence between psychopathy and APD, much of the

---

[28] Hanson et al., *supra* note 25, at 650 (relationship to victim); QUINSEY et al., *supra* note 12, at 130; Vikki H. Sturgeon & John Taylor, *Report of a Five Year Follow-Up Study of Mentally Disordered Sex Offenders Released From Atascadero State Hospital in 1973*, 4 CRIM. JUST. J. 31, 56 (1980) (level of force).

[29] *Cf.* Hanson et al., *supra* note 25, at 650; Rice et al., *supra* note 25, at 385; *with* Abel et al., *supra* note 25, at 230; Marshall & Barbaree, *supra* note 25, at 509; Sturgeon & Taylor, *supra* note 28, at 51.

[30] Abel et al., *supra* note 25, at 230.

[31] Nagayama Hall & Proctor, *supra* note 19.

[32] Howard E. Barbaree & William L. Marshall, *Deviant Sexual Arousal, Offense History, and Demographic Variables as Predictors of Reoffense Among Child Molesters*, 6 BEHAV. SCI. & L. 267 (1988); QUINSEY et al., *supra* note 12, at 131–32; Rice et al., *supra* note 25, at 385.

[33] Abel et al., *supra* note 25, at 230; Robert A. Prentky, Raymond A. Knight, & Austin F. S. Lee, *Risk Factors Associated With Recidivism Among Extrafamilial Child Molesters*, 65 J. CONSULTING AND CLINICAL PSYCHOL. 141, 147 (1997) (Degree of sexual preoccupation with children, presence of a paraphilia, and number of sexual offenses prior to the recidivism predicted sexual recidivism among familial child molesters. Variables reflecting impulsive antisocial behavior predicted violent sexual and nonsexual recidivism.); BARRY M. MALETSKY, TREATING THE SEX OFFENDER 254 (1990).

[34] Furby et al., *supra* note 19, at 27; Hanson et al., *supra* note 25, at 650; Longo & Groth, *supra* note 19; Rice et al., *supra* note 25, at 383–85; Marshall & Barbaree, *supra* note 25, at 509; Nagayama Hall & Proctor, *supra* note 19; Prentky et al., *supra* note 33.

[35] Barbaree & Marshall, *supra* note 32; Rice et al., *supra* note 25, at 383–85.

[36] QUINSEY et al., *supra* note 12, at 130–32. Although psychopathy does not appear in the current edition of the diagnostic manual of the American Psychiatric Association, it has been the subject of substantial research. Psychopathy includes affective, interpersonal, and behavioral characteristics. These include egocentricity; irresponsibility; inability to experience significant emotional feeling; a lack of empathy, guilt, or remorse; pathological lying; manipulativeness; and persistent violation of social norms. Robert D. Hare, *Psychopathy: A Clinical Construct Whose Time Has Come*, 23 CRIM. JUST. & BEHAV. 25 (1996). APD is defined primarily as a "pervasive pattern of disregard for, and violation of, the rights of others that begins in childhood or early adolescence and continues into adulthood." AMERICAN PSYCHIATRIC ASSOCIATION, *supra* note 17, at 645. Associated features include lack of empathy, inflated self-appraisal, superficial charm, and irresponsibility. *Id.* at 647.

[37] Hare, *supra* note 36, at 29.

recent empirical research into the population described by the criteria for psychopathy, and to some extent APD, uses the Psychopathy Checklist (PCL) and the Psychopathy Checklist—Revised (PCL–R) as tools to identify the relevant population.[38]

Psychopathy, as indicated by increasing scores on the PCL, significantly improved predictions of offenders' failures while on parole or mandatory supervision releases beyond the predictive inferences provided by factors such as age at release, release type (parole or mandatory supervision), and criminal history.[39] One study found that psychopathy as measured by the PCL–R was the greatest single predictor of violent recidivism.[40] Others have found positive correlations between psychopathy as measured by different techniques in addition to the PCL or PCL–R and violent recidivism.[41] Among a sample of mentally disordered offenders released from a maximum security psychiatric hospital, individuals who met the PCL criteria for psychopathy were more likely to violently reoffend than those who had similar histories of past violent offending and maladjustment but did not meet PCL criteria for psychopathy.[42] Using the PCL to assess psychopathy, researchers found that approximately 40% of a sample of rapists were psychopathic.[43] Moreover, psychopathy has been shown to be predictive of sexual offense recidivism.[44]

In summary, although conclusions must be drawn tentatively in light of the limitations of the research, the following are correlated with recidivism: offender characteristics, characteristics of preferred victims, and the relative violence of prior offenses. Offender characteristics that increase the probability of future sexual offending include youth, unmarried status, unemployment, deviant sexual preferences, and a diagnosis of psychopathy. Conversely, offender characteristics that suggest a relatively lower risk of sexual offense recidivism include older age, marriage, employment, and the lack of deviant sexual preferences and psychopathy. Characteristics of victim selection that increase the likelihood of sex offense recidivism include the preference for relatively younger children by child molesters and a less direct

---

[38] ROBERT D. HARE, MANUAL FOR THE REVISED PSYCHOPATHY CHECKLIST (1991).

[39] Steven D. Hart, Philip R. Kropp, & Robert D. Hare, *Performance of Male Psychopaths Following Conditional Release From Prison*, 56 J. CONSULTING & CLINICAL PSYCHOL. 227, 229–31 (1988).

[40] Grant T. Harris, Marnie E. Rice, & Vernon L. Quinsey, *Violent Recidivism of Mentally Disordered Offenders: The Development of a Statistical Prediction Instrument*, 20 CRIM. JUST. & BEHAV. 315, 324 (1993). Scores on the PCL–R correlated .34 with violent recidivism (where higher scores on the PCL–R exceed the cutoff for a diagnosis of psychopathy). In other studies, the correlation between psychopathy and violent recidivism or failures on conditional release is similar. *See e.g.,* Vernon L. Quinsey, Marnie E. Rice, & Grant T. Harris, *Actuarial Prediction of Sexual Recidivism*, 10 J. INTERPERSONAL VIOLENCE 85, 102 (1995); Marnie E. Rice & Grant T. Harris, *A Comparison of Criminal Recidivism Among Schizophrenic and Nonschizophrenic Offenders*, 15 INT'L J. L. & PSYCHIATRY 397, 402 (1992); Ralph C. Serin, Ray D. Peters, & Howard E. Barbaree, *Predictors of Psychopathy and Release Outcome in a Criminal Population*, 2 PSYCHOLOGICAL ASSESSMENT 419 (1990).

[41] Ralph C. Serin & Nancy L. Amos, *The Role of Psychopathy in the Assessment of Dangerousness*, 18 INT'L J. L. & PSYCHIATRY 231, 234–37 (1995).

[42] Grant T. Harris, Marnie E. Rice, & Catherine A. Cormier, *Psychopathy and Violent Recidivism*, 15 L. & HUM. BEHAV. 625, 633–34 (1991).

[43] Robert A. Prentky & Raymond A. Knight, *Identifying Critical Dimensions for Discriminating Among Rapists*, 59 J. CONSULTING & CLINICAL PSYCHOL. 643, 648 (1991). These researchers found a similar prevalence of APD among this population, using the criteria of the AMERICAN PSYCHIATRIC ASSOCIATION, DIAGNOSTIC AND STATISTICAL MANUAL OF MENTAL DISORDERS (3d ed. rev. 1987).

[44] Quinsey et al., *supra* note 40.

personal relationship between the offender and the prior victim. The relationship between the preference for same sex versus opposite sex victims and recidivism is unclear, but some evidence suggests that child molesters who offend against both sexes represent a greater risk of recidivism than those who offend against one sex exclusively. Finally, the more violent the previous sexual offense or offenses, the greater the risk that the offender will commit additional sex crimes.

C. Treatment Effects and Recidivism

The literature provides no conclusive link between treatment and recidivism.[45] Various commentators provide mixed reviews concerning the efficacy of treatment upon sex offender recidivism and the attempt to empirically establish a set of variables related to treatment response and subsequent reoffense or relapse.[46] To evaluate the relevant body of research, one must differentiate amenability to treatment, therapeutic change during treatment, and reduced risk of recidivism. Researchers define amenability to treatment as the offender's ability to engage in treatment.[47] Although amenability to treatment is related to recidivism, it does not establish reduced risk of recidivism.[48] Unfortunately, few empirical studies examine the factors that determine an individual's amenability to treatment or correlate such information with recidivism.[49]

Available research provides very little information regarding the manner in which changes during treatment are associated with reduced recidivism.[50] Insofar as offense prevention constitutes the primary social purpose of sex offender treatment and the significance of treatment success for expert testimony regarding commitment rests on its relationship to recidivism, the need for clear information regarding that relationship remains critical.

The available data regarding attempts to identify factors associated with treatment success by sex offenders remain sparse. Gully and colleagues reported that no predictive relationship has been established between offender classification systems or typologies and treatment outcome criteria.[51] They also indicated that although psychometric data suggest that socially competent sex offenders are more likely to complete the treatment program, neither victim age, history of violence, nor violence

---

[45] Furby et al., *supra* note 19, at 22–27; William L. Marshall, Robin Jones, Tony Ward, Peter Johnson, & Howard E. Barbaree, *Treatment Outcome for Sex Offenders*, 11 CLINICAL PSYCHOL. REV. 465, 467 (1991); *but see* William L. Marshall & William D. Pithers, *A Reconsideration of Treatment Outcome with Sex Offenders*, 21 CRIM. JUST. & BEHAV. 10 (1994); Gordon C. Nagayama Hall, *Sex Offender Recidivism Revisited: A Meta-Analysis of Recent Treatment Studies*, 63 J. CONSULTING & CLINICAL PSYCHOL. 802 (1995); QUINSEY et al., *supra* note 12, at 132–34.

[46] Hanson et al., *supra* note 25, at 650.

[47] McGrath, *supra* note 26, at 330.

[48] Richard Rogers & Christopher D. Webster, *Assessing Treatability in Mentally Disordered Offenders*, 13 L. & HUM. BEHAV. 19, 20–22 (1989).

[49] Abel et al., *supra* note 25; Rogers & Webster, *id.*

[50] R. Karl Hanson, Brian Cox, & Carolyn Wocyzna, *Assessing Treatment Outcome for Sexual Offenders*, 4 ANNALS SEX RES. 177, 179 (1991).

[51] Kevin Gully, Christine Mitchell, Clifford Butter, & Richard Harwood, *Sex Offenders: Identifying Who Can Complete a Residential Treatment Program*, 8 BEHAV. SCI. & L. 465, 469 (1990).

during the offense appear to discriminate between offenders who complete residential treatment and those who do not. Kalichman, Shealy, and Craig reported that several Minnesota Multiphasic Personality Inventory scales were found to predict sex offenders' attendance to group therapy and therapist ratings of participation, but these data do not address outcome in the form of reduced recidivism.[52]

Some studies compile outcome data in order to empirically determine a set of variables related to treatment response and to subsequent reoffense or relapse. Abel and colleagues studied a group of 192 nonincarcerated pedophilic individuals who completed a treatment program focused on decreasing deviant arousal, sex education and sex dysfunction, cognitive restructuring, and social skills and assertiveness training.[53] Three variables were significantly related to failure to complete treatment and to subsequent relapse. Level of pressure to participate in treatment was positively correlated with completion of treatment and inversely correlated with relapse. A diagnosis of APD and lack of discrimination in the choice of sexual victim or paraphilic act were positively correlated with failure to complete treatment and with recidivism.

One study evaluated 150 offenders committed for treatment under a Mentally Disordered Sex Offender statute and subsequently discharged from a secure treatment facility.[54] No significant relationship was found between amenability to treatment and offender demographics, offending behavior (including level of force used and type of criminal act), or the offender's pretreatment level of denial or acceptance of responsibility for the sexually assaultive behavior. Offenders described by treatment staff as benefiting from treatment had significantly fewer prior criminal offenses, whether sexual or otherwise. Those who were less discriminating regarding types of victims and more likely to victimize strangers prior to treatment were more likely to reoffend after treatment. Those who reoffended after treatment had criminal histories involving significantly more prior sexual and nonsexual offenses than did those who were not found to have reoffended after treatment.

Although controversy remains regarding the efficacy of treatment, a recent meta-analysis revealed rather heterogeneous treatment effect sizes upon recidivism, with programs using either cognitive–behavioral or hormonal treatments demonstrating higher success rates than other types of treatment.[55] Several authors have reported that strategies that include hormonal or surgical intervention to reduce sexual arousal have successfully reduced recidivism.[56] A separate recent review of reported studies found that treatment of sexual offenders with group and individual psychotherapy has not often been subjected to thorough, controlled evaluation and that those studies

---

[52] Seth Kalichman, Lucinda Shealy, & Mary E. Craig, *The Use of the MMPI in Predicting Treatment Participation Among Incarcerated Adult Rapists*, 3 J. PSYCHOL. & HUM. SEXUALITY 105, 113 (1991).

[53] Abel et al., *supra* note 25, at 230.

[54] Mario J. Scalora, Daniel L. Ullman, Mark DeKraai, & Calvin Garbin, *Sex Offender Recidivism and Amenability to Treatment*, Paper presented at the American Psychology–Law Society Conference, Santa Fe, New Mexico (1994).

[55] Nagayama Hall, *supra* note 45, at 807.

[56] Kirk Heilbrun, Christine Maguth Nezu, Michelle Keeny, Susie Chung, & Adam L. Wasserman, *Sexual Offending: Linking Assessment, Intervention, and Decision Making*, 4 PSYCHOL., PUB. POL'Y, & L.138, 144–51 (1998); QUINSEY et al., *supra* note 12, at 133; William Winslade, T. Howard Stone, Michele Smith-Bell, & Denise M. Webb, *Castrating Pedophiles Convicted of Sex Offenses Against Children: New Treatment or Old Punishment?*, 51 SMU L. REV. 349, 366–76 (1998).

that have evaluated such treatment have not provided evidence of reduced recidivism.[57] The same review found that drugs that lower testosterone levels reduce sexual arousal imperfectly and can result in side effects that induce offenders to avoid the drugs. These authors reported that castration can reduce sex drive but that it may be inappropriate for offenders whose offenses are not limited to sexual ones, those whose offenses are unrelated to hormone levels, and those who do not consent to the procedure. Finally, the authors reported that cognitive and behavioral treatments attempt to normalize deviant sexual preferences and may also address social competence, sex education, anger management, relapse prevention, or other skills. Evaluations of these treatment programs have provided mixed results regarding recidivism.

Follow-up studies of offenders who have received treatment indicate that a variety of factors involving demographics, criminal history, and personal characteristics as well as treatment variables are correlated with recidivism. One study of 136 extrafamilial molesters treated in a maximum security facility and followed for an average of 6.3 years after release revealed the following factors associated with recidivism: higher prior sex crime history, never having been married, a diagnosis of personality disorder, and higher inappropriate responses to phallometric assessment.[58] A separate study that followed 197 treated child molesters for a 10–30 year period found that extrafamilial offenders, those offenders who were never married, and those who had a prior sex offense history were more likely to reoffend.[59] Another study found that treated child molesters with higher levels of deviant and nondeviant sexual arousal during treatment were more likely to commit sexual offenses and that offenders skilled in applying relapse prevention concepts were less likely to reoffend.[60] Although these studies provide some support for treatment programs involving cognitive–behavioral, hormonal, and relapse prevention modalities, they also suggest that actuarial evidence regarding recidivism rests heavily upon factors associated with the pattern of prior offenses, demographic characteristics, and arousal patterns.

Individuals diagnosed with psychopathy or APD are difficult to treat effectively.[61] Hare reported that no sound treatment or resocialization programs have been demonstrated to be effective with psychopathic individuals and cited studies in which treated psychopathic individuals recidivated more often than untreated ones.[62] For example, 27.5% of sex offenders who completed treatment at a "Sexual Behavior Laboratory" at a maximum-security psychiatric facility were convicted of new sexual offenses. Psychopathy, prior criminal history, and phallometric assessment data were positively correlated with recidivism among this population.[63]

In summary, the treatability of sex offenders in general is a matter of some dispute. The available research supports some tentative conclusions regarding the

---

[57] Marnie E. Rice & Grant E. Harris, *The Treatment of Mentally Disordered Offenders*, 3 PSYCHOL., PUB. POL'Y, & L. 126, 153–57 (1997).

[58] Rice et al., *supra* note 25, at 383–85.

[59] Hanson et al., *supra* note 25, at 650.

[60] Janice Marques, Craig Nelson, Mary Ann West, & David M. Day, *The Relationship Between Treatment Goals and Recidivism Among Child Molesters*, 32 BEHAV. RES. & THERAPY 577 (1994).

[61] William L. Marshall & Ralph Serin, *Personality Disorders* in ADULT PSYCHOPATHOLOGY AND DIAGNOSIS 508, 520–22 (Samuel M. Turner & Michael Hersen, eds., 1997).

[62] Hare, *supra* note 36, at 41–42.

[63] Quinsey et al., *supra* note 40, at 94–100.

effect of treatment on sex offender recidivism. Factors that decrease offenders' amenability to treatment overlap with factors directly related to recidivism, such as diagnosis of APD or psychopathy and a lack of discrimination in the choice of victims. Age and the extent of violence of prior offenses, however, appear to be among the factors that may not be related to the ability to complete treatment. Cognitive–behavioral and hormonal treatments seem relatively more successful than some other treatment strategies at reducing recidivism. Individuals who complete treatment recidivate at higher rates when they are unmarried, diagnosed with a personality disorder or psychopathy, or have a longer prior history of sex offending.

III.   Interpreting the Evidence

The review of the statutes, the cases, and the relevant empirical evidence suggests that sexual predator statutes provide an opportunity to examine and articulate consistent parameters for the responsibilities of legal, clinical, and social scientific participants. Experts, lawyers, and courts must direct careful attention to a series of conceptual, normative, and empirical issues in order to avoid offering, seeking, or allowing testimony that violates the boundaries of these responsibilities. For the sake of efficiency, the discussion here addresses the limits on the testimony that expert witnesses should offer, but one could rephrase this discussion in terms of the testimony that the court should allow or that attorneys should seek to admit. A satisfactory framework for the adjudicative process would explicitly recognize the responsibilities of witnesses, lawyers, and judges and provide a consistent set of directives and limits for all.

As compared to ordinary civil commitment statutes, the sexual predator statutes exacerbate the already substantial risk that expert witnesses and courts will fail to recognize the appropriate boundaries of their respective expertise and responsibilities. The risk arises because the statutes articulate the criteria of commitment in a manner that conflates the relevant notions of disorder and of dangerousness. Furthermore, they render it very difficult to differentiate the descriptive and explanatory aspects that fall within the expertise of clinicians and social scientists from the normative components that fall within the responsibility of the courts.

The sexual predator provisions define "sexual predators" and "mental abnormality" in a manner that incorporates risk of harm into these notions. These statutes partially define a sexual predator as one who is likely to engage in acts of sexual violence, and they partially define mental abnormalities as disorders that render the person a menace.[64] Thus, these provisions narrow the range of psychological disorders that can fulfill the statutory requirements to those that generate the appropriate type and degree of risk. At first glance, this suggests that active psychosis represents one type of disorder at issue because recent data indicate an association between active psychosis and increased risk of violence.[65] These statutes address psychosis ambiguously, however, because the statutory definitions and criteria of application would apply to individuals with active psychosis, but the legislative findings specif-

---

[64] KAN. STAT. ANN. § 59–29a02(a), (b) (Supp. 1997); WASH. REV. CODE ANN. § 71.09.020(1), (2) (Supp. 1998).

[65] John Monahan, *Mental Disorder and Violent Behavior*, 47 AM. PSYCHOLOGIST 511 (1992).

ically indicate that these statutes address those who do not suffer disorder of a type that ordinarily qualifies the person for civil commitment.[66]

APD, psychopathy, and paraphilia do not encounter this ambiguity. These disorders do not ordinarily elicit civil commitment, but they support an inference of increased risk of socially harmful conduct because the past patterns of injurious behavior that partially fulfill the diagnostic criteria for these disorders also support an inference of risk of future harmful conduct. Although individuals can qualify for the diagnoses involved in these cases primarily on the basis of their past patterns of criminal behavior, these diagnostic categories do not reduce to those patterns of criminal behavior. The current formulations of paraphilia and of APD allow diagnosis on purely behavioral criteria, but these diagnoses also involve emotional or motivational tendencies.[67] The overt behavior provides the basis for an inference of impaired or distorted psychological processes including, for example, deviant sexual arousal and fantasies or lack of empathy and interpersonal responsiveness. Thus, psychologists can testify regarding the causal interpretation of the statutory criteria without encountering the previously discussed difficulties regarding the strictly discriminative interpretation of those criteria.[68]

Consider two perpetrators, each of whom commits a series of sexual assaults on children over a 2-year period. The first does so in order to satisfy obsessive fantasies and urges regarding sexual contact with children. The second does not experience sexual desires specific to children. Rather, he experiences diffuse sexual arousal that he satisfies by exploiting vulnerable adults or children. In addition, he has developed a profitable business selling private security services, and he has learned that profits increase markedly when local residents fear for the safety of their children. Although he can satisfy his diffuse sexual desires through activity with either adults or children, he periodically molests children in order to satisfy his sexual desires and promote his business. He is indifferent to the suffering of the victims and their families. In summary, the criminal assaults by the first perpetrator reveal obsessive deviant sexual urges, whereas those by the second perpetrator reveal diffuse sexual urges, greed, and lack of empathy and conscience.

Although either of these perpetrators could qualify for a diagnosis of pedophilia under the most current diagnostic criteria, that diagnosis would fail to accurately represent the central pathological process of the second perpetrator who qualifies for that diagnosis primarily under the behavioral disjunct.[69] Competent clinicians with access to sufficient information could provide the courts not only with the diagnostic category, derivable at least partially from the history of criminal conduct, but also with explanations for those patterns of conduct that would differentiate the two perpetrators by virtue of their different emotional states and deficits. Thus, clinicians can provide expert testimony that calls upon the expertise in the field and draws upon the past pattern of criminal conduct but does not reduce to that pattern of conduct.

Although clinicians can describe and explain an offender's clinical impairment

---

[66] KAN. STAT. ANN. § 59–29a02(a), (b), 29a03(Supp. 1997), 59–29a01 (1994); WASH. REV. CODE ANN. § 71.09.020(1), (2), .030 (Supp. 1998), 71.09.010 (1992).

[67] AMERICAN PSYCHIATRIC ASSOCIATION, *supra* note 17, at 649–50 (APD), 528 (pedophilia).

[68] *See* section I.

[69] AMERICAN PSYCHIATRIC ASSOCIATION, *supra* note 17, at 649–50.

and diagnostic category, they cannot offer an expert opinion that the offender suffers (or does not suffer) a mental abnormality or personality disorder. The statutes require that a mental abnormality or personality disorder sufficient for commitment as a sexual predator "makes the person likely to engage in the predatory acts of sexual violence."[70] The statute provides no guidance regarding the degree of probability that would fulfill the requirement that such acts are "likely." The statutory definition of a mental abnormality provides no assistance in clarifying this issue because it reveals a similar pattern. A condition qualifies as a mental abnormality only if it "predisposes the person to commit sexually violent offenses in a degree constituting such person a menace."[71] The statute provides no guidance regarding the degree of predisposition necessary to qualify an individual as a menace.

The court must determine in each case whether the complete body of evidence relevant to the probability and severity of anticipated offenses is sufficient to justify the severe limitation on liberty represented by commitment. Given the availability of relevant information, psychological experts can provide actuarial and clinical testimony relevant to the probability of such conduct. Experts might also inform the court's decision by describing and explaining the offender's pathology, with particular attention to the relationships between the offender's prior offenses and his psychological condition at the times of those offenses and between the offender's psychological condition at the time of those prior offenses and his condition at the time of the hearing. In this manner, experts can inform the court regarding the offender's psychological condition as one potentially relevant circumstance that renders the current risk similar or dissimilar to the risk at the time of the prior offenses. To the extent that clinicians and courts fulfill their respective roles in this manner, they conform to the framework developed in chapter 10, and they discharge the responsibilities appropriate to their professions.[72]

IV. Interpreting the Inability to Control

The discussion by the *Hendricks* majority of Hendricks's putative inability to control his sexual behavior represents one attempt to fulfill the judicial responsibility to articulate a legal conception of mental illness for a particular purpose.[73] Insofar as legislatures or courts articulate an intelligible conception of legal mental illness for this purpose as impairment that renders the individual unable to control sexual behavior, they advance the discriminative and justificatory functions of these provisions. Furthermore, they provide the criteria of admissibility for expert testimony regarding legal mental illness in that clinicians should describe and explain psychological impairment relevant to that conception of legal mental illness. Courts should evaluate such testimony according to the applicable normative criteria in order to determine whether the individual qualifies as legally mentally ill in this sense. As

---

[70] KAN. STAT. ANN. § 59–29a02(a) (Supp. 1997); WASH. REV. CODE ANN. § 71.09.020(1) (Supp. 1998).

[71] KAN. STAT. ANN. § 59–29a02(b) (Supp. 1997); WASH. REV. CODE ANN. § 71.09.020(2) (Supp. 1998).

[72] *See* chapter 10, sections V–VII.

[73] *See* chapter 8, section IV.

indicated in the prior discussions, however, neither the *Hendricks* opinions nor the related Minnesota case to which it referred provides any clear conception of the putative inability to control or any account of what would constitute evidence of such inability. Thus, it remains very difficult to identify the type of testimony that expert witnesses should offer and that courts should admit.

On its face, the claim that Hendricks was unable to control his conduct appears to be the literal claim that he lacked the capacity to direct bodily movement through the psychological decision-making process. One can imagine circumstances in which an individual might engage in harmful behavior as a result of such impairment. Suppose, for example, that the individual suffers an unanticipated seizure while driving an automobile. The seizure might produce involuntary movements causing the automobile to accelerate and veer onto the sidewalk into a stream of pedestrians.[74] Expert testimony by a neuropsychologist or a neurologist regarding the individual's ability to control that behavior might well meet the applicable standard for admissibility in any trial in which the individual's capacity to control the conduct was at issue. Nothing in *Hendricks* or in other cases brought under the sexual predator statutes suggests that these cases involve impairment of this type, however, because the conduct in question is well organized and goal directed. The behavior of Hendricks and of others who were committed under sexual predator statutes was planned and calculated to avoid arrest and punishment. It appears to be precisely the type of behavior that is usually understood as intentional human action under the direction of ordinary behavior-directing processes.[75]

One might cogently argue that certain types of cognitive impairment constitute volitional impairment of a type regarding which psychological experts might appropriately testify. Individuals who suffer psychotic disruption of cognitive process, for example, suffer serious disruption of their ability to direct their conduct through an ordinarily competent process of practical reasoning. Disruption of the ability to direct one's conduct through such a process of competent practical reasoning provides the basis for findings of incompetence for person or of retributive incompetence as discussed in chapters 5 and 7. Although such impairment is usually discussed as cognitive rather than as volitional, it distorts the process by which individuals form intentions, make decisions, and direct their conduct.[76] Thus, to the extent that these functions are considered part of the ordinary volitional process, severe thought disorder constitutes a volitional disorder. The individuals committed under the sexual predator statutes do not manifest severe cognitive impairment, however, and any individuals who engaged in acts of sexual violence while suffering such impairment would qualify for commitment under general civil commitment statutes or under postinsanity acquittal provisions. The legislative findings in the sexual predator statutes explicitly direct these provisions at offenders who do not manifest the types of disorder that ordinarily support civil commitment.[77]

Alternately, the claim that these offenders are unable to control their conduct might be understood as the normative claim that these individuals find it so difficult

---

[74] ROBERT F. SCHOPP, AUTOMATISM, INSANITY, AND THE PSYCHOLOGY OF CRIMINAL RESPONSIBILITY 166 (1991).

[75] *See* section I for a description of the conduct in the cases.

[76] SCHOPP, *supra* note 74, at 201–04, 211–12.

[77] *See* chapter 2, section II.

to resist engaging in this behavior that the state is justified in confining them in order to prevent it. Absent further elaboration, the claim that the inability to control, interpreted in this manner, justifies civil commitment represents the vacuous contention that the state is justified in confining those who find it so difficult to resist engaging in sexual violence that the state is justified in confining them.[78] This interpretation of the claim that the inability to control justifies commitment interprets the conclusion into the meaning of the purported premise, rendering the premise tautological and thus insignificant for the discriminative and justificatory functions. Furthermore, this interpretation provides no basis for exercising this type of state control through mental health commitment rather than through the criminal justice system because it requires no psychological impairment. If one stipulates that the inability to control, interpreted in this manner, must rest upon impairment of psychological process, the interpretation still provides no basis for expert testimony regarding that inability to control, absent some interpretation of the types of impairment appropriately granted such exculpatory significance. According to this interpretation, the conclusion that an individual is unable to control his conduct is premised upon a normative judgment regarding the appropriate criteria of exculpation, rather than upon strictly clinical or empirical determinations that fall within the scope of clinical expertise.

If one interprets the *Hendricks* language regarding the inability to control as appealing to such a normative standard, psychologists could not qualify as experts to offer an opinion that the individual either was or was not able to control the conduct in question because under a normative standard, such an opinion entails an interpretation of the normative force of the impairment. A psychological expert might offer descriptive and explanatory testimony regarding the individual's psychological impairment, but absent a legal articulation of the meaning of the exculpatory inability to control, it is not clear how the expert or the court could identify the relevant descriptive and explanatory testimony.

In principle, psychologists could conceptualize and measure psychological processes and impairments relevant to volitional standards such as those discussed in the *Hendricks* opinion or those included in some insanity provisions.[79] In order to do so, however, those developing and measuring these constructs must have some explication of the normative rationale, indicating what should count as an impairment of the ability to control for specific legal purposes such as exculpation or civil commitment. Although it is possible in principle to conceptualize volitional impairment in empirically measurable terms, determining which conceptualization is relevant to the normative function of a specific legal standard is not an empirical issue. Thus, the central problem with the legal reliance on the lack of ability to control conduct, either for exculpation or for commitment, does not involve imprecision or lack of reliability in measurement. More important, neither the legislatures nor the courts have addressed the central normative task. They have not developed a normative account of volitional impairment or of the inability to control that falls short of the clear cases such as seizure movements yet justifies special legal status for the purposes of civil commitment or exculpation.

---

[78] SCHOPP, *supra* note 74, at 165–74.

[79] Richard Rogers, *APA's Position on the Insanity Defense*, 42 AMER. PSYCHOLOGIST 840, 842 (1987).

V. Conclusion

The sexual predator statutes provide an opportunity to reflect upon the proper scope of expert testimony and the proper distribution of professional responsibility among clinical, social scientific, and judicial participants in commitment hearings. They do so because they exemplify the lack of clear differentiation between clinical and normative notions that permeates mental health law. The analysis presented here demonstrates that clinicians can contribute relevant testimony to questions arising under these statutes, but defining the defensible boundaries of this testimony requires careful interpretation of the conceptual, empirical, and normative components of statutory criteria. This analysis suggests that the judgment that an individual is (or is not) dangerous always falls beyond the expertise of clinicians and social scientists and, thus, that making such judgments must violate the limits of professional responsibility. Yet, clinicians are called upon to make such judgments in many circumstances. Clinicians frequently make decisions regarding discharge or conditional release from commitment, the exercise of off-ward privileges by committed patients, or the need to issue warnings regarding danger posed by their patients. Do clinicians who make such decisions necessarily violate the limits of professional responsibility, or can one provide some explanation that renders those activities consistent with the limits of professional judgment discussed in chapters 10 and 11? Chapter 12 addresses this question.

Chapter 12
PROFESSIONAL JUDGMENT AND RESPONSIBILITIES:
Intrinsic and Delegated

Chapters 10 and 11 discuss the parameters of expert testimony by clinicians and social scientists in commitment hearings generally and regarding sexual predator commitment specifically. The defensible parameters of the roles of various participants in these hearings are defined by the expertise of the professions as well as by the normative framework underlying the integrated body of mental health law. Clinicians and social scientists fulfill a variety of functions that extend well beyond the role of expert witness in commitment hearings. The analysis that generates appropriate parameters of expert testimony can also inform our understanding of the appropriate range of professional judgment and responsibility in a variety of other roles. This chapter examines the considerations relevant to the exercise of professional judgment in some of these roles. It does not provide an exhaustive catalogue of professional roles and their limits; rather, it addresses the roles of information provider and care provider in certain circumstances in order to clarify the relationships among professional roles, the expertise of the professions, and the legal institutions within which these roles are embedded.

I. Clinicians and Social Scientists as Providers of Information and Treatment

Chapters 10 and 11 limit the scope of expert testimony at commitment hearings by clinicians and social scientists to descriptive and explanatory information that falls within the range of their expertise and informs the issues before the court. At least three factors contribute to the definition and defense of these limits. First, experts must testify within the range of expertise of their professions. Second, the meaning of statutory criteria such as mental illness, dangerousness, or likelihood of engaging in crimes of sexual violence partially defines the relevance of the witnesses' expertise. Third, experts must fulfill their roles in a manner that complements the roles of other participants, including judges and juries. These three factors interact with each other in the context of the discriminative and justificatory functions of the legal criteria.

These three factors are also relevant to understanding the proper boundaries of professional judgment and responsibility in roles other than that of expert witness. These roles include, for example, those of program designer, treatment provider, and ward manager. Some of these roles raise particularly troubling questions in the context of sexual predator commitment because the statutory provisions and legislative findings appear inconsistent. The legislative findings suggest that the individuals targeted by these statutes are not appropriately committed for treatment in that they do not manifest a disorder that ordinarily supports civil commitment and they are not amenable to ordinary treatment modalities. Yet, the statutes authorize commitment for long-term care and treatment and specify that this care and treatment must conform to constitutional standards.[1]

II.   Professional Judgment and Responsibility Regarding Treatment or Mere Incapacitation

No more than a small subset of sex offenders suffer serious impairment, such as psychosis or serious retardation.[2] Conventional treatment and behavioral management techniques apply to that small subset of offenders as they do to nonoffenders who manifest similar impairment. Ordinary civil commitment statutes would apply to these offenders, however, and the legislative findings previously discussed indicate that the sexual predator statutes do not target these offenders as their primary subject population. The data reviewed previously indicate a lack of reliable treatment modalities for certain types of offenders as delineated by offense or diagnostic categories, particularly those who manifest traits associated with APD or psychopathy.[3] The cases indicate that the individuals committed under these statutes frequently fall within these categories of offenders who are least likely to demonstrate treatment effects.[4]

Just as the diagnoses of the subjects of commitment in the cases are derived to a substantial degree from the pattern of criminal conduct, treatment success or failure is measured to a substantial degree by success or failure in preventing recidivism.[5] This pattern suggests that the primary function of commitment under these statutes is incapacitation and that the purpose of the treatment for which these individuals are supposedly committed is recidivism prevention in the absence of any serious impairment that would render them appropriate for involuntary treatment intended to ameliorate that impairment. Thus, the statutes appear to serve primarily as a method of social control in the absence of any serious impairment that would ordinarily render these individuals subject to social control through the mental health system rather than through criminal incarceration.[6]

This interpretation suggests the following questions. First, what properties qualify an intervention as treatment rather than as mere incapacitation? Second, what is the significance, if any, of the distinction between treatment and mere incapacitation for the abilities of clinicians and social scientists to practice their professions in conjunction with the legal institution of commitment in a manner that comports with a defensible distribution of responsibility across clinical and legal actors in light of the normative framework underlying mental health law?

---

[1] KAN. STAT. ANN. §§ 59-29a07, 09 (1994 and Supp. 1997); WASH. REV. CODE ANN. §§ 71.09.060(1), 080(2) (Supp. 1998).

[2] See chapter 11, section II.

[3] Id.

[4] See chapter 11, section I.

[5] See chapter 11, section II.

[6] See chapters 7 and 8.

A.   Treatment Versus Mere Incapacitation

The legislative findings discussed previously, the prior convictions of these individuals as criminally responsible, and the measurement of treatment effectiveness in terms of offense recidivism all support the argument that these commitments are intended to incapacitate those who are criminally responsible and subject to the criminal justice system as the primary legal institution of social control. The observation that sexual predator commitments serve to incapacitate does not by itself establish, however, that they serve only or primarily to incapacitate. Some forms of intervention, such as involuntary inpatient commitment of those who suffer thought disorder that generates violent resistance against delusional assaults, can provide treatment in a format that also incapacitates and reduces recidivism. It cannot be the case, however, that every intervention that incapacitates or reduces recidivism qualifies as treatment. If that were the applicable conception of treatment, execution would constitute treatment. Although few would argue that execution constitutes treatment rather than punishment, some advocate surgical or chemical castration as appropriate social responses to these offenses, either as punishment or as treatment.[7]

Careful consideration of the arguments regarding the justification for controversial interventions or regarding the manner in which clinicians or social scientists can responsibly participate in such interventions requires clarification of the question as one regarding punishment, treatment, or mere incapacitation. Courts and commentators tend to recognize the obligations to identify state interventions that constitute punishment and to administer those interventions according to relatively well-established legal and moral principles embodied in the criminal justice system. Chapters 10, 11, and 12 are primarily concerned with identifying the proper scope of participation in legal institutions by clinicians and social scientists rather than with justifying those institutions. As part of this inquiry one must recognize the frequently overlooked distinction between treatment and mere incapacitation in order to clarify the properties of these two types of interventions and the relationships between these properties and psychological expertise. These clarifications facilitate an examination of the defensible roles of psychologists in legal institutions designed to provide treatment or to incapacitate.

Chapter 5 contains an analysis of the appropriate conception of treatment as a subset of care that differs from custodial care, disciplinary programs, or mere incapacitation. That analysis generates a conception of treatment as an intervention that takes the form of an application of clinical skills and knowledge designed to ameliorate a pathological condition or to reduce the injurious effects produced by that condition by increasing the individual's adaptive skills, capacities, or functioning level associated with that impairment.[8]

---

[7] Avital Stadler, Comment, *California Injects New Life into an Old Idea: Taking a Shot at Recidivism, Chemical Castration, and the Constitution*, 49 EMORY L. J. 1285 (1997); William Winslade, T. Howard Stone, Michele Smith-Bell, & Denise M. Webb, *Castrating Pedophiles Convicted of Sex Offenses Against Children: New Treatment or Old Punishment?* 51 S.M.U. L. REV. 349 (1998). The authors recognize that the classification of castration as punishment or treatment might influence the analysis, but they do not address mere incapacitation as a third alternative.

[8] *See* chapter 5, section IV.

B.   The Normative Framework and Professional Judgment

Consider the second question regarding the significance, if any, of the distinction between treatment and mere incapacitation for the abilities of clinicians and social scientists to practice their professions in conjunction with the legal institution of commitment in a manner that comports with a defensible distribution of responsibilities across clinical and legal actors in light of the normative framework underlying mental health law. This question contains two more specific questions:

1. Can clinicians or social scientists practice their professions and exercise professional judgment within the range of expertise of those professions in such intervention programs?
2. Does the status of these programs as either treatment or mere incapacitation alter the manner in which they can participate without violating the normative framework that provides the foundation for mental health law and that partially defines the relevant conceptions of mental illness and dangerousness?

In order to identify more clearly the appropriate limits of professional judgment within an institution of commitment, one must clarify and integrate the nature and function of that commitment, the substance and limits of relevant professional expertise, and the appropriate interpretation and application of the underlying normative framework.

The normative framework underlying mental health law renders that body of law coherent and defensible. By providing principles of political morality that justify the broad body of law, this normative framework enables us to evaluate and interpret any particular provision in order to render it coherent with that broader justification or to reject it as inconsistent with that justification. By guiding the interpretation of specific provisions, the underlying normative framework defines the normative components of the central concepts, determinations, and criteria. In this manner, it partially defines the corresponding limits of professional judgment and responsibility.

The analysis presented in chapter 6 interprets the PJS as a standard according to which clinicians exercise professional judgment regarding clinical care within the boundaries defined by the goals and limits articulated by the substantive legal standards in the cases. Interpreted in this manner, the PJS provides a workable form of procedural protection for the legally protected interests at issue in cases such as *Parham* in which the Court articulates substantive standards that call for judgment regarding matters that fall within clinical expertise. Reliance on this standard raises serious concerns, however, in circumstances such as those presented in *Romeo*, *Harper*, and *Rennie*. As applied in these cases, the PJS requires professional judgment regarding matters that include legal or normative concerns beyond the scope of clinical expertise. Thus, these cases raise two important concerns regarding expertise and authority. They raise a question of expertise because in order to exercise judgment regarding these legal standards, clinicians must be aware of and understand the relevant legal and normative considerations. More fundamentally, however, these cases raise important questions regarding the legitimate authority of clinicians to make legal or normative determinations in a democratic society. To remain consistent with a defensible distribution of responsibility among clinical and legal participants, courts must apply the PJS standards to decisions that fall within the range of clinical expertise, and they must refrain from applying it in such a manner as to abdicate responsibility for normative determinations.[9]

III.   Professional Judgment: Intrinsic and Delegated

The holdings in *Harper* and *Romeo* raise concerns regarding clinicians' understanding, expertise, and authority as they attempt to exercise professional judgment regarding treatment decisions in the context of legally defined standards. Clinicians who exercise professional judgment in the context of commitment under sexual predator statutes encounter similar concerns. These clinicians must address additional difficulties, however, in that the substantive bases for commitment, treatment, and discharge involve the mental abnormality and likelihood of reoffending that seem largely to represent a pattern of criminal conduct. Furthermore, the only interpretation of the mental abnormality available from the Court remains the mysterious inability to control discussed in *Hendricks*,[10] and the statutory findings seem to indicate that the legal purpose of the commitment is merely (or at best primarily) incapacitation. Thus, the statute and the Court's opinion neither provide guidance for the interpretation and application of legal and normative components nor establish criteria likely to naturally converge with the exercise of professional judgment by clinicians involved in a treatment program. To the extent that clinicians involved in evaluation, treatment, or management exercise judgment regarding the statutory commitment criteria, they make the types of legal and normative determinations that place opinions regarding these criteria beyond their expertise in the role of expert witness at the commitment hearing, and to the extent that commitment represents an exercise in incapacitation, they make social policy decisions regarding the degree of danger of recidivism that justifies continued incarceration.[11]

Although *Hendricks* and the sexual predator statutes present these difficulties in a stark form, other areas of mental health law conflate psychological and normative judgments in a similar manner. Clinicians who practice on wards that house patients committed under more conventional civil commitment statutes, for example, sometimes make similar determinations. Although courts or mental health boards make initial commitment decisions, clinicians sometimes have the authority to grant discharge, conditional release, visits, or off-ward privileges. They also make decisions about changes in treatment programs and about the application of seclusion or restraint as required by current indications of danger.[12] In these circumstances, clinicians make judgments regarding both the clinical and the normative components of dangerousness. That is, they must estimate the risk of harmful conduct, and they must decide whether that risk is sufficient to justify certain restrictions on liberty.

These responsibilities suggest that one must distinguish two senses in which clinicians make professional judgments and practice their professions. Professionals

---

[9] *See* chapter 6, section III.

[10] Kansas v. Hendricks 117 s. Ct. 2072, 2080–81 (1997).

[11] *See* chapters 10 and 11.

[12] BARBARA A. WEINER & ROBERT M. WETTSTEIN, LEGAL ISSUES IN MENTAL HEALTH CARE 60–61, 88–91 (1993).

exercise professional judgment in the *intrinsic* sense when their judgments, and their decisions or actions based on those judgments, involve the understanding and exercise of the substantive content of their professions that distinguishes these professionals from those who do not claim expertise in their professions. Social scientists exercise intrinsic judgment, for example, when they gather, interpret, and apply data such as those discussed in chapter 11, (section II). Professionals exercise judgment in the *delegated* sense when their judgments, and their decisions and actions based on those judgments, involve the discharge of responsibilities that are socially allocated to those who practice their profession, although these functions require judgments and decisions that do not require the understanding and application of the substantive content of that profession.Teachers make delegated judgments and discharge delegated responsibilities, for example, when they monitor the schoolyard for suspicious strangers, loose dogs, and other dangers to children or when they report injuries suggesting child abuse. These judgments and responsibilities qualify as delegated rather than intrinsic because they depend on the care and judgment the teachers possess as ordinary adults, rather than on substantive expertise in teaching. Similarly, statutes or court decisions might delegate to clinicians a duty to issue warnings to potential victims or to the police when an outpatient makes a specific threat to an identifiable victim.[13] Neither the ability to recognize specific threats toward identifiable victims nor the ability to dial a telephone and report such threats requires any special knowledge or skill associated with the clinical professions. Clinicians discharge this responsibility in the same manner as would nonclinicians. That is, they listen to statements made by their clients, and they report those that include specific threats to identifiable victims. Jurisdictions that adopt such a duty delegate a public safety function to clinicians, and they provide legal criteria that are accessible to clinicians as they are to any ordinary adult in the circumstances. Thus, clinicians who issue warnings pursuant to legal duties formulated in this manner discharge a delegated duty, but they do not exercise expertise as clinicians. Rather, these clinicians discharge a duty that the state could as well delegate to accountants, lawyers, or bartenders because members of each of these professions are capable of recognizing specific threats and of notifying the specified parties or the police.[14]

Legislatures and courts can delegate public safety functions to various professions, but in doing so, they cannot make those functions part of the expertise of the profession. Rather, they delegate distinct public safety functions that members of the profession can discharge only by applying legal criteria or by acting as reasonable persons in the circumstances. Insofar as the courts and the members of the profession recognize these responsibilities as delegated, the members of the profession can discharge them by exercising the care of ordinary persons in the circumstances, and the courts can hold these individuals to an ordinary standard of care. If the professionals or the courts misconstrue these responsibilities as intrinsic, however, they are

---

[13] Robert F. Schopp, *The Psychotherapist's Duty to Protect the Public: The Appropriate Standard and the Foundation in Legal Theory and Empirical Premises*, 70 NEB. L. REV. 327, 327–41 (1991).

[14] These statutes delegate a public safety function and provide legal criteria for the discharge of that function. Jurisdictions that maintain a duty to warn or a duty to prevent harm to third parties without specific criteria create a delegated responsibility but attempt to enforce it as an intrinsic responsibility. Thus, they create circumstances in which clinicians and courts attempt to address an incoherent responsibility; that is, the responsibility to apply the standards of the profession to a task that does not fall within the scope of the profession.

likely to attempt to develop and enforce illusory standards for nonexistent expertise. Members of the profession may distort the legally relevant issues by attempting to translate them in a manner that makes them more accessible to the profession, and courts may abdicate their responsibilities to make critical legal determinations because they misidentify these determinations as professional judgments to be made by the members of the other professions. Arguably, the courts and experts have manifested this pattern of errors regarding the criteria of commitment under the sexual predator statutes and under general civil commitment provisions.[15]

Clinicians make intrinsic and delegated judgments, and they discharge intrinsic and delegated responsibilities when they act as treatment providers or ward managers for those committed under sexual predator statutes or under more general civil commitment statutes. When statutes or courts delegate to clinicians the responsibilities to make delegated professional judgments, such as the judgment that a person is (or is not) sufficiently dangerous to justify continued confinement, they must provide clear legal criteria or recognize that the clinician can exercise only the ordinary care and competence of a reasonable person in the circumstances regarding the delegated aspects of that decision. That is, a professional judgment regarding a delegated responsibility extends beyond the practice of the profession in the intrinsic sense, and thus, the practitioner cannot discharge all aspects of that responsibility to the standards of the profession because the delegated components of the decision do not involve substantive expertise in the profession. Rather, that professional can discharge the delegated aspects of that responsibility only by applying legal criteria or by acting as an ordinary reasonable person in the circumstances.

One commentator has suggested that the PJS appropriately applies to positive rights but not to negative rights. According to this interpretation, the PJS provides an appropriate standard for determining whether a positive right, such as the limited right to treatment in *Romeo*, has been properly fulfilled, but it does not provide an appropriate standard for determining whether a negative right, such as the liberty interest in freedom from unwanted medication in *Harper*, has been violated.[16] The analysis supporting this position rests partially on the recognition that excessive reliance by courts on the PJS undermines the significance of rights and liberties that lie beyond the scope of professional judgment.[17]

Although this failure to properly address these rights and liberties is an important factor in the misapplication of the PJS, review of the central cases suggests that the distinction between intrinsic and delegated judgment, rather than the distinction between positive and negative rights, defines the parameters of professional judgment. *Harper* and *Parham* address negative rights to freedom from unwanted medication and confinement, respectively. *Romeo* addresses a positive right to minimally adequate treatment for the purpose of preventing unnecessary restraint or injury. If the distinction between positive and negative rights is central to the PJS, that standard should apply to *Romeo* but not to *Harper* or *Parham*. As discussed previously, however, all three cases apply the PJS standard in some form, and that standard applies smoothly to the substantive criteria articulated in *Parham* but not to the substantive

---

[15] *See* chapter 10.

[16] Susan Stefan, *Leaving Civil Rights to the "Experts": From Deference to Abdication Under the Professional Judgment Standard*, 102 YALE L. J. 639, 667–99 (1992).

[17] *Id.* at 670–85.

criteria articulated in *Harper* or *Romeo*.[18] Thus, the degree to which the PJS accommodates the responsibilities raised by the substantive standards established by these cases does not map neatly onto the distinction between positive and negative rights. Rather, the PJS accommodates the cases insofar as the substantive standards call for intrinsic judgment but not insofar as they call for delegated judgment.

The exercise of professional judgment in compliance with *Harper* or *Romeo* differs from the exercise of professional judgment in *Parham* because the judgment called for by the *Parham* opinion falls within the category of intrinsic judgment, whereas *Harper* and *Romeo* call for judgments with both intrinsic and delegated components. *Parham* calls for a clinical judgment regarding the psychological condition of the child and the advisability of admission to a mental health facility as a form of clinical intervention likely to advance the clinical interests of that child. In contrast, *Harper* calls for an intrinsic judgment that the antipsychotic medication is in the prisoner's medical interest and a delegated judgment that the prisoner is dangerous to himself or others. The latter judgment falls in the delegated category because the judgment that the person is (or is not) dangerous includes an intrinsic psychological assessment of risk and a delegated normative decision regarding the level of risk required to justify the intervention in question. Such justificatory judgments necessarily fall beyond the expertise of the clinical professions.

Similarly, *Romeo* calls for training necessary to protect the constitutional liberty interests in freedom from bodily injury and undue restraint. In order to select a treatment program for that purpose, clinicians must exercise intrinsic professional judgment regarding the type of intervention most efficacious for reducing injury and restraint. They must also exercise delegated judgment, however, because the *Romeo* standard neither guarantees freedom from all injury or restraint nor provides any formula for weighing these values against each other or against other important interests of the patient, others affected, or the state. Thus, clinicians must make judgments that involve balancing the probability of further marginal gain or loss in one or both of these values against other potential gains or loss for this patient as well as against potential gains for other patients from reallocation of the available clinical resources. They must also consider costs and benefits to this patient and others that include but are not limited to the two identified constitutional interests.

Consider a number of potential approaches. They could immediately eliminate physical restraint at the cost of increased physical injury, for example, by simply abandoning the use of restraints. The case suggests that they adopted the alternative approach of attempting to eliminate physical injury at the cost of very frequent restraint.[19] Alternately, suppose there were good reasons to believe that Romeo would decrease self-injurious conduct most quickly through a treatment program that included aversive conditioning. The clinicians would have to weigh the cost of experiencing the aversive stimuli against the potential benefit of reducing the self-inflicted injuries. Similarly, massive doses of tranquilizers might reduce bodily injury and mechanical restraint at the cost of markedly reducing his functioning level. These decisions require consideration of matters that fall within the scope of clinical expertise, but they also involve normative judgments regarding individual and social

---

[18] *See* chapter 6, section III.

[19] Youngberg v. Romeo, 457 U.S. 307, 311 (1982).

values. The latter judgments fall beyond the range of professional expertise. Thus, these decisions require intrinsic and delegated judgment.

Many roles filled by professionals involve complex responsibilities requiring intrinsic and delegated judgment. Professionals can discharge intrinsic responsibilities to the standards of their professions, but they can perform delegated responsibilities only by applying legal criteria or by acting as ordinary, reasonable persons. Ideally, legislatures and courts would explicitly identify the delegated responsibilities or components of responsibilities assigned to clinicians, social scientists, or other professionals. These legal actors would make the relevant normative decisions and provide legal standards for the discharge of these delegated responsibilities as well as guidelines for the exercise of delegated judgment. In this manner, they would facilitate the proper functioning of legal institutions and promote appropriate decision making by legal actors and by other professionals.

Unfortunately, legal rule makers often fail to recognize the boundaries between normative judgments and professional expertise. Thus, they fail to differentiate intrinsic and delegated responsibilities, and they provide no legal criteria or guidelines for the exercise of delegated judgment. When statutes and cases fail to articulate clear legal criteria for the delegated components, neither the courts nor the professionals are likely to recognize that these components are delegated rather than intrinsic or to address them satisfactorily. Rather, courts frequently abdicate their responsibilities to make normative judgments and to set legal criteria for these duties, and they call upon professionals to apply nonexistent professional standards. Similarly, professionals often attempt to exercise professional judgment, as expert witnesses or as treatment providers, regarding questions that are not subject to determination through intrinsic professional judgment.

IV. Professional Judgment and Professional Roles

A. *Information Providers*

Because of the interaction of expertise and legal function in defining the proper scope of professional judgment, the appropriate range of judgment exercised regarding a particular matter can vary with one's institutional role. Sexual predator statutes illustrate this pattern because they call upon psychologists to exercise judgment in at least three distinct institutional roles. First, they serve as expert witnesses at the commitment hearings. Second, they evaluate individuals in these programs and recommend extended commitment, discharge, or revision of treatment conditions. Third, they serve as treatment providers in programs designed for those who have been committed under the statutes. As treatment providers, they might design or manage the program or engage in direct treatment.[20] The mutual failure of some courts and professionals to recognize the significance of the specific role in defining the appropriate range of judgment can generate errors of the types discussed.

Recognizing the distinction between intrinsic and delegated responsibilities is necessary but not sufficient for the proper distribution of responsibility across par-

---

[20] KAN. STAT. ANN. § 59-29a05-10 (1994 and Supp. 1997); WASH. REV. CODE ANN. § 71.09.040.080 (Supp. 1998).

ticipants in the legal process. In order to properly allocate responsibilities, define the boundaries of these responsibilities, and evaluate the performance of professionals in discharging them in a particular role, legal institutions must apply two principles corresponding to two conditions that define the relationship between the professions and the legal institutions. Insofar as the responsibility at issue is intrinsic, it calls upon the substantive expertise of the profession, and a principle of *expertise* applies. That is, insofar as these responsibilities and judgments are intended to call upon special professional knowledge and skills, legal institutions should define the parameters of these responsibilities and evaluate the performance of individual members of these professions in terms of the available expertise of the profession. Second, a principle of *support* applies in that legal institutions should define the parameters of these intrinsic responsibilities in a manner reasonably expected to support the values and goals of the legal institutions by rendering them consistent with the underlying normative framework that justifies them. Because of variations in the legal functions of specific roles in specific institutions, the appropriate scope of professional judgment or responsibility authorized might vary despite constant expertise. Thus, these principles of expertise and support provide the criteria for the design, discharge, and evaluation of intrinsic professional judgment and responsibility.

The principle of expertise cannot apply to delegated responsibilities or judgments, in contrast, because these do not apply the substantive expertise of the professions. In defining and discharging delegated responsibilities, therefore, legal institutions and professionals can apply only the support principle. That is, legal institutions must design and interpret delegated responsibilities in a manner expected to support the capacities of these institutions to serve the values and goals that underlie them, and professionals who participate in these institutions must discharge those responsibilities in a manner expected to support the ability of those institutions to function in that manner.

The sexual predator statutes call upon clinicians and social scientists to fulfill roles that reflect this distinction between intrinsic responsibilities properly defined by the principles of expertise and support and delegated responsibilities properly defined by the principle of support. The role of professional witness discussed in chapters 10 and 11 calls upon professionals to discharge their intrinsic responsibilities providing the court with information and explanation that falls within the expertise of the profession. Clinicians and social scientists in this role appropriately exercise intrinsic professional judgment when they consistently apply professional expertise in gathering, interpreting, and communicating the relevant descriptive and explanatory testimony. Properly understood, this role does not call upon experts to exercise delegated professional judgment precisely because the role of expert witness legitimately serves only to provide testimony involving the expertise of the profession.[21] The court retains the responsibilities to integrate this testimony with other evidence, to make the legal and normative determinations, and to generate a final judgment.

Common legal standards of admissibility approximate this distribution of responsibility to experts and courts, and they reflect the principles of expertise and

---

[21] The point here is not that ordinary observational evidence does not or should not play a role in expert testimony by psychologists. It is rather that such observations legitimately fall within the scope of expert testimony only when they are integrated with expertise in the profession in such a manner as to provide testimony that applies that expertise.

support. The *Daubert* Court, for example, interpreted the Federal Rules of Evidence in such a manner as to require that a trial judge rule on the admissibility of proffered scientific evidence by determining whether the expert's testimony "rests on a reliable foundation and is relevant to the task at hand."[22] The reliability component addresses evidentiary reliability, understood as trustworthiness. The Court identified several factors relevant to reliability, including the degree to which the evidence can be and has been subject to scientific testing and to scrutiny through peer review, the known or potential rate of error, and the degree of general acceptance within the scientific disciplines.[23]

The relevance component addresses the relationship between the scientific evidence and the facts at issue in the trial. The Court characterized this concern as involving the "fit" between the scientific information proffered and the factual dispute before the finder of fact.[24] This estimate of fit can be understood as consisting of two steps corresponding to two of the basic rules of evidence. First, does the proffered evidence have the tendency to make some fact at issue in the trial more or less probable?[25] Second, does this probative value outweigh the degree to which it might confuse, mislead, or prejudice the finder of fact?[26] In summary, the reliability and relevance standard provides for the admission of scientific evidence if it is well-grounded in valid science and related to facts at issue in the dispute such that the probative value to the fact finder outweighs the risk that it might undermine the legitimate function of the judicial process.[27]

The *Daubert* reliability and relevance criteria represent specific applications of the more general principles discussed in this book as the principles of expertise and support. The reliability criterion represents the general principle that the professional expertise in question must have a foundation sufficient to warrant reliance by the applicable legal institution. The basis required to meet this requirement might vary with the specific legal institution and with the manner in which that institution must rely on the expertise. Factors relevant to the determination that proffered expertise meets this requirement include, for example, the quality and quantity of scientific evidence available, the availability of alternative sources of information, error preference as between erroneous acceptance and erroneous rejection, and the ability of the legal institution to evaluate the expertise in the circumstances.

The relevance component of the standard represents the general principle that legal institutions should consider and rely upon expertise that applies to the matters before those institutions in such a manner as to support rather than undermine the abilities of those institutions to discharge their legitimate functions. Certain types of expertise involving broad statistical tendencies might apply more appropriately to a

---

[22] Daubert v. Merrell Dow Pharmaceuticals, Inc., 509 U.S. 579, 597 (1993).

[23] *Id.* at 592–95.

[24] *Id.* at 591–92.

[25] *Id.* at 587.

[26] *Id.* at 595.

[27] For more detailed discussion of this standard and its significance, *see e.g.*, David L. Faigman, *The Evidentiary Status of Social Science Under Daubert*, 1 PSYCHOL., PUB. POL'Y & L. 960 (1996); David L. Faigman, Elise Porter, & Michael J. Saks, *Check Your Crystal Ball at the Courthouse Door Please: Exploring the Past, Understanding the Present, and Worrying About the Future of Scientific Evidence*, 15 CARDOZO L. REV. 1799 (1994); Laurens Walker & John Monahan, *Daubert and the Reference Manual: An Essay on the Future of Science in Law*, 82 VA. L. REV. 837 (1996).

rule-making function, for example, than to fact finding or to an adjudicative function. Other types of expertise, such as clinical diagnosis of a specific individual, might apply more appropriately to adjudication. For each legal institution, legal decision makers must determine whether the proffered expertise stands in a relationship to the function of that institution such that accepting the expertise would support rather than undermine the responsible execution of that function. For the sake of convenience, this book refers to the two general principles as the principles of expertise and support, respectively.

Although evidentiary standards for the admission of scientific evidence provide legal rules that govern the responsibility of professionals who fulfill the specific role of expert witness, other roles lack such rules. In order to define the parameters of professional responsibility and judgment in these roles, one must apply the broader principles of expertise and support in light of the distinction between intrinsic and delegated responsibilities.

Clinicians fulfill their second role regarding these commitments when they provide periodic examinations of individuals committed under these statutes and testify at hearings called to consider proposed changes in the commitment status of those individuals.[28] Insofar as clinicians' roles in the posthearing commitments include the responsibility to perform periodic evaluations and to make recommendations regarding continuation or change of treatment status and program, they make intrinsic and delegated judgments. They exercise the same types of intrinsic judgments that apply in their role as expert witnesses in the initial hearings. They exercise additional delegated judgments, however, because recommendations regarding continued commitment, release, or change of commitment and treatment conditions require consideration of normative and legal components addressed by the legislature and by the court in formal hearings. These include, for example, the acceptable degree of risk for a particular disposition and the most defensible allocation of scarce resources.

The statute or court ideally should articulate legal criteria for these normative components, delegating to clinicians only the responsibility to apply these criteria. When legislatures and courts fail to articulate such criteria, clinicians must exercise delegated judgment as reasonable persons in the circumstances because the clinical professions provide no substantive expertise regarding these normative components. Thus, the court should interpret the delegated components of these judgments as the opinions of reasonable persons for the purpose of deciding how much to rely on these delegated judgments and in any litigation regarding liability for these judgments.[29] That is, when addressing professional judgments with delegated components, the courts should recognize that these components do not represent intrinsic professional judgment based on the expertise of their professional. Thus, the courts retain the responsibility to evaluate and decide upon the force of the delegated components of such judgments. Furthermore, courts must differentiate the intrinsic and delegated judgments made by clinicians who participate in this process of evaluation and recommendation because the courts must eventually rule on these recommendations. Thus, courts can fulfill judicial responsibilities only if they recognize that

---

[28] KAN. STAT. ANN. § 59-29a08, 10 (Supp. 1997); WASH. REV. CODE ANN. § 71.09.070, .090 (Supp. 1998).

[29] *Romeo,* 457 U.S. at 307 (discussing the professional judgment standard in context of decisions of liability).

in the hearing, they retain the responsibility to address the normative components delegated to the clinicians in the earlier process of evaluation and recommendation because in the context of a judicial hearing those clinicians serve as expert witnesses providing description and explanation. Their expert testimony can extend only to the limits of their expertise. As such it includes only their intrinsic judgments.

Consider, for example, a graduated treatment program emphasizing the development of empathy for victims and cognitive behavioral skills designed to enable the offender to manage his conduct in such a manner as to avoid reoffending. The program has four sequential levels of treatment, and each offender must successfully complete each level in order to move to the next. Recidivism data indicate that offenders who complete the program before leaving confinement recidivate at a rate of 15% over 5 years, whereas similar offenders who do not complete the program recidivate at a rate of 30% over 5 years.[30]

In designing and administering such a program, psychologists would exercise intrinsic judgment in the processes of treatment design and delivery, offender evaluation, and placement recommendation for the purpose of effective treatment. In making recommendations for release or placement in a less restrictive setting, however, they would exercise delegated as well as intrinsic judgment. These recommendations reflect the intrinsic judgments that the offender has successfully completed all four levels of the program and that such completion reduces the likely recidivism rate from approximately 30% to approximately 15% for the population of offenders who complete all four levels. This recommendation also reflects the delegated judgment that this reduction in risk is sufficient to justify a less restrictive placement. This final component represents a normative judgment about the relative significance of risk to third parties, constraints on offender liberty, and allocations of social resources. These matters do not fall within the expertise of the clinical professions or of the social scientists.

In reviewing and ruling upon such recommendations at hearings, courts must accurately identify the intrinsic and delegated components in order to evaluate the professional testimony and adequately discharge their own responsibilities. Courts can elicit and evaluate professional opinions regarding the intrinsic components, but they should recognize the delegated components as exceeding the scope of professional expertise. Thus, courts retain the responsibilities to limit expert testimony in the hearing to the intrinsic components and to make the normative judgments regarding which professionals can provide only their personal opinions. In this manner, the courts discharge their responsibilities by integrating the intrinsic professional judgments of the experts with the normative judgments of the legislature as interpreted and applied by the courts.

B. Care Providers: Treatment, Custodial Care, and Mere Incapacitation

Psychologists fulfill their third institutional role regarding these commitments when they function as treatment providers and ward managers in programs designed for individuals committed under these statutes. The defensible range of professional

---

[30] I present this hypothetical program for the purpose of illustration. I do not contend that such programs reliably produce such effects.

judgment by psychologists serving in these roles can vary according to the functions served by those programs. These programs can include treatment, incapacitation, and custodial components. The previous analysis of the statutes and court opinions suggests that incapacitation, rather than treatment, represents the primary purpose of these commitments, although that emphasis remains compatible with a treatment function in some circumstances.[31] Any inpatient commitment program necessarily contains a component of custodial care because the state takes on the responsibility to provide for the basic needs of those taken into custody.[32]

It is analytically impossible for professionals to exercise intrinsic professional judgment regarding custodial care. Custodial care consists of nontechnical attention to another's basic needs such as shelter, nourishment, or protection.[33] Attention cannot require intrinsic professional judgment and remain nontechnical. Thus, professionals might take on program management roles that include delegated responsibilities and require delegated judgment regarding custodial care, but these logically cannot constitute intrinsic professional judgments. In setting the parameters of these responsibilities and evaluating professionals' performance of these responsibilities, legal decision makers should apply the support principle in order to define and evaluate these delegated responsibilities in a manner that supports the proper function of the commitment. They should recognize, however, that the expertise principle does not apply: That principle addresses the application of professional expertise, which is not involved in purely delegated duties because such duties do not involve the expertise of the discipline. This recognition should encourage the courts to recognize and discharge their responsibilities to address the legal and normative issues.

Professionals can exercise intrinsic professional judgment regarding the treatment function of these programs. Although the empirical evidence reviewed previously does not support great optimism regarding treatment success, it does provide some information regarding the types of interventions that are more promising than others with certain subsets of offenders and regarding which offenders are more or less likely to succeed according to the outcome criteria of recidivism. Insofar as professionals make use of this information and related research or clinical skills in the process of treatment design and delivery, they exercise intrinsic professional judgment and discharge intrinsic professional responsibilities. Thus, the expertise and support principles both apply to these judgments, and legal decision makers should evaluate the available professional expertise in order to allocate responsibilities in such a manner as to maximize the ability of legal institutions to pursue their legitimate values and goals.

The measurement of treatment success in terms of recidivism reduction suggests that treatment delivery includes a substantial public safety function. An intervention can qualify as treatment while serving a public safety function. Recall the examples involving medication intended to ameliorate the psychotic process that generates assaults in delusional "self-defense" and behavioral management programs that reduce assaultive behavior by increasing a seriously impaired person's adaptive skills. These interventions serve a public safety function, but they constitute treatment rather than incapacitation because they do not serve that public safety function by rendering

---

[31] See chapter 5, sections II and III.
[32] Romeo, 457 U.S. at 307, 317, 324.
[33] See chapter 5, section III.

the individual unable to engage in harmful conduct. Rather, they ameliorate the impairment or reduce the injurious effects of that impairment by improving adaptive skills in areas of dysfunction associated with that impairment.

The research reviewed earlier indicates that some intervention programs designed to reduce sex offender recidivism constitute treatment rather than mere incapacitation. Consider, for example, programs designed to increase empathy for victims or to develop cognitive strategies and techniques that enable the offender to avoid circumstances that promote offending. These approaches constitute treatment in that they involve the application of clinical skills and knowledge in building adaptive skills that the offender can apply in order to reduce the likelihood of recidivism. Clinicians exercise intrinsic judgment insofar as they call upon the substance of the profession in designing and delivering such programs. Insofar as the intervention qualifies as treatment, clinicians must exercise intrinsic judgment because treatment necessarily involves some application of technical knowledge and skills. They also exercise intrinsic judgment in selecting offenders to participate in such programs insofar as they select those individuals on the basis of amenability to treatment.

Clinicians extend beyond the range of intrinsic judgment, however, if they select candidates for such treatment programs on the basis of social policy determinations about the relative importance of risk and amenability to treatment or if they make decisions about such matters as the level of progress needed for release to a less secure environment. These matters require consideration of legal and normative matters beyond the expertise of the profession. As discussed previously, clinicians may exercise delegated judgment in making recommendations about such matters, but neither they nor the legal decision makers are likely to properly discharge their respective responsibilities unless they explicitly identify these judgments as delegated rather than intrinsic. Having identified the various judgments as intrinsic or delegated, legal decision makers should apply the expertise and support principles to the intrinsic judgments but only the support principle to the delegated judgments. The recognition of this distinction should also remind the decision makers to fulfill their own responsibilities regarding the legal and normative components.

Consider, in contrast, interventions designed to protect the public by disabling the offender in some manner. Certain previously discussed interventions, including execution, clearly constitute mere incapacitation rather than treatment. Although execution is not likely to be endorsed as treatment, surgical or chemical castration designed to reduce arousal or the capacity to engage in sexual activity is sometimes discussed as treatment. Although these interventions involve the application of technical skills and knowledge to reduce the injurious effects of the prior patterns of arousal, they do not do so by facilitating adaptive skills, capacities, or functioning level. Rather, they attempt to reduce recidivism by rendering offenders unable to perform certain offenses or less likely to experience arousal that promotes such offenses.[34]

The proper classification of these interventions as mere incapacitation or as both treatment and incapacitation depends partially on the appropriate interpretation of the arousal patterns associated with the offenses. Recognized paraphilias involve

---

[34] I do not discuss here the use of hormonal treatment to reduce obsessive or intrusive sexual fantasies to normal levels. Such intervention may qualify as treatment, particularly in combination with other interventions.

sexual arousal in response to stimuli other than those ordinarily considered normal in society. These include, for example, sexual arousal associated with fantasy or contact involving children, dead bodies, or the infliction of pain.[35] Those who classify such arousal as pathological in itself would categorize interventions intended to reduce it as treatment in that it constitutes an intervention involving the application of clinical skills for the purpose of reducing the pathological arousal that constitutes one type of pathological condition. Similarly, if the individual experiences distress associated with such arousal and the intervention reduces the distress as well as the arousal, it constitutes treatment in that it reduces the subjective suffering that constitutes one aspect of the pathological condition. Insofar as such interventions also render the individuals less able to perform certain offenses, they would constitute incapacitation as well as treatment. Finally, those who deny that such arousal is pathological in itself would classify these interventions as mere incapacitation.

Some applications of these interventions constitute clear instances of mere incapacitation. Suppose, for example, that the offender is a rapist who experiences ordinary heterosexual arousal but who responds to such arousal through forcible rape because of antisocial or psychopathic personality traits. This particular type of offender manifests pathology involving his anger or lack of empathy or constraint rather than a deviant pattern of sexual arousal. Chemical or surgical castration or aversive conditioning in these circumstances would constitute mere incapacitation because these interventions would involve attempts to reduce the probability of recidivism by rendering such offenders unable to experience normal arousal or unable to engage in heterosexual activity. Thus, some types of intervention might represent treatment in some cases, mere incapacitation in other cases, and combined treatment and incapacitation in others.

Although treatment necessarily involves intrinsic judgments and custodial care necessarily does not involve intrinsic judgments, incapacitation may or may not involve such judgments. Certain interventions may involve intrinsic professional judgment and responsibilities, although they qualify as incapacitation rather than treatment or as incapacitation as well as treatment. Surgical or chemical castration or aversive conditioning programs that take the form of mere incapacitation, for example, require expertise in the areas of sexual arousal, hormonal or surgical intervention, or autonomic conditioning. These programs may or may not also call for delegated judgments. Legislatures and courts might preclude delegated judgments regarding legal or normative issues by reserving for the courts the decisions that subject individuals to such interventions. Alternately, they might create delegated responsibilities by calling upon clinicians to decide or recommend which offenders should be subject to such interventions. The latter approach but not the former would require delegated judgment because although the clinical professionals might provide technical information relevant to such decisions, they do not have expertise in making the normative determination that the prior offenses or the risk of recidivism justifies such intervention.

Explicit differentiation of intrinsic and delegated judgments regarding these interventions and explicit recognition that these interventions constitute incapacitation rather than (or in combination with) treatment serve two important functions. First,

---

[35] AMERICAN PSYCHIATRIC ASSOCIATION, DIAGNOSTIC AND STATISTICAL MANUAL OF MENTAL DISORDERS, 522–32 (4th ed. 1994).

differentiating the intrinsic and delegated judgments exposes the normative components, rendering it more difficult for either legal actors or clinicians to avoid confronting the need to justify the normative decisions. Blurring the distinction between the intrinsic and delegated judgments, in contrast, undermines the justificatory requirement by encouraging various participants to misconstrue normative determinations or components as clinical judgments based only on professional expertise. Second, recognition that certain interventions constitute incapacitation rather than (or in combination with) treatment makes explicit the need to justify state action, as well as participation by clinicians in that state action, that involves doing something *to* the recipient, rather than doing something *for* that person.

The claim here is not that states could never justify such intervention or that clinicians could never justify participating in such action. This chapter does not pursue those significant justificatory questions. The claim here is only that explicitly recognizing such action as mere incapacitation or as incapacitation combined with treatment renders it more difficult to indulge the illusion that it constitutes purely clinical treatment of the individual that can be justified solely on the claim that it is "for his own good." Thus, this recognition might render it more likely that legislators, courts, and clinicians will directly confront the justificatory questions, that they will do so in a manner consistent with the normative framework underlying the legal system, and that they will appropriately distribute responsibility among legal and clinical actors.[36]

Although this chapter does not purport to resolve these justificatory issues, I discuss briefly the analytical framework that decision makers must bring to those issues in order to clarify the role of the expertise and support principles for this task. Legal decision makers must justify involuntary intervention in the form of treatment or incapacitation by appeal to the principles of political morality represented by the legal system. Chapters 4 and 7 advance an interpretation of the normative framework underlying central institutions of mental health law in a liberal society. Insofar as justifications appealing to this normative framework or to some alternative framework rest partially on empirical premises regarding the likely effects of such interventions, information from clinicians or social scientists may be relevant to the justificatory argument in the legislative or judicial process. Furthermore, if decision makers conclude that such programs are justified, they may call upon members of those professions to fulfill various roles in the design and implementation of such programs.

Clinicians and social scientists might occupy at least two distinct roles regarding the inquiry into the justification of such programs. First, they may be called upon to provide information grounded in professional expertise regarding the probability that such interventions can reduce recidivism. The information provided is descriptive and explanatory rather than normative, but it informs the normative judgment that the legislature or court must make regarding the costs and benefits that are relevant to the justificatory determination.[37] The expertise and support principles both apply to the intrinsic responsibilities associated with this role. Professionals conform to the

---

[36] Notice that these concerns arise most visibly in the context of commitment and treatment programs for sex offenders, but the same concerns permeate police power civil commitment more generally.

[37] The relevance of such information varies with the justificatory argument. I claim here only that this information is relevant to some plausible arguments.

expertise principle insofar as they provide descriptive and explanatory information that conforms to the boundaries of professional expertise. They conform to the support principle insofar as they facilitate the legitimate function of the legal institution by presenting this information in a manner that clearly identifies it as empirical and differentiates it from the relevant normative judgments. Information presented in this manner clarifies the distinction between the empirical and normative components and facilitates the proper functioning of the legal institution by assisting the legal decision makers in identifying the normative questions that they must address. In contrast, if clinicians or social scientists present the same information in a manner that blurs the boundary between the empirical and normative issues, they undermine the proper functioning of the legal institution by increasing the probability that legal decision makers will fail to recognize and address the normative issues.

Clinicians and social scientists occupy a second role regarding the justification of such programs in that they must make independent ethical decisions regarding the justification for participating (or for refusing to participate) in such programs. Individual clinicians or social scientists as persons might endorse a variety of moral principles that would provide good reasons to participate (or to refuse to participate) in such programs under a variety of circumstances. Similarly, professional associations of clinicians or social scientists might collectively endorse principles that support or preclude such participation. Insofar as they clearly recognize and address these moral decisions as distinct from the specialized information and technical skills they possess as practitioners of their professions, the expertise and support principles do not apply.[38] That is, these decisions involve individual or collective ethical decisions to participate in particular legal institutions or to refuse to do so. The expertise and support principles address the manner in which legal institutions should define and evaluate the proper roles of professionals as such in the operation of those institutions. These principles address the proper distribution of responsibilities in the legal institutions representing underlying principles of political morality. They do not purport to address all of the various principles of critical morality that individual professionals or their associations might defensibly endorse.[39]

V.   Conclusion

Clinicians and social scientists exercise professional judgment and fulfill professional responsibilities in a variety of roles within the legal institutions that implement mental health law. The three chapters comprising part IV of this book examine the parameters of professional judgment and responsibility in several professional roles associated with sexual predator statutes specifically and with civil commitment generally. These chapters demonstrate that the proper definition and execution of professional responsibility require attention to the expertise of the profession and to the function of the role in the legal institution in which it is embedded.

Professional judgment and responsibility occur in the context of a complex set

---

[38] Although the moral decisions are distinct from the empirical expertise, that empirical expertise might provide information relevant to those decisions.

[39] Robert F. Schopp, *Verdicts of Conscience: Nullification and Necessity as Jury Responses to Crimes of Conscience*, 69 S. CAL. L. REV. 2039, 2065–74 (1996).

of related roles and responsibilities that contribute to the functioning of legal institutions. These institutions rest upon an underlying normative structure that explains and justifies a coherent body of mental health law. Just as the underlying normative structure defines the defensible form and function of specific institutions of mental health law, it also defines the proper scope of professional judgment and responsibilities within these institutions.

The distinction between intrinsic and delegated responsibilities and the associated principles of expertise and support fulfill a crucial function in the definition and execution of professional roles, responsibilities, and judgments. They do so because they facilitate recognition of the empirical and normative components of various roles, responsibilities, and judgments. Thus, they promote our ability to distribute responsibility appropriately among clinicians, social scientists, and legal participants. The study of mental health law as an integrated body of law representing an underlying normative structure promotes our understanding of each of the component institutions and of the proper roles of various participants in these institutions.

Some readers might question various components of the integrated set of *parens patriae* and police power institutions of mental health law advanced in the first three parts of this book. Some might also question the approaches to specific roles, responsibilities, and judgments discussed in the last part. Insofar as they do so by arguing that alternative formulations of those institutions or roles more effectively implement the broader underlying principles of an integrated body of mental health law, they will advance the project this book pursues.

Chapter 13
THE FRAGMENTED STRUCTURE OF MENTAL HEALTH LAW REVISITED

This book advances and defends an integrated body of mental health law reflecting a coherent normative structure. The principles of political morality underlying the legal institutions of a liberal society provide a general normative framework that unifies two separate sets of justificatory principles and two corresponding sets of legal institutions. The principles represented by the patient-centered approach to health care support *parens patriae* institutions of mental health law, and the principles represented by standards of criminal responsibility support police power institutions of mental health law. These principles and institutions share a more abstract foundation in the liberal principles of political morality underlying a comprehensive set of legal institutions. The *parens patriae* and police power institutions reveal two distinct but related applications of a common conception of competence. Competence for person lies at the core of the patient-centered principles of health care represented by the *parens patriae* institutions, and retributive competence fulfills an analogous function in developing complementary institutions for the exercise of the police power. Legal mental illness as psychological impairment rendering an individual incompetent in the relevant sense fulfills the discriminative and justificatory functions for each specific legal purpose.

The interpretations of the central *parens patriae* and police power institutions advanced in parts II and III demonstrate that this approach can generate plausible and coherent institutions for the application of such a body of mental health law. I do not contend that these are the only possible formulations that can represent a coherent and defensible normative structure. One might advance alternative institutions representing similar underlying principles or some alternative set of principles. I advance this particular set of institutions and this particular normative framework primarily for the purpose of demonstrating that this general approach can generate an integrated body of law that promotes understanding of a variety of problematic issues and applications. This project does not purport to displace conventional doctrinal analysis or empirical inquiry. Rather, it provides a more abstract conceptual and normative framework intended to promote integration of doctrinal and empirical study. This framework informs our understanding of the most defensible approach to the formulation, interpretation, and application of law and of the appropriate distribution of responsibility among legal actors, clinicians, and social scientists.

This approach generates institutions that share many characteristics with their current counterparts, although they also depart significantly from current provisions and practices. The central Supreme Court cases addressing mental health law reflect principles generally consistent with those discussed in this book. Thus, these cases are amenable to interpretation consistent with the analysis presented here. When interpreted as a formal principle of justice in constitutional adjudication, the reasonable relationship principle from *Jackson* requires a certain relationship between the state intrusion and substantive principles that justify the intrusion as consistent with the Constitution.[1]

The ambiguous conclusion in *O'Connor* specifies that a nondangerous mentally ill person who can live safely in the community cannot be held in simple custodial confinement.[2] By limiting the conclusion to those who are not dangerous and can live safely in the community, the Court addresses only *parens patriae* commitments. If one interprets the category of mentally ill persons as limited to those who suffer impairment rendering them incompetent for the purposes of decisions regarding their own well-being, the *O'Connor* conclusion addresses the subsequent issue of placement through *parens patriae* intervention in a manner consistent with the approach advanced in this book.[3] The approach advanced here would authorize *parens patriae* intervention intended to return the individual to competence, to provide therapeutic benefit short of that goal, or to provide custodial care needed to protect the individual from harm or further deterioration. The phrase regarding the ability to live safely in the community limits the Court's conclusion to those who do not need custodial care for protection, however, and the limitation to simple custodial confinement defines the scope of the holding narrowly such that it does not address cases in which the hospitalization is necessary to provide some treatment benefit. Thus, the narrow rule only rules out protective placement of a civilly incompetent person in circumstances that reduce his well-being and liberty without providing any benefits such as positive treatment effect or needed custodial protection that would render the disposition in that person's best interests.

Jones is the case that most closely approximates requirements of mental illness and dangerousness for commitment. The court explicitly stated that the insanity acquittal established that Jones was mentally ill and dangerous, and it stated that an insanity acquittal entitles the government to confine him in a mental institution until he is no longer mentally ill or no longer dangerous.[4] Although the Court did not explain why psychological impairment sufficient to establish an insanity defense would necessarily suffice for commitment, the proposal advanced in this book explains why such impairment would justify social control through institutions other than conviction and punishment in the criminal justice system. The insanity acquittal identifies the defendant as one whose impairment is such as to render him retributively incompetent and thus, ineligible to participate in the retributive criminal justice system. The mere fact of retributive incompetence would not justify inpatient commitment, however, unless the complex balance of individual and social interests precluded a less intrusive method for managing the risk. The Court approximated this conclusion by calling for release when the individual is no longer dangerous.

One plausible objection to the *Jones* case concerns the doubt that Jones was dangerous. Jones engaged only in a relatively minor property crime, and the opinion provides no evidence that he demonstrated risk of further harm either by virtue of

---

[1] *See* chapter 2, section III.

[2] O'Connor v. Donaldson, 422 U.S. 563, 576 (1975).

[3] The assumption that "mental illness" establishes civil incompetence for person is made for the purpose of interpreting *O'Connor* in context of the proposal in this book. I do not suggest that the Court drew this conclusion or even considered the question.

[4] Jones v. United States, 463 U.S. 354, 363–70 (1983).

the manner in which he committed the crime or by later conduct.[5] One might reasonably speculate that this problem arises in *Jones* precisely because the statute in question, like most postinsanity acquittal statutes, conflates questions regarding impairment and disposition and focuses attention on disposition.[6] By separating the issues of retributive competence and disposition in the police power function, the proposal in this book would require that the court first determine retributive competence and then address disposition as a distinct question if the individual is not competent in the relevant sense. Furthermore, by framing these issues in such a manner as to distinguish the questions of competence and placement, these provisions might enhance the probability that the courts would recognize and exercise dispositions less restrictive than inpatient confinement.

In *Foucha*, the Court accepted the characterization of the petitioner as one who has an antisocial personality but is not mentally ill.[7] If Foucha suffers no psychological impairment at all, he cannot suffer legal mental illness for any purpose because legal mental illness entails functional impairment.[8] If one understands the claim that Foucha suffered no mental illness as meaning that he suffered no impairment sufficient to justify continued hospitalization as mentally ill and dangerous, the language in the plurality and concurring opinions that implied reliance on the reasonable relationship principle seems apt.[9] This analysis provides little explanatory force, however, because it seems only to deny that the state can justify hospitalizing a person who suffers no psychological impairment that would justify hospitalization.

The proposal advanced here accommodates *Foucha* in a manner that explains the case as consistent with the broader framework. One might understand the characterization of Foucha as indicating that he qualifies for a clinical diagnosis of APD or that he engages in antisocial conduct but manifests no psychological impairment sufficient to qualify him for any clinical diagnostic category. In either case he demonstrates no impairment of the psychological capacities needed to engage in a process of competent practical reasoning about either self-regarding decisions or the rule-based criminal justice system. Thus, the court should never address the issue of placement in a hospital, because Foucha does not meet the threshold condition of incompetence for either the *parens patriae* or police powers. Because he is retributively competent, he is eligible for the status of criminally responsible in the primary police power institution of the liberal state.

This interpretation of *Foucha* appears problematic because the previous insanity acquittal indicates that he was not retributively competent. Despite the insanity acquittal, a review panel of clinicians at the facility at which Foucha was held reported that he had demonstrated no evidence of mental illness since admission. Expert testimony at a release hearing indicated that Foucha was probably experiencing a drug-induced psychosis at the time of the crime for which he was acquitted by reason of insanity and that he had recovered from that disorder.[10]

If Foucha committed the crime while manifesting a psychotic episode associated with voluntary ingestion of illegal drugs, the case raises at least three difficult ques-

---

[5] *Id.* at 359–61.
[6] *Id.* at 357 and n3.
[7] Foucha v. Louisiana, 504 U.S. 71, 75–83 (1992).
[8] *See* chapter 3, section III.
[9] *Foucha*, 504 U.S. at 79 (plurality) and 88 (O'Connor, J., concurring).
[10] *Foucha*, 504 U.S. at 74–75.

tions, but none of these are specific to the notion of retributive competence advanced here. First, the case raises the difficult general question regarding the significance for a defendant's defense that he caused the conditions of that defense.[11] The second question addresses the manner in which voluntary intoxication purportedly causes impairment that gives rise to an insanity defense or to a claim that the defendant failed to form the mental state required by the offense definition. Although intoxication clearly affects mental states and processes, it is not clear that it frequently does so in a manner that supports either defensive claim. Given the testimony reported by the Court indicating that Foucha had demonstrated no evidence of mental illness from the time he was admitted to the hospital, one should consider the possibility that the central problem regarding postacquittal commitment in this case arises from an inappropriate insanity acquittal.[12]

Finally, if a defendant is appropriately acquitted and committed because of the effects of voluntary intoxication, the third question involves the manner in which the state ought to frame the release criteria. Should the authority making the decision regarding release of such an individual consider only that person's condition at the time of the petition, or should that authority also consider the probability that the individual will again become intoxicated and commit another crime? Regardless of the approach one takes to these difficult issues, they emphasize the importance of developing complementary police power institutions for those who possess retributive competence and for those who lack such competence.

The petitioners in cases brought under the sexual predator statutes, such as *Hendricks*, *Young*, and *Blodgett*, illustrate a pattern similar to that of Foucha insofar as they manifested no impairment raising a colorable question of incompetence for either the *parens patriae* or police power functions at the time of potential release.[13] At first glance, the Court's opinion in *Hendricks* seems to suggest a basis for a determination of retributive incompetence for the police power function when it describes Hendricks as unable to control his pedophilic behavior.[14] The Court provides absolutely no indication, however, what this claim means or what reason one has to believe it. Both the nature of this putative volitional impairment and the explanation for its compatibility with the prior determination of criminal responsibility remain mysterious. Thus, these cases also resemble *Foucha* in that they reveal the difficulties created by the failure to develop a complementary set of police power institutions with a consistent set of criteria of eligibility for each. Although they do not adopt the approach advanced in this book, they cogently illustrate the need for such an approach.

The central cases addressing the right to refuse treatment mandate neither the approach taken in this book nor any other single alternative. They suggest certain considerations and principles, however, that are consistent with the approach proposed here. The Court's substantive holding in *Harper* authorizes the involuntary administration of antipsychotic medication to a prisoner with serious mental illness "if the inmate is dangerous to himself or others and the treatment is in the inmate's

---

[11] Paul H. Robinson, *Causing the Conditions of One's Own Defense: A Study in the Limits of Theory in Criminal Law Doctrine*, 71 VA L. REV. 1 (1985).

[12] *Foucha*, 504 U.S. at 74–75.

[13] *See* chapter 8, section IV.

[14] Kansas v. Hendricks, 117 S.Ct. 2072, 2080–81 (1997).

medical interests."[15] If serious mental illness is limited to disorders that render the individual incompetent for person and retributively, then this holding addresses circumstances in which the prisoner's treatment interests converge with the state's police power and *parens patriae* functions.

The court opinions in the *Rogers* series discuss police power and *parens patriae* cases as distinct categories. The First Circuit adopted the findings of the Massachusetts supreme court that allowed involuntary medication under the police power without prior court approval only to prevent imminent harm and only in keeping with the applicable rules regarding restraints.[16] Similarly, the Massachusetts supreme court addressed *parens patriae* cases as requiring a finding of incompetence for person and a substituted judgment.[17] The *Rennie* opinions differ from the *Rogers* opinions in that the latter but not the former require judicial determinations of incompetence for involuntary treatment under most conditions. The *Rennie* opinions accept statutory procedures that allow clinicians to make and review decisions to administer involuntary treatment. These opinions discuss the parameters of the clinician's duty in terms that include professional judgment, least restrictive alternatives, and traditional police power and *parens patriae* considerations without clarifying the relationships among these.[18]

Collectively, these cases recognize the importance of competence, the *parens patriae* and police powers, professional judgment, and the balance of individual and social interests. They provide no consistent analysis that reconciles these considerations, however, nor do they provide any clear, consistent framework for judicial or clinical decision making regarding involuntary treatment of mental health patients. Chapters 6 and 9 develop an interpretation of the PJS that integrates these central considerations and allows the exercise of professional judgment regarding treatment by clinicians within the boundaries set by legal standards. This approach applies the central notions of retributive competence and competence for person in order to address circumstances in which involuntary intervention is justified under the police power, the *parens patriae* function, or both. This analysis interprets and integrates central notions discussed in the cases including the PJS, the least restrictive alternative, competence, and the balance of state and individual interests. In doing so, it articulates the justification for and limits on involuntary treatment, and it allocates responsibility among legal and clinical actors in a manner that comports with their expertise and with the underlying principles that provide the normative framework for mental health law and for the larger legal system in a liberal society.

Laws that authorize the state to treat some people differently than it treats most citizens merely because of their religion or race would clearly violate the Constitution and the underlying principles of political morality. In order to establish a coherent and defensible body of law that authorizes the state in treating some people differently because they suffer mental illness, mental health law must articulate conceptions of legal mental illness that explain and justify differential treatment according to the applicable principles of political morality. This book advances a conceptual

---

[15] Washington v. Harper, 494 U.S. 210, 227 (1990).

[16] Rogers v. Com'r of Dept. of Mental Health, 458 N.E.2d 308, 321–22 (Mass. 1983); *see* chapter 6, section II.

[17] *Rogers*, 458 N.E.2d at 312–19; *see* chapter 6, section II.

[18] *See* chapter 6, section II.

and normative framework that provides the basis for an integrated and defensible body of mental health law in a liberal society. It draws upon current law and broader principles consistent with that law in order to provide that normative structure. I do not contend that this approach represents the only defensible normative framework or the only possible interpretations of these legal institutions. Neither does it displace traditional doctrinal or empirical inquiry. Rather, it seeks a more abstract framework intended to facilitate doctrinal and empirical scholarship in a manner that promotes our abilities to establish a coherent and justifiable body of mental health law and to appropriately distribute authority and responsibility among legal actors, clinicians, and empirical scientists.

TABLE OF AUTHORITY

Cases

Laws, Regulations, and Rules

AUTHOR INDEX

SUBJECT INDEX

ABOUT THE AUTHOR

Robert F. Schopp completed a PhD in psychology and practiced clinical psychology for approximately 10 years, during which he encountered a variety of clinical circumstances that raised perplexing legal and moral questions. These circumstances involved, for example, criminal competence and responsibility, civil competence and commitment, involuntary treatment, treatment using aversive stimuli, and the management or release of individuals who had demonstrated a pattern of violent or suicidal behavior. These individuals and circumstances raised questions regarding the limits of clinical competence and responsibility, the clinician's responsibilities to the individual and the community, the relationship between the criminal justice and mental health systems, and the relationships among the clinician's legal and moral responsibilities as a clinician and as a person.

Dr. Schopp turned to the study of moral philosophy and law in an attempt to understand more clearly some of these questions. After completing a JD and a PhD in philosophy, he joined the faculty of the College of Law and the Department of Psychology at the University of Nebraska, where he teaches and writes as a member of the Law–Psychology program. His teaching and scholarship tend to focus on questions that arise at the intersection of law, psychology, and moral philosophy. These questions often occur in the fields of mental health law, criminal law, jurisprudence, and professional ethics. His prior books include *Automatism, Insanity, and the Psychology of Criminal Responsibility* (1991) and *Justification Defenses and Just Convictions* (1998).